FOOD FROM AN AMERICAN FARM

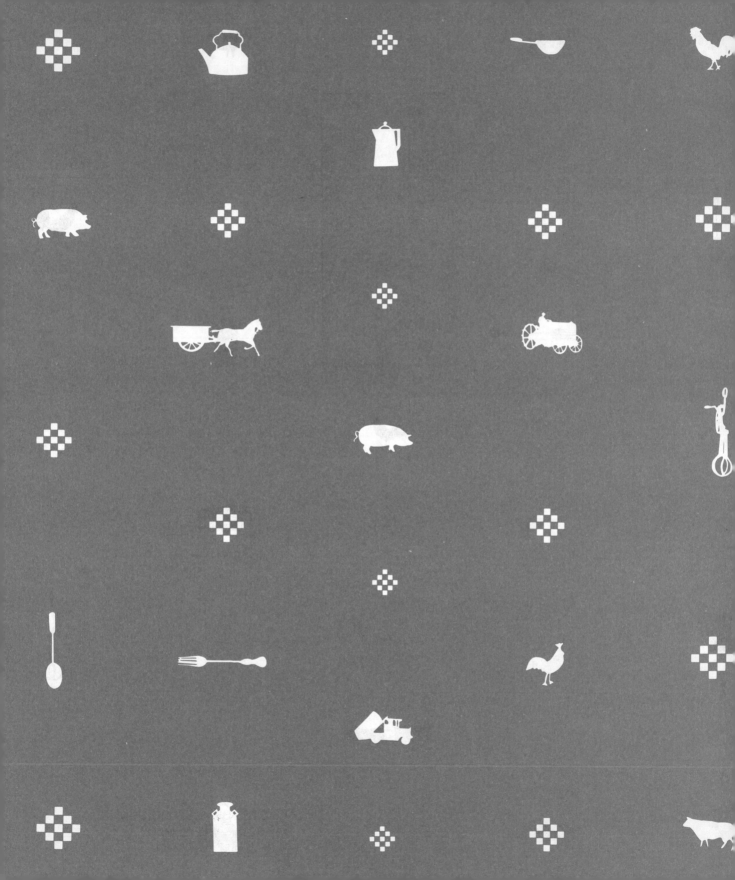

FOOD

FROM

AN

AMERICAN

FARM

❖❖❖

**JANEEN
ALETTA SARLIN**

Simon & Schuster

*New York   London   Toronto   Sydney
Tokyo   Singapore*

Simon & Schuster
Simon & Schuster Building
Rockefeller Center
1230 Avenue of the Americas
New York, New York 10020

Copyright © 1991 by Janeen Sarlin

SIMON & SCHUSTER and colophon are
registered trademarks
of Simon & Schuster Inc.

Designed by Bonni Leon

Manufactured in the United States of
America

10 9 8 7 6 5 4 3 2 1

Library of Congress Cataloging in
Publication Data
Sarlin, Janeen.
    Food from an American farm/Janeen
Aletta Sarlin.
        p.   cm.
    Includes bibliographical references and
index.
    1. Cookery, American.   I. Title.
TX715.S245   1991
641.5973—dc20   90-25608
                            CIP

ISBN 0-671-68499-X

The author gratefully acknowledges permission to
use the following material:

    Photographs on pages 7 and 205 courtesy of
Successful Farming; photographs on pages 64, 69,
192, 205, and 207 courtesy of *The Farmer;*
photographs on pages 30 and 180 courtesy of *Ford
Farming Magazine;* photograph on page 85
courtesy of Mrs. Nelva Prinsen.
    The recipe "Fattigmand" from *What to Cook for
Company* by Lenore Sullivan, Iowa State
University Press, 1952, is reprinted with
permission from the publisher.
    The recipe "Mom's Zesty Pork Chops" from
Farm Journal magazine, May 1968, is reprinted
with permission from Farm Journal, Inc.
    The excerpt "Sandwich Advice" from
Granddaughter's Inglenook Cookbook edited by
Genevieve Christ and Elizabeth Weigle, Brethren
Publishing House, 1942, is reprinted with
permission from the publisher.

For Grams,

Mom, Aunt Bets, and Aunt Rubye

A Special Note of Thanks
to
My Entire Family—
Past, Present, and Future

and to
Kerri Conan for her
guiding enthusiasm, clear
eagle eye, true-blue sense of
family, and ability to make my
nonsense sound sensible;
and to Bonni Leon
for using her creative green
thumb to design a pattern
of chapters that literally
bloom.

Contents

▼▼▼▼▼▼▼▼▼▼▼▼▼▼▼▼▼▼

INTRODUCTION

There's No Place Like Farm

Farm life is about the balance between nature's way and human needs. Farmers provide food—both directly to the people and for the animals that nourish people, who in turn nurture the land—that supports the food chain. Farm life is seasonal: frantic summer fieldwork; the satisfying fall harvest; winter —when we "rest," repair the machinery, fix things around the house; and then spring and the blossoming of new life. This cyclical phenomenon directs, undermines, and surprises, breathing life and death with an even hand. In the barnyard, the strong and the hearty live, but the weak and the sickly pass on. The old dog dies, but each year of her life she whelped a litter of puppies.

Farmers talk freely about these everyday occurrences. They are friendly, curious, and interested. Because the drive down an unpaved gravel road in the country is slower than on smooth, paved state highways, the farmer can observe the progress of a crop, determine the immediate condition of the farmyard and the buildings, check out the progress in the garden, and notice that a new calf is nursing.

If you on your drive observe a farmer (or his wife) plowing, cultivating, picking corn, combining soybeans, or cutting hay, wave to him. He will wave back, often wondering to himself, "Who is that fellow (or that lady)? That's a different car for these parts. I wonder where he (or she) is going." His concern is genuine, though guarded at times in front of strangers.

The farmer conducts his business face-to-face; he would no more think of calling you on the phone for an appointment than he would give his prize bull away. Instead, he will hop in his pickup and drive over to see you about the business at hand. Food naturally is incorporated into all visits—a cup of coffee and a fresh doughnut at the neighbors, the extra chair pulled up to the dinner table for someone who "just happened to be in the area." Even a quick trip to town to get a part fixed ends with an ice cream cone and a "Fine weather we're having . . ." at Hansen's drugstore. Then there are the daily meals, organized gatherings, impromptu socials, and grand traditional holiday family dinners.

Most babies in the nineteenth century and the early part of the twentieth century were birthed in the same beds where their mothers and grandmothers were born. Not only Grams and Granddad, but Mom and Dad as well were born on the "home place" where their families farmed. Although my brother and sisters and I were born in a hospital, we thrived, learned, loved, and laughed on our farm.

"Our Farm"—the setting where this food is fixed —is a 160-acre piece of land in southern Minnesota. It is located in the section of this great country that borders the northern edge of the Iowa Corn Belt. As the crow flies over the fertile rolling hills heading north, he'll see strips of rich black dirt and green alfalfa or clover. There next to that patterned field is a cluster of buildings, surrounded by trees, with a vegetable garden and flower patch and the dog—the home place.

Life on our farm was romantic, humorous, and full of adventure. We shared sadness and happiness with our friends, family, and neighbors, and everyone worked very hard. This book, then, becomes one joyous celebration of that life, beginning generations before Grams and Granddad, nurtured by the devotion of my parents, promising continuity and sustenance to future generations.

The Home Place, 1980s

The Home Place

"The home place" never refers to a house in the city or suburbs. It is *pure* country, in our case *pure farm,* meaning not only a house but a garden, a barn, a pasture, and animals, fields, machinery, and trees.

In the late 1790s, a wise man by the name of Kerwin found a particular piece of land in southern Minnesota. He knew that the rolling hills verdant with woods and underbrush were covered with fertile topsoil that would produce abundant crops and provide a good living for himself and his family, and for the future generations of farmers who would inhabit this land.

Congress passed the Homestead Act in 1862, authorizing the acquisition of 160 acres from U.S. public lands by the head of a family after he had cleared and settled the area and promised to live on it for five years. Accordingly, Kerwin established a tract of land in southeastern Minnesota. (The name Minnesota comes from the Dakota Indian word for "land of sky-tinted water.")

My great-grandfather, Darius Broadwater, purchased a quarter-section from Kerwin in 1889, thirty-one years after Minnesota became a state and the year my grandfather, Frank Walker Broadwater, was born. Darius continued clearing and cultivating the land, raising crops, livestock, and his family of five children on the home place.

Following in his father's footsteps, Granddad, at age twenty-two, bought the home place in 1911, one year before he married Grams. Granddad further cleared just about all the land (making the farmland as it is today), cultivated the soil, and improved the homestead by building a new barn in 1916 and a new house in 1925. Both structures exist today. Together with Grams and hired hands, he farmed the land, fed livestock, milked cows, and reared three daughters: Mom, Aunt Rubye, and Aunt Bets.

In 1934 Mom and Dad first met at a mutual friend's home in Lewiston, Minnesota, a year later at Bethany Seminary in Chicago, and then "off and on" over the next two years. After the three-year "hodgepodge" courtship, they were married in Grams and Granddad's flower garden on September 5, 1937. Their honeymoon trip took them to Middlebury, Indiana, where they rented Grandpa Schrock's farm. Six years later, they returned to the Minnesota home place, which they first rented and subsequently purchased from Granddad Broadwater in 1946.

Dad then began what we now call "sustainable agriculture." Originally, the land was tilled straight up and down the hill. He implemented the unconventional (according to Granddad) contours and terraces around the rolling hills to hold the fertile topsoil in place. On the newly laid-out strips—some a mile long—he planted a five-year crop rotation program. He started with two years of corn or soybeans—"cash crops"; then devoted one year to oats—also a "cash crop"; and finally, reserved two years for alfalfa—a "nurse crop" that retains runoff water and feeds natural nitrogen back into the soil, both while simultaneously producing two crops of hay each year: a quadruple benefit! This planning resulted in higher yields using less fertilizer, no need for pesticides or herbicides, and the land replenishing itself. And he made a good living to boot!

Dad's farming practices soon allowed him to buy the "Eighty," another 80-acre farm two-and-a-half miles southeast of the home place in 1950. From then on, he farmed the entire 240 acres of land, heeding sound earth conservation methods that produced bumper crops even during the dry spells. He milked a fifty-head herd of Brown Swiss dairy cows (until his last kid was out of college), and raised pigs, sheep, chickens, horses, and beef cattle, as well as various cats and dogs. Together with Mom, he provided for, nurtured, and brought up four children: Joel, myself, Judy, and Joany—all on the home place.

Mom and Dad live in the house that Granddad designed and built with the help of the Masons in 1925. Ahead of his time (or so they all said), Granddad intentionally constructed the basement thirteen cement blocks high (instead of the usual eleven): This left him enough room to swing an ax when he split the wood for fuel in the furnace room. The basement tank room housed the new running water system. Previously, the windmill pumped all water into the pumphouse, and Grams carried it by bucket into the house. He devised a way to pipe water directly into the tanks in the house instead.

The first and highest tank held the drinking water. The second tank performed the role of refrigerator: Chains hung from the ceiling beams, suspending metal pails in the cold water. Cottage cheese and other perishable foodstuffs were sealed in large glass jars and sunk in this middle-level "fridge." Granddad used the third and lowest tank to chill the cans of cream that the milkman picked up every other day and transported to the Granger Creamery. We used this tank to float, and thereby chill, foods like watermelons. Ingeniously, he also thought about water overflowing. He laid an underground pipe from the house to the barn that carried this runoff water directly into the tanks of water for the cattle inside the barn—a sophisticated practice for the time.

Although electricity was unavailable to the Greenleafton rural community in 1925, Granddad —with foresight—installed electrical wiring and outlets in the new house. The juice arrived three years later. (Prior to 1928, every wall light fixture —indeed, the lighting for all the farm buildings— was fueled by gas made from powdered carbide, piped directly into the house from the tank near the windmill.) After 1928, he also instituted a complete water pressure system, whereby hot and cold running water was pumped into both the kitchen and the upstairs bathroom. Grams and Granddad had the most modern house for miles around. Most 1928 farmhouses were set up with only cold water pumped into the kitchen—much like Grams's old house. The "plumbing" was an outhouse or "privy," fully equipped with either a two-holer or a three-holer seat (depending on the size of the family), and a Sears & Roebuck catalog (later replaced by real toilet paper!).

The deep foundation of the new farmhouse basement also served as an alternative kitchen and dining room for the threshing crew during the dog days of summer, as well as a constantly cool vegetable room for all the crocks, vessels, and crates of homegrown produce. Here, too, the shelf-lined room provided storage space for the multitude of quart jars filled with sparkling fruits, beautiful vegetables, and their juices to be opened during off-season. Alongside were the sweet and sour crunchy pickles and relishes. Jars of dried apples and mincemeat stood nearby, ready to be popped into a fresh piecrust. Even with the addition of freezers and Dad's woodworking equipment, the basement larder remains the same room full of delicious farm food.

The cement-block, slate-sided farmhouse provides warm shelter from the blustery snow, sleet, and wind of winter, and is a cool oasis out of the blistering hot summer sun. Ivy continues to grow from the roots that Grams planted in 1938, partially covering the south and north sides of the house. Sometimes "the pesky stuff" winds its way into the sill of one of the forty-eight windows in the house. This may not sound like a lot of windows, but to Grams, it was a major improvement from the traditional window-or-two-to-a-room farmhouse. ("And small ones at that!")

Being "big, in the sunshine department," Grams tended numerous pots of green plants and flowers year-round in her sun parlor. Separated from the living room by French doors, this room was Grams's pride and joy—a brilliantly conceived in-house greenhouse. With vigor and acumen that would "do Grams real proud!" Mom continues her mother's tradition. "Sometimes, it gets like a jungle in there," laughs Mom, "and I have to give plants away!"

Grams's old (pre-1925) farm kitchen was a multifunctional room according to times of day and seasons: In the evening, it was transformed into a tub-room for family bathing; in the spring, a space behind the wood-burning stove served as an egg hatchery; and before every meal, the whole clan washed up in a round basin sitting inside a dry sink, and dried their hands on a white linen roll-towel hanging on the wall next to the stove. Don't forget the food preparation and preservation tasks performed there, and its role as the family dining room and social center.

In sharp contrast, her new kitchen was devoted strictly to these latter functions of food preparation, preservation, and family dining. In no uncertain terms would Granddad (or any other person alive) even dare to think about arriving at her dinner table with a speck of dirt on his shoes, sporting unchanged overalls or barn clothes—in short, unkempt or disheveled in any fashion. To Grams, cleanliness was next to godliness! (And Mom isn't much different!)

During my parents' remodeling, a powder room and laundry room were added on the first floor. Mom's efficient, state-of-the-art kitchen is still where the family gathers for breakfast, dinner, and supper around the same one-hundred-year-old oval oak table that was once used for carving meat in the basement. It is not only where the food preparation and preservation takes place, but our farm kitchen is generally the hub around which most daily activities occur.

Leading up from the dining room is an open staircase—the location of childhood imaginary places, where we played for hours. At the top, a long hallway joins the four, aptly named bedrooms: the North, East, and South rooms, plus a sleeping porch one the West and the large bathroom with a dressing area and linen closet in the middle. During Mom's childhood—and for that matter, mine as well—each bedroom was filled to capacity. There is always "room in the inn" at Opal and Troy's.

At present, the tillable fields are rented by younger neighbor farmers who observe sustainable agriculture procedures similar to Dad's. While overseeing the progress of the crops, Dad still takes out his trusty hoe during the evening hours before sunset "to catch a weed or two in the bean row." During the winter months, you will find him in the basement busy as a bee, creating handcrafted cedar baskets, carriers, trivets, or whatever strikes his fancy. Mom continues with her chores *de rigueur* in between her many civic obligations and, as Dad calls them, "her galavantings." If she's not whipping up a cake for company, late at night, you might find her in the North room tailoring one of the latest fashions.

Meanwhile, both of them, in their prime golden years, are fit as a fiddle, joyfully digging in the good earth, planting, harvesting, and reaping the bounty of beautiful flowers, fruits, and vegetables from their various garden patches. Mom preserves the fruits of their labor according to the best and latest methods, "just in case someone needs it." They provide enough food to feed all the friends and family members forever dropping by the home place, who are always grateful for the hospitality and accompanying care packages they take away. And remember, "there's lots more where that came from!"

The Home Place Family Tree

GRANDDAD'S SIDE OF FAMILY

▼▼▼▼▼▼▼▼▼▼▼▼▼▼▼▼▼▼▼▼▼▼▼▼▼▼▼▼▼▼▼▼▼▼▼▼▼▼

Cornelius Broadwater, m *Mary "Piper,"*

BORN IN BRISTOL, ENGLAND   BORN IN ENGLAND, DATES UNKNOWN

CAME TO MARYLAND, USA, 1804

▼

William Broadwater, m *Rebecca "Green"*

BORN IN ENGLAND, 1784,

5TH CHILD

▼

Robert Broadwater, m *Rebecca "Ogg"*

BORN IN USA, 3RD CHILD

▼

Darius Broadwater, m *Mary "Drury,"*

1ST CHILD, 1851–1935   1861–1938

▼

Frank Walker Broadwater,   m ▶

"Granddad"

B. 6/15/1889   D. 10/16/76

4TH CHILD, PRESTON, MINN.

Note: Emmett Crowe's Father and Mother:

Joseph Crowe, both birth and death dates unknown, left his wife, Sara Rapp, 1 daughter, and 3 sons to seek gold in 1860.

Sara Rapp, B. 8/24/1833, Germany, D. 6/24/16, Minn. From Maryland, they traveled by covered wagon to "the West."

GRAMS'S SIDE OF FAMILY

▼▼

Thomas Curtis,   m   *Elizabeth "Adams,"*

BORN IN LONDON, ENGLAND, 1792 CAME   B. 1790, LONDON, ENGLAND

TO MARYLAND, USA, 1800 D. 8/13/1849   D. 5/31/1873, MARYLAND

▼

Archibald Frisby,   m   *Elizabeth "Curtis,"*

B. 12/15/1824, MARYLAND   B. 1/7/1828 7TH CHILD,

D. 7/24/1874   MARYLAND D. 3/28/1862

▼

John Morgan Mansfield, m   *Alice "Frisby,"*

B. 1/10/1847, IOWA   D. 4/22/13, S.D.   B. 5/16/1850 1ST CHILD, IOWA D. 3/19/24

▼

Emmett Emerson Crowe,   m   *Esther Eliza Mansfield,*

B. 12/5/1859, WISCONSIN   B. 4/11/1868 1ST CHILD, IOWA D. 11/11/20, MINN.

MOVED TO S.D. 1870 D. 12/15/45, CA.

▼

Arlone Aletta "Crowe,"

"Grams"

B. 10/28/1891 2ND CHILD, ABERDEEN, S.D.   D. 7/5/75, MINN.

▼

Opal Ruby "Broadwater,"   m   *J. Troy Schrock,*

"Mom"   *"Dad"*

B. 10/17/13 1ST CHILD,   B. 12/30/10

PRESTON, MINN.   8TH CHILD, MIDDLEBURY, INDIANA

▼

Janeen Aletta "Schrock," m   *Richard Peter Sarlin*

author   B. 6/22/37, NEW YORK CITY

B. 4/14/41   M ON 12/27/64

2ND CHILD, GOSHEN, INDIANA

▼   ▼

Scott Peter Sarlin,   *Paige Heather Sarlin,*

B. 4/22/67, NEW YORK CITY   B. 9/23/71, NEW YORK CITY

The Cast
of Characters

In case you wonder who so-and-so is, in the recipe section, I have listed each person in order of appearance in the recipes (not on earth). Some family members are listed with birth and death dates—for obvious reasons—while other family members are still living and playing out their major roles as they see fit. All the other characters, most of whom were cast long before I arrived on the scene, merely have their relationship to our family explained. Whether the role was major or minor, each character's performance was important.

Grams: Arlone Aletta Crowe Broadwater, my maternal grandmother; born second child of twelve on 10/28/1891 in Aberdeen, S.D.; died 7/5/75 in Preston, Minn.

Granddad: Frank Walker Broadwater, my maternal grandfather; born third child of five on 6/15/1889 and died 10/16/76 in Preston, Minn.

Dad: J. (Joseph) Troy Schrock, my father; born eighth child of thirteen on 12/30/10 in Middlebury, Ind.

Mom: Opal Ruby Broadwater Schrock, my mother; born first child of three on 10/17/13 in Preston, Minn.

Aunt Rubye: Rubye Esther Broadwater Riehl, Mom's sister; born second child of three on 3/29/16 in Preston, Minn.

Great-Grandmother Broadwater: Mary Drury Broadwater, Darius Broadwater's second wife, Granddad's mother; born in 1861 and died in 1938 in Preston, Minn.

Gordon Snyder: Farmer neighbor who lived three-quarters of a mile south of the home place on the same farm as Aunt Isla and Uncle Sam (Grams's sister and brother-in-law).

Aunt Mabel: Mabel Irene Schrock Snider, Dad's sister; born seventh child of thirteen on 10/2/09 in Middlebury, Ind.; lives in New Paris, Ind.

Grandmother Schrock: Flora Edith Gephart, wife of J. (James) Harvey Schrock, Dad's mother; born second child of two on 9/19/1878 in Elkart, Ind.; died on 8/14/65 in Middlebury, Ind.

Lyle Austin: owner of Austin's meat locker, ice cream parlor, and soda fountain in Preston, Minn., 1940 to 1960s.

Edna Nagel: Distant cousin of Granddad's; farm neighbor who lived three-quarters of a mile south of the home place next to Gordon Snyder's farm.

Dave Ogg: Farmer neighbor who lived on the adjacent farm a half mile south of the home place. (He was probably the most wealthy farmer of the area from the turn of the century into the 1930s, with a smokehouse, an icehouse, and a "moonshine still" in the woods!)

Read Brothers: Ed and Bill Read owned the grocery store in Preston, Minn., where Grams purchased her provisions, from the turn of the century into the 1940s.

Aunt Marguerite: Ethel Marguerite Schrock Burke, R.N., Dad's oldest sister; born first child of thirteen on 9/21/1898; died on 4/22/83 in Middlebury, Ind.; married Dr. Homer Burke and they became missionaries in Africa.

Charlie Vanderbie: Owner of Vanderbie's General Store in Greenleafton, Minn., one mile west of the home place as the crow flies, where Grams and Mom purchased groceries, from the turn of the century into the 1940s; cousin by marriage to Granddad.

Charlie Keehn: Owner of the Charlie Keehn Meat Market (later Keehn & Son) in Preston, Minn., from 1924 to 1958, where all the meat was ground with a hand grinder and Great-Grandmother Broadwater, Grams, and Mom purchased weiners, salami, etc.

Great-Grandmother Crowe: Esther Eliza Mansfield Crowe, Grams's mother; born first child of three on 4/11/1868 in Iowa; died on 11/11/20 in Foley, Minn.

Joany: Joanita Austrid Schrock Brantl, my youngest sister; born fourth child of four on 3/21/51 in Harmony, Minn.

Aunt Janie Broadwater: Uncle George Broadwater's wife, Granddad's sister-in-law; lived in Preston, Minn.

Joel: Joel Frank Schrock, my older brother, born first child of four on 6/29/38 in Goshen, Ind.

Dorothy Burkholder: Neighbor, fellow church-woman, who lived next to the parsonage, one mile east of the home place.

Judy: Judith Ann Schrock Aufenthie, my younger sister, born third child of four on 10/31/49 in Cresco, Iowa.

Jeff: Jeffrey William Heitner, Aunt Bets's oldest son, my first cousin; born on 7/7/52 in Wykoff, Minn.

Judd: Judson Walker Heitner, Aunt Bets's youngest son, my first cousin; born on 3/25/58 in Wells, Minn.

Julie: Julie Ann Riehl, Aunt Rubye's only daughter, my first cousin; born on 2/15/56 in La Crosse, Wisc.

Grams's Great-Grandchildren (in birth order):

Susan—Joel's oldest child; born on 2/11/66 in West Chicago, Ill.
Scott—Janeen's oldest child; born on 4/22/67 in New York, N.Y.
Jay—Joel's second child; born on 5/7/68 in Winfield, Ill.
Bill—Judy's oldest child; born on 9/15/70 in Austin, Minn.
Stacey—Joel's youngest child; born on 6/3/71 in Geneva, Ill.
Laurie—Judy's second child; born on 8/18/71 in Austin, Minn.
Paige—Janeen's youngest child; born on 9/23/71 in New York, N.Y.
Todd—Judy's youngest child; born on 10/5/72 in Austin, Minn.
Jodi—Joany's only child; born on 10/4/73 in Denver, Colo.

Marie M. Kruegel: Farm woman, contemporary of Grams's, who lived in Carimona.

Aunt Isla: Isla Crowe Broadwater, Grams's older sister and wife of Uncle Sam Broadwater; born on 5/26/1890 in South Dakota; died on 9/26/72 in California; lived on a farm, one mile south of the home place, before moving west.

Jessie Tammel: Jessie Broadwater by birth, married to Jake Tammel, cousin and contemporary of Granddad's; farm neighbor who lived two miles east of the home place, fellow church-woman.

Charlotte Snyder: Gordon Snyder's oldest daughter, older neighbor friend of mine.

Nora East: Charlie Vanderbie's daughter, distant cousin, Mom's contemporary.

Aunt Bets: Betty Gene Broadwater Heitner, Mom's youngest sister; born third child of three on

7/16/27 in Preston, Minn.; married Maynard Heitner; lives in Wells, Minn., about eighty miles west of the home place.

Uncle Roy: Roy K. Riehl, Aunt Rubye's husband; born on 12/25/12 in Preston, Minn.

Uncle Buzz: Maynard G. Heitner, Aunt Bets's husband; born on 1/31/27 in Preston, Minn.

Hershel Ogg: Very distant cousin and young contemporary of Granddad's who lived one mile south of the home place, across from Edna Nagel.

E. J. Maloney: Irish hired hand who worked for Dad and other various farmers.

Marilla Heusinkveld: Wife of Ed Heusinkveld, my "other" grandmother and mother of Marjorie, Arlen, Leland, and Bethy; farm neighbor woman and fellow church-woman; contemporary of Grams's who lived one mile southeast of the home place.

Marcheta: Marcheta Tate, farmer's wife, mother, and teacher, living in Indiana; Manchester College classmate of mine.

Joan: Joel's wife, my sister-in-law.

Uncle Lee: Dr. Lee Burrous, Dad's brother-in-law, husband of Aunt Viola; second child of thirteen; lived in Indiana.

Grandfather Schrock: J. (James) Harvey Schrock, Dad's father; born first child of two on 4/16/1874 and died on 4/15/63 in Middlebury, Indiana.

Barbara Alexander: Barbara Alexander Storey, Kenneth and Rebecca Alexander's daughter who lived one mile north of the home place; contemporary childhood playmate of mine, now living in Texas.

Marvin and Jerry Rindels: Marvin is married to Gwenland Broadwater Rindels, a young contemporary and distant cousin of Mom's. (Gwen's and Mom's grandfathers were first cousins.) Jerry—Marvin and Gwen's son—enjoys big-game hunting with his dad. Both families live near Greenleafton.

Darius Broadwater: Granddad's father; born in 1851 in Allegheny, Penn.; died in 1935 in Preston, Minn. Darius's great-grandfather, Cornelius Broadwater, was born in England and came to Maryland in 1804; his father, Robert, moved to Fillmore County, Minnesota, in 1855. Darius bought the home place from Kerwin in 1889.

Kerwin: Homesteader of the property that my great-grandfather purchased as the home place in 1889, the year Granddad was born. Granddad purchased the home place in 1911; my dad rented the home place from his father-in-law in 1944 and bought it in 1946.

Ila Bloom: Mom's distant cousin, contemporary, and good friend.

Vilda Mandelko: Next-door neighbor lady, married to Carl Mandelko, contemporary of Mom's.

Doris Nagel: Neighbor lady, wife of Norris Nagel, Dorothy Burkholder's twin sister, Prairie Queen mother, and contemporary of Mom's.

Uncle Glen: Rev. Glen Montz, Grams's brother-in-law (husband of Aunt Iris, Grams's sister); Brethren Church minister who lived in the parsonage next to the Brethren Church, one mile east of the home place, and later moved to California.

Violet: Violet Iola Crowe Hayworth, Grams's sister who lived with Aunt Iris; twelfth child of twelve.

Irene Nagel: Wife of Perlam Nagel, Dorothy Burkholder and Doris Nagel's sister; neighbor lady who lived in Greenleafton.

Mary Bestor: Born Mary Broadwater, Granddad's first cousin on the Broadwater side (my third cousin); lived 99 years.

Veva Bestor: Mary Bestor's daughter, my second cousin.

Uncle Paul: Paul Christian Schrock, Dad's oldest brother, husband of Gladys Guffey; born third child of thirteen born on 2/4/02 in Middlebury, Ind.; died on 4/25/46 in Goshen, Ind.

Straight
Farm Talk

Here's a list—like a glossary—of words we use to describe things around the farm.

CLABBER: To become thick in souring (used in reference to milk).

COMING DOWN THE PIKE: An anticipation of the next event, happening, or behavior, based on previous experience and knowledge. Example: "I can see it coming down the pike."

DRUGSTORE—WRAP: Place a sandwich in the center of a sheet of waxed paper. Bring the two opposite sides together over the center, folding them over in small creases until the paper lies flat over the sandwich. Then fold the ends into a triangular shape and tuck them under the sandwich.

FOLEY FOOD FORK: A kitchen utensil with a six-pronged fork, at the end of an angled 10-inch handle that is made by Foley Company. We use it to mash potatoes, cut shortening into flour for piecrust, smash tomatoes or apples for sauces or butter—an all-around handy tool.

GRAMS'S BLACK BOOK: Grams's personal record and compilation of newspaper clippings and handwritten recipes (often spelled "receipt") in an unlined (originally blank) book with a black hard cover. She kept it in the linen tea towel drawer.

GUNNYSACK: Burlap material bag used for holding 100 pounds of oats or feed for cattle.

INGLENOOK COOK BOOK: A cookbook that traditionally was passed from generation to generation of American farm women. Preserved in the book are cherished recipes contributed by sisters of the Brethren Church, subscribers, and friends of the *Inglenook Magazine*. It was first published in 1901, then reprinted in 1911 and again in 1970 by the Brethren Publishing House, Elgin, Illinois.

KIT 'N CABOODLE: Everyone or everything, plus all the trappings.

MAKE OUT: To shape bread.

RAZZING: Teasing someone, using a sharp sense of humor.

RENNET: A preparation—usually a tablet or extract—of the rennet membrane, the lining of the fourth stomach of a calf. It is used to curdle milk, for making junket, ice cream, or cheese.

ROUND UP: Placing bread dough oiled side up in bowl, before allowing bread to rise.

SEN SEN: A tiny, black, strong-flavored licorice candy that looks like confetti; position on or under the tongue to melt. Sen sens come in small paper envelopes.

SOAP SOCK: A clean work sock, filled with homemade soap and tightly knotted, placed in hot-water washtub or washing machine for laundering clothes.

SUNNY: A small sunfish, found in freshwater creeks and rivers.

TRUCK PATCH: An area of land, too small for cash crops, that is planted with vegetables to be consumed by the family and sometimes to be marketed locally. Usually the plot is far enough away from the farm buildings that a truck is used to transport the produce.

WINNOWING: The act of cleaning the chaff from corn or grain. When done by hand, the dried corn is poured from one pan that is held 12 to 14 inches above another pan, outside in a good brisk breeze.

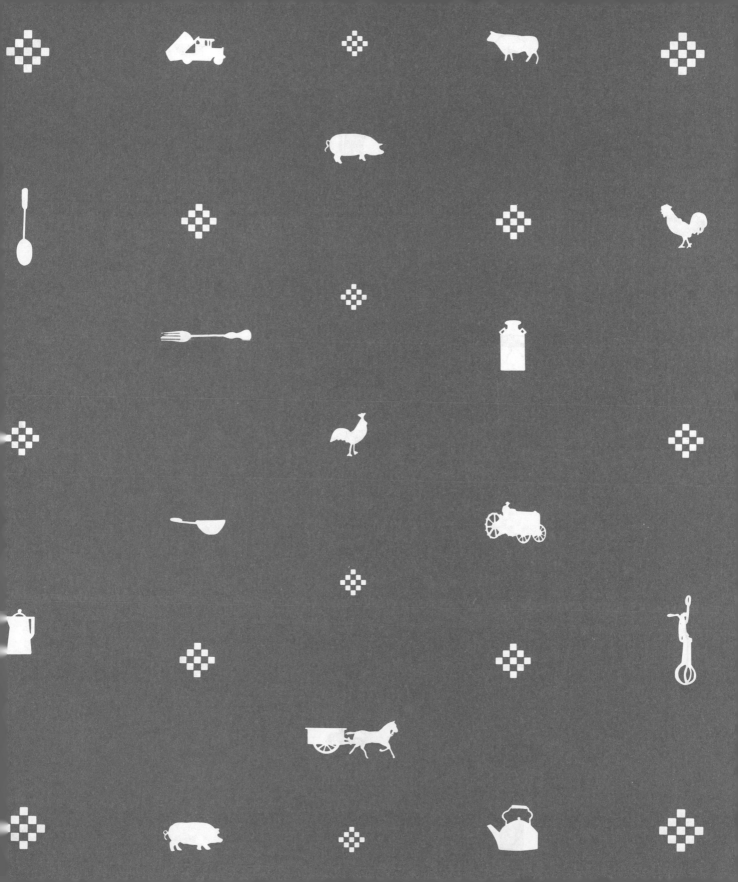

EARLY
BIRD
BREAKFAST

On the farm, dawn is ushered in by a symphony of bird songs. They begin with a few clear, high flute-like chirps and melodies, and are soon joined by the "bill and coo" soothing middle tones to form harmonious intricate warbling duets. The sudden punctuation of a rooster's "cock-a-doodle-doo" is the trumpet call to the rest of the chicken flock, sending the hens into their arias of "clucks." Introduce the booming, bass notes from the barnyard cattle, accented with a rolling "bleat," a mud-muffled "snort," or a winsome "whinny," to give the beginning-of-the-new-day chorus the support of a full symphony orchestra.

Like the birds, Dad was an early riser. "I like to get a head start on the day's work," he'd say. His objective was to be in the field, with his team of horses, as the sun came up over the horizon, even if this meant he milked the cows in the dark. His morning milking routine often started at new light to the accompaniment of the barnyard concert. The clink of the milkers that he carried to the barn was a sure signal for the cows to let down their milk.

Meanwhile back in the house, Mom stayed in bed as long as she dared. Judging from the size of the dairy herd, and what she planned to fix, she timed breakfast to be ready when Dad re-entered the house. We kids were on our way down from upstairs as Dad leapt up the basement steps, taking them two at a time—our own ballet to the kitchen table.

Breakfast truly meant "breaking the fast" on the farm. It was a bountiful meal, which usually began with healthful whole-grain cereals sprinkled with crumbled brown sugar and rich top milk. We had freshly laid eggs with their upright yolks and transparent whites fried to perfection in sizzling bacon grease, or a stack of mile-high buttermilk pancakes hot from the griddle, topped with flavor-rich, hand-sugared maple syrup. These were sided with crisp, home-cured, smoked bacon or a corn-fed steak, and breakfast fries from home-grown potatoes. A big bowl of untainted berries or seasonal citrus fruit accompanied everything. Woven into the edible composition were breakfast rolls, sweet butter, freshly brewed coffee, orange juice, and milk.

After this hearty breakfast, everyone had sustenance for the work at hand: We kids either trudged off to school or pitched in with the chores—outside or in; Dad continued his workday and Mom commenced her post-breakfast duties.

On your next trip to farm country, wake up at the sound of the first chirping note, then listen as the ensuing musical tribute unfolds, ringing in a resplendent new day. Then head downstairs for some breakfast.

Not-So-Gruelsome Graham Cereal

❖

Graham and whole wheat flour are interchangeable (not to be confused with whole grain, but a close relative to it). Grams and Mom called this cereal graham. But I call it a wonderful, thick, whole-flavored wheat cereal and enjoy it still whenever I can.

To keep this cereal free from those gruesome lumps, the whole trick is to mix the flour into the cold water before adding it to the hot water. Whoo-lah! Now "you ain't just whistling 'Dixie'!"

In saucepan, bring 6 cups water and salt to a boil. In small bowl, stir ½ cup cold water into flour; mix until smooth, adding any additional water, up to ¾ cup amount, until desired consistency is achieved.

Pour flour mixture into boiling, salted water, stirring constantly. Reduce heat to medium-low and cook, stirring often, for approximately 25 minutes, or until water is absorbed. Cereal should be thick and smooth.

Just before serving, stir half-and-half or milk into cereal. Pour into bowls and serve with brown or white sugar.

6 CUPS WATER
½ TEASPOON SALT
½ TO ¾ CUP COLD WATER
2 CUPS GRAHAM FLOUR

1½ CUPS HALF-AND-HALF OR MILK
BROWN OR WHITE SUGAR

SERVES 6

Winsome Whole-Grain "Grub"

"Oats, peas, beans, and barley grow. Whether or not, nor anyone knows, how oats, peas, beans, and barley grow." This songwriter obviously was not raised on a farm! We not only knew how it grew, but we knew how good whole-grain "grub" tasted. Around the turn of the century, Grams would soak whole wheat berries overnight to soften the tough outer shell. Next morning, she drained off the soaking water and cooked the berries into cereal. (Some say the soaking water, with a bit of sugar and lemon juice, will reduce a fever!)

Thanks to modern mechanical means, only about thirty minutes are necessary to make this rich-with-natural-sweetness, generally pleasing, whole-grain "grub" for your family.

....

In medium saucepan, bring water and salt to a boil. Stir oats and wheat berries into water; return to a boil and reduce heat. Cover and simmer for approximately 30 minutes, or

6 CUPS WATER
PINCH SALT
1½ CUPS STEEL-CUT OATS
1½ CUPS WHEAT BERRIES

MILK OR HALF-AND-HALF
BROWN SUGAR

until grains are tender to the bite. Stir often. Add a bit more water if necessary to keep grains from sticking to bottom of pan.

Remove from heat. Serve with milk and brown sugar. In season, top with blackberries, blueberries, strawberries, or raspberries.

NOTES Wheat berries are available in most health-food stores or in the gourmet, grain, or cereal section of your supermarket. Package labels may not indicate "wheat berries"; they may read either "hard" (or) "soft" wheat. Wheat berries are brown, round, and about the size of a kernel of unpopped popcorn; after cooking they become firm yet extremely palatable, granular, nutty-flavored cereal. Any leftovers can be transformed into a pilaf or a salad for another meal.

Do not substitute Quaker oatmeal or Scotch oatmeal for the steel-cut oats because the consistency is not the same.

S E R V E S 6

Maize, a generous gift from the Indians to our forefathers, sprouts up at almost every meal. Here for breakfast the grain is cooked with water, milk, and salt—to pour out of the pan like liquid gold into the cereal bowl. Left to chill overnight, it becomes a firm golden nugget, ready to be sliced and fried for another breakfast or supper. Truly a-maize-ing stuff.

"A-Maize-ing" Cornmeal Mush

❖

3 CUPS WATER
½ CUP MILK
PINCH SALT
1 CUP YELLOW CORNMEAL
½ CUP COLD WATER

MILK OR HALF-AND-HALF
SUGAR

In medium saucepan, bring 3 cups water, ½ cup milk, and salt to a boil.

In small bowl, mix cornmeal and cold water together until well combined. Briskly stir meal mixture into liquids on stove; continue to stir constantly until mixture in saucepan boils. Reduce heat and simmer partially covered, approximately 30 minutes; stir every so often. It will be thick, bubbly, and spattering away.

Pour into bowls and serve, topped with milk and sugar.

Pour leftover mush into loaf pan that has been rinsed with cold water. Cover with plastic wrap and refrigerate until firm. To store, remove from pan, wrap in plastic, and refrigerate up to 2 weeks.

S E R V E S   6

Fried Cornmeal Mush

❖

1 LOAF OF COLD CORNMEAL
MUSH
2 TO 3 TABLESPOONS BUTTER
2 TO 3 TABLESPOONS VEGETABLE
OIL (MOM USED LARD)

Preheat oven to 375°.

Slice firm loaf "nugget" into ¼-inch-thick pieces (or slice sizes according to personal preference). In skillet, heat butter and oil until sizzling. Fry cornmeal slices over moderately high heat until crisp and brown on both sides; loosely cover pan to reduce splattering.

Drain crisp slices on baking sheet lined with brown paper bag. Keep hot in warm oven until all slices are fried. Serve with *Master Homemade Sausage* (page 46) and *Old-Fashioned Griddle Cake Syrup* (page 36).

S E R V E S   4   T O   6

FROM GRAMS'S GRIDDLE

After morning milking (believe me, she milked her share of cows), Grams got cleaned up and stirred up a batch of pancakes. She didn't need a recipe. After all, she served them for breakfast every day, along with bacon and eggs or ham, because Granddad wanted his pancakes! Rumor has it that the "plain old pancakes" of Great-Grandmother Broadwater (Granddad's mother) were stacked high on the back of the stove, making them soggy and tough. Bearing that in mind, Grams served her pancakes straight from the griddle.

And straight from Mom's griddle come the basic recipe and variations. It takes a bit of practice to make them by heart like Grams did.

Some Threesome
Aunt Rubye, Mom, and Janeen

Master
Pancake
Recipe

❖

In small mixing bowl, beat eggs with rotary eggbeater (or process until frothy in food processor).

Add flour, sugar, baking powder, salt, milk, and butter or oil; beat or process just until smooth.

Heat griddle or frying pan until very hot. (When a few drops of water skitter across the pan, it's ready.) Lightly grease with oil and pour ⅓ cup batter onto pan. Cook until puffed and dry on edges; flip over and cook until golden brown. Serve immediately (I bring the batter and electric skillet right to the table). Top according to personal preference with butter, *Old-Fashioned Griddle Cake Syrup* (page 36), or *Homemade Applesauce* (page 153).

VARIATIONS

Apple or Banana Pancakes Stir in ½ teaspoon cinnamon and pinch of nutmeg. Add 1 cup apple, peeled, seeded, and chopped or thinly sliced; or 1 cup banana, thinly sliced.

2 EGGS
2 CUPS FLOUR
2 TABLESPOONS SUGAR
2 TABLESPOONS BAKING POWDER
1 TEASPOON SALT
1½ CUPS MILK
4 TABLESPOONS BUTTER (MELTED) OR VEGETABLE OIL

1 TO 2 TABLESPOONS VEGETABLE OIL FOR GREASING PAN

Blueberry Pancakes Add pinch of freshly grated nutmeg to batter; stir in 1 cup fresh blueberries, washed, picked over, and well drained.

Buckwheat Pancakes Substitute 1 cup buckwheat and 1 cup whole wheat flour for all-purpose flour; use 2 cups milk.

Buttermilk Pancakes Substitute 2 cups buttermilk for regular milk. Decrease baking powder to 2 teaspoons and add 1 teaspoon baking soda.

Cornmeal Pancakes Substitute 1 cup cornmeal for 1 cup flour.

Rye Pancakes Substitute 1 cup rye flour for 1 cup all-purpose flour; add ¼ cup more milk.

Whole Wheat Pancakes Substitute 2 cups whole wheat flour for all-purpose flour. Add ¼ cup more milk and substitute brown sugar for white sugar.

MAKES 12 SIX-INCH PANCAKES

Old-Fashioned Griddle Cake Syrup

❖

This was the only syrup on the breakfast table during Grams's era. However, Mom added little pitchers of white and dark corn syrup, as well as sorghum, to our selection. After Dad and his friend, Gordon Snyder, began "sugaring"—(making maple syrup), we poured "Dad's Maple Syrup" over our pancakes.

In medium saucepan, stir brown and white sugar into water until sugar is

½ CUP BROWN SUGAR
½ CUP WHITE SUGAR
1 CUP WATER

½ TEASPOON MAPLE FLAVORING (OPTIONAL) (GRAMS USED WATKINS IMITATION MAPLE FLAVORING)

dissolved. Stop stirring, bring to a boil, and boil to desired thickness.

Suggested cooking times are 5 minutes for very thin syrup and 10 minutes for medium syrup (my favorite).

Remove from heat; flavor if desired (I don't). Pour into small pitcher set on plate; serve hot.

MAKES ¾ TO 1 CUP

"Boil some water, dump in part brown and white sugar and boil it. Add maple flavoring if desired."
Mom

36

THE CHICKEN OR THE EGG?

✦

Which came first, the chicken or the egg? Previous generations of farm families have never agreed on the answer and I doubt if future generations will. Ours couldn't. This issue aside, here is the rest of the "chicken (s)coop."

Grams gathered eggs from the nests of what we now call "free-range chickens" every morning and evening. Such chickens are allowed "free run" of the grounds surrounding the farm buildings. The hen-house (or coop) was designed with roosts hanging along one wall at an angle. Every evening just before sundown, the chickens "came home to roost." In fact, the term "tuck yourself in" comes from the resting habits of chickens: They sleep with their heads tucked under their wings.

Along another wall of the coop stood a double row of "nesting boxes," each large enough for a chicken to fit inside. Part of the chicken chores was to keep clean straw in those boxes so that the chickens would lay eggs in them.

I dreaded gathering the eggs that were under an "old dumb clucker." With her beak, she tried to dissuade my reaching under her. Talk about "hen-pecked"! Taking matters into my own hands (what else could I do?), I distracted her vicious attack with a stick, while slipping the other hand underneath her feathers and quickly fetching the eggs. Some-times as many as twelve eggs were in one nest! Mind you, one chicken did not lay all of them. Other hens also used the same nest. Upon squatting and feeling lots of eggs under her, the hen "naturally got the notion to nest!" That's why she didn't want me to gather the eggs.

Most healthy chickens lay one or two eggs a day. But in hot weather they go into a "molt" and lay fewer. In anticipation of this, Grams saved extra eggs for baking by putting them in a gallon glass jar covered with a saltwater solution. These eggs were then stored in a crock in the cool basement. Grams never served these preserved eggs for breakfast, but she used them for baking.

A fresh egg yolk stands high up in the center of a clear, almost stiff white with very little water on the edge. The yolk of an older egg is flattened some-what; the whites are not as clear and have a more watery edge. For the best eggs, try to buy them straight from the farmer.

Next best, check the date that is stamped on the carton in the grocery store. Open the carton, check each egg for cracks, and see whether or not it moves freely in the slot.

Because the shells are porous, eggs readily absorb any and all aromas surrounding them. (Some restaurants put a truffle in the center of the egg carton to flavor the eggs that are used to make omelets.) I store eggs in their cartons away from the vegetable drawer and use the egg-keeper spaces in the door of the refrigerator to store a half of a lemon or lime, small leftovers, little bags of herbs that could otherwise be overlooked, and my vitamins.

Cholesterol was not a word in my family's vocabulary when I was young. Today, with all the nutritional information available about food and its effect on personal health, I cannot recommend eating two fried eggs every morning. However, most of us may enjoy eating a fresh egg every so often.

Grams's and Dad's Fried Eggs

✦

6 TABLESPOONS BUTTER
6 FRESH EGGS
SALT
BLACK PEPPER, FRESHLY GROUND

Grams's Perfect Egg Story

One summer Saturday morning I accompanied Grams to church for the purpose of being her "young apprentice." She was going to make breakfast for 150 people who were attending "District Meeting," an annual event that was held at different churches within the district.

After frying what seemed to me pounds and pounds of bacon in a huge, black, cast-iron skillet over a kerosene stove, Grams carefully cracked a dozen eggs into a china bowl and gently slipped them one by one into the remaining hot bacon grease. Each egg sat-up majestically in that heavy skillet as she spooned the flavorful fat over them—twelve perfect eggs sunny-side up. What a pro! I was impressed.

Dad's Perfect Egg Story

Contrary to anything I've led you to believe, Dad entered into the cooking scene too. His elaborate, specific procedure for "two perfect fried eggs, sunny-side up" begins with the proper pan: Grams's old, six-inch, black Griswold cast-iron skillet with the red lid that fits perfectly inside. Dad melts butter in the skillet over high heat on the electric stove. After adding two fresh eggs and covering the pan with the red lid, he turns off the heat, leaving the pan on the element. The eggs are cooked to perfection in a few minutes. (The time varies depending on personal preference.) This method works *only* on an electric stove with a cast-iron skillet because only that combination of element and skillet holds just enough heat to complete the cooking process.

All you need is a heavy skillet and farm-fresh eggs to produce a perfect egg story of your own.

Melt butter in heavy skillet over moderately high heat until bubbly. Break eggs into bowl. Carefully slip into skillet, one at a time. Reduce heat. Cook over low heat, spooning butter over egg yolks until whites are set, or until they are done according to personal preference.

Remove eggs from heat; season to taste. Serve immediately, garnished with sprig of parsley.

S E R V E S 6

OPAL'S OMELET SECRETS

❖

Learning from her grandmother, Mom's secret to successful omelet-making is a well-seasoned skillet. The inside story is this: Fill the skillet (any skillet will do) with an ample amount (1 to 1½ inches deep) of vegetable oil or shortening. (Mom used lard.) "Heat" the oil for fifteen to twenty minutes on the stove over moderate heat. Or, if the skillet is ovenproof, "bake" at 375° for fifteen to twenty min-utes. Remove from the stove top or oven. Pour the hot oil into a bowl and reserve for another use. Im-mediately sprinkle two to three tablespoons salt into the *hot* skillet. With a triple thickness of paper tow-eling or a brown paper bag, vigorously rub the salt into the surface of the skillet. Wipe out the excess salt and discard. *Do not wash the skillet in soap and water.* Cool and reserve the skillet for omelet-making.

Oven-Baked Omelet

❖

When a meal included "just the family," meaning no hired hands or extra men to feed, both Grams and Mom sometimes whipped up a baked omelet for supper, accom-panied by fried potatoes or a cheese sauce poured over the top.

■ ■ ■ ■ ■ ■ ■ ■ ■ ■ ■

Preheat oven to 400°.

Place butter in 10-inch cast-iron skillet or heavily buttered 8- or 10-inch au gratin or quiche dish, and heat in oven.

5 TO 6 TABLESPOONS BUTTER
9 LARGE EGGS, SEPARATED
PINCH SALT
4 TABLESPOONS FLOUR
8 TABLESPOONS CREAM OR
 HALF-AND-HALF
BLACK PEPPER, FRESHLY
 GROUND

Beat egg whites with salt until stiff but not dry. In another bowl, beat yolks until thick and lemon-col-ored. Beat in flour, cream, and pep-per; fold egg whites into yolk mixture.

Remove skillet from oven. Pour egg mixture into hot skillet and re-turn to oven. Bake for 5 to 10 min-utes. *Reduce heat* to 350° and bake for another 15 to 18 minutes, or until light brown on top and firm when pressed with finger.

Slice into wedges and serve im-mediately.

S E R V E S   6

Stove-Top
Omelet

Be sure to use "new" eggs and a newly seasoned skillet when preparing this "old" recipe. Count 2 eggs per person, up to three people. At that point, count about 1½ eggs per person.

Beat eggs and water with fork; season with black pepper.

Heat butter in seasoned skillet over moderately high heat until foam subsides; pour eggs into skillet all at once. Shake skillet back and forth rapidly over heat. At the same time, stick table fork into center of eggs, allowing raw eggs to flow through to cook on bottom. Continue to cook until eggs are lightly browned on edges and slightly firm but moist over most of surface. (Put the filling in at this point.)

"Jerk" or tilt pan away from you and, with the help of a fork, quickly fold omelet in half. Cook a few seconds longer. Turn out onto plate.

9 EGGS
4 TABLESPOONS COLD WATER
BLACK PEPPER, FRESHLY GROUND
4 TO 5 TABLESPOONS BUTTER

Pour hot butter from skillet over top and serve immediately, garnished with fresh herbs.

VARIOUS FILLINGS
Cheese Omelet Sprinkle with ⅓ to ½ cup shredded cheddar, American, or any variety of cheese you wish.
Herb Omelet Sprinkle with ¼ cup total chopped fresh parsley and chives. (Add dash of other herbs—for example, chervil, tarragon, or thyme—if desired.)
Onion Omelet Sauté ¼ to ⅓ cup chopped onions or scallions in 1 to 2 tablespoons butter until soft and translucent. Season to taste with salt and pepper.
Potato Omelet Sauté 1 large baked potato, cubed, in 2 to 3 tablespoons butter until crisp and brown. Season to taste with salt and pepper. Sprinkle omelet with chopped fresh parsley.

S E R V E S   6

Brown and White Breakfast Fries

If starting with raw potatoes, scrub potatoes but do not peel. In large pot of boiling salted water, boil potatoes approximately 20 minutes or until tender to point of fork. Drain well and cut into thick slices of desired size; reserve.

6 LARGE POTATOES OR LEFTOVER COOKED POTATOES
3 TABLESPOONS BUTTER
1 TABLESPOON LARD OR OIL
SALT
BLACK PEPPER, FRESHLY GROUND

Heat butter and lard or oil in skillet until sizzling. Add sliced potatoes. Fry until crisp and brown, stirring occasionally. Season to taste.

S E R V E S   6

Great Grandparents Esther and Emmett Crowe, Wedding Photo, 1880

High-Strung Breakfast: Steak and Eggs

◈

It was common practice to have a hind quarter of beef hanging on a meat hook attached to a ceiling beam in the cool tank room in the basement of our house. Breakfast steak presented no difficulty: Mom cut off a thick or thin slice of beef according to the number of us eating and fried it! This arrangement, ordinary to me, is not a high-strung story. However, you may need to pull high strings for a fresh slice of steak for an Early Bird Breakfast!

▪▪▪▪▪▪▪▪▪▪▪▪▪▪▪▪▪▪▪▪▪▪▪▪▪▪▪▪▪▪▪▪

Trim meat and cut into 6 serving pieces. Pound with meat hammer or

1 ROUND STEAK, ABOUT 1½ POUNDS
APPROXIMATELY ¾ CUP SALTINE CRACKERS, CRUSHED
2 EGGS
APPROXIMATELY 1½ TABLESPOONS MILK
BLACK PEPPER, FRESHLY GROUND
4 TO 5 TABLESPOONS BUTTER
1 TO 2 TABLESPOONS VEGETABLE OIL (MOM USED LARD, GRAMS USED BUTTER)

wooden mallet to tenderize. (Grams used the edge of a china plate.)

Crush crackers in plastic bag with rolling pin, or process until fine; empty onto plate.

In small bowl, beat eggs with milk; season with pepper to taste. Dip steak into egg and then into cracker crumbs.

Heat butter and oil in skillet until hot. Add steak; brown on both sides. Reduce heat and partially cover. Continue to cook until done to order.

Serve immediately with plain scrambled eggs. Garnish with fresh herbs.

S E R V E S 6

Crazy Creamed Eggs

❖

The party-line telephone system was the only one available to rural communities until the late 1950s. One line connected ten to twelve families, each family having its own ring code—such as one long and two short, four short and two long, two long and one short, and so on. Upon hearing your "ring," you picked up the phone. But as expected, everyone else on the line did likewise! (Now you know the origin of the term "rubbernecking.") Some folks were even so bold as to break in on your conversation with their "two cents"!

Aunt Mabel (Dad's sister) explained, "When central [the telephone operator] heard either exciting news or there was an emergency, she rang a lot of little rings in succession. People ran like crazy when they heard that ring!" The operator then instructed everyone where to send help. Also, this party-line system eliminated the need for written invitations. When a hostess planned a party or had a baby, she called "central" with one long ring. Every person ran "like crazy" to the phone to hear the news!

There is no reason to run like crazy from this delicious Pennsylva-

CREAM SAUCE
■ ■ ■
3 TABLESPOONS BUTTER
3 TABLESPOONS FLOUR
PINCH SALT
BLACK PEPPER, FRESHLY
  GROUND
1 ½ TEASPOONS DRY
  MUSTARD
1 ½ CUPS HOT MILK

ASSEMBLY
■ ■ ■
6 HARD-COOKED EGGS
6 SLICES TOAST, BUTTERED
AND HALVED DIAGONALLY

nia Dutch–style recipe of Grandmother Schrock's. It is an easy one to make, adaptable to your own personal preference, and if the phone rings, go ahead and answer—the eggs will be fine.

Melt butter over low heat in heavy saucepan. Blend in flour, salt, pepper, and mustard with wooden spoon or wire whisk. Cook for 2 to 3 minutes, stirring constantly. Do not brown.

Off heat, add hot milk all at once, stirring constantly. Return to heat and cook 2 to 3 minutes longer. Remove from heat again; taste and correct seasonings.

Sauce can be done ahead. Transfer to nonreactive bowl, place plastic wrap directly on sauce (so no air pockets or skin forms on top), and refrigerate. Reheat in double boiler or microwave 1 to 2 minutes until hot.

TO ASSEMBLE Peel cooked eggs; cut into quarters. Fold quartered eggs into hot cream sauce; season to taste. Serve on toast points.

S E R V E S   6

43

I'm sure a breakfast of bacon and eggs immediately conjures up a picture of your favorite eggs with slices of bacon on the side. Taste this old-fashioned family recipe that combines the flavors.

▪▪▪▪▪▪▪▪▪▪▪▪▪▪▪▪▪▪▪▪▪▪▪▪▪▪▪▪▪▪

Crumble cooked bacon into small pieces; place in skillet with butter. Heat bacon and butter over moderate heat until sizzling.

Beat eggs with fork in bowl; pour over bacon and butter in skillet. Cook over moderate heat until

M om and Aunt Rubye, in typical farmer fashion, sometimes bartered a roast beef (of ours) for a ham (of Rubye's). This system works well for farmers because they have goods to trade.

If the barter system is not good for you, either buy a piece of ham, or use leftover baked ham for this breakfast.

▪▪▪▪▪▪▪▪▪▪▪▪▪▪▪▪▪▪▪▪▪▪▪▪▪▪▪▪▪▪

Slice ham thinly. Melt butter in skillet until sizzling; fry ham until browned on both sides. Remove

Farmer-Style Crumbled Bacon and Eggs

7 TO 8 SLICES COOKED BACON
3 TEASPOONS BUTTER
8 EGGS

Bartered Breakfast Ham and Eggs

6 SLICES BAKED HAM, ¼ TO ½ INCH THICK
3 TO 3½ TABLESPOONS BUTTER
6 LARGE EGGS
BLACK PEPPER, FRESHLY GROUND

edges are set. Stir up once and continue to cook until eggs are completely set.

Shake skillet to loosen eggs, carefully slip flat-sided wooden spoon or pancake turner under one edge, and quickly lift eggs up and over, as if turning a pancake. Don't worry if it's not perfect!

Continue to cook 1 to 2 minutes longer.

Remove to platter. Slice into wedges and serve immediately, garnished with fresh herbs.

S E R V E S   6

meat to platter lined with paper towels or brown paper bag to absorb excess fat; keep warm in oven or near stove.

Crack eggs separately into bowl. Gently slip eggs all at once into hot skillet; reduce heat. When edges of whites are set, either turn or spoon hot butter over eggs to cook top sides.

Remove paper towels from ham platter. Place an egg on top of each slice of ham. Season with black pepper to taste and serve immediately.

S E R V E S   6

HOMEMADE HEIRLOOM SAUSAGE

◆

Making sausages by hand was a long and arduous process. Both Grams and Granddad took turns at the handle of the meat grinder and manually forced the odd cuts of boned pork meat into the hopper. The ground meat pushed out the end of the grinder and dropped into a large dishpan set on the floor. This was one of Grams's "messy" jobs, originally done in the pump house. After our bigger house was built, she worked in the basement. Grams mixed salt, pepper, and sage into the ground meat with her hands and placed the meat mixture into a metal two-gallon "lard press."

The lard press was similar to a small milk can. It was round and metal, but the lid was a heavy metal plate with a large auger handle. On the bottom the spout would be fitted with a six-inch metal funnel for stuffing sausages. The press had two functions.

Dave Ogg's Family Table

One procedure extracted cracklings from the hot liquid pork fat—or lard; the second stuffed sausages.

Grams first prepared the cleaned hog-gut casings by washing them several times in salted water. Just before she attached the casing to the spout, she scraped the inside with a silver table knife, keeping to her own sanitary code. Grams put the seasoned meat in the lard press, fitting the metal plate snugly on top. Then Granddad cranked the handle on the lid to move the heavy plate down, compressing the meat into firm, air-bubble-free sausage while he held the casing on the spout with his other hand. As the sausage flowed into the casing, Grams twisted the filled portion every two to three inches to form breakfast sausages. Whew! This was an all-day process!

Mom and Dad made sausages the same way until the late 1950s. After that they took the butchered hog into Austin's and asked Lyle to process all the meat into sausages . . . "whole hog sausage." (I'll tell you all about Austin's and Lyle a little later.) The sausages were smoked and packaged into meal-sized portions (for six) and frozen. Granddad took some of the raw sausages up the road to Dave Ogg's smokehouse. After the sausages were smoked, Grams canned them for safekeeping. A neighbor, Edna Nagel, preserved her sausages by putting the smoked links in a crock jar and pouring hot lard on top. She stored the crock in the cool basement. After the lard hardened, it formed an airtight, but not foolproof, seal on top of the meat. Whenever she needed sausages, she went into the basement, scraped off some of the lard, took out what she needed, and fried them in that lard. After the sausages were brown, she poured the hot lard back on top of the remaining sausages in the crock!

"For heaven's sake, do not do that now!" cries Mom. "It's amazing that no one died from food poisoning after eating those."

As for the sausages that had not been smoked, Grams poached them in a brine for twenty minutes and then canned them while they were still hot for variety.

This non-vintage method comes from a former student, Tanya Tesa: If a sausage stuffer is not in your larder, poach fresh sausage meat in cheesecloth.

Master Homemade Sausage (with Grams's Down-Home Flavor)

❖

1½ POUNDS GROUND PORK, LEAN
1½ TEASPOONS SALT
1½ TEASPOONS BLACK PEPPER, FRESHLY GROUND
1½ TEASPOONS GROUND SAGE

Bone and trim pork; grind in food processor to desired texture, then weigh meat. Or ask butcher to grind lean pork as if for meat loaf.

Place ground meat in bowl; thoroughly mix in salt, pepper, and sage. An electric mixer is all right, but not a food processor (so meat remains coarse, not smooth).

Fry a tablespoonful of raw meat in small skillet to check seasonings; adjust according to taste.

Place meat on sheet of plastic wrap, set on top of tea towel.

Bring edge of plastic nearest you over top of meat; then, using towel as a cradle, firmly roll meat into cylinder shape, sealing edges as you work, and remove towel. Refrigerate immediately until ready to poach.

WHEN READY TO POACH SAUSAGE In large saucepan, bring water, salt, and sugar of poaching brine to a boil; boil 20 minutes.

Cut cheesecloth to a length of approximately 24 inches, dampen with water, and unfold to double thickness, then lay flat on clean counter. Remove sausage roll from refrigerator and remove plastic wrap by unrolling meat onto cheesecloth; tightly re-roll meat into "log" shape. Securely twist each end and knot. Tie with kitchen string to keep shape.

Poach in boiling brine to cover, 35 to 40 minutes. Test internal temperature with thermometer; it must reach 170°. Remove sausage from liquid, chill in cloth (wrapped in plastic bag), and refrigerate overnight. Can be stored in freezer up to one month, or in refrigerator meat cooler 1 to 2 days.

TO SERVE Slice off patties; add a few drops of olive oil or butter if sausage is very lean. Heat skillet and brown patties on both sides. Drain on brown paper bag and serve immediately.

VARIATIONS
Top Note Sausage Add 1½ teaspoons rosemary (ground in mortar and pestle) to master recipe.

POACHING BRINE
■ ■ ■
4 QUARTS WATER
½ CUP SALT
1 CUP SUGAR

Hot and Tasty Sausage Add 1 teaspoon rosemary and 1 teaspoon thyme (ground in mortar and pestle), plus 2 medium cloves garlic (minced), and pinch of cayenne pepper to master recipe.

Christmas Breakfast Sausage Add 1 teaspoon thyme (ground in mortar and pestle), pinch of cloves, and ⅛ teaspoon freshly ground nutmeg to master recipe.

French Pâté–Flavored Sausage Add 1 tablespoon brandy and 1 medium clove garlic (minced) to master recipe.

S E R V E S   6

Imagine a grease-marked handwritten note: "Brine recipe: 1 gal water, ½ cup salt, 1 cup sugar. Let come to boil, then stuff sausage. Put in about 1 gal sausage, let boil 20 min, pick with fork so won't burst. Can while hot. Will keep fine." Grams's Black Book

Sausage, to make: "Take 20 pounds of pork (¾ lean and ¼ fat), 6 ounces of salt, 1 ounce of pepper, 1½ ounces of sage. Put the meat through a meat grinder, and mix all together well." Inglenook Cook Book, 1901

Bride's Breakfast Rolls

❖

Both Grams and Mom were famous for their bread-baking ability. We seldom ate store-bought bread even though I secretly wished for some. Whenever the bread supply was low, another batch of *Potato Water Bread* (page 57) was waiting in the wings.

Mom also liked to have an ample supply of rolls on hand for our breakfast. Although she generally made various rolls from the dough for *Potato Water Bread,* the recipe here was a good backup for her emergency supply.

This recipe is suited for those of us, myself included, who, unlike pioneer women, are not near the hearth/home the required amount of time needed to execute a "proper" bread recipe. It was named by Grams, who declared it "so simple that even a young bride can make it!"

▪▪▪▪▪▪▪▪▪▪▪▪▪▪▪▪▪▪▪▪▪▪▪▪▪▪▪▪▪▪▪▪

THE NIGHT BEFORE Proof yeast, sugar, and ¼ cup warm water in small bowl, 15 to 20 minutes. (Test temperature with a few drops on your wrist; it should feel warm, not hot.)

In large mixing bowl, combine water, sugar, and 4 cups flour. Beat until smooth; add yeast mixture and

2 PACKAGES DRY YEAST
1 TEASPOON SUGAR
¼ CUP WARM WATER

2 CUPS WARM WATER
½ CUP SUGAR
8 CUPS FLOUR TOTAL,
 DIVIDED INTO TWO 4-CUP
 PORTIONS
1 TABLESPOON SALT
2 TABLESPOONS LARD OR
 BUTTER, MELTED
2 EGGS, BEATEN

mix well. Add remaining ingredients—salt, lard, beaten eggs, and remaining 4 cups flour; mix until smooth. It will seem sticky, but do not add more flour.

Cover with large plastic bag inverted over top of bowl and refrigerate overnight. Be sure to put another bag under bowl on shelf also. (I forgot to use the second bag one time and as a result, the dough rose over the top and down the sides of the bowl, making a sticky mess throughout the refrigerator! I didn't forget it again!)

Prepare 2 or 3 jelly roll pans and/or several cake pans for baking depending on size of each slice you cut and amount of dough desired. I use 2 jelly roll pans for a generous (13 to 14) baker's dozen of rolls and three 9-inch cake pans for a snug-generous (6 to 7) half-dozen cluster. But do not worry about the exact inches of the pan for rolls; "take a cake, that's another story!" Grease pans heavily with lard or solid vegetable shortening and, if desired, sprinkle with sugar (see variations).

TO MAKE ROLLS Remove dough from refrigerator, turn onto floured board, and cut in half with knife. Roll out one portion of dough with rolling pin to form square approximately 12 inches by 15 inches.

Spread desired filling over dough and roll up in jelly roll fashion. Tightly pinch dough along seam to close. Cut off slices ¾ to 1 inch thick and arrange flat on prepared baking pan. Roll out second half of dough and continue in the same manner. Cover all rolls with damp tea towel. Set in warm "friendly place to rise." (The best place is near the oven, but not over the pilot light.) Allow approximately 30 to 45 minutes for dough to double in bulk. Preheat oven to 400° during this time.

TO BAKE Bake for 15 minutes; reduce heat to 350°. Continue to bake approximately 20 minutes longer or until evenly brown. Rolls should sound hollow when tapped with knuckle. Remove from oven and turn out onto cooling rack; cool completely.

TO STORE If not eaten immediately, wrap rolls in plastic. Place in plastic bag, seal tightly, and freeze until needed.

TO DEFROST Remove from freezer and allow to come to room temperature on counter overnight. Or, microwave according to manufacturer's directions. Or, remove from freezer and unwrap plastic wrap; rewrap rolls in tin foil and reheat in 350° oven for approximately 15 minutes or until hot.

VARIOUS FILLINGS

Caramel Nut Rolls Sprinkle ¼ cup brown sugar evenly over greased baking pan. Melt ½ cup butter; lightly brush butter over dough. Mix 1 cup brown sugar with approximately ⅓ cup heavy cream (or more), until mixture is just thin enough to spread with table knife. Spread on top of buttered dough. Sprinkle with ½ cup pecans (coarsely chopped), and roll up as directed.

Christmas Morning Cinnamon Rolls Melt ½ cup butter; lightly brush butter over dough. Mix 1 cup white sugar, 1 tablespoon cinnamon, and 1 teaspoon vanilla with approximately ⅓ cup heavy cream (or more), until mixture is just thin enough to spread with table knife. Spread evenly on top of buttered dough and roll up as directed.

Cinnamon Raisin Rolls Follow directions for cinnamon rolls, then sprinkle 1 cup raisins over dough before rolling up and continue.

Orange Rolls Sprinkle ¼ cup white sugar evenly over greased baking pan. Melt ½ cup butter; lightly brush butter over dough. Mix 1 cup white sugar, grated rind of 1 large orange, and approxi-mately ⅓ cup heavy cream (or more), until mixture is just thin enough to spread with table knife. Spread evenly on top of buttered dough, sprinkle with ½ cup chopped nuts, if desired, and roll up as directed.

Walnut Rolls Sprinkle ¼ cup brown sugar evenly over greased baking pan. Melt ½ cup butter; lightly brush butter over dough. Mix ½ cup white sugar and ½ cup brown sugar together with approximately ⅓ cup heavy cream (or more), until mixture is just thin enough to spread with table knife. Spread evenly on top of buttered dough, sprinkle with ½ cup walnuts (chopped), and roll up as directed. (When Mom and Dad lived in Indiana, Mom used hickory nuts and butternuts from their own trees. After moving to Minnesota, she used black walnuts from the trees growing next to the chicken coop. English walnuts were considered a delicacy and therefore they were used sparingly!) Pecans can be substituted for walnuts, if desired.

MAKES 3 TO 4 DOZEN ROLLS

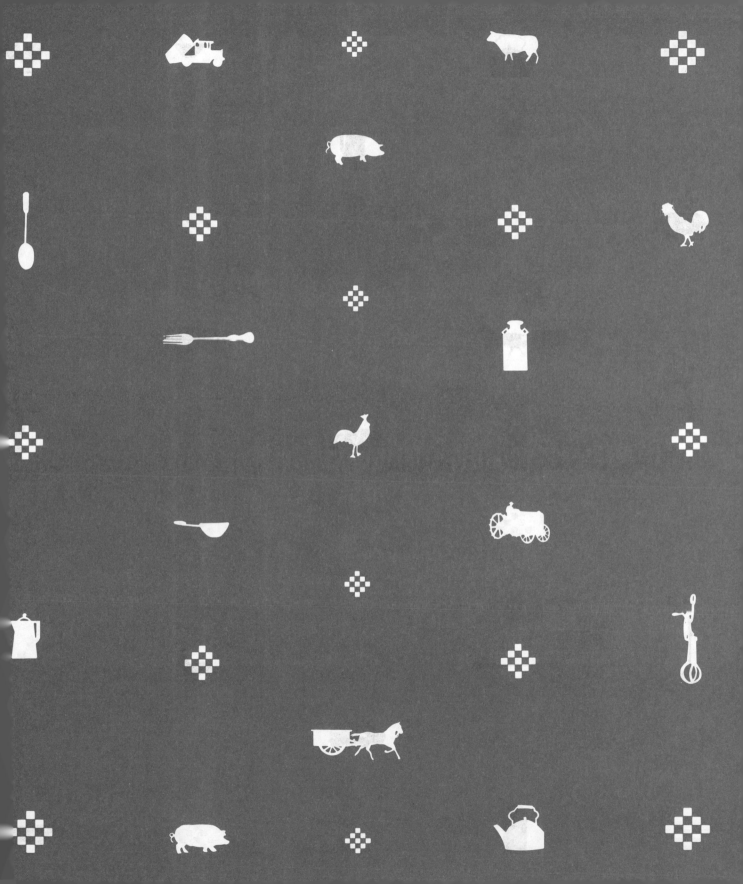

"A LITTLE SOMETHING TO TIDE YOU OVER" LUNCH

Lunch was served to men on the farm at around 10 A.M. between breakfast and dinner, and then again at around 3 P.M. between dinner and supper. Grams offered the first "little something to tide you over" (between meals) as a preface to more substantial noontime fare, which was "dinner" in farm language. Granddad always stopped for lunch because he wanted to give the horses a rest from their work supplying the power for the farm equipment—the plow, disc, drag, mower, rake, and wagons. The men were also thankful for the respite.

When Mom and Aunt Rubye were young, they walked barefoot out to the hayfield to deliver lunch to the men. Grams sometimes made a ginger "brew" from powdered ginger, sugar, water, and vinegar. Like most farm women, Grams simply mixed up this concoction, poured it in a big crock jug, wrapped the jug in a damp gunnysack to keep it cool, and sent the refreshing drink to the men working outside.

The two girls also carried out sandwiches and cookies. When they arrived, Granddad loosened the harness on the mares so their colts that followed behind could nurse while the men ate their lunch. (This image of horses is so peaceful compared to the large, looming, diesel-powered tractor that Dad uses for farm work today!)

On the way back to the house, the two sisters caught grasshoppers in their hands. Just for good, clean, farm-style fun they put the insects in the empty gunnysack and watched the bag hop. Later, they released them onto the lawn; the girls then would go back to their household chores.

Unlike Granddad (and more than anyone else I know), Dad was always in a hurry to get things done, and he preferred to have an uninterrupted work morning and afternoon. However, after he became accustomed to his Minnesota neighbors' farm work habits, he learned to enjoy lunch. (Dad's workday began at 5 A.M. during planting and harvest season. He took a ten-minute nap on the dining room floor after dinner whenever he needed rest.)

When I was little, we served lunch "on site" wherever the men were working. However, I did not walk out to the field barefoot. I either rode on an empty haywagon with food in hand or, when I was older, I drove the pickup to deliver lunch. When the men saw me coming, their faces lit up with big smiles.

Mom filled a white enamel coffeepot with *Egg Coffee* (page 72), for the men to drink, along with a jug of refreshing well water. In the summer we filled a gallon glass jar or metal pail with lemonade, Kool-Aid, or iced tea for a cool alternative to coffee or water. Dad always drank water and the Kool-Aid or lemonade, but Granddad drank black coffee. I passed out the delicious overstuffed sandwiches and large cookies or whopping big pieces of cake to the men. They ate with gusto to replenish the calories they burned off with their rigorous work. These days Dad comes into the house for an apple or a handful of peanuts when he needs a rest. If a crew of men are working for him, they come into the house for lunch, instead of Mom taking it to them.

On the home front, Grams, Mom, and Aunt Rubye simply drank a cup of coffee and ate a cookie on the run for their lunch. Typical of most farm women, they didn't take the time for a rest during their normal morning or afternoon work. But, whenever Mom and I went to town, morning or afternoon, we ate lunch at Grams's before we headed "up the hill"—home. In the afternoon, Grams always served tea. This tradition was a legacy from her English heritage, no less. I loved to have tea with her! While Grams put up a pot of tea, I set the table with cups and saucers, sugar, jam or jelly, and a small pitcher of milk. I opened the familiar red cookie tin hoping to find white sugar cookies inside.

Sometimes she stored wonderful mouthwatering ginger creams in it. If she had baked bread that morning, we'd all have a fresh bun with butter and jam, plus a cookie or two. Grams also brewed a fresh pot of coffee for Mom. Obviously, neither caffeine nor calories were a household concern in those days.

THE GRANDMOTHER OF BREAD

◆

Great-Grandmother Mary Drury Broadwater, an Oregonian by birth, grew hops in her garden. The small cone-shaped flower from a "hop" vine—dried, then reconstituted—was the catalyst that transformed flour, sugar, and water into a starter or yeast for bread. She would mix up a batch of starter and place it in a crock jar, fashioning a lid by draping a tea towel over, with a plate on the top. This allowed the starter to "work." From this starter she made a basic white bread. We call it sourdough bread.

Unlike Great-Grandmother Broadwater, Grams neither grew hops in the garden nor fermented the starter. She purchased the hops from Read's Grocery. In her *Black Book* was her handwritten yeast recipe: "Take twelve good-sized potatoes, boil and mash fine; save the water they were boiled in and

Grams, High School
Graduation

have a small handful of hops, boiled in a separate pan; strain the hop water; add 1 tea-cupful of sugar and the same of salt; put all together to make 1 gallon. Always save a pint of the yeast to start with when you make again. Keep corked in a jug or crock jar in a cool place."

Grams kept the starter down in the tank room. She kept it alive with the addition of sugar and potato water when it was necessary, per her directions. Later, around 1920, Grams began using small compressed yeast cakes. They were troublesome because it took a long time for the sugar and warm water to start the yeast's growth.

Because Mom and Grams served potatoes in one form or another every day, the vitamin-filled potato water was an abundant and natural base for bread. The dough was formed into loaves,

55

rolls, pan rolls, sandwich buns, or whatever shape they needed at that time.

Continuing in the family tradition, I too save potato water to make this creamy-colored, flavorful, and lightly textured bread. If a delay is necessary, I refrigerate the potato water in a plastic container. When I am ready to mix up the bread, I reheat the water in the microwave until it is warm.

▼▼▼▼▼▼▼▼▼▼▼▼▼▼▼▼▼▼▼▼▼▼▼▼▼▼▼▼▼▼

Potato Water for Bread

❖

Peel and halve 1 large or 2 medium potatoes, place in medium-size saucepan, cover with 1 quart of cold water, and bring to a boil. Add 1 teaspoon salt and continue to cook, approximately 20 minutes, or until very tender to point of knife. Cooking time will vary according to size and type of potato. Off heat, remove potato and "rice" it directly back into hot cooking water, then cool to room temperature. Proceed according to recipe or refrigerate in glass jar for up to 1 week.

MAKES APPROXIMATELY 1 QUART

▲▲▲▲▲▲▲▲▲▲▲▲▲▲▲▲▲▲▲▲▲▲▲▲▲▲▲▲

Potato
Water
Bread

◈

Proof yeast in warm water with sugar. Stir well and set aside to "work" about 10 minutes. Be careful: If left longer, it will grow out of the container.

Heat potato water to about 105 to 115°. It should feel comfortable when a drop is placed on the inside of your wrist (as if testing a baby's bottle). In large bowl, mix proofed yeast, potato water, sugar, and 3 cups flour. With wooden spoon beat until smooth and elastic; beat in salt and lard or butter. Continue to beat while adding remaining 4 to 4½ cups flour, a half-cupful at a time; dough will still be sticky, but pulls away from side of bowl.

Turn dough onto floured board or pastry cloth and cover with clean towel; let rest 5 to 10 minutes. Meanwhile, rub 2 to 3 tablespoons flour around edges of bowl to clean and add these dough particles to mass of dough on board. Wash bowl, grease with lard, and set aside. Knead dough on floured board until smooth and elastic for about 7 to 10 minutes. It's good therapy.

TO TEST Stick two fingers into

2 PACKAGES DRY YEAST
½ CUP WARM WATER (110 TO 115°)
1 TABLESPOON SUGAR
1¾ CUPS WARM POTATO WATER (SEE RECIPE, PAGE 56)
2 TABLESPOONS SUGAR
7 TO 7½ CUPS ALL-PURPOSE FLOUR TOTAL, DIVIDED INTO PORTIONS OF 3 AND 4 TO 4½ CUPS
1 TABLESPOON SALT
2 TABLESPOONS LARD OR BUTTER, MELTED AND COOLED

ball of smooth dough, and if impression stays, it is ready to rise. Place dough in greased bowl and "round up." Cover with damp linen towel; let rise in warm place (approximately 80°) until double in bulk. This first rise should take about 1½ hours. Punch down; cover again with towel and let rise for approximately 30 more minutes.

TO MAKE OUT AND BAKE Generously grease inside of two 9-by-5-by-3-inch (2-pound) loaf pans, or two 8-by-4-by-2-inch (1½-pound) loaf pans plus one 7-by-3-by-2 (1-pound) loaf pan with lard; grease hands as well. Divide dough into two equal portions; spank ball of dough to remove any large air bubbles. Shape into 2 loaves, and place dough in prepared pans; let rise 20 minutes more. Preheat oven to 425°.

Bake 10 to 15 minutes; reduce heat to 400°. Continue to bake approximately 15 to 20 minutes longer. Bread is done when it is evenly browned on all sides and sounds hollow when pan is rapped with knuckle on bottom. When done, remove bread from pan and cool on rack. Slice after it is completely cool.

NOTE A finished loaf of bread should have an even brown crust on the outside and a creamy white–colored, even-textured grain inside. Large holes mean that there was too long a rising period before the bread was baked. A coarse texture will result after too short a kneading process. Do not be discouraged. It takes practice to bake a finished loaf of bread. At the ripe age of thirteen, I baked one loaf of bread every day to practice for the annual 4-H Bread Baking Contest. I won grand champion at the county level and went on to receive a blue ribbon at the State Fair!

VARIATIONS
To Shape Potato Water Sandwich Buns Grease baking sheet and hands. Pinch off piece of dough about size of large egg; place dough in palm of hand and squeeze into ball between thumb and forefinger. Place your other hand over top of ball and in downward motion, "pull" top layer of dough over ball (as if taking your arm out of a sweater sleeve and

> *"Put the flour in a warm place in an open pan to dry thoroughly before using. Take 1 quart of warm potato water, 1 small tea-cupful of yeast, flour enough to make a stiff batter; let rise overnight in a warm place. In the warmest weather let rise about 3 hours; then add flour enough to knead without sticking to the pan, knead ½ hour; set to rise again, when risen sufficiently, knead 10 minutes without using more flour; mold into loaves; set to rise, and bake 1 hour."* Inglenook Cook Book, 1901

bringing the cuff with you) until top is smooth. Then spank out excess bubbles, squeeze/twist off excess dough below your thumb, and tuck rough edges under ball as you place "bun" on prepared baking sheet. Flatten with hand to finish bun's shape. Let rise another 15 to 20 minutes. Bake at 400° for 12 to 15 minutes.

To Shape Pan Rolls Grease four 7-by-3-by-2-inch (1-pound) loaf pans and hands. Pinch off piece of dough about size of large egg, place in palm of one hand, and with other hand, roll into cylinder shape. Place dough at one end of prepared loaf pan. Continue with about 5 or 6 more cylinders until pan is full. Let rise 15 to 20 minutes and bake following loaf directions above.

TO STORE When bread or rolls are completely cool, place in plastic bag, seal airtight, and refrigerate or freeze until needed.

TO DEFROST Remove bread from freezer. Defrost 3 to 4 hours or overnight at room temperature, or follow manufacturer's directions for microwave defrosting.

MAKES 2 LARGE LOAVES OR 2 MEDIUM LOAVES PLUS 1 SMALL LOAF

Cinnamon
Raisin
Bread

◆

Nothing was a better welcome home from school than the aroma of freshly baked bread. I'd barely remember to shoo the flies off the back-porch screen door before I opened it: the yeasty aroma of fresh bread was as inviting to the insects as it was to me. Imagine walking into a kitchen where the counters were covered with loaves of freshly baked bread; Mom never made a small batch.

Because I had a sweet tooth, cinnamon raisin bread was my first choice. This recipe is equally suitable for a tasty cream cheese–filled tea sandwich or comforting breakfast toast.

■■■■■■■■■■■■■■■■■■■■■■■■■

Proof yeast in warm water with sugar; stir well and set aside.

Place potato water and milk in mixer bowl. Add sugar, proofed yeast, and 2 cups all-purpose flour and beat well.

Add nutmeg, cinnamon, salt, eggs, and butter; beat until smooth and elastic. Mix raisins into batter. Continue to beat while adding 4 to 5 cups flour, a quarter cupful at a time, to make stiff dough.

1 PACKAGE DRY YEAST
½ CUP WARM WATER (110 TO 115°)
1 TABLESPOON SUGAR
¾ CUP WARM POTATO WATER (SEE RECIPE, PAGE 56)
¾ CUP WARM MILK
¼ CUP BROWN SUGAR
6 TO 7 CUPS ALL-PURPOSE FLOUR TOTAL, DIVIDED INTO PORTIONS OF 2 CUPS AND 4 TO 5 CUPS
½ TEASPOON NUTMEG, GROUND
1 TEASPOON CINNAMON
1 TEASPOON SALT
2 EGGS, BEATEN
¼ CUP BUTTER, MELTED AND COOLED
2 CUPS RAISINS

TOPPING
■ ■ ■

¾ TO 1 TEASPOON CINNAMON, OR TO TASTE
2 TABLESPOONS SUGAR
1 TO 2 TABLESPOONS BUTTER, MELTED

Turn dough onto floured board or pastry cloth. Cover with clean towel and let rest 5 to 10 minutes. Clean bowl and grease with lard and set aside. Knead dough until smooth and elastic; add a little more flour to board only if necessary to keep from sticking. Place dough in greased bowl, round up, and cover with damp towel. Let rise until double in bulk (see page 57). Punch down; let rise again for approximately 30 minutes.

TO MAKE OUT AND BAKE Generously grease 2 medium 8½-by-4½-inch (1½-pound) loaf pans. Divide dough in half; spank dough and shape into loaves. Place in pans and let rise until almost double for approximately 30 more minutes. Preheat oven to 425°.

Mix cinnamon and sugar together. Brush loaves with melted butter. Sprinkle half of cinnamon and sugar mixture on each loaf. Bake for 25 to 30 minutes or until rich brown. Remove bread from pan and cool on rack.

MAKES 2 MEDIUM LOAVES

Whole Wheat (Graham) Bread

◈

Mom made whole wheat—graham—bread by substituting whole wheat flour for the white flour in the basic *Potato Water Bread* recipe (page 57). I use 2 cups of all-purpose flour to start, then whole wheat, whole-grain, and/or brown rice flour interchangeably according to my whimsy. For a crunchy variation, add ½ cup raw sunflower or toasted sesame seeds before kneading.

································

Proof yeast in warm water with sugar; stir well and set aside.

Place potato water in large bowl. Add sugar, proofed 2 tablespoons yeast, and 2 cups all-purpose flour; beat until smooth and elastic (can be done in electric mixer with a dough hook).

Beat in salt and lard; continue to beat while adding wheat flour, ½ cupful at a time. (For electric mixer method: When dough starts to work up mixer paddle, remove paddle. Add rest of flour with wooden spoon until dough pulls away from side of bowl, but is still a bit sticky.) Add ½ cup seeds at this time, if desired, for variation.

2 PACKAGES DRY YEAST
½ CUP WARM WATER (110 TO 115°)
1 TABLESPOON SUGAR
2 CUPS WARM POTATO WATER (SEE RECIPE, PAGE 56)
PINCH BROWN SUGAR
2 CUPS ALL-PURPOSE FLOUR
1 TABLESPOON SALT
2 TABLESPOONS LARD OR BUTTER, MELTED AND COOLED
APPROXIMATELY 4 TO 5½ CUPS WHOLE WHEAT FLOUR (OR 7 TO 8 CUPS DIFFERENT FLOURS TOTAL, INCLUDING 2 CUPS *ALL-PURPOSE* FLOUR ABOVE)

Turn dough onto floured board or pastry cloth. Cover with clean towel and let rest 5 to 10 minutes. Clean bowl; grease with lard and set aside. Knead dough until smooth and elastic. Add a little more flour only if necessary to keep from sticking to board. Test with two fingers (see instructions, page 57).

Place dough in greased bowl, round up, and cover with damp linen towel. Let rise in warm place until double in bulk (approximately 2 hours). Punch down let rise again for approximately 30 minutes.

TO MAKE OUT AND BAKE Generously grease 2 medium 8½-by-4½-inch (1½-pound) loaf pans. Divide dough into four equal portions. Spank ball of dough to remove large air bubbles. Make out as for *Potato Water Bread* (page 57). Let rise until almost double (approximately 30 to 45 minutes). Preheat oven to 400°.

Bake 45 to 55 minutes, or until loaves are evenly browned on all sides and sound hollow when rapped with knuckle on bottom. Remove bread from pan and cool on rack.

MAKES 4 SMALL OR 2 LARGE LOAVES

Mom's Swedish Rye Bread

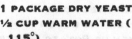

This wonderful, moist cakelike bread is from Mom's repertoire. At family celebrations, she added thin slices of this marvelous rye bread to the brimming basket of rolls on the table. We slathered a thick layer of rich creamery butter on top.

This sweet molasses-flavored bread tastes especially good when combined with a slice of either longhorn cheese or turkey breast. Add a crisp lettuce leaf and top with another slice to make a sandwich.

Proof yeast in warm water; add pinch of sugar.

Combine rye flour, molasses, lard or butter, and salt. Add boiling water and blend well; cool until lukewarm.

Beat in yeast from above. Add additional flour a cup at a time, beating well after each addition. Cover with damp tea towel and let rest 10 minutes.

Turn out onto floured board or pastry cloth; knead until smooth and

1 PACKAGE DRY YEAST
½ CUP WARM WATER (110 TO 115°)
PINCH SUGAR
2 CUPS RYE FLOUR
¾ CUP LIGHT MOLASSES
⅓ CUP LARD OR BUTTER
2 TEASPOONS SALT
2 CUPS BOILING WATER
6 TO 6½ CUPS ALL-PURPOSE FLOUR

"satiny." Add more flour only if necessary to keep from sticking to board. Place dough in greased bowl and round up. Cover with damp tea towel and let rise in warm place until double in bulk, about 1½ to 2 hours. Punch down; let rise again for 30 minutes.

TO MAKE OUT AND BAKE Turn dough onto lightly floured surface and divide into thirds. With greased hands, spank out excess air bubbles. Form into round loaves, tucking ends under smooth top. Place loaves on greased baking sheet and cover with damp towel. Let rise 20 to 30 minutes. Preheat oven to 350°. Before baking, beat 1 egg with 1 teaspoon cold water; brush tops of loaves with egg glaze.

Bake approximately 35 to 40 minutes or until bread is browned and sounds hollow when tapped with knuckle. Cool completely on rack.

MAKES 3 LARGE FREE-FORM LOAVES

Farm
Fried
Bread

❖

Both the Schrocks and the Broadwaters served homemade bread with every meal. Mom continued with the tradition. Whenever we had eaten all the bread in the house, and Mom had a new batch rising but not baked, she made this recipe for dinner. She heated lard in the old Griswold cast-iron skillet, cut off a few slices of dough after the second rising, and fried them golden brown. The result was similar to a very light–textured English muffin. Oblivious to calories, we slathered butter over the bread and topped it with strawberry jam.

I like to serve fried bread for a special breakfast treat to weekend guests.

APPROXIMATELY ONE-QUARTER THE DOUGH FROM A BATCH OF *POTATO WATER BREAD* (PAGE 57) OR *BRIDE'S BREAKFAST ROLLS* (PAGE 48)
3 TO 4 TABLESPOONS LARD OR BUTTER

Cut off six slices of raw dough (each approximately 5 to 6 inches long) after second rising.

Heat butter in skillet (10 to 12 inches) until hot. Add slices of dough and fry until golden brown, turn, and continue to fry until browned on other side.

Remove from skillet; pat dry with paper towels. Serve immediately with butter and jam.

MAKES 6 SERVINGS

C.B.Y.F.
Barbecued
Beef Buns

When the C.B.Y.F. (Church of the Brethren Youth Fellowship) or the 4-H Club met at our house, Mom served barbecued beef buns. The recipe was a favorite of everyone, including Mom. The preparation is easy and the result is a terrific-tasting sandwich for people of all ages. Mom served homemade dill pickles, and carrot and celery sticks on the side. We drank chilled apple cider or homemade *Grape Juice* (page 80). Popcorn balls and *Aunt Rubye's Brownies* (page 97) were dessert.

This infallible recipe is ideal for a hearty weekend lunch or late-night supper. I serve a tossed green salad on the side and top it off with a frosty glass of beer.

Cook meat in dry skillet or 3-quart saucepan over high heat until lightly browned (some bits of beef will stick to the bottom).

Add chopped onions and continue to sauté until onions are soft. Season

1 POUND 80% LEAN GROUND BEEF
2 MEDIUM YELLOW ONIONS, PEELED AND CHOPPED
½ TEASPOON SALT
1 TEASPOON BLACK PEPPER, FRESHLY GROUND
1 TEASPOON SUGAR
½ TEASPOON GARLIC POWDER
1 TEASPOON YELLOW MUSTARD
1 TABLESPOON WORCESTERSHIRE SAUCE
SPLASH TABASCO SAUCE
GENEROUS ½ CUP CATSUP (MOM PREFERS HUNTS)
8 SANDWICH BUNS

to taste with salt and pepper. Add sugar, garlic powder, mustard, Worcestershire sauce, Tabasco, and catsup. Bring to a boil, lower heat, and simmer until thick but not dry (approximately 30 to 40 minutes).

If necessary, add some water or tomato sauce to keep mixture moist, yet firm enough so it doesn't soak through bread. Taste and correct seasonings.

TO SERVE Remove from heat and spoon equal portions into buttered buns. Serve with garlic dill pickles and your favorite relishes. Filling may be made ahead.

TO STORE FILLING AND USE LATER Place in airtight container and refrigerate 3 to 4 days or freeze up to 3 months. Defrost in refrigerator until thawed, then reheat until piping hot. Spread generous portion of BBQ meat onto buttered sandwich buns.

MAKES APPROXIMATELY 8 SANDWICHES

Aunt Rubye's Harvest Bologna Filling

❖

During hay and harvest season I helped Aunt Rubye prepare and serve the lunches—and other meals as well—for the men. All farm women were expected to manage every aspect of housekeeping as well as the food preparation without outside help. Not hired help, certainly —only men had that privilege!

When the men saw us coming down the pike, they instantly stopped working; they knew these sandwiches were in the lunch box that we carried.

████████████████████████

Grind bologna in meat grinder; or, cut into chunks and process in food processor until coarse grind. Remove to mixing bowl.

1 RING COOKED BOLOGNA (FINE GRIND, HORMEL OR SCHWIGERT, 1 POUND)
4 EGGS, HARD-COOKED
6 MEDIUM SWEET PICKLES
Approximately ⅔ CUP HOMEMADE SALAD DRESSING OR MAYONNAISE (RUBYE USED MIRACLE WHIP)

A Bumper Harvest

Peel eggs and coarsely grind with pickles. Add to meat and mix by hand; regrind if necessary. Stir salad dressing into meat mixture; add more if needed to bind. Taste and correct seasonings.

NOTE If Hormel or Schwigert bologna is unavailable, use Hebrew National brand.

TO STORE Cover mixture with plastic wrap and refrigerate until serving time. This may be done 2 to 3 days ahead.

TO SERVE Spread generous amount of filling (⅓ to ½ cup) on lightly buttered bread or sandwich buns.

MAKES 10 GENEROUS SANDWICHES

River Bank Beefsteak Sandwich Filling

✦

Twice a year Granddad hitched up Roxy and Topsy (his best matched team of strong work horses) to a steel-wheeled flat wagon bed. Aunt Rubye went along for the six-mile ride south of the farm to Granger, Minnesota. The mission was to dig sand from the banks of the Iowa River.

Most of the sand was used for insulation around the livestock water tanks. The remainder was either shoveled into piles outside the barn doors to collect the excess dirt and mud (a doormat for the farm animals) or scooped into a pan for the chickens. According to Granddad, "Any fool knew that to get good eggshells, there had to be a pan of sand in the coop!"

This day was always a banner day for Aunt Rubye because Granddad seldom invited her to tag along. She quickly fetched her doll, along with a few pails and small jars to store the odd shiny pebbles and small smooth stones that she gathered from the clear shallow riverbed. Knowing her intentions, Grams warned, "Don't go near the water! Don't fall in! Be careful of the cattle in the pasture!"

2½ POUNDS LONDON BROIL
½ TEASPOON BLACK PEPPER, FRESHLY GROUND
1 MEDIUM ONION, SLICED
½ CUP BEEF BROTH

4½ CUPS GROUND COOKED BEEF
¾ CUP ONION, COARSELY CHOPPED
4 SWEET PICKLES, CHOPPED
1½ TABLESPOONS DIJON MUSTARD
1 CUP MAYONNAISE (OR MORE, TO TASTE)
1 TEASPOON CELERY SALT
2 TO 3 TEASPOONS BLACK PEPPER, FRESHLY GROUND

After those instructions, the trip was twice as enticing and dangerous.

Grams packed a hearty lunch for the two of them to eat. She filled a quart jar (usually used for canning fruit) with hot black coffee for Granddad and a large glass jug with fresh cool well water for both travelers to drink. Each container was wrapped separately in newspaper. Then it was placed in a clean gunnysack for insulation.

They often carried these savory and satisfying ground beef sandwiches, made with a mixture of leftover roast beef, onion, and sweet pickles (hand-ground together in the meat grinder)—moistened with cooked salad dressing and seasoned with salt and pepper. Grams buttered the buns and generously filled the sandwiches, then cut them in half and packed each sandwich in a drugstore wrap of waxed paper. These bundles sat on top of two apples in the bottom of a gallon pail; a separate package of ginger cream cookies and an oatmeal raisin cookie or two completed their pail lunch.

While Granddad shoveled the sand from the river onto the wagon bed, Aunt Rubye gathered her stones, without any mishaps. The cushioned smooth return trip was slow because the wagon loaded with sand was heavy.

Make these treats whether you plan a trip to the riverbank or not. Although this recipe works well in the food processor (Grams used the meat grinder), be careful not to over-process—this is not a pâté.

■■■■■■■■■■■■■■■■■■■■■■■■■■■■■

TO PREPARE FROM SCRATCH
Preheat oven to 350°.

In heavy casserole with lid, sear meat on both sides. Season with pepper to taste.

Strew onion slices over meat; pour in broth. Cover and bring to a boil. Bake 45 to 50 minutes, or until well done and tender.

Allow meat to cool in broth and refrigerate in broth until ready to prepare. Can be done 1 to 2 days before preparation.

TO PREPARE FROM LEFTOVER BEEF Remove fat from meat; discard cooked onion. Cut meat into 2-inch cubes. In small batches, process

8 to 10 pulses or until coarsely ground in grinder, then remove meat to bowl. Continue until all cubes are processed. Measure ground meat. For 1 quart loosely packed meat, proceed as follows:

Place half of meat in food processor bowl; add half of chopped onion and pickles and process 2 to 3 pulses to mix. Add half of mustard, mayonnaise, celery salt, and pepper. Process until mixture is an even grind (looks like hamburger).

Repeat process with other half of ingredients remaining to be ground. After all meat is processed, mix together thoroughly. Add more mayonnaise if necessary; taste and correct seasonings. Filling should be moist and have coarse even texture with slightly spicy zest. Can be made 1 to 2 days ahead; keep refrigerated.

TO SERVE Butter both sides of sandwich bun; add lettuce leaf, tomato slice, and desired amount of sandwich filling.

MAKES APPROXIMATELY 1 QUART FILLING

In October we served these aromatic hot sandwiches to the crew of corn pickers. When the men opened the sandwich bags, fragrant steam curled out. These delicious sandwiches also warmed their cold fingers.

If there was a large crew, we filled and wrapped all the sandwiches at once. We placed them in a large dry roasting pan. Mom covered the pan and heated them in a hot oven for approximately ten minutes. I carried the whole business directly out to the men.

Mom used a stewing chicken to make the filling, but I prefer a fat roasting chicken. *Be sure* to butter the sandwich buns generously on both sides before adding the hot chicken, so the chicken does not soak into the bread. I serve these sandwiches topped with a skewered sweet pickle on top of the bun. For a casual Sunday evening supper, add a tossed mixed green salad and crisp potato chips.

Cut chicken into pieces; place in large stockpot with lid (dark meat on the bottom and white meat on the top). Generously season with salt and pepper. Add carrot, onion, and celery to meat. Cover with enough cold water to come ¾ way up side of meat. Cover pan and bring to a boil. Reduce heat and simmer over low heat for approximately 1 hour, turning over once or twice, or until well done (meat should fall off the bones).

Autumn Sandwiches

◈

1 FOUR-POUND ROASTING CHICKEN WITH FAT AND NECK, BUT NO GIBLETS
1½ TEASPOONS SALT
1 TEASPOON BLACK PEPPER, FRESHLY GROUND
1 CARROT, PEELED AND SLICED
1 MEDIUM ONION, PEELED AND STUCK WITH 2 CLOVES
2 STALKS CELERY, SLICED

¼ TEASPOON SALT
DASH CAYENNE PEPPER
½ TEASPOON BLACK PEPPER
½ CUP GREEN PEPPER, FINELY CHOPPED

WHEN MEAT IS DONE Set strainer over large bowl; pour chicken, vegetables, and broth into strainer. Shake off excess broth, then return broth collected in bowl to pot. Bring to a rolling boil and reduce broth until only 2 cups remain; this will take approximately 20 to 25 minutes. Set aside to cool and allow fat to surface.

MEANWHILE Separate chicken meat from skin, bones, and fat. Cut meat across grain into cubes 1½ to 2 inches thick. Discard skin, giblets, bones, connective tissue, excess fat, and vegetables. Place cubed chicken in bowl and set aside.

TO ASSEMBLE Skim fat off broth and discard; pour reduced broth over chicken. Season chicken with salt, cayenne, black and green pepper; taste and correct seasoning.

TO SERVE Remove from heat and spoon large serving of chicken into buttered sandwich bun; serve immediately or reserve a short while.

TO STORE Place mixture in airtight container; refrigerate overnight or up to 4 days.

TO REHEAT Place seasoned chicken pieces along with jellied broth in saucepan; cover and slowly bring to a boil; remove from heat. To serve, proceed as directed above.

MAKES 6 TO 8 SERVINGS

Ladies Aid Pressed Chicken

✦

1 FOUR-POUND STEWING/ ROASTING CHICKEN WITH FAT, GIBLETS, HEART, ETC.
1½ TEASPOONS SALT
1 TEASPOON BLACK PEPPER, FRESHLY GROUND

To make this economical yet rich-flavored sandwich filling, both Grams and Mom cooked a stewing hen (an old chicken that no longer laid eggs on a regular basis). Before cholesterol and calories were important dietary concerns, Mom ground the skin, giblets, and stringy neck meat twice before she added them to the rest of the chicken. Now, neither Mom nor I add the skin.

On the first Thursday of every month, the church women gathered for Ladies Aid. These admirable women were the service arm of the church; they "went about doing good." For a Ladies Aid luncheon, Mom cut thin slices of the pressed chicken and placed them on individual beds of shredded lettuce garnished with olives and sweet pickles. She topped each slice with a dollop of homemade whipped salad dressing and served hot homemade rolls on the side.

▪▪▪▪▪▪▪▪▪▪▪▪▪▪▪▪▪▪▪▪▪▪▪▪▪▪▪▪▪

Cut chicken into pieces; place in large stock pot with lid. Place dark meat and giblets on bottom, and white meat on top; generously season with salt and pepper.

Cover with enough cold water to come ¾ way up side of meat; cover pot and bring to boil. Reduce heat; cook over moderate-low heat, turning over once or twice, for approximately 1 hour, or until well done (until the meat falls off the bones).

For more flavor, add 1 carrot (peeled and quartered), 1 medium onion (washed, whole, but unpeeled —to color the broth yellow), and 1 stalk celery (washed and quartered) to raw chicken. Cook as directed above; reduce salt if vegetables are added, because natural flavor will compensate for reduction.

WHEN MEAT IS DONE Set strainer over large bowl; pour chicken and broth into strainer. Shake off excess broth, then return broth collected in bowl to pot. Bring to a rolling boil and reduce broth until only 2 cups remain; this will take approximately 20 to 25 minutes. Set aside to cool and allow fat to surface.

MEANWHILE Separate chicken meat from skin, bones, and fat. Cut meat across grain into pieces ½ to ¾ inches thick; place in clean bowl. Cut off flesh part of gizzard, heart, neck, and about ¼ of liver. Chop these pieces into ¼-inch dice. Discard skin, bones, connective tissue, and fat.

Mix all chopped meat together. Season with approximately ¾ teaspoon celery salt and ½ teaspoon black pepper, freshly ground. Skim all but 2 tablespoons fat off reduced broth. Stir liquid into meat mixture; combine thoroughly. Taste and correct seasoning (more salt and/or pepper may be needed). Mixture should be moist and loosely held together. Spoon mixture into large, 9-by-5-by-3-inch, Pyrex glass loaf pan or very clean bread pan; seal top with plastic wrap.

TO PRESS AND STORE Set another bread pan filled with 2 or 3 unopened soup cans on top of meat; refrigerate overnight or up to 3 to 4 days.

"Pressed chicken. Stew the chicken quite soft, also let it boil almost dry. When done, pick the meat off the bones in rather small pieces. Put back in liquid; season to taste with salt and pepper. Pour all in a mold, under a press, in a cool place. Eat cold." Inglenook Cook Book, 1911

Man at Work

TO SERVE Unloaf by running sharp knife around inside edge of pan, dip bottom of pan into bowl of hot water for 30 seconds, and wipe water from pan. Invert pan on top of serving plate, unloaf with firm "jerk" or shake, and cut pressed chicken into approximately ½-inch slices or according to personal preference.

Fill buttered sandwich bun or bread, then dress with mayonnaise and a lettuce leaf. Or place sliced chicken on bed of shredded lettuce, garnish with pickles and/or olives, and top with whipped salad dressing (serving rolls on the side).

MAKES 6 TO 8 SERVINGS

Old-Fashioned Grilled Sandwiches

Ｗe ate the most unusual grilled sandwiches when I was growing up. Even though the technique was always the same, the fillings were as varied as Mom could imagine! First, I generously buttered one side of each slice of homemade bread. I put the two buttered sides together, leaving one un-buttered side of the bread facing up, then I lined them up on the counter. Mom placed the filling she had in mind on top of the bread and covered the whole affair with a damp tea towel. This procedure eliminated a last-minute scramble to butter, fill, and grill at the same time.

When we heard Dad open the back door, we heated the griddle very hot and started grilling the assembled sandwiches. By the time he had washed up in the basement and was sitting at the kitchen table, the sandwiches were hot off the griddle.

Cut bread into ½-inch slices; generously butter each slice. Face two

**12 SLICES HOMEMADE BREAD
APPROXIMATELY 6
 TABLESPOONS BUTTER,
 SOFTENED
APPROXIMATELY ¼ CUP—OR
 3 OR 4 THIN SLICES—OF
 MEAT, CHEESE, AND/OR
 VEGETABLES FOR EACH
 SANDWICH**

buttered sides together and place on clean counter top. Continue until all are prepared. Evenly spread filling over unbuttered side. Cover with damp tea towel or plastic wrap until grilling time.

When ready to eat, heat grill or skillet until drop of water skitters across pan. Uncover prepared sandwiches and separate buttered sides. Place buttered side of bread holding filling on grill (buttered side down), then put other slice on top of filling (buttered side up). Adjust heat to moderate. Grill until evenly browned; then turn with pancake turner. Grill other side until done. Halve each sandwich diagonally, or quarter by making an additional diagonal slice. Serve immediately.

NOTE Use your imagination for various other fillings.

MAKES 6 SANDWICHES

Black Coffee

The Crowe and Broadwater families drank black coffee every meal and in between, too. Even the babies were weaned from bottles with coffee-flavored milk in a teacup. Great-Grandmother Broadwater brewed coffee in an old-fashioned, twenty-four-cup, white, enameled coffee-pot. She simply filled the pot with cold water, dumped in a combination of coffee extended with ground chicory, and boiled it on top of the wood-burning stove.

The first few cups were delicious, but she kept the pot hot all day long. Rumor had it that by afternoon her coffee was so strong and bitter that a spoon stood straight up in the cup.

Because Grams did not like the taste of chicory, she used only freshly ground coffee beans. She purchased the beans from Read's Grocery Store in Preston. Ed Read scooped the beans from a two-hundred-pound

FOR THE BEST CUP OF COFFEE, FOLLOW THESE RULES

1 Use freshly ground coffee.
2 Use the right grind for the coffee maker.
3 Use a clean coffee maker.
4 Start with fresh cold water.
5 Use enough coffee for desired strength.
6 Serve coffee immediately after grounds are settled.

Two Coffee Drinkers

Great Uncle Leslie
and Great-Grandfather Crow, 1936

sack that was sitting on the floor into a brown paper bag, then weighed them. Grams bought five or ten pounds each trip.

Some customers had the beans ground at the store, but Grams ground her own. She used a square wooden coffee grinder with a black handle on top. A little drawer in the bottom held the ground coffee. As soon as ground coffee in vacuum-packed cans was available, Mom bought three-pound tins of Butternut.

The coffeepot was always on at our house; most every farmer or his wife would think it inhospitable if you did not offer him or her a cup of coffee. To us, a regular cup of coffee meant black. But as some easterners have noted, midwestern coffee is so weak you have to drink the whole pot to get a kick out of it.

Egg Coffee

❖

This method is perfect for coffee made on the stove top. Because Grams and Mom were excellent coffee makers, they were asked to make egg coffee for church meetings or suppers. When egg is added to coffee grounds, a "glob" is formed; it is a natural filter. The coffee flavor remains in the water and the coffee itself does not become cloudy or bitter. Egg coffee can be made ahead and reheated successfully.

6 QUARTS FRESH COLD WATER
1½ CUPS GROUND COFFEE
1 EGG, BEATEN
APPROXIMATELY ¼ CUP WATER

Fill 24-cup enamel coffeepot with 6 quarts cold water; bring to a boil.

Mix coffee with egg and add enough water (approximately ¼ cup) to form thick paste (this is a "glob"). Stir egg-coffee mixture into hot water; bring to a boil, turn off heat, and allow grounds to settle to bottom (about 5 minutes). Serve immediately. Can be made ahead; remove "glob" and reheat if necessary.

MAKES 24 CUPS

A Traditional Family

Great-Grandmother and Grandfather
Alice and John Mansfield, 1880

BREWS AND TEAS

Sassafras Tea

Every spring Granddad asked Grams to make sassafras tea because he thought it "thinned the blood." The Schrock family drank gallons of this tea because they believed it was good prevention against an upset stomach. It also tasted good, as a first cousin to the flavor of root beer.

The tea was made from pieces of either the bark or the new roots of the sassafras tree, then simply boiled in a pan of water and steeped until they developed a strong-flavored brew. Both of my grandmothers added sugar and fresh water before serving the tea.

Each July at the annual Schrock reunion, Dad's oldest sister, Aunt Marguerite, brewed a big batch of iced sassafras tea for the whole clan (anywhere from 100 to 150 people) to drink. Here again, modern herb books inform us that the oil extracted from the sassafras root and bark is unsafe for humans to drink. So don't go making any!

Pennyroyal Tea

One of Dad's favorite drinks in the spring was tea made with pennyroyal, a fern-shaped leafy plant that grew in a shady part of the flower garden. Mom hated the acrid taste, but brewed the tea for Dad anyway. She picked the green leaves from the plant, poured boiling water over them, and steeped the tea for approximately twenty minutes. The "brew" was cooled and Dad added two to three tablespoons of sugar to each glassful before he drank it. We now know that pennyroyal leaves are poisonous and not recommended to use for tea!

Root Beer

Mom bought Hires root beer extract from Charlie Vanderbie's general store in Greenleafton. It was packaged in a pint bottle, with the directions for making the drink included. She filled a five-gallon milk can with hot water, then stirred the contents of the bottle into the water along with a cake of yeast and some sugar. After the brew started to ferment, Mom poured the beer into two 1-quart glass jars and sealed the tops with mason jar lids. The filled jars were sunk in the bottom of the cool (50 to 60°) water tanks in the basement, halting the fermentation process —our homemade soda pop. The extract is now extinct, because store-bought soda put it out of business.

Do not despair, my family made other teas and brews without harmful side effects and non-extinct that I *can* recommend to drink! Read on!

Black or Green Tea

1 QUART FRESH COLD WATER
2 HEAPING TABLESPOONS
  LOOSE TEA

Grams kept black tea leaves in a tall orange tea tin with an Oriental motif that I now use for tea bags. When I was little, she served either black tea or green tea. They were the only flavors available in Preston. Surely other teas were available elsewhere, but no one ever asked.

Grams would fill the kettle with cold water and bring it to a boil. We rinsed the china teapot with hot water, put tea leaves in the pot, and set it next to the kettle on the stove. The minute the water boiled, she poured it over the leaves and steeped it for five minutes.

Bring about a quart of water to a boil. Place tea in sufficiently large teapot rinsed with hot water. Pour boiling water over tea and steep 5 minutes.

TO SERVE For straight black tea, strain into cups. For tea with milk and sugar, put desired amount of milk in cup, then add hot tea and sweeten to taste.

MAKES 1 QUART

Iced Sun Tea

1 QUART FRESH COLD WATER
4 TEA BAGS

After tea bags were available, Grams started making sun tea in the summertime. This tea does not get cloudy and takes little effort to make. I like to add a few spearmint sprigs to the tea after it is the strength that I want. It's best to refrigerate it before serving.

Fill jar with water; add tea bags, leaving tags over top. Cover with lid; set in sun 1 to 2 hours or until desired strength. It works without the sun, but it takes longer. Remove tea bags and refrigerate tea until serving time.

TO SERVE Fill glasses with ice, pour cold tea over top, and sweeten to taste with sugar.

VARIATIONS

1   Add 3 or 4 sprigs of mint to tea after tea bags are removed, chill, and serve as directed above.
2   Add 3 or 4 slices of lemon to tea after tea bags are removed, chill, and serve as directed above.
3   Add one 3-inch cinnamon stick and 2 slices of orange to tea after tea bags are removed, chill, and serve.

MAKES 1 QUART

Mint Tea

2 CUPS MINT LEAVES,
  LOOSELY PACKED
2 QUARTS COLD FRESH COLD
  WATER

There are many varieties of mint plants. Spearmint was our family favorite. Actually, we called it a weed; once planted, mint will take over a whole flowerbed or section of the lawn. In fact, a spearmint bed grows right between the stones at the end of our driveway in Long Island.

Wash mint leaves; place in one 2-quart jar (or two 1-quart jars). Bring water to a boil, pour over leaves, and steep 2 hours at room temperature for iced mint tea; refrigerate until serving time.

TO SERVE Pour into ice-filled glasses and garnish with a sprig of fresh mint. Sugar and lemon can be added according to taste.

VARIATION For hot mint tea, follow directions for *Black or Green Tea* (above), substituting 1 cup fresh mint leaves for 2 tablespoons loose tea.

MAKES 2 QUARTS

Chocolate Milk

CHOCOLATE SYRUP
...

3 CUPS SUGAR
2 CUPS WATER
1 CUP COCOA
2 TABLESPOONS CORN SYRUP
2 TEASPOONS VANILLA
¼ TEASPOON SALT

From my perspective, life on a dairy farm had advantages and disadvantages. One advantage was when I got to help Dad feed and milk the cows, as a diversion from my regular housework. The abundance of fresh milk, butter, cream, and cheese to eat was another plus. But in the spring, after Dad turned the cows out to pasture, the milk had a dreadful green grass taste—a *big* disadvantage. Mom made chocolate milk so we would drink the required three glasses of milk a day. No, chocolate milk does not come from brown cows!

Mom used this chocolate syrup recipe to flavor the cold milk. It can also be used as a topping on ice cream.

Combine sugar, water, cocoa, and corn syrup in saucepan; bring to a boil. Boil 10 minutes without stirring, then remove from heat. Add vanilla and salt.

Cool to room temperature. Pour into glass container and store in refrigerator. The syrup can be stored, refrigerated, for months. A bottle is a good Christmas gift for a chocolate lover.

NOTE For one 8-ounce glass chocolate milk, place 1½ tablespoons chocolate syrup in bottom of glass; pour in cold milk while stirring vigorously with long-handled spoon. Taste and add more syrup if necessary.

MAKES APPROXIMATELY 1¾ QUARTS

Hot Cocoa

Method I

**2 SQUARES
UNSWEETENED
CHOCOLATE,
CHOPPED
1 CUP WATER
⅓ CUP SUGAR
PINCH SALT
3 CUPS MILK**

MARSHMALLOWS

In saucepan or top of double boiler, melt chocolate and water, stirring constantly. Add sugar and salt; bring to a boil. Boil 4 minutes, stirring. Slowly stir in milk and heat until scalded. *Do not boil.* Set aside, off heat.

Just before serving, beat with rotary beater to break up skin formed on top. Place a marshmallow in cup and pour hot cocoa on top. Serve with spoon.

When there was a chill in the air, hot cocoa was our favorite drink for after school or when my friends came to visit. If it was snowing in the morning, we could count on hot cocoa in our school thermos. Mom knew we would be glad for a hot drink at noon.

For a snack, we put a large marshmallow in the bottom of the cup before pouring in the hot cocoa. The heat partially melted the marshmallow and I found it impossible to wait until I was finished drinking the cocoa to eat it. So, I put two marshmallows in my cup—one to eat halfway and the other when I was finished.

VARIATIONS

1 Add one 3-inch cinnamon stick to each cup; pour in cocoa.
2 Sprinkle cinnamon on top of each serving of cocoa.
3 Top cocoa with dollop of whipped cream.

MAKES 1 QUART

Method II

**⅓ CUP
UNSWEETENED
COCOA
⅓ CUP SUGAR
PINCH SALT
½ CUP WATER
3½ CUPS MILK
1 TEASPOON
VANILLA**

MARSHMALLOWS

Mix cocoa, sugar, salt, and water together in saucepan. Over low heat boil 1 minute, stirring constantly. Slowly stir in milk and heat until scalded. *Do not boil.* Set aside, off heat.

Beat in vanilla with rotary beater or whisk. Place a marshmallow in cup and pour hot cocoa on top. Serve with spoon.

Mom's Instant Cocoa Mix

❖

Along with my clothes and various other things, I took a two-quart jar of instant cocoa mix with me to college in Indiana. When Mom mailed me a box of cookies, she included a refill supply. A hot cup of cocoa tasted great at midnight on pre-exam all-nighters.

On the home front, Mom kept a handy supply ready for us kids to make ourselves a cup of cocoa whenever we wanted. Make a large batch, and store it in an easy-to-reach, airtight container for all the cocoa lovers in your family.

1 ⅓ CUPS DRY MILK
3 TABLESPOONS COCOA, UNSWEETENED
3 TABLESPOONS SUGAR

Mix dry milk, cocoa, and sugar together. Store in airtight container.

To Make Cocoa

Bring 4 cups water to a boil; stir in cocoa mix from above. Heat until hot, but do not boil. Stir in ½ teaspoon vanilla.

Serve immediately, topped with cinnamon or marshmallows.

FOR 1 CUP Bring 1 cup water to a boil, add generous ⅓ cup mix to water, and stir well. Add a few drops of vanilla and serve, or follow hot cocoa variations (page 76), if desired.

MAKES 1 QUART

Eggnog

4 EGGS
⅓ TO ½ CUP SUGAR
1 TABLESPOON VANILLA
3½ CUPS COLD MILK
½ TEASPOON FRESHLY
GRATED NUTMEG

For some people, drinking an eggnog conjures up festive holiday celebrations, but I am reminded of the many bouts that I had with tonsillitis as a child. Because my throat was so sore and my taste buds were gone, I refused to eat my regular meals. So, Mom insisted, "At least drink an eggnog!" She used plenty of sugar, vanilla, and nutmeg to encourage my cooperation. I drank it with restrained caution then and now I don't drink it at all.

For Christmas celebrations Mom added rum flavoring, but not real rum, to the eggnog. (Maybe I would have liked it if she had added real rum.)

Because some commercial eggs are found to be contaminated with a harmful virus, use *only* absolutely fresh eggs gathered from free-range chickens for this recipe.

Beat eggs until frothy in mixer or blender (Mom used a rotary beater). Beat in sugar until dissolved. Add vanilla and milk; mix well. Stir in nutmeg; taste and correct flavorings.

Serve immediately or refrigerate until serving time.

MAKES 1 QUART

All Gussied Up 1920s

JUICY FRUIT DRINKS

The Schrock Clan, circa 1912

The Schrock side of our family consumed inordinate amounts of fruit juice drinks. Whenever juice formed in the bowl from fresh fruit, Grandma Schrock saved it. The untouched juice was either drunk as is, transformed into a multi-flavored fruit punch, thickened with cornstarch for a dessert sauce, or preserved into jelly.

Of course Grandma Schrock also pressed apples for cider and cooked tomatoes into juice. When she stewed and pureed various dry and tart fruits for sauces, she reserved the juices to drink as well.

Apple and plum trees grew at the "Eighty." Dad had a second, eighty-acre farm, two miles east of the homestead. Even though it would seem natural for Mom to press the apples for cider, the time and labor was too involved to warrant it; instead, we bought our cider from the local orchard.

Imagine bushels and bushels of shiny red apples stacked in a large shed. The air was filled with a tart-sweet aroma. The schmushing sound of the press whet my palate for a must-have ladle of fresh cider as it spewed from the wooden trough into a barrel. We brought three to four gallons home and kept them cool in the basement storage water tank. It tasted terrific.

Because a "waste not, want not" philosophy prevailed on the farm, Mom prepared raspberry and strawberry juice from culls or blemished berries. When I asked her for the recipe, she replied, "I just cooked up the berries and canned the juice!" She also stewed rhubarb for a fruit sauce and strained off the juice to process. Just before serving, she mixed one part canned pineapple juice with two parts rhubarb —pineapple-rhubarb juice. But our favorite, grape juice, was made especially for us to drink.

Grape Juice

❖

6 CUPS CONCORD GRAPES
3 CUPS SUGAR

Every fall we stocked our larder shelves with two-quart jars of rich grape juice. Mom bought Concord grapes from the grocery in wire-handled wooden baskets containing a half peck (three to four pounds) each of the fruit. We washed and stemmed the grapes, put equal amounts of grapes and sugar in a mason glass jar, and filled the jar with cold water. She sealed the lid and processed the juice in a water bath. The jars of juice were then cooled and stored. Do not use this method (now deemed unsafe by the USDA). Instead, follow the procedure in the recipe below.

Mom doled out grape juice sparingly. We saved it for special occasions. When my friends assembled at our house, she chilled a jar of full-bodied, rich-flavored grape nectar for us to drink. Don't be surprised if this homemade grape juice becomes a favorite drink request.

·····································

SPECIAL EQUIPMENT 8-quart canner and six 1-quart jars with lids.

TO PREPARE JARS AND LIDS Wash new jars in hot soapy water, rinse well, cover with hot water, and set aside. Several minutes (5 to 10) before ready to process juice, pour water out of jars and invert them on towel to drain. Follow manufacturer's directions to prepare lids.

Fill canner half full of water; heat until hot, but do not boil.

Wash, drain, and stem grapes. Measure and place a heaping cup of grapes in each prepared jar.

To make medium sugar syrup, cook sugar and 4 cups water until sugar is dissolved; remove from heat. Keep hot, but do not continue to boil. (This can be done ahead, kept in refrigerator, and reheated.) Meanwhile, boil 4 cups water; keep hot.

Pour ½ cup hot sugar syrup over each jar of grapes. Fill with approximately 3 cups hot water (190–200°) to come up to neck of jar. (The idea is to make a grape concentrate and then dilute it.) Wipe off top and screw threads of jar. Place hot metal lid on jar and firmly screw down metal band.

When sealed, place jars on rack in canner. Allow enough space for the water to circulate. Add hot (but not boiling) water to cover jars by 1 to 2 inches. Cover canner and heat to a boil; reduce heat to a slow gentle boil. Process for 30 minutes. Remove jars; check seals. The metal lids should be flat.

Tap each lid with teaspoon; a dull thud sound is a sign of a good seal. If it sounds fishy, refrigerate jar and drink juice in next few days or so; or reprocess it, using new lid and/or jar if necessary (one or both may be defective), and proceed according to recipe. Stand jars on wooden board or rack away from drafts and allow to cool to room temperature (about 12 hours). Date lid and store in cool, dry place. For full flavor or best taste, store 2 to 3 months before drinking.

MAKES 6 QUARTS

Tomato Juice

❖

When the tomatoes were ripe, the cream of the crop were sliced and eaten fresh at every meal. Grams and Mom chose very red, almost overripe tomatoes to make juice. They removed the cores and cut off the green and dark spots. The tomatoes were cooked in a large pot until soft and run through the Foley food mill. Each batch was seasoned with salt, pepper, and sugar.

Three stalks of raw celery and three slices of raw onion were placed in each jar. The hot seasoned juice was poured into the jar and then processed. Sometimes the juice spoiled due to a low acidity in the tomatoes. When spoilage occurred, the juice was simply thrown out. "All that work for nothing!" Mom would say.

Mom and Grams used slightly overripe and spotted tomatoes because they were so thrifty. However, they *knew* what to do if the tomato juice was "bad," in other words, they threw it out. On the other hand, I cannot afford to have even one person slightly sick from food poisoning after making tomato juice from this recipe. So, I felt the reader needs to follow safe practices in this process and use only perfectly ripe, unbroken, beautiful tomatoes. I know

10 QUARTS FIRM TOMATOES, UNBLEMISHED (NO BROKEN SKIN OR SPOTS)
3 MEDIUM ONIONS
3 STALKS CELERY WITH TOPS
1 LARGE GREEN PEPPER
3 TO 4 MEDIUM BAY LEAVES

readers who are farm women will use slightly over the hill ones, but "they take their chances and live with them!" Ha!

The following recipe is a safe, USDA-recommended method to preserve tomato juice. (Mom uses it now, too.) It is also healthy because the additional seasonings can be tailored to fit each individual's needs. Finally, the juice is an economical winter taste treat from last summer's bumper crop of tomatoes.

▪▪▪▪▪▪▪▪▪▪▪▪▪▪▪▪▪▪▪▪▪▪▪▪▪▪▪▪▪▪▪▪

SPECIAL EQUIPMENT 8-quart canner, seven 1-quart jars with new lids, and large kettle, stainless steel or enamel (10-to-12-quart capacity).

TO PREPARE JARS AND LIDS See instructions on page 80.

Choose ripe, but not overripe, unblemished tomatoes. I recommend Jet Star or Celebrity varieties. Remember that one small spot can spoil and make the whole batch toxic. Wash, drain, core, and quarter; place in large enameled kettle (we called it a granite kettle).

Peel and chop onions, slice celery, chop green pepper, and add with bay leaves to tomatoes. Cover kettle, bring to a boil, reduce heat, and cook until vegetables are soft, 30 to 40 minutes.

Remove from heat. Run through sieve or Foley food mill set over large bowl. Can be done in food processor and strained. Discard seeds and skins.

Season juice according to taste (see note below), and add lemon juice or citric acid (as the USDA recommends for safety).

Fill canner half full of water; heat until hot, but do not boil. Fill prepared jars with hot juice to come up to neck of jar. Wipe off top and screw threads of jar. Place hot metal lid on jar and firmly screw down metal band. Then proceed with instructions on page 80 from the point of placing jars in canner to storing fully processed juice. When sealed, place jars on rack in canner. Allow enough space for water to circulate. Add hot (but not boiling) water to cover jars by 1 to 2 inches. Cover canner and heat to a boil; reduce heat to a slow gentle boil. Process for 50

minutes. Remove jars; check seals. The metal lids should be flat. Tap each lid with teaspoon; a dull thud sound is a sign of a good seal, as discussed on page 80. Stand jars on wooden board or rack away from drafts and cool to room temperature (about 12 hours). Date lid and store in cool, dry place. For full flavor or best taste, store 2 to 3 months before drinking.

Total ingredients needed for seasoning *6 to 7 quarts* of tomato juice (adjust amounts according to personal preference or dietary restrictions):
1 to 2½ tablespoons salt
1 to 2½ tablespoons black pepper, freshly ground
1 to 2½ tablespoons sugar
6 to 7 tablespoons lemon juice

NOTE The USDA suggests using the following proportions as guidelines: For *1 quart,* use 1 teaspoon salt, 2 tablespoons concentrated lemon juice, 1 teaspoon sugar, and ½ teaspoon black pepper.

MAKES 6 TO 7 QUARTS

Grand Old-Fashioned Lemonade

If given but one drink to drink, I would choose this grand, old-fashioned fresh lemonade. I still savor my memories of those long hot summer days, rocking in the green wooden swing on Grams's front porch, sipping lemonade from a tall frosty glass. Grams's lemonade ritual was very simple, with excellent results.

Wash lemons. With your hand, roll each lemon on counter a few rolls to release juice. Cut in half and juice into tall glass pitcher. Slice rind of

3 LARGE LEMONS
⅔ CUP SUGAR

2 lemons and add to juice; discard rest.

Add sugar to juice and rind. With wooden spoon, stir vigorously until sugar is dissolved. Fill pitcher with 2 quarts of fresh cold water. Stir until mixed well. Taste and correct sweetness. It should taste tart yet sweet.

TO SERVE Pour lemonade into ice-filled glasses and garnish with lemon slice cut from center to edge, slipped over edge of glass.

MAKES 2 QUARTS

SCHOOL DAYS, SCHOOL DAYS, DEAR OLD GOLDEN RULE DAYS

"Readin', and writin', and 'rithmatic

Taught to the tune of a hickory stick..."

The Broadwater side of the family, including Granddad, Mom, and myself, learned to read and write in a one-room country school. Regardless of the weather, we walked or rode our bicycles the half-mile south of the farm to Prairie Queen, District #62. But in Indiana, the Schrock side of the family, including Dad and all twelve of his brothers and sisters, had simply walked across the front yard to the school next door.

In 1933, before she was married, Mom taught school at Flying Cloud, District #61, located five miles south of the farm. Her salary was the handsome sum of thirty-five dollars a month! Granddad exclaimed, "But Opal, that's mighty good money!" Mom walked to work in good weather, but on rainy days she drove a Model-T Ford—a runabout, with one seat. When the road was impassable with muddy ruts too deep for the wheels of the car, after spring thaw and rain, Granddad escorted her via a horse-drawn, two-seat Democrat Wagon.

Her daily routine was the same as that of the other country schoolteachers of that era. Upon arrival, Mom built a fire in the potbelly stove, wrote the assignments on the blackboard, and sent two strong boys to the nearest farmhouse with a four-gallon water pail to fetch the drinking water. Between 9 A.M. and 4 P.M. she taught every subject to all eight grades, including a kindergarten class in the spring. Then, she performed the janitor's job before return-

ing home late in the day. At home, Mom prepared her lessons and helped Grams with household chores —a Renaissance woman!

Picture this enchanting setting of my one-room schoolhouse, Prairie Queen. In the schoolyard were a softball diamond, four sturdy swings, and four teeter-totters, surrounded by lots of space for running races and other games. The square schoolhouse was built with solid west, south, and north walls for protection from cold winter winds. During the morning, sunshine streamed through the floor-to-ceiling windows on the east side of the room. The crisp clean smell of freshly waxed floors and wood shavings from the pencil sharpener filled the air (especially on the first day of school).

We students sat in assigned according-to-grade-and-height seats at wooden desks of various sizes that were arranged in neat rows facing the front of the room. All the seats were attached to the floor by a metal runner. Each desk top had an inkwell in the upper right-hand corner, a thin groove for pencils along the top, and an open bookshelf underneath. The teacher's large looming wooden desk faced us. All the classes were conducted around a large low table surrounded by eight chairs, next to her desk. Every morning we recited the Pledge of Allegiance to the flag that hung over the upright piano. Behind the piano a small, limited library area was used for

A One-Room School (Janeen is second from right, by window)

quiet "research" and sometimes not so quiet "conferences," too.

The scene was completed by a charming objet d'art sitting in the center of the room. This large, black potbelly stove not only heated the room but also cooked our lunches. We poked raw potatoes into the red-hot coals on the bottom to bake by lunch time. And some of us warmed up small jars of leftovers brought from home in a pan of water sitting on the top (circa 1930–40s *bain marie*). Later on, a furnace was installed and we brought hot foods to school in thermos bottles.

Lunch was the best part of my school day. I can still smell the marvelous aroma of potatoes baking while my stomach rumbled. It was hard to wait for the clock to strike 12 noon. My potato had a charcoal-black hard skin with the inside baked to perfection. A large chunk of sweet creamery butter disappeared instantly into the pearly white center.

My favorite lunch box was a gallon tin pail that originally contained syrup, because the thin metal handle easily slid over one of the handlebars on my bike and the lid fit very tight, securing my lunch for the bumpy ride on the gravel road. Later on, I used a real, store-bought lunch pail. Just like a workman's, the food fit in the bottom section and a thermos clipped into the lid. On winter days, Mom filled my thermos with either steaming hot cocoa or a rib-sticking soup. In warm weather, she gave me cold chocolate milk. I wished for coffee or tea, but to no avail!

Mom packed a perfect ripe pear, a peach, a crisp apple, or a large yellow banana on the bottom of the pail. Carrot sticks, cucumber slices, green pepper slices, or tiny yellow pear tomatoes and red juicy cherry tomatoes were tucked into old-fashioned waxed paper sandwich bags. (These were the days pre–plastic bags and Baggies.)

Mom had hated the fact that Grandmother Broadwater gave her, and the other high school students boarding at the house, only two boring sandwich poppyseed cake or a white caraway seed cookie—every high school day for the three years she boarded at her house, Mom never made or packed them in *my* lunchbox. Instead, I found a delicious cookie or a fat rich brownie carefully wrapped in waxed paper to either trade or eat. Once in a while, she surprised me with a Hershey's or Baby Ruth candy bar that was hidden under all the other little packages of food.

My all-time favorite was a Graham Cracker Cookie. The recipe is very easy: Mix powdered sugar and softened butter together; add vanilla and enough heavy cream to the mixture until it is a smooth frosting. Spread the frosting on top of a graham cracker

SANDWICH ADVICE:

"As much care is needed in selecting and preparing the food for the child's lunch at school as for other meals served to the child. If the lunch is inadequate or lacking in food essentials throughout the school year, the child's whole food nutrition will be seriously affected, and his work at school will suffer. The school lunch is one of three meals, not just a snack, and should possess the following characteristics:

1 It should be abundant in amount for a hungry, healthy child.

2 It should be chosen with regard to the nutritive needs of the child and in relation to the whole day's food.

3 It should be clean, appetizing, wholesome, and attractive." Inglenook Cook Book, 1942

choices: raspberry jam and butter or Charlie Keehn's bologna with butter. Therefore, I had a different school lunch every day, but the sandwiches were always made with homemade bread. My favorite sandwich was and still is made with mellow slices of longhorn cheese fresh from the creamery topped with crunchy green pepper slices tucked into a buttered *Potato Water Sandwich Bun* (page 58).

With my sweet tooth, I could not imagine a school lunch without dessert. Because Grandmother Broadwater gave Mom only two choices—a piece of square, top with another square, and continue until enough cookies are assembled. These are great do-it-yourself cookies for kids of all ages.

If I included the recipe for every sandwich that I consumed during my school days, this book would weigh a ton! Instead, I have compiled a list of various family "secrets" and other suggestions for sandwich combinations. I hope they will pique your interest and serve only as a guideline for successful personal sandwich creations.

Sandwich Secrets and Combinations

My Sandwich Secrets

1 Use homemade bread or a top-quality wholesome fresh bread.
2 Spread a thin coat of softened sweet butter over the entire area of the bread or bun to prevent the filling from soaking into the bread.
3 Make the filling fresh, wholesome, interesting, and appropriate for the person eating the sandwich.
4 Consider the following points before making your final choice of sandwich:
   - Available preparation time
   - Budget and palate preferences
   - Weather and storage conditions for safe consumption
   - Thickness of bread
   - Amount of filling

A Few Favorite School Sandwich Combination Suggestions

Start with buttered homemade *Potato Water Bread* (page 57).

APPLE BUTTER or apple butter and cream cheese

CHIVES or chives and cream cheese

COTTAGE CHEESE and cinnamon, raisins, or chopped nuts

CREAM CHEESE and sliced green olives, chopped nuts, chopped green peppers, jelly, or sliced tomatoes

DRIED BEEF and sliced raw onion

FRIED EGG with chopped bacon, dill pickles, or catsup

GARDEN RADISHES, salted, on dark bread

HONEY BUTTER (equal parts honey and butter mixed together to make a thick spread)

HONEY PEANUT BUTTER (equal parts honey and peanut butter mixed together to make a thick spread)

LONGHORN CHEESE with green peppers, scallions, tomatoes, or pickles

NEW ONIONS or scallions, salted, on rye bread

PEANUT BUTTER and dill pickles, chopped bacon, sliced banana, raisins and coconut, chocolate chips, or strawberry jam

SLICED TOMATOES, salt, and pepper on white bread

VELVEETA CHEESE with mustard and dill pickles

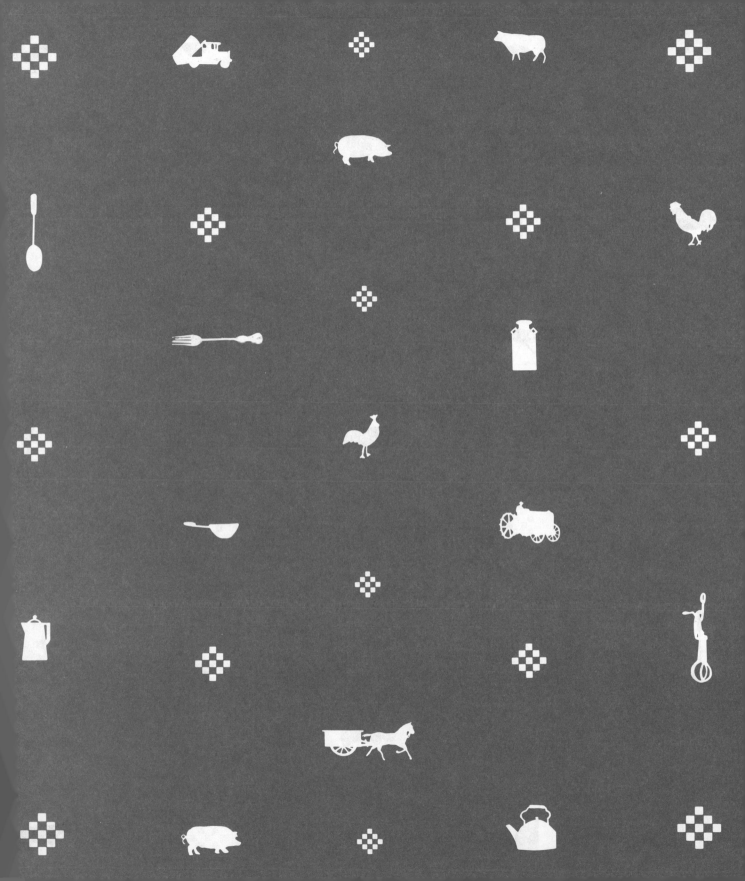

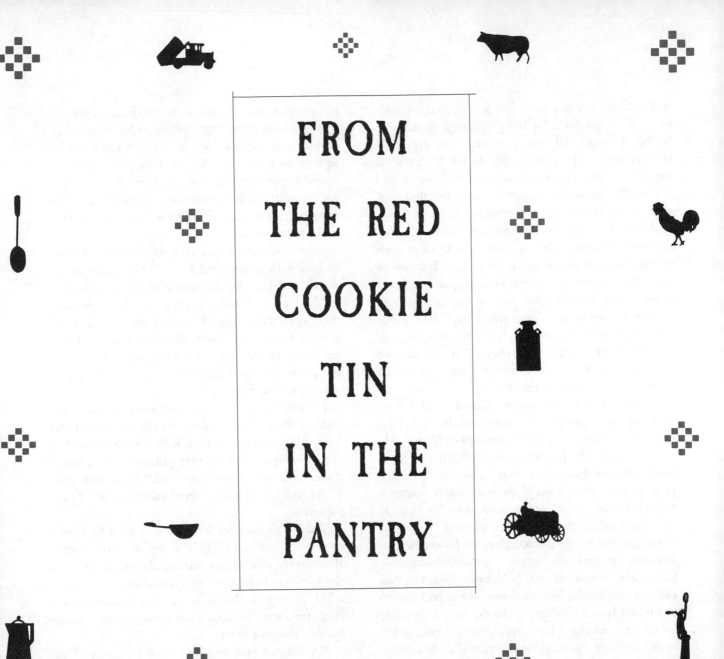

FROM
THE RED
COOKIE
TIN
IN THE
PANTRY

Because the typical farm fare was fresh but bland, or "just simple food," a farm wife took great pride in her baking. All baked goods—but especially cookies—were the perfect vehicle for her personal expression and experimentation with sweets and spices. The hungry farm family found freshly baked cookies irresistible, no matter what the flavor.

All farm women, including Grams, baked cookies in a wood-burning stove without benefit of an oven thermometer or any temperature gauge. This was in the 1800s—pre-kerosene stoves, or gas or electric ovens. They built a good fire in the fire box and waited for the oven to heat up. They literally put their hand inside the oven to check the temperature. If it felt "hot enough to the hand," it was time to bake cookies. A more foolproof test was (and still is) to bake a test cookie in the oven.

Instead of a cookie sheet, Grams used Great-Grandmother Crowe's hand-me-down black baking tin designed by my Great-Grandfather Crowe. He carefully shaped, pounded, and soldered a thick black sheet of tin into a "box" that measured approximately three inches high on the sides, fourteen to fifteen inches wide, and seventeen inches long. It was handcrafted to fit into the oven of the wood-burning stove with just enough room for the heat to circulate around the edges. Great-Grandmother Crowe and Grams not only baked cakes, breads, and rolls on the inside, but they turned the pan upside down and baked cookies on the bottom. One other baked item emerged from this practical baking tin—cat and dog biscuits! Grams mixed up a concoction of ground corn and/or oats, lard, and buttermilk into a dough. The raw dough was "baked until done" and cut into biscuits. These animal biscuits were similar to a healthy buttermilk corn biscuit that we humans eat today. It's a shame that Grams and her mom didn't serve them to the family too.

Grams's red cookie tin sat in the pantry filled to the brim with cookies. (Now, it's not quite so red.)

It seemed to us grandkids that magical happenings sprang forth from that pantry. Her white sugar cookies never seemed to run out; the soft creams—equally as tasty—nestled in a flat cake pan with waxed paper between them to keep the frosting in good condition; and much to our delight, candies and chocolates were stuffed into jars. A wealth of sweet riches for sure!

From the time I was able to stand up, I baked cookies with Grams and Mom. They mixed up the dough and I licked the spoon. (Some people think the best part of cookie baking is licking the utensils.) Mom would say, "Don't eat that dough. You'll get sick from it!" Frankly, she wanted all the dough for baked cookies. With a resigned sigh, I licked every last bit from the sides of the bowl. P.S.: I never got sick from it.

I fondly recall the sweet and spicy aroma of oatmeal raisin cookies cooling on the newspaper that Mom placed on the kitchen table. After we read, in the newspaper no less, that poisonous lead was in the ink, we immediately stopped that practice. Now I cool cookies on an oversized cake rack or a brown paper bag.

Truthfully, cookies are my first choice for dessert or snack. I can say, "This is my favorite cookie," about every recipe that follows. Mom can attest to the fact that I ate more than my share of cookies as a kid. Even now, Mom bakes extra cookies before I come for a visit because I am often caught with my hand in the cookie jar!

We did not exactly have a cookie jar when I was small; all cookies were stored in a round tin. It sat on the end of the counter—underneath the dish cupboard and next to the toaster—filled to the brim. Another similar tin is sitting there now in the same condition, filled with enticing cookies for every farm visitor. If it is empty, look in the lower cupboard or on the back porch counter—any old tin could be hiding some fantastic cookie treat.

THE OATMEAL COOKIE FAMILY

A chewy yet crisp oatmeal cookie conjures up various childhood memories for most of us. As Grams was mixing up the batter for oatmeal cookies, Mom and Aunt Rubye played under the heirloom oak kitchen table. The two actresses mimicked the horses by eating dry rolled oats from a bowl they put on the floor. They chewed, snorted, neighed, tossed their heads, and stomped around on all fours. Wish that I could have witnessed that act!

"2 cups sugar, 2 eggs, butter size of an egg, 3 Tbsp milk, 3 cups oatmeal, pinch of salt, flavor with vanilla."
Grams's Black Book

Each of the following oatmeal cookie recipes was part of the Broadwater or Schrock heritage. I am sure our family was not unique in the fact that we always had on hand one variation or another of an oatmeal cookie. Go ahead and try them all.

Three Cookie Eaters Judy, Janeen, and Joany

The Great-Grandmother Oatmeal Cookie

✦

Grams did not include instructions for this recipe in her little black book. She assumed anyone would know exactly what to do with the list of ingredients. Joany, my sister, reminded me, "Oh, Grams always rolled those cookies between two sheets of waxed paper." Both Grams and Mom preferred a crisp cookie, so they rolled the dough thin. However, I like a chewy cookie, so I roll it thick. Take my word for it, all the cookies will be eaten, whether thick or thin. The only unquestionable thickness will be around the waistline.

2 TABLESPOONS BUTTER
2 CUPS SUGAR
2 EGGS
3 TABLESPOONS MILK
PINCH SALT
1 TEASPOON VANILLA
3 CUPS ROLLED OATS

Preheat oven to 375°.

Cream butter and sugar together. Add eggs and milk; mix well. Stir in salt and vanilla. Stir in oats and mix well.

Roll dough between two sheets of waxed paper—thick for chewy, thin for crisp. Cut with 2½-inch round cutter; place on greased baking sheets and bake 8 to 10 minutes, or until browned on edges and firm. Cool completely on rack.

Store baked cookies in cookie tin. Can be kept in cool place 2 to 3 weeks or frozen 2 to 3 months.

MAKES 3 TO 4 DOZEN

Grandma Schrock's Boston Cookies

◈

Why Grandma Schrock named this recipe "Boston Cookies" is still a mystery to the whole family. Nevertheless, they are Dad's favorite cookie. Grandma Schrock packed a few into each teenager's lunch bag to be consumed during the ride to and from Middlebury High School in Indiana where my father grew up. On school mornings, the Schrock clan crowded into two buggies with their books and lunch, plus a bag of oats and hay for the horses. Then off they went on the five-mile trip. They drove directly to the stable behind the school. Other students followed suit. At lunch time, Dad and his brothers or sisters gave the horses their bag of oats to eat. After school, the horses were hitched up to the buggies and they all merrily journeyed home. My less-exciting trip home from school also ended with a few of these cookies.

Both Grandmother Schrock and Grams used the following recipe. It yields more cookies than most other recipes and requires equal amounts of flour and oatmeal. If I had a family of thirteen children, I would want to economize both time and money too.

½ CUP BUTTER
½ CUP LARD OR SOLID
  SHORTENING
1 CUP SUGAR
2 EGGS
¼ CUP MILK
1 TEASPOON BAKING SODA
2¼ CUPS FLOUR
1 TEASPOON CINNAMON
PINCH SALT
1 CUP CHOPPED RAISINS
2 CUPS ROLLED OATS

Preheat oven to 375°.

Cream butter, lard, and sugar together until light and fluffy. Stir in eggs and milk.

Add soda, flour, cinnamon, and salt; mix well. Dust raisins with some flour mixture, then add them and oats to batter; mix well.

Drop by teaspoonfuls onto greased baking sheets. Bake 10 to 12 minutes, or until lightly browned on the edges and firm. Cool completely on rack.

Store baked cookies in cookie tin. Can be kept 2 to 3 weeks in cool place or frozen 2 to 3 months.

MAKES 5 TO 6 DOZEN

"Take 1 cup of sugar, ½ cup of butter, ½ cup of lard, 2 eggs, twelve teaspoonfuls of sweet milk, 1 teaspoonful of soda, 2 cups of flour, 1 teaspoonful of cinnamon, one cup of raisins and 2 cups of oatmeal added last with a pinch of salt. Mix with a spoon and drop by spoonfuls into a greased pan like cookies." Inglenook Cook Book, 1911

Aunt Janie Broadwater's Rolled Fruit Cookies

Aunt Janie, Granddad's sister-in-law, always made this recipe with black walnuts. These walnuts have such a distinctive flavor that people either adore or abhor them. The strong, rich, dense, nutty, almost musty flavor is totally unlike English walnuts. Black walnuts are obviously colored black and are smaller than other walnuts.

A black walnut tree is still growing near the machine shed on the farm. Like Granddad, Dad has spent many hours in the basement, cracking and picking out the walnut meats from the shells during cold winter months. Dad's unending perseverance is matched only by his love for nuts. The extremely hard outer shells are impossible to crack with a normal nut cracker. Dad uses a hammer. However, for some obstinate nuts, he uses a vise.

½ CUP BUTTER
½ CUP LARD OR SOLID
  VEGETABLE SHORTENING
2 CUPS SUGAR
1 CUP DARK RAISINS
3 EGGS
1 TEASPOON VANILLA
1 TEASPOON BAKING SODA
4 TABLESPOONS SOUR MILK
  (PLACE ¼ TEASPOON LEMON
  JUICE IN WHOLE MILK TO
  SOUR)
PINCH SALT
1 ½ TEASPOONS CINNAMON
¼ TEASPOON CLOVES
4 CUPS FLOUR
¾ CUP BLACK WALNUTS,
  CHOPPED FINE

If black walnuts are not your cup of tea, substitute regular walnuts in this recipe. You will still love them.

Cream butter, lard, and sugar together until light and fluffy.

Grind raisins with eggs in food processor until finely ground. Add butter mixture and vanilla; process until combined with raisins. Remove to mixing bowl.

Dissolve soda in sour milk; beat into batter. Mix dry ingredients together and stir into batter; mix well. Add nuts and combine well. Refrigerate dough 1 to 2 hours or overnight.

Preheat oven to 375°.

To roll cookies, place half of dough on floured board, roll ¼ inch thick, and cut into 3-inch cookies. Place 2 inches apart on greased baking sheets. Bake 8 to 10 minutes, or until browned on edges and firm. Cool completely on rack.

Store baked cookies in cookie tin. Can be kept 2 to 3 weeks in cool place or frozen 2 to 3 months.

MAKES APPROXIMATELY 6 DOZEN

"3 eggs, 2 cups sugar, 1 cup shortening, 1 cup ground raisins, 1 tsp soda dissolved in 4 Tbsp sour milk, 1½ tsp cinnamon, ¾ tsp cloves, ½ tsp nutmeg, ½ cup ground black walnuts, flour to roll." Grams's Black Book

Aunt Rubye's Brownies

There were two reasons I yearned to stay overnight at Aunt Rubye's. First, she had an old glass-covered candy dish filled with what I considered "the best" candy. It was accessible to my eager little fingers, sitting on a shelf inside a glass-front dish cupboard. I always quietly opened the door and the lid so as not to be found out. Second, I loved to devour her brownies. They are better than any candy!

Joany, my chocoholic sister, would eat at least one every meal if given the chance. They are moist, rich, and chewy. Even after two weeks in a cookie tin, they are irresistible. I wrap them individually in plastic and store them in the freezer. Unfortunately, my family has a passion for frozen brownies. They knowingly raid the freezer and leave none for me.

Preheat oven to 350°. Grease and "flour" with unsweetened cocoa an 11-by-17-inch jelly roll pan.

Melt butter in microwave or over low heat; stir in sugar and cocoa. Cool slightly. With wooden spoon, mix in eggs and vanilla. Blend well, but do not beat.

1 CUP BUTTER, MELTED
2 CUPS SUGAR
¼ CUP COCOA
4 EGGS AT ROOM TEMPERATURE
1 TEASPOON VANILLA
1½ CUPS FLOUR, SIFTED
1 TEASPOON SALT
½ CUP NUTS, CHOPPED (PECANS ARE RUBYE'S FIRST CHOICE)

Sift flour and salt together and add to batter. Fold in nuts and combine well.

Pour batter into prepared baking pan and bake 20 to 25 minutes. Watch carefully; bake just until toothpick inserted in center comes out clean. Set pan on rack and frost while still warm.

MAKES APPROXIMATELY 5 DOZEN

Rubye's Chocolate Frosting

2 TABLESPOONS MARGARINE
1 ONE-OUNCE SQUARE UNSWEETENED CHOCOLATE
1 CUP SUGAR
⅓ CUP MILK
2 TEASPOONS VANILLA
1½ TO 2 CUPS POWDERED SUGAR

Aunt Rubye told me if she had fifty cents for every time she has made this frosting, she would be able to take a few trips around the world.

Bring margarine, chocolate, sugar, and milk to a boil; boil exactly 3 minutes, stirring constantly. Remove from heat and add vanilla. Beat in powdered sugar until frosting becomes spreading consistency.

Spread on top of warm brownies; cut into bars when cold. Store in airtight camouflage containers 1 week, placing waxed paper between layers of bars. Can be kept 2 to 3 weeks in freezer.

MAKES APPROXIMATELY 1¾ CUPS

Aunt Rubye's Frosted Pumpkin Bars

B ar cookies are Rubye's favorite because they require less time and fuss than a drop or rolled cookie. These princely pumpkin bars are akin to a royal rich cake. Rubye promises that her standard frosting "won't be grainy and it always sets up nice. I always use this frosting for bar cookies, especially if I am bringing them to someone!" These bars taste terrific any time of year. If your family will accept it, serve them for a Thanksgiving Day dessert and skip the pumpkin pie. Horrors!

▪▪▪▪▪▪▪▪▪▪▪▪▪▪▪▪▪▪▪▪▪▪▪▪▪▪▪▪▪▪

Preheat oven to 350°.

Beat eggs in mixing bowl until frothy; add sugar and continue to beat until thick. Blend in oil and pumpkin.

Measure out remaining dry ingredients and sift together. Sprinkle reserved 2 tablespoons flour over nuts and raisins. Add flour mixture to batter and mix well; fold in nuts and raisins.

Pour batter into prepared baking pan. Bake 20 to 25 minutes, or until toothpick inserted into center comes out clean. Set on rack and frost in pan while still warm.

MAKES APPROXIMATELY 6 DOZEN

◆ ◆ ◆ ◆ ◆

4 EGGS
2 CUPS SUGAR
1 CUP VEGETABLE OIL
1 CUP PUMPKIN, MASHED, CANNED, UNSWEETENED (FREEZE ANY LEFT OVER)
1 TEASPOON SALT
2 TEASPOONS CINNAMON
1 TEASPOON BAKING SODA
1 TEASPOON BAKING POWDER
2 CUPS FLOUR, UNSIFTED (WITH 2 TABLESPOONS REMOVED)
1 CUP NUTS, CHOPPED
½ CUP RAISINS

Caramel Frosting

▼▼▼▼▼▼▼▼▼▼▼▼▼▼▼▼▼▼▼▼▼▼

◆
◆ ◆
◆

2 TABLESPOONS MARGARINE
1 CUP BROWN SUGAR
⅓ CUP MILK
2 TEASPOONS VANILLA
1½ TO 2 CUPS POWDERED SUGAR

This frosting is the non-chocolate version of Rubye's standard frosting. It has the most marvelous caramel flavor—the favorite of the whole family.

Bring margarine, sugar, and milk to a boil; boil exactly 3 minutes, stirring constantly. Remove from heat and add vanilla. Beat in powdered sugar until frosting becomes spreading consistency: "Beat 'n beat it."

Spread over warm cookies; cut into bars when cold. Store in cookie tin, placing waxed paper between layers of bars. Can be kept 5 to 6 days in cool place. This recipe does not freeze well.

MAKES APPROXIMATELY 1¾ CUPS

▲▲▲▲▲▲▲▲▲▲▲▲▲▲▲▲▲▲▲▲▲

Grams's Oatmeal–Chocolate Chip Cookies

◆

Because Grams liked oatmeal better than chocolate chips, her idea of a good chocolate chip recipe contained nutritious oatmeal. Just out of the oven, these cookies are soft and chewy; when cool, they are crisp and still chewy! This relatively new recipe was written in Grams's handwriting on onion-skin paper that was slipped into her little black book.

Prior to 1939, clever farm women used a round, sharp-edged chocolate chopper to cut a chocolate bar into "chips." Most old recipes call for "chocolate, the size of a pea."

■■■■■■■■■■■■■■■■■■■■■■■■■■■■■■■■■

Preheat oven to 375°.

Cream butter and sugars together until light and fluffy. Add eggs and vanilla; mix well. Blend in flour, salt, and dissolved soda. Stir in oats, nuts, and chocolate chips; combine well.

1 CUP BUTTER
¾ CUP WHITE SUGAR
¾ CUP BROWN SUGAR
2 EGGS
1 TEASPOON VANILLA
1½ CUPS FLOUR
½ TEASPOON SALT
1 TEASPOON BAKING SODA,
  DISSOLVED IN 1 TEASPOON
  HOT WATER
2 CUPS ROLLED OATS
1 CUP NUTS, CHOPPED
1 CUP CHOCOLATE CHIPS

> "1½ cups flour, 1 tsp soda, 1 tsp salt, 1 cup fat, ¾ cup w. sugar, ¾ cup b. sugar, 2 eggs, 1 tsp hot water, 1 pkg chocolate chips, 1 cup nuts, 2 cups rolled oats. 375° for 10, 350° for 5."
> Grams's Black Book

Drop by teaspoonfuls 1 to 2 inches apart onto greased baking sheets. Bake 8 to 10 minutes, or until browned on edges and firm. Cool completely on rack.

Store baked cookies in cookie tin. Can be kept 2 to 3 weeks in cool place or frozen 2 to 3 months.

MAKES APPROXIMATELY 4 DOZEN

Dorothy Burkholder's Date-Filled Cookies

Dorothy is noted for her fabulous baking ability along with her zealous good deeds. Her son Gale was the only boy in my class of five girls for all eight grades at Prairie Queen School. He weathered assorted girlish giddiness with the mark of a real trouper.

Dorothy's date-filled cookies, more affectionately known as "Toads in a Hole," vanished instantly from the dessert table at church suppers. I suspect that the same magic will occur soon after you bake them.

■■■■■■■■■■■■■■■■■■■■■■■■■■■■■■■

TO PREPARE FILLING In small saucepan, bring raisins, dates, sugar, and water to a boil. Cook until thick, about 30 minutes; remove from heat. Stir in butter, vanilla, and nuts. Cool filling to room temperature, then proceed with cookie recipe. The filling can be done ahead and refrigerated for 2 to 3 weeks.

TO MAKE THE COOKIE DOUGH Preheat oven to 375°.

Cream butter, lard, and sugar together until light and fluffy. Add eggs, one by one, beating well after each addition. Dissolve soda in hot water; add to butter mixture and mix well. Add flour and salt; mix well.

Drop dough by tablespoonfuls 2

FILLING
■ ■ ■

1 HEAPING CUP RAISINS
1 CUP CHOPPED DATES
½ CUP SUGAR
½ CUP WATER
1 TABLESPOON BUTTER
1½ TEASPOONS VANILLA
½ CUP CHOPPED NUTS

COOKIE DOUGH
■ ■ ■

½ CUP BUTTER
½ CUP LARD OR SOLID
  VEGETABLE SHORTENING
1 CUP BROWN SUGAR
1 CUP WHITE SUGAR
3 EGGS
1 TEASPOON BAKING SODA
1 TABLESPOON HOT WATER
3½ CUPS FLOUR
½ TEASPOON SALT

inches apart onto greased baking sheet. Indent each cookie with back of tablespoon and place ½ teaspoon filling into indent. Top with approximately ¼ teaspoon more dough and bake in 375° oven 12 to 15 minutes, or until lightly browned on edges and firm. Cool completely on rack.

Store baked cookies in cookie tin. Can be kept 2 to 3 days in cool place or frozen 2 to 3 weeks.

MAKES APPROXIMATELY 6 DOZEN

"1 cup fat, 1 cup brown sugar, 1 cup white sugar, 3 eggs, salt, 1 tsp soda in 2 Tbsp hot water, 3⅓ cup flour. Filling, 1 large cup raisins, 1 cup dates, ½ cup sugar and ½ cup water. Boil until thick, add 1 Tbsp butter, vanilla and nuts. 1 Tbsp dough, indent to ½ tsp filling and dough on top. Drop cookies, 375°, 15 mins." *Mom's recipe file*

Grams's Red-Skinned Peanut Cookies

Dad has always been a loyal fan of red-skinned peanuts. Sitting on his desk in the back porch room is a green-covered dish filled with peanuts. Whenever he walks past, he pours a handful out and pops them into his mouth. This recipe is on top of his cookie list.

Even though the vintage recipe suggests rolling the dough, I prefer to make a soft version by dropping the dough. This recipe is perfect for the peanut lovers of your family. The salty red-skinned peanuts not only counterbalance the sweetness, but add a sparkle of color too.

- -

◈

1 CUP BUTTER OR MARGARINE (OR ½ CUP BUTTER AND ½ CUP SOLID VEGETABLE SHORTENING)
2 CUPS BROWN SUGAR
2 EGGS
1 ½ TEASPOONS VANILLA
1 TEASPOON CREAM OF TARTAR
1 TEASPOON BAKING SODA
3 CUPS FLOUR
1 GENEROUS CUP WHOLE RED-SKINNED PEANUTS

Preheat oven to 350°.

Cream butter and sugar together until light and fluffy; beat in eggs and vanilla.

Mix cream of tartar and baking soda with flour; add to butter mixture and blend well. Stir in peanuts and combine well.

Drop by teaspoonfuls 2 inches apart onto greased baking sheets. Bake 10 to 12 minutes, or until browned on edges and firm. Cool completely on rack.

Store baked cookies in cookie tin. Can be kept 2 to 3 weeks in cool place or frozen 2 to 3 months.

MAKES APPROXIMATELY 6 DOZEN

"*2 cups brown sugar, 1 cup shortening, 2 eggs, 3 cups flour, 1 tsp soda, 1 tsp cream of tartar, 1 cup chopped peanuts. Make as butter cake, chill dough, then roll out.*" *Grams's* Black Book *and* Inglenook Cook Book, *1942*

Grams's Famous White Sugar Cookies

Each and every one of us grandchildren affectionately reminisce about eating Grams's famous white sugar cookies that were stored in the noted red round cookie tin that sat on a shelf in her pantry. (There are seven of us, each with a name beginning with the letter *J:* Joel, Janeen, Judy, Joany, Jeff, Judd, and Julie.) This sugar cookie passion and lore were passed down to the next generation of her nine great-grandchildren. (But not all their names begin with the same letter; they are: Susan, Scott, Jay, Bill, Stacey, Laurie, Paige, Todd, and Jodi.)

If you tried to follow the vintage recipe, the result of a perfect cookie can hardly be guaranteed. It is our good fortune, then, that Mom chronicled the recipe in its present state. I once questioned Mom, "Why do your sugar cookies finally taste like Grams's?" Her sage reply was, "Because I finally got the knack of it!" Practice is the key element to a successful sumptuous soft sugar cookie like Grams made.

Cream fats and sugars together until light and fluffy. Add eggs and sour cream; blend thoroughly. Add baking powder, soda, nutmeg, cinnamon, salt, and vanilla; mix well. Add 3 cups flour (more, if necessary to stiffen). Stir until flour is incorporated.

The secret is to keep the dough soft like a cake batter. It is very tricky to handle. Cover dough with plastic wrap and chill at least 12 hours before rolling. Dough can be done ahead and refrigerated 2 to 3 days.

TO ROLL COOKIES AND BAKE
Preheat oven to 350°.

Heavily flour board or pastry cloth by heaping ½ cup flour in center and speading it all over surface. Place half of dough on top of floured board. With rolling pin, roll out approximately ¼ to ½ inch thick (¼ inch for thin, ½ inch for fat). Dip 4-inch cookie cutter into excess flour. Cut dough into cookies. Place cookies 2 inches apart on ungreased baking sheet. Bake in 350° oven 9 to 10 minutes, or until lightly browned on edges and firm. Cool completely on rack.

Store baked cookies in cookie tin, preferably a red one. Can be kept 2 to 3 weeks in cool place if hidden or frozen 2 to 3 months.

MAKES APPROXIMATELY 5 DOZEN 4-INCH COOKIES

½ CUP LARD (IF YOU DO NOT USE LARD, USE ALL BUTTER)
½ CUP BUTTER
1 CUP BROWN SUGAR
1 CUP WHITE SUGAR
3 EGGS
1 CUP SOUR CREAM
2 TEASPOONS BAKING POWDER
1 TEASPOON BAKING SODA
⅛ TEASPOON NUTMEG, FRESHLY GRATED
¼ TEASPOON CINNAMON
¼ TEASPOON SALT
2 TEASPOONS VANILLA
APPROXIMATELY 3½ CUPS FLOUR

"2 cups sugar, 1 cup butter, 1 cup sour cream, not too rich, according to the butter, 3 eggs, 1 tsp soda, more than a level, not very stiff." Grams's Black Book (Anyone had to be a mind reader to understand this!)

Hummingly Good Honey Jumbles

❖

Our family often spent Sunday afternoons in Forestville, now a Minnesota state park. It was our favorite site for picking spring flowers, picnicking in the summer, and tromping through the leaves in the fall. Not many people lived in Forestville; therefore, it was the perfect location for Mr. Wilbright, the local beekeeper. For two generations, we purchased raw, natural unfiltered honey from Wilbright's. The honey was still in the comb.

Around 1960, we received a windfall of honey. During a major summer electrical storm, with thunder, lightning, and wind not to be believed—almost of tornado intensity—an old, almost-dead oak tree west of the house blew over. In doing so, the trunk split in half and out flowed gallons and gallons of honey. Silver lined those dark clouds!

Dad would advise, "Bees will not sting you if you leave them alone!" But I choose to buy honey at the store or stay a reasonable distance from the hive. I prefer clover blossom honey, but any honey will be just fine for this hummingly good recipe.

**3 EGGS, BEATEN
1 CUP HONEY
1 TEASPOON CINNAMON
¼ TEASPOON GINGER
1 TEASPOON BAKING SODA
½ TEASPOON SALT
APPROXIMATELY 3 CUPS FLOUR, DIVIDED INTO PORTIONS OF 2½ CUPS AND ½ CUP
½ CUP SUGAR**

"1 cup sugar, 1 cup strained honey, 1 cup lard, 1 egg, 1 teaspoonful soda, 1 cup sour milk, add sugar, lard, egg and honey—thoroughly blended. 1 teaspoon ginger, 1 teaspoon cinnamon, pinch salt, mix, soft, roll ¼" thick." Grams's Black Book

This recipe, originally published in the Preston Republican paper, is adapted from Marie M. Kruegel. Expect a very soft spongelike cookie. Be sure to allow room on the baking sheet for the dough to spread.

Preheat oven to 350°.

In mixing bowl, beat eggs until frothy; stir in honey.

Mix cinnamon, ginger, baking soda, salt, and 2½ cups flour together. Stir these dry ingredients into honey mixture; as Marie says, "Beat it all good!" Fold in sugar.

Add more flour, up to ½ cup if necessary, to make a drop cookie. (Bake one cookie—a dropped teaspoonful for 8 to 10 minutes—to test the amount of flour necessary.)

Drop by teaspoonfuls 3 to 4 inches apart onto greased baking sheets. Bake 8 to 10 minutes, or until lightly browned on edges and firm to the touch in center. Cool completely on rack.

Store baked cookies in cookie tin. Can be kept 2 to 3 days in cool place or frozen 2 to 3 weeks.

MAKES APPROXIMATELY 4 DOZEN

Grams, Aunt Isla, 1890s

Aunt Isla, Grams, circa 1905

Aunt Isla's Gingersnaps

Aunt Isla (Grams's sister) and Uncle Sam had a farm that was three-quarters of a mile south of Grams and Granddad's. Prior to 1929 they were considered wealthy farmers. When the Depression hit, they packed their belongings and drove westward to California, seeking a better fortune. Despite their hardships, Aunt Isla's reputation as a fabulous baker remained behind in Minnesota. You will see what I mean after tasting this snappy-thin crisp cookie. They are perfect cookies to dunk in coffee.

▪▪▪▪▪▪▪▪▪▪▪▪▪▪▪▪▪▪▪▪▪▪▪▪▪▪▪▪▪▪▪

Cream butter, shortening, and sugar together until light and fluffy; mix in molasses. Dissolve soda in hot water and stir into butter mixture.

½ CUP BUTTER
½ CUP SOLID VEGETABLE SHORTENING
1 CUP SUGAR
1 CUP BLACKSTRAP MOLASSES (BRER RABBIT, GREEN LABEL)
1 TABLESPOON BAKING SODA
½ CUP HOT WATER
1 TABLESPOON GROUND GINGER
½ TEASPOON SALT
3¾ CUPS FLOUR (OR MORE)

Add ginger, salt, and flour; beat dough well. Add more flour to form a stiff dough if necessary. Cover and refrigerate 1 to 2 hours or overnight.

Preheat oven to 350°. Turn half of dough onto heavily floured board or pastry cloth. Roll out ¼ inch thick; cut into 3-inch cookies. Place on ungreased baking sheet and bake for 8 to 10 minutes, or until lightly browned on edges and firm. Completely cool on rack.

Store baked cookies in cookie tin. Can be kept 2 to 3 weeks in cool place or frozen 2 to 3 months.

MAKES APPROXIMATELY 7 DOZEN

"1 cup sugar, 1 cup butter and lard mixed, 1 cup black molasses, 1 Tbsp ginger, ½ tsp salt, 1 Tbsp soda, ½ cup hot water." Grams's Black Book

(There is no mention of flour.)

Jessie Tammel's Chocolate Chews

❖

Jessie and Jake Tammel, contemporaries of Grams and Granddad, were highly respected pillars of strength in the community. Because Jessie was an excellent cook, her invitation to Sunday dinner was greeted with savory anticipation. When she was in her nineties, Jessie penned her autobiography and published it for friends and family. She died at the ripe old age of ninety-eight.

These ageless chocolate treats are crisp on the outside with soft and chewy centers.

································

Cream butter, shortening, and sugar together until light and fluffy. Add vanilla, then eggs, and mix well. Stir in cooled chocolate.

¼ CUP BUTTER
¼ CUP SOLID VEGETABLE SHORTENING
1⅔ CUPS SUGAR
2 TEASPOONS VANILLA
2 EGGS
2 ONE-OUNCE SQUARES UNSWEETENED CHOCOLATE, MELTED AND COOLED
2 TEASPOONS BAKING POWDER
½ TEASPOON SALT
2 CUPS FLOUR
⅓ CUP MILK
½ CUP WALNUTS, CHOPPED

½ CUP POWDERED SUGAR
1 TEASPOON CINNAMON

Sift together baking powder, salt, and flour. Add dry mixture and milk to egg batter alternately, mixing well after each addition. Fold in nuts.

Cover with plastic wrap and chill 2 to 3 hours or overnight in refrigerator.

Preheat oven to 350°. Form dough into 1-inch balls. Mix powdered sugar and cinnamon together. Roll balls in this mixture. Place 3 inches apart on greased baking sheets. Bake 8 to 10 minutes, or until browned on edges and firm. Cool completely on rack.

Store baked cookies in cookie tin. Can be kept 2 to 3 weeks in cool place or frozen 2 to 3 months.

MAKES APPROXIMATELY 4 DOZEN

"½ cup shortening, 1⅔ cup sugar, 2 tsp vanilla, 2 eggs, 2 1-oz squares of unsweetened chocolate, melted, 2 cups sifted flour, 2 tsp baking powder, ½ tsp salt, ⅓ cup milk, ½ cup walnuts. Cream shortening and sugar. Add vanilla. Beat in eggs, then chocolate. Sift dry ingredients together, add alternately with milk. Stir in nuts. Chill 2–3 hours. Form into balls, 1 inch in diameter, roll in ½ cup powdered sugar and 1 tsp cinnamon. Place on sheets 3" apart and bake in moderate oven." Handwritten by Jessie on lined note paper, folded in Grams's Black Book

Mom's Orange Drop Cookies

Because Mom loved citrus fruit, she added this recipe to the lengthy Christmas cookie list. The cookies were met with such acclaim that she made them for every season. These soft, moist, mini-cake cookies have a zesty bite of orange peel. For variation, part lemon or lime zest can be added, but I prefer the pure orange flavor. Use caution when grating the orange rind into zest, because the white pith is very bitter: Be sure to stop after the orange skin.

Preheat oven to 400°.

Cream butter and sugar together until light and fluffy. Beat in eggs, one by one, blending well after each addition.

Grate orange rind, then squeeze out juice from 1 orange. Stir rind and juice into egg batter, combining thoroughly.

In separate bowl, mix soda, salt, and flour together. Alternately add sour cream and flour mixture to batter, beating well after each addition.

Drop dough by teaspoonfuls, 2 inches apart, onto greased and floured baking sheets. Bake approximately 8 minutes, or until no longer shiny on top and ever so slightly browned on edges and firm to the touch. Cool completely on rack.

1 CUP BUTTER
2 CUPS SUGAR
3 EGGS
Grated rind from 3 oranges
Juice from 1 orange (approximately 1 cup)
1 TEASPOON BAKING SODA
½ TEASPOON SALT
3½ CUPS FLOUR
1 CUP SOUR CREAM

FROSTING
###

JUICE AND GRATED RIND OF 1 ORANGE
1 TEASPOON BUTTER, MELTED
1½ CUPS POWDERED SUGAR

"1 cup butter, 2 cups sugar, 3 eggs, 1 cup sour cream, 3 oranges, grate rind, add 1 juice ... 1 tsp soda, ½ tsp salt, 3½ cups flour. Mix as butter cake, drop frost with juice and rind of 1 orange, add water and 1 tsp butter. Bake 425° don't brown, 85 cookies." Mom's recipe stack, circa 1950

TO FROST Grate orange rind and squeeze juice into bowl. Add butter and powdered sugar until mixture becomes spreading consistency. (If too thin, add sugar; if too thick, add juice or water.) Frost tops of cooled cookies; allow to dry completely before storing.

Store in airtight cookie tin, placing waxed paper between layers of cookies. Can be kept 2 to 3 days in cool place or frozen 2 to 3 weeks.

MAKES APPROXIMATELY 7 DOZEN

Mother's Molasses Cookies

✦

One of my favorite places to play was at the home of Charlotte Snyder, who was five years my senior. We played "house" in an empty corn crib. She had old kitchen plates, spoons, pots, and pans just like the rest of us farm girls, but her mother allowed us to practice with molasses. With sticky molasses as a base, we concocted pies, cakes, cookies, soups, and whole meals by adding various sticks and stones to simulate the real thing. I was in paradise. (At home I just used my imagination.)

Molasses cookies were common farm table fare. Each farm woman used her own special variation of the same basic recipe. The "mother" of this recipe title is Grams. She used it so often that the ink was very faint on the grease-spotted page. It makes a very crisp cookie with a definite rich flavor.

■■■■■■■■■■■■■■■■■■■■■■■

Cream butter, shortening, and sugar together until light and fluffy. Add molasses and egg; beat well.

½ CUP BUTTER
½ CUP SOLID VEGETABLE SHORTENING
1 CUP SUGAR
1 CUP GOLDEN MOLASSES (BRER RABBIT OR GRANDMA'S)
1 EGG
1 CUP MILK
1 TEASPOON LEMON JUICE
1 TEASPOON BAKING SODA
PINCH SALT
1 TEASPOON GINGER
1 TEASPOON CINNAMON
3¾ CUPS FLOUR

"1 cup sugar, 1 cup lard, 1 egg, 1 cup molasses, 1 cup sour milk, 1 teaspoonful soda, pinch of salt, 1 teaspoonful ginger and 1 of cinnamon. Mix, soft, roll ¼" thick." Grams's Black Book

Sour milk by adding lemon juice; let stand 2 to 3 minutes.

In separate bowl, mix baking soda, salt, ginger, cinnamon, and flour together. Alternately add dry ingredients and milk to egg batter, beating well after each addition. The dough should be soft, yet rollable.

Cover with plastic wrap. Chill completely 2 to 3 hours in refrigerator or overnight.

Preheat oven to 350°. Place half of chilled dough on floured board or pastry cloth. Roll ¼ inch thick and cut into cookies with 3- or 4-inch cutter. Place 2 inches apart on ungreased baking sheets; sprinkle pinch of sugar on top of each cookie. Bake 8 to 10 minutes, or until lightly browned on edges and firm. Repeat with remaining dough. Cool cookies on rack. Store in cookie tin. Can be kept 2 to 3 weeks in cool place or frozen 2 to 3 months.

MAKES APPROXIMATELY 4 DOZEN

Mom's Prune- Walnut Bars

Granddad bought Sunsweet Quality, nature-flavored, tree-ripened prunes in a twenty-five-pound wooden box. They were shipped to the grocer from San Jose, California, by railroad. That generous supply lasted the whole winter. I have one of his prune boxes as an artifact in our living room. I wish it could tell where it has traveled and what it was used for after the prunes were eaten.

Mom purchased prunes in two-pound cellophane bags. She always had at least one or two on hand. They needed to be pitted and plumped up before adding to the dough. She used dried fruits too often for my palate as a child. I considered prunes poisonous, then. Now, I favor their natural flavor in most forms.

This easy-to-make recipe gets a special pizzazz from the grated orange peel. Lemon peel tastes equally good.

⅓ CUP BUTTER
1 CUP BROWN SUGAR
2 LARGE EGGS
1 TEASPOON GRATED ORANGE PEEL
¾ CUP FLOUR
½ TEASPOON SALT
½ TEASPOON BAKING POWDER
1 CUP UNCOOKED, PITTED PRUNES, SNIPPED INTO ¼-INCH PIECES WITH SCISSORS
½ CUP CHOPPED NUTS

½ CUP POWDERED SUGAR

Preheat oven to 325°.

Cream butter and sugar together until light and fluffy. Add eggs and orange peel; mix well. Stir in flour, salt, and baking powder; mix well. Fold prunes and nuts into batter; mix well.

Pour batter into greased and floured 9-inch-square cake pan. Bake for 30 minutes, or until brown on top and toothpick comes out clean when inserted into center.

Cut into bars while warm. Cool on rack. When cool, roll bars in powdered sugar, or dust top with powdered sugar.

Store in cookie tin, placing waxed paper between layers of bars. Can be kept 2 to 3 days in cool place. Does not freeze well.

MAKES APPROXIMATELY 1½ DOZEN

Nora East's Apple Bars

❖

Nora East's father, Charlie Vanderbie, owned a country store in Greenleafton. This little burg is one mile west of the farm as the crow flies. Grams and Granddad bought necessary items from Charlie to supplement the provisions that they purchased on the large shopping expeditions to Preston.

Mom and I stopped in to buy various items, including bologna and my favorite, longhorn cheese. The large wheel of golden cheese sat on the counter under a large glass dome. With great fascination and the anticipation of a sliver to taste, I watched him precisely cut off a wedge of cheese with a lethal-looking knife. The store is still standing there today with modern cases for the meats and cheese.

Nora and Mom grew up together. Nora's children and we kids were good friends, too. Although we now are in various parts of the country, we manage to keep up-to-date via our mothers. Nora and Ray live in Harmony, about twelve miles east of the farm.

Nora's special recipe is a mini-apple-pie cookie. If you like apples, you will love this generous apple "tart."

CRUST
■ ■ ■

1 CUP BUTTER (OR LARD)
2½ CUPS FLOUR
1 TABLESPOON SUGAR
2 EGG YOLKS PLUS ENOUGH
   MILK TO EQUAL ⅔ CUP

APPLE AND SUGAR FILLING
■ ■ ■

6 TO 7 LARGE TART APPLES,
   GRANNY SMITH OR
   GREENINGS
½ TEASPOON NUTMEG,
   FRESHLY GRATED
1 TEASPOON CINNAMON
1 CUP SUGAR

ASSEMBLY
■ ■ ■

1½ CUPS CRUSHED
   CORNFLAKES
1 TABLESPOON BUTTER, CUT
   IN TINY PIECES
1 EGG WHITE, BEATEN

TO MAKE CRUST In food processor, cut butter into flour and sugar until it becomes coarse meal; remove to mixing bowl.

Stir milk-egg mixture into flour mixture until it forms dough. Gather into ball, then divide dough in half. Turn onto floured board or pastry cloth and cover with towel to rest 10 minutes.

TO MAKE FILLING Peel, seed, and thinly slice apples; measure to make about 1½ quarts.

Mix nutmeg, cinnamon, and sugar together in small bowl; set aside.

"2½ cups flour, 1 cup lard, 1 Tbsp sugar, 1 egg yolk and enough milk to equal ⅔ cup. Roll out half to fit jelly roll pan. Spread 2 handfuls of crushed cornflakes on top.

10 large apples or 1½ quarts. 1 cup sugar, cinnamon and nutmeg, dot the top with butter. Put rest of crust over top, brush with beaten egg white. Bake 400° for 60 mins. Glaze with 1 cup p. sugar, ⅓ cup milk and vanilla, drizzle over hot pie." <u>Mom's recipe stack</u>

TO ASSEMBLE AND BAKE Preheat oven to 400°. Roll out half of rested dough to fit bottom of ungreased 11-by-17-inch jelly roll pan. Line pan, leaving an inch overhanging edges.

Spread crushed cornflakes over crust. Place sliced apples on top of cornflakes. Sprinkle sugar mixture evenly over apples.

Dot top with butter cut into pieces. Roll out other half of crust. Place on top of whole affair. Seal edges with crimp, as if for pie. Cut a few slits in the crust to vent steam.

GLAZE

• • •

1 CUP POWDERED SUGAR
⅓ CUP MILK
1 TEASPOON VANILLA

Brush crust with egg white. Bake for 45 minutes, or until brown on top and apples are tender. Set on rack.

TO GLAZE Mix sugar, milk, and vanilla together; it will be runny. Pour glaze over hot crust. Cool completely and cut into bars.

Store in pan, covered with plastic wrap. Can be kept in cool place 1 to 2 days. Does not freeze well.

MAKES APPROXIMATELY 6 DOZEN

Christmas in the Country

Christmas began even before Thanksgiving, when we started preparing our school Christmas program. We selected the plays, skits, and songs, and psyched ourselves up for the season. The Monday after Thanksgiving we began laying the groundwork by building the stage (with the help of a father or two), borrowing or creating the costumes, and painting the scenery. We learned our lines, practiced the songs (I was the school pianist), and planned the lighting—all the while attending to our schoolwork.

Once the floor-to-ceiling Christmas tree was lit, we knew that our big production was imminent. Classes ended ten days prior to the performance. We rehearsed, re-rehearsed, and dress-rehearsed. Finally, on opening (and closing) night, every family (all dolled up), plus grandparents and friends, jammed into the schoolhouse in anticipation of the show. Most of us suffered from the jitters, stage fright, stomach butterflies, or some other sign of excitement. But once we donned costumes and a hefty dose of makeup and the curtain went up, we became real troupers, giving another smashing performance. Afterwards, our mothers and grandmothers cried, and our brothers and sisters cheered as our fathers proudly beamed their approval.

Yuletide events dominated every segment of our lives. Extra choir practices, rehearsals for the church Christmas pageant, and the usual holiday social events filled our calendar every day. Although the family's elaborate baking preparations began even earlier, the decorations were put up about three weeks before Christmas. Dad always brought Mom a poinsettia plant or fresh flowers before Christmas

as part of his gift to her. Later, with her strict instructions, he selected a suitable pine tree from our windbreak out north of the house or one from a neighbor's thinned-out grove. After he chopped down the tree, Dad carried it to the basement to become acclimated to a warmer environment. This process took at least twenty-four hours, and it seemed longer to me. As kids, we thought a subtitle to Christmas should read, "Wait, wait, and wait some more!"

At the appointed time, Dad brought the tree up and set it in the designated spot in front of the staircase in the dining room. Most of our holiday traditions remained the same, except that Mom had a different decoration scheme planned for the tree each year: It was adorned various years with fifty red cardinals, several dozen red-and-white, polka-dot strawberries, all gold balls with gold swags, or all silver ornaments tied on with big red satin bows. However, four special ornaments, commemorating each child's first Christmas, *always* hung on the pine boughs. (Joel has a red—by now tarnished—ball. Mine was a glass bell with red, white, and silver tinsel inside. Judy's bell is red; Joany's is green.) One year, Dad found a tree that was naturally decorated with three birds' nests.

We knew that Mom enjoyed the anticipation of Christmas as much as we did. Fresh wreaths with huge red bows and pine cones decorated the front and back doors; the cornices were filled with candles, angels, angel hair, and pine boughs. One year, Mom strung a garland of greens on the banister of the staircase. Unfortunately, the next morning, Joel slid down the banister and brought the garland with him . . . Oops! No matter what, our house was perfumed from basement to attic with the scent of Christmas.

Traditionally, Grams entertained the family for *Christmas Eve Oyster Soup* supper (page 274). We kids were glad for a shortened menu because we were itching to hang our stockings at home. Before climbing the stairs on Christmas Eve, we each hung a stocking (one of Dad's big work socks, in hopes that it would be completely filled) by the register in the dining room. The lack of a fireplace did not dissuade our belief that Santa slid down a chimney. I left a plate of his favorite cookies and a glass of milk on the kitchen table with a note, explaining my errors and frailties, asking that they be overlooked, then up to bed with visions of sugar plums. . . .

Santa always stuffed a tangerine in the toe of the sock and filled the leg with a new toothbrush, a few English walnuts in the shell, a special chocolate Santa or store-bought candy, a candy cane, and a new pencil box or pens, plus hair ribbons or a new pair of mittens. Mom, already preparing dinner, served warm cinnamon rolls and hot cocoa. We were a happy lot! Our family opened the important presents after dinner, but before dessert. (Thank goodness!)

After extra leaves extended the table, the top padded and spread with the Christmas green linen tablecloth, I set the table according to Emily Post's instructions: White linen napkins, Lenox china, Fostoria goblets, water glasses, and polished silverware marked each place. We created a spectacular and festive mood with the help of cut glass and Fostoria candlesticks, lettered place cards, festive favors, fresh flowers, and a centerpiece of fruits and nuts. Christmas music played in the background. As the one o'clock dinner hour neared, with every detail checked and ready, we changed into dress clothes for dinner.

On rare occasions, other guests were invited, but mostly Christmas dinner was for the immediate family. (There were fifteen of us.) The order of arrival of family members and their cargoes was predictable. Grams and Granddad came first—Grams carrying the basket of buns, an extra two-crust pie (usually sour cream raisin), the filled red cookie tin, and the cranberry relish and "mould." Granddad had the big box of gifts for under the tree. Aunt Rubye, Uncle Roy, and cousin Julie were next. Rubye brought a box of krumkaka, rosettes, lefse, Jell-O salad, or bar cookies. Roy added another big box of gifts. Aunt Bets, Uncle Buzz, and cousins Jeff and Judd would finally arrive from Wells. Bets carried her special cookie platter, assorted candies, and watermelon rind pickles. Buzz followed with a big box of gifts for under the tree. That was one huge heap of presents!

After Dad led us by singing the blessing, we sat down to Christmas dinner. It was served family style: According to "Hoyle and Emily Post," we passed every dish from left to right, holding the bowls and platters for our dinner partner. It is joked among this generation's in-laws (the family newcomers) that those gathered around the table were so busy passing the dishes that they never got a chance to eat their food! (Family members knew how to sneak bites between handoffs.) Contests among and between the menfolk, razzing about who was the bigger "hog" (of the potatoes and gravy), and all sorts of corny jokes were the usual banter. One observer claimed, "The whole kit and caboodle are rascals!" We often laughed until our sides ached.

We kids wished for less frivolity because opening the gifts was the next order of business. With cameras flashing, hugs and kisses—and screeches of "Oh! That's just what I wanted!"—generally good-natured mayhem prevailed in the living room.

Next? Delicious desserts. Mom's famous three-tier table was laden with individual two-and-a-half-inch tarts: chocolate and vanilla custard, glazed strawberry, raspberry, lemon, pecan, mincemeat, apricot, and pumpkin.

Alongside were large platters heaped with sweets from our back-porch candy-land. Christmas would not be Christmas without at least a taste of each variety. Mom's candy inventory included Mary Bestor's bologna candy, caramels, crystal-cut candies, divinity, fudge, penuche, holiday mints, peanut brittle, popcorn balls, *The Broadwaters' Caramel Corn* (page 337), taffy, toffee, turtles, and innumerable other confection variations. Then there were Aunt

Rubye's light-as-a-feather Norwegian rosettes and krumkaka. Given the highest place among the sweets was *Great-Grandmother Esther Mansfield Crowe's White Fruit Cake* (page 344). Somehow we inserted an *Angel Food Cake* (page 313), in honor of Uncle Roy, into the sweet mix. The entire group raised voices in song and best wishes because it was his real birthday, poor chap. And of course we always had fresh-churned *1990s Old-Fashioned Vanilla Ice Cream* (page 342) that was offered with toppings of every imaginable description.

Great-Great Grandmother Sara "Rapp" Crowe, circa 1860

CHRISTMAS COOKIES

◈

Our lengthy Christmas gift list compelled Mom and me to commence baking cookies right after Thanksgiving. We began with fruitcakes, fruit-and-nut cookie varieties, candies, and fattigmand (Scandinavian fried cookies). They all possess lengthy storage capabilities under the proper conditions. The all-butter cookies, including spritz, were next on the to-do list. Mom has always been a genius with the cookie press. She colored the dough with harmonious hues of food coloring: green for trees and wreaths, pink for poinsettias, and yellow for stars. I did not take one breath as I watched with awesome respect while she expertly turned the black round handle on the gray metal press. Each perfectly formed cookie magically emerged from the bottom onto the baking sheet. Then they were baked, cooled, and set aside for decoration. On another day, we baked white sugar cookies, the chocolate and ginger creams, and of course my favorite, gumdrop cookies, to complete our list.

The kitchen table was an incredible sight! Dozens and dozens of tiny cookies waiting to be decorated covered every inch of table. I arranged each shape into clusters to simplify the next step. Mom reserved a whole afternoon to perform her favorite task, decorating cookies. She colored the powdered sugar frosting with food coloring and set out cereal bowls filled with shots, sprinkles, and silver balls. Then with decorating tubes in hand, we spent hours placing red holly berries and pink bows on the wreaths. Mom put pink candles with yellow flames on some trees; on others we put garlands of red or yellow swags. Green swirls outlined the yellow stars. I was the right-hand assistant. My main job was placing the shots, sprinkles, and silver balls on top of the frosting. After the frosting hardened, I carefully stored the cookies in tins and plastic containers. Waxed paper was placed between each layer to protect the frosting. Each tin went unlabeled because I just *knew* where every cookie was!

All the empty tins, plastic boxes, pails, and containers in the house were laden with Christmas cookies. The unheated back-porch cupboard soon became a cookie lover's—or a cookie monster's—heaven. After all the cookies were baked, I packed an assortment into gift boxes of various sizes. The lucky recipients were our family's friends, the milkman, the mailman, shut-ins, and older people who no longer baked their own. Even though Mom admonished me not to eat any, the irresistible temptation to snitch at least one was overpowering.

Do not think for one moment that we gave every Christmas cookie away. We indulged ourselves by serving a special plate of assorted cookies along with dessert at all the holiday dinner parties as well as at our family meals. Not one person mentioned weight gain nor did they restrain themselves from tasting every one on the plate—me included!

Best Frosted Chocolate Creams

To me, Grams's chocolate creams tasted better than Mom's. I was positive that the reason had something to do with her pantry. It was filled with a combination of lavender, onion, garlic, and chocolate aromas. My every visit was rewarded with some savory or sweet surprise.

Grams tried every variation of this recipe. "Best" was noted next to the list of ingredients for this cookie . . . no explanation necessary.

Chocolate was ever present at the conclusion of our family Christmas celebration. Uncle Buzz, a veteran chocoholic, and Uncle Roy, a devout lover of food in general, along with Dad—who was part and party to these shenanigans—egged each other on during dinner to see who could consume the most. Our family gatherings were not solemn affairs.

This soft cakelike cookie melts in your mouth—a chocolate lover's idea of heaven.

"1 cup sugar, 2 eggs, ¾ cup milk, 1 cup nuts, ½ cup fat, 1 tsp soda, 2½ cups flour, 2 squares chocolate, vanilla."
Grams's Black Book

½ CUP BUTTER
1 CUP SUGAR
2 EGGS
2 OUNCES (SQUARES) UNSWEETENED CHOCOLATE, MELTED AND COOLED
1 TEASPOON VANILLA
1 TEASPOON BAKING SODA
2½ CUPS FLOUR
¾ CUP MILK

FROSTING

2 OUNCES UNSWEETENED CHOCOLATE
2 TABLESPOONS BUTTER
2 CUPS POWDERED SUGAR
2 TEASPOONS VANILLA
APPROXIMATELY 2 TEASPOONS HEAVY CREAM

60 PECAN HALVES FOR GARNISH

Preheat oven to 400°.

Cream butter and sugar together until light and fluffy. Add eggs, melted chocolate, and vanilla; mix well.

Combine soda and flour together. Alternately add flour mixture and milk to egg batter, beating well after each addition.

Drop by teaspoonfuls, 2 inches apart, onto ungreased baking sheets. Bake 8 to 10 minutes, or until dull on top and firm to the touch. Remove cookies from sheets immediately and cool on rack.

TO FROST Melt chocolate and butter in saucepan; remove from heat. Stir in sugar, vanilla, and enough cream to become spreading consistency.

Frost cookies after they are completely cool (but the frosting should still be slightly warm). With table knife or small spatula, swirl frosting around top of cookie. Place a perfect pecan half on top before frosting is set. Let frosting set while cookies are on rack.

Store in cookie tin, placing waxed paper between layers of cookies. Can be kept 5 to 6 days in cool place. This recipe does not freeze well.

MAKES APPROXIMATELY 5 DOZEN

Aunt Bets's Peanut Cookies

Christmas Day was exciting because the whole family came for dinner. Everyone, dressed in their best "bib 'n tucker," arrived with packages and their culinary contribution to the feast! First, the joyous greeting "Merry Christmas," then came hugs and kisses, and finally the food parcel was unveiled.

Aunt Bets (Mom's youngest sister) and Uncle Buzz—short for Betty Gene and Maynard—live in Wells, Minnesota, about eighty miles west of our farm. Mom and I would keep watch out the kitchen window for the first glimpse of their car. We'd announce, "They're here!" —and the unspoken tension was over.

Aunt Bets brought a platter of distinctive cookies. On that platter she always included these spicy, rich-flavored, peanut-topped cookies. They were eaten almost "as fast as a cat could wink its eye!"

Do not blink or they will be gone.

¾ CUP BUTTER
1 CUP SUGAR
4 TABLESPOONS MOLASSES (BRER RABBIT, ORANGE LABEL)
1 EGG
2 TEASPOONS BAKING SODA
2 CUPS FLOUR, PLUS UP TO 1 CUP MORE AS NEEDED
1 TEASPOON GINGER
1 TEASPOON CINNAMON
½ TEASPOON CLOVES
PINCH SALT

FROSTING

1 ½ CUPS POWDERED SUGAR
3 TABLESPOONS BUTTER, MELTED
2 TEASPOONS VANILLA
APPROXIMATELY 2 TABLESPOONS HEAVY CREAM

½ CUP RED-SKINNED PEANUTS

Preheat oven to 375°.

Cream butter and sugar together until light and fluffy. Add molasses and egg; mix well.

Add soda, 2 cups flour, ginger, cinnamon, cloves, and salt; mix well. Add more flour as needed so dough can be rolled into balls.

Roll into walnut-sized (1-inch) balls. Place 2 inches apart on greased baking sheets. Flatten with fork or bottom of glass. Bake 12 to 15 minutes, or until lightly browned on edges and firm. Cool on rack.

TO FROST Mix sugar, melted butter, vanilla, and enough cream to become spreading consistency. With table knife or small spatula, frost cooled cookies. Top each cookie with a peanut. Let frosting set and cool cookies completely on rack.

Store in cookie tin, placing waxed paper between layers of cookies. Can be kept 2 to 3 weeks in cool place, or frozen, unfrosted, 2 to 3 months.

MAKES APPROXIMATELY 6 DOZEN

Christmas
Fruit
and
Nut Bars

Grams made these bars right after Thanksgiving because they have a long shelf life. She could proudly check this off her list of things to do. At first glance, I thought these cookies would be strange. Surprise, surprise, they are chewy, full of fruits

¾ CUP FLOUR
1 CUP POWDERED SUGAR
1½ TEASPOONS BAKING POWDER
1 TEASPOON BAKING SODA
2 EGGS
3 TABLESPOONS BUTTER, MELTED AND COOLED
1 TEASPOON VANILLA
1 CUP CHOPPED WALNUTS
1 CUP CHOPPED PITTED DATES
¼ CUP CANDIED ORANGE PEEL, CHOPPED
¼ CUP CANDIED LEMON PEEL, CHOPPED
¼ CUP CANDIED PINEAPPLE, CHOPPED

½ CUP POWDERED SUGAR

and nuts, and much better than any traditional fruitcake (to my taste).

Preheat oven to 275°.

In mixing bowl, combine flour, sugar, baking powder, and soda.

With fork, beat eggs well. Stir eggs and butter into center of flour mixture; blend until completely smooth.

Add vanilla, stirring well. Fold in nuts and fruits.

Spread dough into greased and floured 8-inch-square cake pan. Bake for 1 hour, or until toothpick comes out clean when inserted in center. Cool completely on rack, then cut into tiny (1-by-1¼-inch) bars.

Roll each bar in powdered sugar. Store in cookie tin, placing waxed paper between layers of bars. Can be kept 3 to 4 weeks in cool place, or frozen 3 to 4 months. After storing, redust with powdered sugar just before serving.

MAKES 4 DOZEN TINY BARS

"¾ cup flour, 1 cup powdered sugar, beat 2 eggs, beat in 1½ tsp baking powder, 1 tsp soda, 3 Tbsp shortening, melted. Stir in 1 cup walnuts, 1 cup date, ¼ cup each, orange, lemon and pineapple peel. Bake 40 minutes, 275°, cool. Spread batter in 8" pan." Grams's Black Book

Fattigmand

These Scandinavian fried cookies were one of Grams's favorites. She made them early for Christmas holiday entertaining. I was mesmerized by the magic of the white stocking-covered rolling pin as she rolled out the dough onto a white linen tea towel with her deft hands. My own first attempt was a disaster!

This recipe comes from Lenore Sullivan's cookbook, *What to Cook for Company;* she was a home economist from Iowa State University, Ames campus. Mom and Grams devoutly followed her scrupulous recipes.

Cardamom, the seed from a ginger-family plant, has a pleasant pungent aroma and delicious sweet flavor. It is a popular spice used to flavor sweet baked goods in Scandinavian and Arab countries. One taste and you will become a cardamom convert too!

Beat egg yolks in mixing bowl until light and lemon-colored. Add sugar and cream; continue beating. Add salt, vanilla, cardamom, and ¾ cup flour; mix well. Add ¼ cup more

6 EGG YOLKS
2 TABLESPOONS SUGAR
2 TABLESPOONS HEAVY CREAM
¼ TEASPOON SALT
1 TEASPOON VANILLA
½ TEASPOON GROUND CARDAMOM
¾ TO 1 CUP SIFTED FLOUR

SOLID VEGETABLE SHORTENING OR PEANUT OIL FOR FRYING
APPROXIMATELY ½ CUP POWDERED SUGAR FOR DUSTING

flour if dough is too sticky to roll.

Turn dough out on lightly floured board and roll ⅛ inch thick. Cut in diamond shapes about 4 inches long. Make slit about 1½ inches long in center of diamond and pull one corner through, turning it inside out, just like pulling your sleeve through an armhole.

TO FRY Fill deep-fat fryer with solid vegetable shortening or peanut oil. (Grams used Crisco, Mom used leaf lard, and I use peanut oil.) Preheat fryer to 370°.

When oil is hot, fry one cookie to test, taste, and readjust the temperature if necessary. Fry approximately 3 to 4 minutes or until lightly browned, darker brown on edges. Drain on rack set over brown paper bags to absorb oil.

Cool completely. Sprinkle with powdered sugar just before serving. Store *unsugared* in airtight container. Can be kept 3 to 4 weeks in cool place, or frozen 3 to 4 months.

MAKES APPROXIMATELY 2½ DOZEN

Grams's Best Ginger Creams

◆

One of my fondest memories of Grams is the familiar aroma of ginger wafting through the whole house. My, how she loved ginger cookies! *Grams's Black Book* has no less than three variations of ginger creams. She made a notation on each and every ginger cookie recipe that she found and obviously tested.

This spicy cookie can be either crisp or soft. Grams rolled the dough thick for a soft cookie. On the other hand, Mom rolls the dough thin for a crisp cookie. Because the dough is soft and sticky, I roll the dough about ¼ inch thick. The result is a melt-in-your mouth soft cookie. Do not despair when rolling out the dough: Heavily flour the board and use a gentle touch on the rolling pin. I use a thin pancake turner to transfer the raw cookie to the baking sheet. The extra flour on the cookie will be hidden by frosting.

▪▪▪▪▪▪▪▪▪▪▪▪▪▪▪▪▪▪▪▪▪▪▪▪▪▪▪▪▪▪▪

Cream butter and sugar together until light and fluffy. Add molasses and eggs; mix well.

To sour milk, add lemon juice and let it sit for 2 to 3 minutes.

> "1 cup sugar, 1 cup lard, half butter, 1 cup dark molasses, 2 eggs, 1 cup sour milk, 3 tsp soda, 2 tsp cr. of tartar, 1 big tsp ginger, heaping, 1½ tsp cinnamon, enough flour to roll."
> Grams's Black Book

1 CUP BUTTER, OR ½ CUP BUTTER AND ½ CUP LARD
1 CUP SUGAR
1 CUP MOLASSES (GRANDMA'S, NOT BLACKSTRAP)
2 EGGS
1 CUP MILK AND 1 TEASPOON LEMON JUICE (OR 1 CUP BUTTERMILK)
3 TEASPOONS BAKING SODA
2 TEASPOONS CREAM OF TARTAR
1 HEAPING TEASPOON GINGER
1½ TEASPOONS CINNAMON
3¾ TO 4½ CUPS FLOUR (SEE NOTE)

FROSTING
▪▪▪

3 TABLESPOONS BUTTER, MELTED
2 CUPS POWDERED SUGAR
2 TEASPOONS VANILLA
2 TO 3 TABLESPOONS HEAVY CREAM

Mix dry ingredients and sift onto waxed paper. Alternately add dry ingredients and sour milk to batter, beginning and ending with flour. Mix well after each addition; continue beating until evenly mixed. Cover with plastic wrap; refrigerate until firm, 2 to 3 hours or overnight.

TO BAKE Preheat oven to 350°. Place half of dough on heavily floured board or pastry cloth. Flatten ball with hand; then with rolling pin, roll ¼ inch thick. Dip 2½-inch cookie cutter into excess flour; cut dough into cookies. Place cookies 2 inches apart on greased baking sheet and bake 8 to 10 minutes, or until lightly browned on edges and firm.

Repeat with remaining dough. Cool completely on rack.

TO FROST Mix butter, sugar, and vanilla together. Stir in enough cream to make spreading consistency. When cookies are completely cool, spread frosting on top with kitchen knife. Return to rack until frosting is set.

Store in airtight container, placing waxed paper between layers of cookies. Can be kept 2 to 3 weeks in cool place. Unfrosted cookies can be frozen 2 to 3 months, but frosted cookies do not freeze well.

NOTE Use 3¾ cups flour if using all butter; 4½ cups flour if using lard and butter.

MAKES APPROXIMATELY 6 DOZEN

Gum-drop Bars

Great-Grandmother Crowe always made these spicy jewel-like bars for her family at Christmas. Grams continued the tradition and Mom always made a double batch for us. Not wanting to break this family tradition, I include these savory bars on my Christmas baking list.

Use spice gumdrops, but omit the black ones: The strong licorice taste overpowers the other flavors. My early contribution to this recipe was eating all the black gumdrops. Now, Paige continues the tradition. Christmas would not be Christmas without them.

- -

Preheat oven to 325°.

Beat eggs until frothy. Add sugar and continue to beat until thick and light-colored. Beat 1 tablespoon warm water into egg mixture.

Sift flour, salt, baking powder, and cinnamon together; fold into egg mixture.

Snip gumdrops in half. Dust with flour to prevent sticking. Add pecans to gumdrops and fold into batter.

Pour into greased and floured 11-by-17-inch jelly roll pan, spreading dough to edges. Bake approximately 20 minutes or until toothpick comes out clean. Frost while still warm.

4 EGGS
2 CUPS BROWN SUGAR
2 CUPS FLOUR, SIFTED
PINCH SALT
2 TEASPOONS BAKING POWDER
1 TEASPOON CINNAMON
1 CUP SPICE GUMDROPS
PINCH FLOUR
½ CUP CHOPPED PECANS

FROSTING

3 TABLESPOONS BUTTER, SOFTENED
2 TABLESPOONS ORANGE JUICE
1 TEASPOON GRATED ORANGE RIND
APPROXIMATELY ½ CUP POWDERED SUGAR

"4 eggs, 2 c. B sugar, 2 t B powder, 1 T cold water, 2 c. flour, ¼ t salt, 1 t cinnamon, ½ c. chopped pecans, 1 c. shredded gumdrops (omit licorice). Beat eggs, add sugar and water add dry materials, fold in gum drops and nuts. Bake in slow oven while warm ice. 3 T butter, 2 T orange juice, 1 t grated rind, powdered sugar." Grams's Black Book

TO FROST Mix butter, juice, and rind with wire whip, blending well. Add powdered sugar until mixture becomes thin frosting.

Spread on warm baked contents of pan; cool on rack. When cold, cut into bars with wet sharp knife.

Store in airtight container, placing waxed paper between layers of bars. Can be kept 2 to 3 weeks in cool place. These do not freeze well.

MAKES 4 TO 5 DOZEN

Christmas Macaroons

These pretty, pale, pink-and-green, melt-in-your-mouth confection/cookies were not only good to eat, but economical to make. Egg whites were an abundant commodity on the farm, and both Grams and Mom added "whatever they had on hand" to create macaroons.

For Christmas, Mom divided the white batter in half, and added a few drops of red food coloring to one and green coloring to the other. The light-as-a-feather confections were a colorful addition to our overflowing cookie platter. They remind me of cotton candy from the County Fair. An added bonus: Macaroons are a perfect dessert for the no-cholesterol member of the family.

Preheat oven to 325°.

In very clean, dry mixing bowl, beat egg whites with salt until frothy. Gradually add sugar and continue to beat until very stiff and glossy. *Do not underbeat!* This may take 8 to 10 minutes.

Beat in vanilla and almond extract; divide batter in half. Add red color to half of batter and green to

4 EGG WHITES
PINCH SALT
1⅓ CUPS SUGAR
1 TEASPOON VANILLA
1 TEASPOON ALMOND EXTRACT
2 TO 3 DROPS RED FOOD COLORING
2 TO 3 DROPS GREEN FOOD COLORING

4 CUPS CORNFLAKES

1 CUP CHOPPED NUTS (OPTIONAL)
1 CUP COCONUT (OPTIONAL)

"325° when put in, 350° in about 20 minutes, run up to 375°. 4 egg whites, 2 cups sugar, 4 cups corn flakes, walnuts, or coconut (1 c.), pinch salt, vanilla. Use greased and floured pans."
<u>Grams's Black Book</u>

other half. Keep the intensity the same for each hue.

Stir 2 cups of cornflakes into each batter. Similarly, add nuts and coconut, if desired; fold into batter.

Drop by teaspoonfuls, 2 inches apart, onto baking sheets (greased and floured, or covered with parchment paper). Bake for about 20 minutes, or until set and lightly browned on edges.

If using parchment paper, remove paper with baked macaroons, then lay wet towel on each hot baking sheet. Place paper of cookies on towel; let stand 1 minute. Steam will loosen cookies. Slip off with spatula and cool on rack.

If using prepared baking sheets, remove from baking sheets immediately with spatula and cool on rack.

Store in airtight container. Can be kept 2 to 3 weeks in cool place. These do not freeze well.

NOTE Substitute your favorite mixture of dry cereal and nuts, cracker crumbs, and/or granola, for the cornflakes, nuts, and coconut listed here.

MAKES APPROXIMATELY 3½ DOZEN

Mocha Cakes

It is my suspicion that Great-Grandmother Broadwater flavored the frosting in this recipe with a bit of strong coffee, thus the name, "Mocca Cake." However, Grams and Mom used maple flavoring instead.

Chopping the peanuts in the nut chopper was my job. It was a small manual metal rectangular shaped box, fitted with a set of sharp teeth, that screwed onto the top of a glass pint-sized jar marked on the side for measures of ½, 1, and 1½ cups. I filled the box with a few whole nuts, turned the handle, and the chopped nuts fell into the jar. It took me a long time to chop 1 cup of nuts—a perfect job for a budding young baker; a food processor now performs this task in seconds.

Crunchy ground peanuts surround these sweet, moist white cake fingers. My brother ate these tasty morsels almost as fast as we could roll them in the peanuts.

Preheat oven to 350°.

Beat eggs until frothy; add sugar gradually and continue to whip until thick and lemon-colored. Beat in cream.

Alternately fold flour and baking powder and hot water into egg batter, beginning and ending with flour. Spread into 11-by-17-inch

3 EGGS
2 CUPS SUGAR
8 TABLESPOONS WHIPPING CREAM
2 CUPS FLOUR, SIFTED
2 TEASPOONS BAKING POWDER
½ CUP HOT WATER

FROSTING

2 CUPS POWDERED SUGAR
2 TABLESPOONS BUTTER, MELTED
1 TEASPOON MAPLE FLAVORING
1 TEASPOON VANILLA
1½ TO 2 TABLESPOONS MILK

2½ TO 3 CUPS ROASTED, UNSALTED PEANUTS, CHOPPED FINE

jelly roll pan, greased and heavily floured.

Bake for 20 to 25 minutes, or until cake is firm but springy to the touch in middle. Cool in pan set on rack; cut into 1½-by-3-inch "fingers."

TO FROST In small bowl, mix sugar, butter, flavorings, and enough milk to make thin frosting. Completely coat "fingers" with frosting; immediately roll in peanuts in pie plate to cover. Place on rack set over baking sheet to dry.

When completely dry, store in air-tight container, placing waxed paper between layers of "fingers." Can be kept 4 to 5 days. These do not freeze well.

MAKES APPROXIMATELY 4 DOZEN

"Mocca Cake. 3 eggs, 2 cups sugar, 8 tablespoons cream, 2 cups flour, 2 teaspoons baking powder, ½ cup hot water. Powdered sugar & butter, roll in chopped peanuts." Penned by Great-Grandmother Broadwater in Grams's Black Book

Pineapple-Nut Drop Cookies

Great-Great-Grandmother Crowe —a dainty, petite, "scrubbed clean" lady with snow-white hair pulled back into a conservative bun—was quiet, reserved, and soft-spoken. Although she was English, her cooking was influenced by her live-in, dominating, German mother-in-law. Sweet and rich cooking was the rule of thumb.

"Pineapple Cookies: 2/3 cup fat, 1½ cups brown sugar, ¼ tsp grated lemon rind, ½ cup nuts, broken, 3½ cups flour, 2 eggs beaten, 1 tsp vanilla, ½ tsp lemon, 2/3 cup crushed pineapple, 1 tsp baking powder, 1 tsp soda. Cream fat and sugar. Add eggs, beat well. Blend in other ingredients, chill dough. Drop on greased sheets, flatten and bake 10 min in a moderate oven." Grams's Black Book

⅓ CUP BUTTER
⅓ CUP SOLID VEGETABLE SHORTENING
1½ CUPS BROWN SUGAR
1 TEASPOON VANILLA
½ TEASPOON LEMON EXTRACT
½ TEASPOON LEMON RIND
2 EGGS, BEATEN
3½ CUPS FLOUR
1 TEASPOON BAKING POWDER
1 TEASPOON SODA
⅔ CUP CRUSHED PINEAPPLE, CANNED, WELL DRAINED
½ CUP CHOPPED PECANS OR WALNUTS

BROWNED BUTTER FROSTING

3 TABLESPOONS BUTTER
3 CUPS POWDERED SUGAR
1½ TEASPOONS VANILLA
2 TO 3 TABLESPOONS MILK

4 DOZEN PECAN HALVES

Cream butter and shortening together with sugar until light and fluffy. Add vanilla, lemon extract, and rind; mix well. Beat in eggs. Blend in flour, baking powder, and soda; mix well. Stir in drained pineapple and nuts; mix well.

Cover with plastic wrap and refrigerate until firm, 1 to 2 hours or overnight.

TO BAKE Preheat oven to 350°. Drop chilled batter by teaspoonfuls onto greased baking sheets; with back of spoon, flatten slightly. Bake for 10 minutes, or until firm to the touch and lightly browned on edges. Cool on rack. Frost when completely cool.

TO FROST In small saucepan, over moderate heat, melt butter and continue to cook until it turns brown and has nutty smell. Do not let it burn. Remove from heat. Add sugar, vanilla, and milk; mix well, until frosting is spreading consistency and smooth.

Frost cookie, then place a perfect pecan half on top. Cool completely before storing.

Store in airtight cookie tin, placing waxed paper between layers of cookies. Can be kept 2 to 3 days in cool place, or if unfrosted, frozen 2 to 3 weeks.

MAKES 4 TO 5 DOZEN

This recipe is not to be confused with *Grams's Famous White Sugar Cookies* (page 102). These cookies were made only for Christmas. They were rolled thin, cut into Christmas shapes, and decorated with colored frosting. Mom had the standard requirements of a purist: blue bells, green trees and wreaths, yellow stars, white angels, red Santas, and the remaining shapes were frosted with the leftover colors.

Following in her footsteps, I taught a children's Christmas cookie baking class at my school. Students from ages four to fourteen came to make cookies. I set only one hard and fast rule: *Absolutely no mothers allowed in class!* Each person rolled and cut out his or her dough. Some free-form cookies were beautiful. After the baked cookies were cool, the fun began.

My large seven-by-eight-foot center island was covered with bowls of thin and sticky colored icing, oodles of paint brushes (all sizes and shapes of watercolor brushes from the dime store), mugs filled with colored and chocolate sprinkles, silver balls, confetti, miniature marshmallows, peanuts, chocolate chips, and coconut —plus any edible food that came to my mind to be used for decoration. The kids ate the decorations while they painted their cookies—and themselves—and decorated the tops. Some of their creations were very traditional while others were avant-garde. Each one was a work of art.

White Christmas Sugar Cookies

✦

½ CUP VEGETABLE
  SHORTENING
½ CUP BUTTER
1 CUP SUGAR
2 EGGS
3 TABLESPOONS MILK
1 ½ TEASPOONS VANILLA
3 CUPS FLOUR
1 TEASPOON BAKING POWDER

ICING FOR DECORATING
■ ■ ■
1 CUP SIFTED POWDERED
  SUGAR
PINCH SALT
½ TEASPOON VANILLA
1 TO 2 TABLESPOONS MILK

For months later, we found silver balls, confetti, and sprinkles in the corners of the room.

■■■■■■■■■■■■■■■■■■■■■■■■■■■■

Cream shortening and butter together with sugar until light and fluffy. Add eggs, milk, and vanilla; mix well.

Stir in flour and baking powder; mix well. Refrigerate, covered with plastic wrap, until dough is firm. This can be done a day ahead.

TO BAKE Preheat oven to 375°. Divide dough into quarters. Roll one portion at a time on floured board. Cut with Christmas cookie cutters. Place 1 inch apart on greased baking sheets. Bake 8 to 10 minutes, or until firm and light brown on edges. Cool on rack. Cool completely before decorating.

TO DECORATE In small bowl, mix sugar, salt, vanilla, and milk until easy to spread or brush.

For brushes, more water or milk may be necessary to thin icing. Divide icing into small bowls; color with food coloring. Decorate cookies as desired; dry completely before storing.

Store in airtight cookie tin, placing waxed paper between layers of cookies. Can be kept 1 to 2 weeks in cool place, or frozen 1 to 2 months.

MAKES APPROXIMATELY 5 DOZEN

Spritz
Cookies

**1 CUP LAND O LAKES
LIGHTLY SALTED BUTTER
⅔ CUP SUGAR
3 EGG YOLKS
3 TEASPOONS ALMOND
EXTRACT
2½ CUPS SIFTED FLOUR**

ICING FOR
DECORATING
∙∙∙

**3 CUPS POWDERED SUGAR
1 TEASPOON ALMOND
EXTRACT
3 TO 4 TABLESPOONS MILK
FOOD COLORING**

On Christmas Eve, after the church program and an oyster stew supper at Grams's, we kids put out a plate of spritz cookies on the kitchen table for Santa. The cookies were accompanied by a misspelled note that attested to our virtuous conduct throughout the past year. We also suggested that he help himself to a glass of milk or juice. (Later, after we suspected who Santa was, we put out a coffee cup too.)

The fact that we had no fireplace did not dissuade us from hanging our stockings. Even though the chimney went directly to the basement furnace, our common-sense logic predicted that Santa would come up from the furnace room to fill all our stockings that were hung by the register with care.

Before daylight on Christmas morning, we quietly crept down the stairs. To our delight, we found our stockings filled with a premium orange, tangerine, or shiny red apple, along with whole walnuts and store-bought Christmas chocolate (our own personal favorite kind)—plus a new toothbrush and a special surprise gift.

The plate in the kitchen was not always empty, but the evidence proved that "he" had been there. Sometimes, Santa left a note in return, explaining his haste or his problem with fitting the surprise gift into our stocking. Then, we had an unbearable wait until after the big family Christmas dinner to open it. (How cruel!)

To me, the best-tasting spritz cookie is made with Land O Lakes lightly salted butter. (This is the *only* time I use lightly salted butter, *ever!*) Keep the dough cool, but not cold or hard, until ready to press out onto baking sheets. Don't be discouraged: Mom once told me, "The reason I do it so quickly and exactly is because I have had thirty more years' experience than you have doing it!" From start to finish, Mom and I annually spent a day making spritz cookies before Christmas.

∙∙∙

The rich buttery almond flavor of a spritz cookie is a universal favorite of everyone. I suggest hiding them in the back of the vegetable drawer of the refrigerator because they are irresistible.

Cream butter until light and fluffy; beat in sugar. Add egg yolks, one by one, beating well after each one. Beat in flavoring.

Add flour and mix well. Cover and refrigerate dough for 1 to 2 hours. This can be done ahead and refrigerated overnight.

TO BAKE Preheat oven to 375°. Remove dough from refrigerator. Dough should be pliable: not hard, yet cool. You may need to let it sit at room temperature for a few minutes. Divide it into four parts. (If desired, color each part with food coloring. Use an equal amount of coloring in each portion.) Place dough in cookie press and carefully

"1 cup butter, 2/3 cup sugar, 3 egg yolks, 1 tsp almond extract, 2 1/2 cups flour. Press onto cookie sheets and bake." Grams's Black Book

press out cookies onto *ungreased* baking sheet. (Take your time, it is a tricky business.) Bake for approximately 8 to 10 minutes, or until just set, not shiny or brown. Remove from baking sheet and cool on rack.

TO DECORATE Mix sugar, flavoring, and enough milk to make smooth, medium-soft-consistency icing (one that can be used in a decorating tube). Divide icing, according to number of colors desired, into bowls. Add 1 drop of food coloring to each portion of icing; mix well. Add more coloring if desired.

Mom used a metal decorating tube, but I prefer a parchment paper cone for each color. Decorate as desired, or as described in the *Christmas Cookies* introduction (page 115). Dry completely before storing.

Store in airtight cookie tin, placing waxed paper between layers of cookies. Can be kept 2 to 3 weeks in cool place, or frozen 1 to 2 months.

MAKES APPROXIMATELY 5 DOZEN

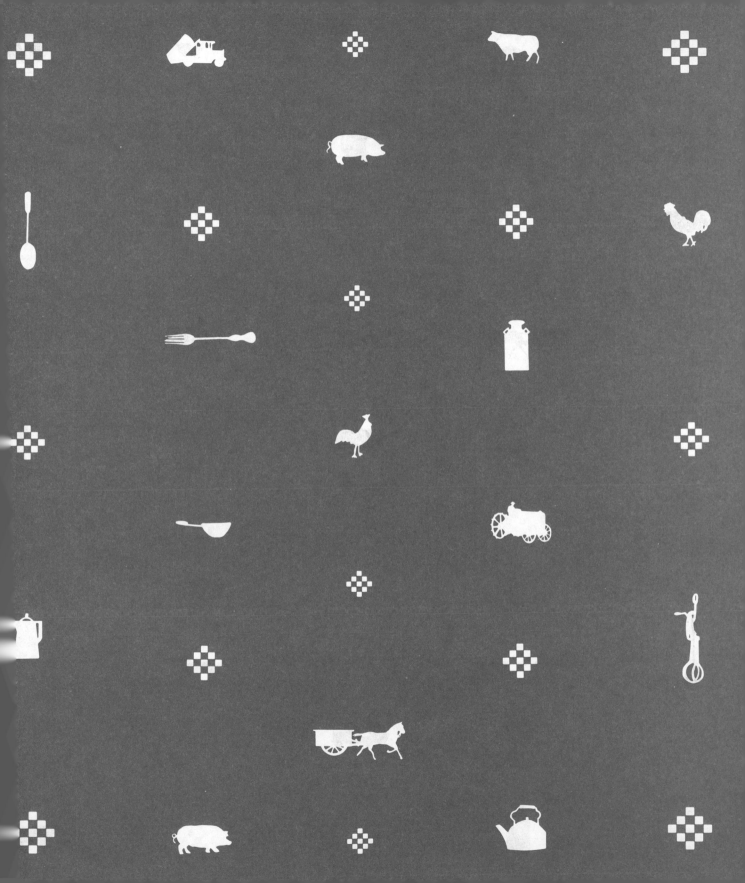

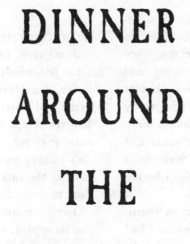

DINNER AROUND THE KITCHEN TABLE

Farm family members gathering for dinner have an intimate connection with the food because they raised most of it. Plowing, seeding, cultivating, and harvesting—each involves its own noises—but at dinner the sounds are purely human. We began by saying grace, because obviously man alone cannot provide such abundance. After that there was talk of today's work and the weather, plans for tomorrow's labor, and the satisfying chewing sounds of home-raised meats and just-picked vegetables.

Granddad came in for dinner at 12 noon sharp. Because Dad was not punctual, either Mom or I had to signal him—"Dinner is on!"—by putting the windmill in gear. Later, a 120-year-old former church and school bell "that still rings as good as new" was the signal for Dad to come in from the field for dinner.

Dinner, for the most part, was simple: well-prepared meat and vegetables that were only a few minutes from the garden or larder. A typical everyday dinner menu started with a brimming platter of some sort of meat, potatoes—usually mashed—two or three cooked vegetables, and a raw vegetable salad. Piping hot bowls and plates were carefully passed from one person at the table to the other, each one helping himself, family style. Pickles, fresh bread and butter, homemade jam, and salt and pepper were already on the table. Freshly baked pie, coffee, well water, and lots of milk for the children completed the meal.

After everyone had a second, and sometimes a third, helping, Mom cut a large piece of the pie for each of us. We placed the pie plate directly on top of our licked-clean dinner plate. (Mom offered second helpings of dessert too . . . but only a very hungry young hired hand was able to eat two pieces of pie!) After the third or fourth cup of coffee, the satiated men straggled out to rest in the shade of the old oak tree. Dad retired to the dining room floor for a ten-minute catnap. While Mom finished her coffee, I gathered up the dishes and put away the bread and butter, and so on. She would scrape the leftover scraps from our plates onto another plate, hand it to me, and say, "Take that out to the dog; he's hungry too!" Our grateful happy pooch would bark at the cats while he gobbled up the food. The cats, of course, got their own portion.

For generations—and even now—our family did not serve veal, lamb, or suckling pigs. Baby animals were needed for future livestock, when they would be valuable cash commodities. On the other hand, because poultry was less expensive to raise, spring chickens, duckling, and geese were acceptable farm table food.

Grams served pork or beef twice a day and poultry twice a week. Her basic preparation for a roast was simple: Season with salt and pepper, flour and sear in bacon drippings or lard, place in a roasting pan, cover and bake until tender (which meant very well done). She took a similar no-nonsense approach to chops and steaks. They were breaded and fried on top of the stove. With the advent of the electric stove in 1945 (at our house), both Grams and Mom broiled steaks and chops.

Potatoes—indeed, our staff of life—were served at dinner and later with supper along with other fresh vegetables, cooked and raw.

The following family recipes were everyday dinner fare. I indicate our customary accompaniments with each recipe. Sunday and holiday dinners were more elaborate ("gourmet," I suppose), and you'll hear more about them later.

Farm Roast Beef

❖

Months before we needed the meat (unless a "suitable" animal broke its leg), Dad fed rich corn and grain meal to a particular steer that would be butchered in early winter and later be eaten at the family table. When he was in college, he had worked in an Idaho slaughterhouse every summer, earning money for tuition, so Dad was an expert butcher. He butchered all our meats and even the cattle and pigs of our neighborhood friends. Buckled around his waist on a leather strap was a nifty metal knife box that jingled as he walked. The encased knives were razor sharp. We kids were forbidden to go near them. Whenever Dad visits Joany or me, he packs his whetstone in his suitcase to sharpen our household cutlery.

In the tank house and then later in the basement, Granddad and Hershel Ogg cut the killed animal into manageable roasts, steaks, and chops, ground some of it, then carted it into Austin's Locker. Dad, on the other hand, hung the slaughtered animal, hind feet first, in a special wooden and metal yoke that was rigged up to a large limb of an elm tree growing next to the granary. With great fascination and curiosity I watched Dad's deft strong hands split the hide down the belly and skillfully peel it from the meat. If the hide was "a beauty," it was dried—and sometimes tanned—to be used for a lap robe, throw, or jacket. Left as is, it became a rug.

Dad's College Graduation, 1933

Watching Dad butcher gave me firsthand knowledge of anatomy and biology. Dad tirelessly answered my eager questions with direct, no-nonsense, explicit, and informative answers. He did not laugh at my curiosity as he explained the functions of the heart and liver and identified all the inner parts of an animal.

Using the skill of a surgeon, first he removed every edible part of the animal, washed them in a spotless bucket of fresh cool well water, and set the pieces aside to be processed. Then with a large handsaw he cut the carcass into quarters. He laid the fresh meat in the back of the pickup on top of clean muslin sheets. In the winter Dad hung part of a hind quarter in the tank room for immediate consumption. The remainder of the meat was hauled into Austin's Locker.

Lyle Austin custom-cut, packaged, labeled, and froze the meat. An average beef steer "dressed out" to 600 to 700 pounds of meat. Individual metal boxes stuffed with meat lined the walls and hallways of a huge walk-in freezer. Each farm family had a locker. On the way home from Grams's, Mom stopped by Austin's for the week's supply of meat. She picked up our numbered key, which hung on a small hook inside a thick accordion-style metal cabinet. When she disappeared inside the ominous freezer, it was spooky and surreal to me. I sat at the soda fountain counter, drinking a five-cent cherry Coke, praying that she would return.

Grams and Mom prepared all the meat well done. A rare roast beef was unheard of! Because our steer was fattened to our family's lean palate, it was often prepared with tenderizing moist heat. (Grams used water, Mom used vegetable broth, and I use wine.)

....

Preheat oven to 325°.

Trim any excess fat from meat; wipe dry. Mix flour, pepper, and paprika together; dredge meat with mixture.

Heat oil in roasting pan larger than meat (fitted with a lid, to be used later) until hot; sear meat on all sides until brown. (If a less tender cut is used, pour the optional liquid around the meat; bring to a boil before roasting.) Cover and bake approximately 2 hours; remove lid and continue to roast until meat is tender. Estimated total cooking time: 2½ to 3 hours, or 25 to 30 minutes per pound or according to personal preference (see page 140).

Remove meat to warm platter; keep warm. Let rest 15 to 20 minutes before carving.

1 SIX-POUND BONELESS EYE ROUND ROAST BEEF (OR ROLLED RUMP)
APPROXIMATELY ½ CUP FLOUR
1 TABLESPOON BLACK PEPPER, COARSELY GROUND
1 TEASPOON PAPRIKA
1 TABLESPOON VEGETABLE OIL
½ TO ¾ CUP BEEF BROTH, RED WINE, OR WATER (OPTIONAL)

GRAVY (4 CUPS)
■ ■ ■

8 TABLESPOONS BUTTER OR PAN DRIPPINGS/OIL
8 TABLESPOONS FLOUR
4 CUPS LIQUID (PAN BROTH— NOW DEFATTED—PLUS BEEF BROTH OR HOT WATER TO EQUAL 1 QUART IN TOTAL)
SALT, FRESHLY GROUND BLACK PEPPER, DASH CELERY SALT

TO MAKE GRAVY Pour broth from pan into bowl; allow fat to rise. (Aunt Rubye adds a few ice cubes to the hot broth to attract the fat. I use a gravy strainer.) Skim off fat, measure, and add enough butter or oil to equal 8 tablespoons. Heat until melted.

Stir flour into fat/oil. Cook over low heat, stirring constantly until mixture is smooth. (Bubbles will cover entire bottom of pan.) The mixture should be the color of a brown paper bag; remove from heat.

Whisk in hot liquid; return to heat. Bring to a boil, then boil 2 minutes, stirring constantly.

Taste and season according to personal preference. If lumpy, strain through strainer into sauceboat.

TO SERVE Slice meat; garnish platter with bouquets of fresh parsley. Serve with *Grams's Horseradish Sauce* (page 135), mashed potatoes, and steamed vegetables.

VARIATION
Au Jus Sauce Remove broth and fat from pan. Allow fat to rise and skim off; return broth to pan. Add ¼ cup Madeira to broth. Bring to a boil; reduce the amount by a third. Taste and correct seasonings; pour into sauceboat.

SERVES 8 TO 10 GENEROUSLY

Grams's
Horseradish
Sauce

❖

Grams gave Mom the sad task of grinding—by hand—the horseradish for this recipe. The strong vapors from the horseradish rising from the grinder made Mom cry and cry every time. "But it was worth it!" she says.

> "1 cup horseradish ground or grated, 2 Tbsp granulated sugar, 1/2 cup heavy cream, 1 cup cider vinegar, mix well." Grams's Black Book

1 TO 2 FRESH HORSERADISH ROOTS (TO YIELD 1 CUP FRESHLY GRATED HORSERADISH)
2 TABLESPOONS SUGAR
1/2 CUP SOUR CREAM
1/2 CUP CIDER VINEGAR
2 TABLESPOONS HEAVY CREAM
1/4 TEASPOON WHITE PEPPER (OPTIONAL)

This sauce is excellent with ham and roast pork, too.

▪▪▪▪▪▪▪▪▪▪▪▪▪▪▪▪▪▪▪▪▪▪▪▪▪▪▪▪▪▪▪

Peel and wash roots. Cut into 2-inch lengths; shred in food processor. Replace shredding blade with chopping blade; process until chopped fine. Measure it.

Mix horseradish well with sugar, sour cream, vinegar, and heavy cream. Taste, correct sugar, and season with pepper to taste if desired. Can be done 2 to 3 days ahead.

Cover and refrigerate. This sauce may be kept 3 to 4 weeks, refrigerated.

MAKES APPROXIMATELY 2 CUPS

Mom's New England Pot Roast

Upon returning for Christmas vacation my first year of college, Mom asked, "What are you hungry for?" I replied, "New England pot roast." Thereafter, Mom served me this delicious robust form of comfort food for my first dinner at home. My children now make the same request at my house.

■■■■■■■■■■■■■■■■■■■■■■■■■■■■■

"Wipe roast. Dredge with flour, sprinkle with salt and pepper and place in baking dish. Sear meat at high temperature for 10 minutes. Reduce heat to moderate and bake until tender. The last hour of roasting place carrots, onion and potatoes over and around roast. Other vegetables may be used if desired." Inglenook Cook Book, 1942

1 SIX-POUND BLADE POT ROAST (OR ROUND, BEEF BOTTOM, OR ARM POT ROAST)
1 TABLESPOON BLACK PEPPER, FRESHLY GROUND
½ TEASPOON CELERY SALT
1 CLOVE GARLIC, MINCED
1 CUP WATER
½ CUP BEEF BROTH

VEGETABLES

■ ■ ■

8 MEDIUM POTATOES, PEELED AND CUT INTO HALVES OR QUARTERS
12 MEDIUM CARROTS, PEELED AND CUT LENGTHWISE INTO QUARTERS
12 SMALL YELLOW ONIONS, PEELED AND SCORED ON ROOT END WITH LARGE X TO PREVENT THE LAYERS FROM SLIPPING OFF
6 STALKS CELERY, WASHED AND CUT INTO 2½-INCH LENGTHS (OPTIONAL)
6 MEDIUM WHITE TURNIPS, WASHED AND CUT IN HALF (OPTIONAL)

GRAVY

■ ■ ■

PAN JUICES
¼ CUP FLOUR
½ CUP COLD WATER

Preheat oven to 325°.

In heavy casserole or Dutch oven, sear meat fat side down first over high heat; season with pepper, celery salt, and garlic. Add water and broth; cover and bring to a boil. Transfer to oven and bake 2 to 2½ hours.

After that period of time, add vegetables to pot with meat; cover and continue to bake until tender, approximately 1 hour. When vegetables are done, remove meat to center of large warm platter, surrounded by vegetables. Tent with foil and keep warm in turned-off oven.

TO MAKE GRAVY Skim excess fat from broth and discard. Measure pan juices, adding more broth or water if necessary to make total of 2½ cups; transfer to saucepan, and bring pan juices to a boil. Mix flour and water together; gradually pour flour mixture into boiling liquid. Boil, stirring constantly, for 2 minutes. Taste and correct seasonings.

TO SERVE Carve meat; pour gravy into sauceboat. Serve with *Grams's Horseradish Sauce* (page 135) and tossed green salad.

SERVES 8 GENEROUSLY

THE THRESHING RING

As was the custom, in those days before powerful tractors and fast modes of transportation were available, a group of ten to twenty farmers within a reasonable distance of each other formed a "ring" or cooperative. This "association" traveled from farm to farm harvesting the grain crop at each place, according to the maturation and ripeness of the oats, and some unwritten prescribed order. Before the "ring" was due to arrive, each farmer cut the oats with a binder that tied the grain into sheaves (or bundles) with twine and then "shocked" them. (Shocks look like teepees and serve to naturally dry the oats in the field.)

As with all farmers and folks who live off the land, harvesting the crops and seeing the "fruits of one's own labor" was downright significant! Thus every man, woman, and child contributed, sympathized, and rejoiced with the work at hand.

Grams, Mom, and Rubye—and later myself— commenced the preparations well in advance. After the groceries—50 pounds of flour, 100 pounds of sugar, quarts of vanilla, 5 to 10 pounds of dried beans, 25 pounds of salt, red "Jell-O," and 25 pounds of coffee—were stocked, the cookie baking began. Next, menus were planned, and the basement scrubbed and set up. Because it was the coolest

Threshing on the Home Place

"It was a red-letter day," Mom explained, "when that big old black steel-wheeled threshing machine rolled into the yard!" Along with it came the "engineer" who fed the coal into the fire box that ran the steam engine, plus a "tank-man" who kept the thousand-gallon tank filled with water (using a hand pump, no less!). This was a *big deal*.

place in the house, the men ate there, at long tables covered with red-and-white-checked oilcloth. We ordered luncheon meats, weiners, and cheese from the butcher, and all other things were in a general state of readiness.

When Dad knew the day "they" were coming to our house, he informed Mom, and that in turn set off a flurry of immediate preparations. We were capable of feeding forty or so men, four and sometimes five meals a day, for at least three days in succession! We were "combat-ready"!

Every able-bodied man, hired hand, and young boy available, along with their horses and wagons (in Grams's era) or tractors and wagons (these days), were en route to our farm.

Mom's day began about 4:30 A.M. with pie baking; Grams arrived from town about 6:30 to serve breakfast to the early birds and lend a hand with lunch preparations. The actual food service began at 9 A.M. when I took lunch out to the field.

The next meal, dinner, was served at noon on the dot; lunch went out to the field again at 3. They ate supper in shifts from 5 to 7:30. Mom's evening was spent in preparation for the next day. The number of men in the threshing ring increased according to the amount of grain to be harvested, but more to the point, according to the ability of the cook—so we had a mess of men to feed!

Sample Threshing Menus

DINNER

- Roast beef, gravy, boiled potatoes, creamed corn (men liked creamed vegetables), cabbage salad, sliced tomatoes, pickles, jams, bread and butter, apple pie, coffee, water, and iced tea.

- Baked ham, mashed potatoes with gravy, hot apple sauce, creamed peas, coleslaw, sliced tomatoes, pickles, jams, bread and butter, cherry pie, coffee, water, and iced tea.

- Oven-fried chicken, riced potatoes with gravy, creamed beans, cucumber and onion salad, sliced tomatoes, pickles, jams, bread and butter, raspberry pie, coffee, water, and iced tea.

- Boiled beef and noodles, mashed potatoes, creamed peas (yes, again), coleslaw, sliced tomatoes, pickles, jams, bread and butter, peach pie, coffee, water, and iced tea.

SUPPER

- Cold sliced ham, hot baked beans, coleslaw, sliced tomatoes, pickles, jams, bread and butter, orange-and-banana Jell-O (men liked Jell-O), spice cake, coffee, water, and iced tea.

- Cold sliced roast beef, cheddar and longhorn cheese, scalloped potatoes, sliced tomatoes, relishes, pickles, jams, bread and butter, cherry and banana Jell-O (men liked especially red Jell-O), chocolate cake, coffee, water, and iced tea.

- Weiners and sauerkraut, hash-browned potatoes, cottage cheese, slices of cheddar or American cheese, sliced tomatoes, pickles, jams, bread and butter, stewed fruit, walnut cake, coffee, water, and iced tea.

- Meat loaf, potato salad, browned potatoes, sliced tomatoes, pickles, jams, bread and butter, fresh peaches, yellow cake, coffee, water, and iced tea.

Thresher's Meat and Potatoes

Farmhands thought dinner was not complete without meat and potatoes on the table. Whether or not it was well prepared was not important to them, although it was to us. For this group, Mom and Grams cooked on two stoves, an electric stove in the kitchen and an oil stove in the furnace room, which helped to keep the house as cool as possible.

This recipe will stand you in good stead with a crowd of hungry folks.

■■■■■■■■■■■■■■■■■■■■■■■■■■■■■■■■

Preheat oven to 350°.

Sear meat in large roasting pan over high heat; brown on all sides. Season with salt and pepper to taste. Strew onions around meat; add approximately ½ to 1 cup water. Cover and roast approximately 4½ to 5 hours, or until cooked to desired doneness. (A meat thermometer should register 170°.)

Meanwhile, halve or quarter potatoes, place in large kettle and cover

15 TO 20 POUNDS BLADE OF CHUCK ROAST BEEF
SALT
BLACK PEPPER
2 TO 3 MEDIUM ONIONS, SLICED

25 POUNDS POTATOES, PEELED
2 TO 3 TABLESPOONS SALT

GRAVY

■ ■ ■

APPROXIMATELY 4 QUARTS POTATO WATER
1 CUP FLOUR
2 CUPS WARM POTATO WATER
SALT
BLACK PEPPER

with cold water. Add salt, cover, and bring to a boil. Boil until potatoes are done when pierced with fork.

Drain potatoes and save water for gravy; place potatoes back in hot kettle to "dry." Turn off heat; keep lid ajar until serving time.

TO MAKE GRAVY When meat is done, remove from roasting pan to platter. Add potato water to pan juices; on top of stove, bring liquid to a boil.

Stir flour into 2 cups warm potato water; mix thoroughly. Gradually stir flour mixture into boiling pan juices. Continue boiling, stirring constantly until smooth and thick enough to coat spoon. Season with salt and pepper; taste and correct seasoning. If color is "sad looking," add a drop or two of Kitchen Bouquet to darken. Pour gravy into bowls. Serve with carved meat and brimming bowls of hot potatoes.

S E R V E S   4 0

Dad butchered and cut up a prime beef cow approximately eight weeks before Christmas in order to have a perfectly aged rib roast available for the holiday dinner. Even on the farm back then, a prime rib roast was considered special. It is probably one of the easiest—but most expensive—festive meats to prepare.

Order a five- or six-rib roast from the loin end, a week or two ahead of time. Figure one pound per person plus another pound for leftovers. If the butcher is reliable, ask him to trim and tie it for you. Be sure to have him save the "cap" layers of fat and meat, with most of the fat trimmed out, and grind it into hamburger meat. Tell him you want the ends of the shortened rib bones and chine bone for stew. (You pay for it anyway.) Better yet, make friends with a beef farmer nearby and purchase a side of beef the next time he is butchering one.

Plan to put the roast in the oven about 4 to 4¼ hours before serving time to be on the safe side. After removing the roast from the oven, allow it to "rest" for 20 minutes before carving. During that time, make the natural sauce and put final touches on the rest of the dinner.

■■■■■■■■■■■■■■■■■■■■■■■■■■■■

Preheat oven to 400°.

Trim fat and tie roast securely with kitchen string for easier handling. Place roast, fat side up, on

Christmas Prime Rib Roast Beef

◆

1 FIVE-RIB ROAST BEEF, APPROXIMATELY 12 POUNDS
BLACK PEPPER, FRESHLY GROUND (OPTIONAL)
1 CLOVE GARLIC, CRUSHED (OPTIONAL)

3 MEDIUM ONIONS, CUT INTO EIGHTHS

½ CUP PORT OR MADEIRA

rack set in shallow roasting pan. If desired, season by rubbing meat with pepper and crushed garlic.

Place in preheated oven and reduce heat to 325°; roast to desired doneness.

RARE 12 to 13 minutes per pound (or 120°)
MEDIUM RARE 14 to 16 minutes per pound (or 125° to 130°)
MEDIUM 17 to 20 minutes per pound (or 140°)
WELL DONE 21 to 25 minutes per pound (or 160°)

After first hour, check roast and rotate pan; baste with pan juices. Strew onions on bottom of pan. Continue to bake, basting every so often until meat is done (use meat thermometer as a guide). Remove roast from oven; discard strings. Place on platter and let rest 20 minutes.

TO PREPARE NATURAL SAUCE
Remove onions with slotted spoon, place in serving bowl, and keep warm. Pour pan juices into gravy strainer; allow fat to rise to top. Meanwhile, deglaze roasting pan with ½ cup port or Madeira; reduce by half. Return defatted pan juices to pan; bring to a boil. Taste and correct seasonings. Pour into small pitcher and serve.

Or serve with *Grams's Horseradish Sauce* (page 135).

SERVES 12 TO 14

A Shaggy-Dog Lover's Swiss Steak

◆

At an early age I became a dog lover. One of my most treasured childhood pastimes was playing with our favorite dog, Sparky. (She was actually one of many.) She was smart, carefully herding the cows in from the pasture (on Dad's command), as well as catching and fighting the coons and other predators without chasing the chickens. She *also* had a litter of puppies twice a year! This last attribute was the most important to me.

After Sparky whelped her litter of puppies, she hid them under the granary. I, self-appointed guardian, helped her take care of the puppies. For hours and hours, I dressed the puppies in doll clothes, hugged them, unsuccessfully tried to feed them milk, and—as Mom put it—"wallowed around in the dirt with the dogs." I was often asked, "Have you been out there with those puppies again?" I simply replied, "No!" —but the condition of my clothes and face told the truth. Mom insisted that I take a bath, wash my hair, and change my clothes before eating dinner (practically before entering the house!). I followed her orders especially when Swiss steak was on the menu for dinner that day.

The addition of tomato both tenderizes and imparts a savory flavor to the round steak, transforming it from an ordinary to an extraordinary dinner dish. Mom made it often.

■■■■■■■■■■■■■■■■■■■■■■■■■■■■■■

1 FOUR-POUND ROUND STEAK, CUT 1½ TO 2 INCHES THICK
1 TEASPOON DRIED BASIL
1½ TEASPOONS BLACK PEPPER, FRESHLY GROUND
1 TABLESPOON VEGETABLE OIL
1 TABLESPOON BUTTER
1 MEDIUM ONION, CHOPPED
3 CLOVES GARLIC, MINCED
1 TWENTY-EIGHT-OUNCE CAN TOMATOES, OR 5 MEDIUM RIPE TOMATOES, PEELED, SEEDED, AND CHOPPED

½ TEASPOON DRIED BASIL
¼ TEASPOON SALT
PINCH SUGAR

Preheat oven to 325°.

Trim excess fat off steak and score edges; season with basil and pepper. Heat oil and butter until it sizzles in large heavy casserole (with a lid to be used later). Sear steak on both sides until brown; reduce heat.

Add onion, garlic, and tomatoes. Add extra tomato juice or beef broth to bring liquid up to top edge of meat if necessary. Season with more basil, salt, and sugar. Cover and bring to a boil.

Remove to oven and bake for 1 to 1½ hours, or until tender. Or finish cooking on stove top: Simmer on low heat for approximately the same amount of time.

TO SERVE Remove meat to large platter with lip. Cut meat into serving-size pieces; top with tomato sauce from pan. Serve with boiled potatoes, green vegetables, and tossed salad.

SERVES 6 TO 8

E. J. Maloney, a hired hand who was shared by several neighbors, was a quick-witted, warmhearted character with a particular love for spirits (of the bottled type). When he worked for Dad, he was on the wagon. My favorite wise Irish phrase of his—"Well, he didn't just lap that up off the floor!"—has become our family's down-to-earth explanation for inherited behavior and traits. E.J. loved to eat Mom's cooking. He said she was the only one who served him T-bone steak.

T-bone steak is Dad's favorite. Mom fried it to perfection: well done on the outside but still juicy inside. Then she made gravy from the pan drippings for the meat.

Trim steaks; season with pepper.

A "Lapped-Up" T-Bone Steak

6 T-BONE STEAKS, ¾ TO 1 INCH THICK
BLACK PEPPER, FRESHLY GROUND, TO TASTE
1 TABLESPOON LARD OR OIL
1 TABLESPOON BUTTER

PAN GRAVY
3 TABLESPOONS FLOUR
1 CUP BEEF BROTH
1 CUP WATER, BOILING (OR 1 CUP WATER AND 1 CUP MILK)
SALT TO TASTE

Heat lard and butter until very hot and smoking. Add steaks to pan, turning over about 3 to 4 times until crusty brown on outside and juicy on inside (according to personal taste). Remove to warm platter.

TO MAKE GRAVY Add flour to pan drippings; stir until color of brown paper bag. Whisk in liquids and continue to stir constantly for 3 minutes. Taste and correct seasoning.

TO SERVE STEAK AND GRAVY Garnish platter with herb bouquet. Serve with *French Fries* (page 231), buttered lima beans, and *Mom's Carrot Salad* (page 298).

S E R V E S 6

1990s Option

Preheat broiler.
Trim steaks; season with pepper. Slather ½ tablespoon mustard on top of each steak. Broil until brown, according to personal taste.

6 T-BONE STEAKS
1 TABLESPOON BLACK PEPPER, FRESHLY GROUND
6 TABLESPOONS GRAINY MUSTARD

Turn, slather mustard on other side, and broil until brown (approximately 2 minutes on each side). Serve immediately.

S E R V E S 6

"Beefsteak: Take either round or T-bone steak, having it at least an inch thick. Remove the bone, and cut off the skin on the edge. Remove everything that cannot be eaten. Then if thought necessary give it a good beating with the rear edge of a flat-iron. Turn and beat and cut again at right angles till the entire steak is broken in fibre. Cut into as many pieces as there are portions to be served. Take half and half of water and rich milk in a bowl. Salt this to taste, and if you like it a dash of catsup or Worcestershire sauce, or paprika, to taste. Have this prepared and at hand. Some put a spoonful of flour in the bowl and beat it in. Now put the pan on the stove, in it put some of the fat of the steak, or butter will do, and let this pan get hot, not warm, but seething hot. Put the plate on which the steak is to be served in the oven of the stove to warm. The rest of the meal must be ready and all other things prepared. Now with a plate of butter near by drop the pieces of steak in the smoking hot pan. Turn them immediately, and keep on turning them throughout the whole process. After turning 3 or 4 times put thin slices of butter on the cooking steak as you turn it over. The meat must be so cooked that it is a crinkly crusted brown on the outside, and juicy within. Then, when done, whip up the material in the bowl with a fork, and pour all in the sizzling hot pan. The moment it boils, pour into a clean bowl or gravy float and serve all immediately. Garnish with Saratoga Chips. Each guest to salt the portion served." Inglenook Cook Book, 1901

[Wow! What terrific directions.]

A Tromping-Good Meat Loaf

❖

Grams and Granddad often chose a crisp sunny fall day to tromp in the woods. Their favorite wooded spot with a trout stream for Granddad was Isinours, the 1870 site of Carrollton township railway junction. The spot was named after George Isinour on whose land it stood. From here the train passengers were transported by stage coach to The Tibbetts' House, the depot in Preston. After 1900 the train traveled directly to Preston.

I sometimes went with them. With her customary metal pail in hand and wearing the old walking shoes that she stowed under the front seat of the car ("just in case!"), Grams and I walked down the railroad tracks to pick perfectly shaped milk pods, interesting weeds, and colorful leaves. Later Grams would spray the weeds with silver, gold, or white paint, and arrange them into beautiful winter floral bouquets.

The cedar and decomposing leaves together with grassy moss in the damp areas filled the air with an unmatchable fragrance. Together, we pondered the wonders of life in general, marveled at the vibrant hues of certain leaves, and simply enjoyed ourselves. We wrestled with prickly sprays of bright orange bittersweet that Mom would later make into fall arrangements.

Meanwhile Granddad would be fishing in the nearby trout stream, but his labor of love sometimes proved fruitless. Knowing his excuse would be "Fishing is for men!" (as though the females in attendance had jinxed his chances!), Grams usually had a meat loaf at home—mixed, shaped, and ready to be baked. We would put up a pot of tea and inspect our bounty of weeds and leaves while it baked.

Mom's hint: Wear rubber gloves a size larger than normal to mix the meat loaf contents. When the phone rings, leave a glove in the mess of

⅔ CUP PLAIN DRY BREAD CRUMBS (OR 2 THICK SLICES WHITE BREAD, STALE AND CUBED SMALL)
1 CUP MILK
1½ POUNDS GROUND BEEF
½ POUND GROUND PORK
2 EGGS, BEATEN
1 SMALL ONION, GRATED (⅓ CUP)
½ TEASPOON SALT
1 TEASPOON BLACK PEPPER, FRESHLY GROUND
½ HEAPING TEASPOON DRIED SAGE

TOPPING

∎ ∎ ∎

3 TABLESPOONS BROWN SUGAR
¼ CUP KETCHUP
1 TEASPOON DRY MUSTARD
⅛ TEASPOON NUTMEG

"⅔ cup diced bread crumbs, 1 cup milk, 1½ cups ground beef, ½ cup sausage, 2 beaten eggs, ¼ cup grated onions, 1 tsp salt, ⅛ tsp pepper, ½ tsp sage. Soak crumbs in milk and add rest of ingredients. Topping: 3 Tbsp B. sugar, ¼ c. catsup, 1 tsp dry mustard, dash nutmeg. Bake 1 hour in 350°." *Grams's Black Book*

the ingredients and slip out your clean hand to answer the call.

▪▪▪▪▪▪▪▪▪▪▪▪▪▪▪▪▪▪▪▪▪▪▪▪▪▪▪▪▪▪▪▪▪

Preheat oven to 350°.

Soak bread crumbs in milk until mushy. Add beef, pork, eggs, onion, and seasonings; mix well with gloved hands. Form into oblong loaf shape and place in 9-by-13-inch baking pan.

TO MAKE TOPPING Mix sugar, ketchup, mustard, and nutmeg together; pour over raw meat.

Bake loaf for 1½ to 2 hours, or until brown and knife inserted into center is too hot to hold on your lower lip (to an internal temperature of about 180°). Remove from oven and let rest 10 minutes.

TO SERVE Serve with baked potatoes and creamed green beans. Slice leftover meat loaf for a sandwich on *Mom's Swedish Rye Bread* (page 61).

S E R V E S   6

Old-Fashioned Meat Balls

❖

1 CUP CRACKER CRUMBS, SALTINE-STYLE (APPROXIMATELY 18 TO 20 SMALL SQUARES)
1 CUP MILK
2 POUNDS GROUND CHUCK
2 EGGS, BEATEN
1 MEDIUM ONION, GRATED
1 SMALL CLOVE GARLIC, MINCED AND SAUTÉED IN BUTTER
1 TEASPOON BLACK PEPPER, FRESHLY GROUND
1 TEASPOON WORCESTERSHIRE SAUCE

¼ CUP VEGETABLE OIL

GRAVY/SAUCE
▪ ▪ ▪

¼ CUP FLOUR
1 CUP HOT BEEF BROTH
1 CUP HOT WATER
SALT AND BLACK PEPPER, FRESHLY GROUND, TO TASTE

The Schrocks, as well as Grams and Granddad, bought large barrels of saltine-style crackers. (With a family of thirteen, it took a barrel of crackers to fill them up!) When the "youngins" were hungry, they grabbed a handful of crackers from the barrel on the back porch and went about their work. Before food processors, children—myself included—were drafted by their mothers to roll the crackers between two sheets of waxed paper with the rolling pin. I, by the way, was not an accomplished cracker roller.

We did not think meatballs and spaghetti were the perfect match. Grams and Mom made meatballs frequently, but they always served a gravy-and-potatoes, not a tomato, sauce. Dad liked gravy made with milk; however, Mom preferred a lighter version using beef broth.

▪▪▪▪▪▪▪▪▪▪▪▪▪▪▪▪▪▪▪▪▪▪▪▪▪▪▪▪▪▪▪▪▪

Preheat oven to 300°.

Roll crackers in plastic bag with rolling pin, or process 3 to 4 pulses in food processor. Soak crackers in milk until soft and mushy. Mix soggy crackers into meat. Add eggs, onion, garlic, pepper, and Worcestershire sauce; mix well with gloved hands.

Test seasonings by frying small ball in skillet; taste and correct seasoning. With wet gloved hands, shape mixture into 1½-to-2-inch balls.

TO FRY In skillet, over medium high heat, fry balls in oil ; turn every so often until brown (this takes about 20 minutes). Remove meatballs to a large jelly roll pan lined with foil; keep warm in oven. Continue until all are fried.

TO MAKE GRAVY Add flour to pan drippings; stir up bits of meat. Cook until flour is color of brown paper bag, stirring constantly. Whisk in hot liquid of broth and water all at once. Bring to a boil, stirring constantly; boil 1 to 2 minutes.

Remove from heat; taste and correct seasonings. Pour sauce over meatballs in pan. Can be kept in warm oven 20 to 30 minutes until serving time.

TO SERVE Place meatballs and gravy in large bowl. Complete meal with mashed potatoes, broccoli, and *Mom's Carrot Salad* (page 298).

VARIATIONS
Baked Meatballs Place meatballs on prepared baking pan. Bake in 400° oven, uncovered, for approximately 25 to 30 minutes, or until crispy brown. Prepare gravy from pan drippings or serve without sauce. Serve with fried potatoes and green vegetable.
Broiled Meatballs Place meatballs on broiler pan. Broil for approximately 4 minutes, turn, and

"Mix 2 lbs ground beef with 1 cup rolled cracker crumbs, 1 cup milk, 2 beaten eggs and 1 shredded onion. Season with salt, pepper and worcestershire sauce. Make into balls, fry in hot lard. Make your gravy with whatever is on hand." Mom

continue to broil until crispy brown. Serve with favorite pasta or potatoes.
Swedish-Style Meatballs Add a pinch of both ground cloves and allspice to raw meat; continue per recipe. Substitute milk for broth and water in sauce; cook as directed. Serve with noodles or riced potatoes.
Tomato Sauce for Meatballs Prepare meatballs per recipe above. To pan drippings add enough oil to equal 2 tablespoons (if necessary). Sauté 1 large onion (chopped) and 2 cloves garlic (minced) until pieces are soft and translucent. Add ½ cup chopped parsley, 1 teaspoon dried basil, ½ teaspoon dried oregano, 1 bay leaf, and 2 twenty-eight-ounce cans whole tomatoes in thick puree (I prefer Red Pack). Mix well; add 2 tablespoons tomato paste, ¼ teaspoon sugar, ½ teaspoon black pepper, and salt to taste. Mix well; bring to a boil. Reduce heat and simmer 30 to 40 minutes. Add water if necessary, stirring every so often. Taste and correct seasonings.

(If home-canned tomatoes are used, add approximately ⅓ cup ketchup, and increase the tomato paste to 4 tablespoons.)

Remove bay leaf, add meatballs, and heat through. Serve with spaghetti (Italian style) or riced potatoes (Minnesota style). Sauce can be done ahead. Covered and refrigerated, it keeps for 2 to 3 days; frozen, it keeps for 1 to 2 months.

S E R V E S   6

THIS LITTLE PIGGY WENT TO MARKET

◆

Granddad raised a few pigs until 1943 and Dad did likewise until 1975. Each year about a hundred went to market, plus one to the butcher for the family table. Uncle Roy and Aunt Rubye were the family hog farmers. Every year Roy sent around six hundred hogs to market, keeping thirty sows for breeding purposes. Sows (female hogs) farrow a litter of ten little pigs twice a year. The sow and her piglets were confined in a small pen for eight weeks. Then they were weaned from their mother. The babies squealed and squealed for about a day or so, after which they decided to give up hope. They slept in the hog house and were free to roam in the farmyard, root under fences, push each other around, and generally make pigs of themselves.

Hog farmers today keep their pigs confined to small pens inside temperature-controlled feeding barns. The sows never see the sun, exercise, or get slopped. One of Rubye's hog producer magazines suggests, "To relieve the pigs' stress, farmers should throw old rubber tires or large plastic balls into the pens." Totally amused, I queried, "Why? That sounds crazy!" Rubye said, "If you were packed in with a bunch of pigs, you'd have stress, too!"

Feeding the pigs raw slop of orange and apple peelings, onion skins, and other scraps from the kitchen was my chore. With one glimpse of me and the bucket, they crowded against the gate, pushing and shoving each other out of the way trying to hog it all. (The terms, "slopping the pigs" and "making slop of something" originated from the "hog lot." The farmer or his wife mixed oats and barley together with water in a large wooden barrel, stirring it up real good, allowing the grains to soak and ferment. This slop, all bubbly and sometimes foaming over the top of the barrel, was a nutritious food that aided the pigs' digestion. The result was a yard full of pigs that ate more corn and gained weight faster, ending in more profit in the farmer's piggy bank.) Our pigs were also fed a special corn mixture that fattened them up to the perfect weight of 200 to 250 pounds. Then they went to market.

Both the farmer and his wife participated in the butchering process. Granddad slaughtered the animal, skinned the hide off the carcass, and quartered the meat. He saved the bacon pieces and the hams for Grams to soak in brine before hanging them in Dave Ogg's smokehouse. They cut the meat into meal-size pieces and stored them in the pump house.

Meanwhile, Grams, being an economical housewife, used every possible scrap of meat and edible portion of the animal. The large meat scraps were made into sausage (see page 45). The knuckles were either pickled or made into souse. She made souse by boiling the knuckles in water until tender. After removing all the fat and bones, the lean pieces of meat were seasoned with vinegar, salt, pepper, onion, bay leaf, and allspice. She pressed the seasoned mixture into a glass dish or loaf pan and covered it with "boiled down" (reduced) broth from the original cooking liquid. The natural gelatin from the knuckles gelled the souse as it cooled in the tank room. Grams sliced it and served it cold for supper or stuffed it into sandwiches.

Headcheese was made from the obvious. Grams loved it, Mom loathed it. I agree with Mom!

Some farm families, like many ethnic families, even used the blood, which was saved in large clean washtubs, then boiled down and transformed—with pieces of lean meat from meat scraps and seasonings

—into blood sausage. Mom warns, "God forbid, don't do it now! They didn't know any better. . . . Lots of stomachaches were food poisoning!" Mom did not make any of these "delicacies" when I was growing up and I am grateful.

However, both Grams and Mom rendered lard from the fat between the skin and the meat. Mom placed a large pot on top of the kerosene stove in the basement, where the fat melted slowly over a low flame. The inviting rich aroma filled the basement and wound its way upstairs during the long process. The tempting tasty cracklings (brown crispy pieces of meat) were hard to resist when I passed that pot. Mom poured the melted fat into a press (see the sausage recipe, page 46) to extract the air bubbles and press out the lard, which was poured in its pure white state into clean jars and containers. They were chilled and stored in a dry cool spot to be used later in baked goods and for frying. After making lard we often stirred up a big batch of *Aunt Gladys's Light Doughnuts* (page 338), and generally made pigs of ourselves!

Would You Believe a Pig-Farmer?

Granddad, early 1900s

"Wash as many heads as you wish, scrape clean, take out eyes, put in kettle with sufficient water to cover and keep water over the top till the meat begins to drop from the bones; set off the fire and let cool. When cold enough to put bare hands in, put in a pan, then take your hands and take out all the bones; to each gallon of meat allow 1 Tablespoonful of pepper, 2 teaspoonfuls of ground sage, 1 teaspoonful of salt; with the hands squeeze all up together, taking out all the lumps that will not mash up, then mold in dish or granite pan and set in a cool place; when cold, slice in thin slices and serve." Inglenook Cook Book, 1901

Grams's Fried Ham

Grams wrapped the smoked hams in bleached linen sheets and tied clean gunnysacks securely over the sheets. She buried the package deep in the oats stored in the granary for safekeeping. At the turn of the century, the temperature stayed well below freezing all winter in Minnesota. (Due to global warming, it is milder now.) These buried edible treasures were dug out of the granary only on special occasions. (Once in a while, one of the hams was unfit to eat or spoiled, and it was tossed out immediately.)

For weekday table food, Grams kept one ham hung in the tank room. She sliced off as much as she needed for the number of people eating dinner and panfried it.

Trim off excess fat and score edge of meat. In large skillet, over moderate heat, melt butter. Add meat and brown, turning often until done (approximately 15 to 20 minutes, total cooking time). Remove meat to hot platter. Keep warm.

TO MAKE GRAVY Pour off all but 2 tablespoons of pan drippings/butter. Stir in flour and cook until it is color of brown paper bag, stirring constantly. Whisk in hot milk

1 ONE-INCH-THICK LARGE SLICE OF PRECOOKED SMOKED HAM (APPROXIMATELY 2 TO 2¼ POUNDS)
1 TABLESPOON BUTTER

GRAVY

2 TABLESPOONS PAN DRIPPINGS
1½ TABLESPOONS FLOUR
1 CUP HOT MILK
BLACK PEPPER, FRESHLY GROUND

"Cut off a 1" thick slice of ham, add a little butter or lard to pan and fry, turning frequently until brown and done. Remove to hot platter. Add flour and make a gravy with 1 cup top milk. Pour over ham and serve."

Mom [This is also called red-eye gravy.]

and continue to stir until mixture comes to a boil; boil 1 minute. Taste and correct seasonings.

Pour gravy over steak. Serve with riced potatoes and fresh baby lima beans.

VARIATION
Raisin Sauce Plump ⅓ cup raisins in ⅔ cup warm water overnight. Or pour water over raisins and microwave 2 to 3 minutes; rest 3 to 4 minutes. Add 4 tablespoons brown sugar, 2 tablespoons white sugar, 1 tablespoon cider vinegar, 2 tablespoons lemon juice, ½ teaspoon dry mustard, ⅛ teaspoon grated lemon peel to raisins; bring to a boil. Mix 1 tablespoon cornstarch with 1 tablespoon water and stir into sauce. Cook 3 to 4 minutes longer or until clear; remove from heat. Add dollop of butter (1 teaspoon) and pinch of salt if desired.

After meat is fried, pour out all pan drippings. Add ¼ cup dark rum to skillet, raise heat, and reduce to 1 tablespoon, stirring up bits from bottom of pan. Add reduction to sauce. To serve, spoon 1 to 2 tablespoons sauce over meat, pass remainder in bowl; accompany with mashed potatoes and fresh green beans.

S E R V E S 6

Roast Pork

✦

Family dinner pork roasts were shoulder or blade cut; a crown roast or loin roast was saved for special dinners when company came. Grams typically served sauerkraut or cabbage of some sort and potatoes with a pork roast. Mom often accompanied roast pork with sautéed Grimes Golden apples, applesauce, or pickled apples. Vary this recipe according to your personal preference.

▪▪▪▪▪▪▪▪▪▪▪▪▪▪▪▪▪▪▪▪▪▪▪▪▪▪

Trim excess fat from meat; wipe dry. With point of knife, make slits every so often in meat; insert garlic.

Mix sage, salt, pepper, and thyme together. Rub seasonings into meat, coating completely. Let stand 20 to 30 minutes (can be done ahead). Cover and refrigerate several hours or overnight.

Preheat oven to 350°. In roasting pan, over high heat, sear roast, fat side down, until brown on all sides. Or broil at 550° until brown on both sides. This takes about 5 to 6 minutes each side.

Place roast, fat side up, on rack in roasting pan. Strew onions around meat. Roast uncovered in oven for 30 minutes. Cover, continue to roast about 1½ hours, or until meat thermometer reads 170° (approximately

1 SIX-TO-SEVEN-POUND SHOULDER PORK ROAST OR
1 FIVE-TO-SEVEN-POUND PORK LOIN BONE-IN ROAST
2 CLOVES GARLIC, SLIVERED
1 TABLESPOON RUBBED SAGE
½ TEASPOON SALT
1 TEASPOON BLACK PEPPER, FRESHLY GROUND
1 TEASPOON DRIED THYME OR 1 TABLESPOON FRESH THYME

2 MEDIUM ONIONS, SLICED

SAUCE OR GRAVY

▪ ▪ ▪

¼ CUP PAN DRIPPINGS
3 TABLESPOONS FLOUR
2 CUPS HOT WATER

> *"Season with salt, pepper and sage. Brown on top of stove, roast in covered roasting pan in slow oven until meat is tender and done."* <u>Mom</u>

30 minutes per pound total cooking time, or about 3 hours in total or according to personal preference).

Remove roast from pan; rest on warm platter 10 to 15 minutes.

TO MAKE SAUCE OR GRAVY Pour off all but ¼ cup pan drippings and fat. On top of stove, over moderately high heat, add flour to pan. Cook, stirring constantly, until it is color of brown paper bag. Whisk in hot water; continue stirring until mixture comes to a boil; boil 1 to 2 minutes. (If lumpy, pour through strainer into sauceboat.)

TO SERVE Accompany with riced potatoes and *Scalloped Cabbage* (page 197) or *Old-Fashioned Coleslaw* (page 299). Garnish platter with parsley.

VARIATIONS
Down-Home After first 30 minutes' roasting time, add 7 to 8 potatoes (peeled and quartered), 8 to 10 small (2 inches round) onions (peeled and X cut in root end), 7 carrots (peeled and cut into 1½-inch lengths), and ½ cup water or chicken broth to roasting pan. Continue to roast according to recipe. Place meat on large platter; garnish with vegetables. Strain natural cooking juices into sauceboat and serve with mashed potatoes.
Apple 'n Kraut After first 30

minutes' roasting time, add 1 pound sauerkraut (rinsed and drained), 1 medium onion (peeled and sliced), 3 medium green apples (peeled, cored, and quartered), and ¾ cup apple juice to roasting pan. Continue to roast according to recipe. Arrange sauerkraut, onion, and apple mixture on large platter; place meat on top. Strain natural cooking juices into sauceboat, serve with boiled potatoes, and garnish with fresh apple rings and sprigs of fresh thyme.

Sweet Potato and Pineapple After first 30 minutes' roasting time, add 6 to 7 medium sweet potatoes (peeled and cut in half), 1 medium onion (peeled and sliced), and 1 can (13¼ ounces) pineapple spears with natural syrup to roasting pan. Continue to roast according to recipe. Place meat on platter; garnish with potatoes and pineapple. Strain natural cooking juices into sauceboat and serve with buttered green beans.

S E R V E S   6   T O   8

Marilla's Fried Pork Chops

❖

6 ¾-INCH-THICK LOIN PORK CHOPS
1 TEASPOON RUBBED SAGE
1 TEASPOON BLACK PEPPER, FRESHLY GROUND
1 SPRIG FRESH SAGE
1 SMALL ONION, SLICED
2 TABLESPOONS OIL
JUICE OF HALF A LEMON
1 TABLESPOON WHITE WINE OR BRANDY

FLOUR FOR DUSTING
2 EGGS, BEATEN
1 TEASPOON VEGETABLE OIL
1 CUP FINE CRACKER CRUMBS (I USE SALTINES)

1 TABLESPOON BUTTER
1 TABLESPOON VEGETABLE OIL

I magine a determined, barefooted four-year-old riding bareback down a country road. I had untied the Old Blind Mare from the stall in the barn, led her over to a nearby fence that I agilely climbed up, mounted her, and rode up the hill to pay a visit to Marilla Heusinkveld, who was like another grandmother to me. The Old Blind Mare (that was really her name and her condition!) knew the way there and back by heart.

Marilla and Ed's four children were in their teens and twenties—

Mitty and Her Foal

big stuff to me. Bethy, my idol and their youngest daughter, wore store-bought dresses, nail polish, and high-heeled shoes. Plus, she had a boyfriend, played "How Much Is That Doggie in the Window?" from sheet music on their player piano, and drank Coke directly from the green glass bottle. This was fast living!

If Bethy was in school, Marilla and I played hide-and-seek because she preferred playing with me to housework. Her favorite hiding place was in the army hammock that was tied between two apple trees growing in the orchard east of the house. It was a gift from her oldest son, my imaginary beau. She meowed like a cat so I could find her. Later, the two of us drank lemonade or iced tea and ate cookies for lunch on the front porch.

Feeling right at home with their family, I frequently ate dinner there also. Marilla's pork chops fried in a black cast-iron skillet were one of my fondest preschool recollections.

I now tenderize and add flavor to the chops with a marinade.

"Pound chops with side of a plate. Sprinkle with salt, pepper and flour and pound until tender. Dip into beaten egg and roll in cracker crumbs. Fry in butter until done." Marilla Heusinkveld, 1945

Trim fat and score edges of meat. Place in shallow glass dish in one layer; sprinkle with sage, pepper, onion, oil, lemon juice, and wine. Cover with plastic wrap and marinate 1 to 2 hours, or overnight in refrigerator, turning meat twice.

TO FRY Remove chops from marinade, strain out onion and herbs, and reserve liquid. Dry chops with paper towels and lightly dust with flour.

Beat eggs with oil; dip chops into egg-oil mixture. Roll chops in cracker crumbs.

Heat butter and oil in skillet until hot. Brown chops on both sides (3 to 4 minutes each side). Reduce heat; pour reserved marinade in pan. Partially cover and simmer approximately 20 to 25 minutes or until tender.

Remove chops to platter, pour pan juices into sauceboat. Serve immediately with boiled potatoes and buttered carrots.

S E R V E S   6

Pork Chops and Applesauce

The universal combination of pork chops and applesauce is part of every family's tradition. Our family was no exception to the rule. To make applesauce, Grams baked the apples all day in a large roasting pan, set in a slow oven. Mom filled a large electric roaster with apples to cook slowly unattended.

I fill a Crockpot with apples in the morning, and by evening they are perfectly cooked. For a full rich apple flavor, do not peel or core the apples before cooking. For a rosy-colored sauce, I add red apples.

Preheat oven to 350°.

Trim fat and score edges of chops, then season with celery salt, sage, cayenne, and black pepper. Lightly dust chops with flour.

Heat butter and oil in heavy casserole (fitted with a lid to be used later). Brown chops over moderate heat (5 to 6 minutes each side). Add

6 LOIN CHOPS (OR SHOULDER), ¾ TO 1 INCH THICK
½ TEASPOON CELERY SALT
1 TEASPOON DRIED SAGE
¼ TEASPOON CAYENNE PEPPER
1 TEASPOON BLACK PEPPER, FRESHLY GROUND
FLOUR FOR DUSTING
1 TABLESPOON BUTTER
1 TABLESPOON OIL
4 CLOVES GARLIC, WHOLE AND UNPEELED
1 MEDIUM ONION, SLICED
1 MEDIUM APPLE, PEELED, CORED, AND SLICED
¼ CUP APPLE JUICE

"Sear chops in a small amount of fat. Season with salt and pepper. Add some apple cider or juice, cover and simmer until tender. Serve with applesauce and fried potatoes." Mom

garlic, onion, and apple to casserole; pour apple juice around meat and vegetables. Cover and bake 30 to 45 minutes, or until tender to point of fork.

Remove chops to platter; keep warm. Strain out vegetables and reduce pan juices over high heat to half of original amount. Taste and correct seasonings if necessary; pour into sauceboat. Serve immediately with the applesauce that follows and *Fried Potatoes* (page 230).

S E R V E S 6

Homemade Applesauce

8 TO 10 TART APPLES (VARIETY ACCORDING TO PERSONAL PREFERENCE), HALF GREEN AND HALF RED
¾ CUP WATER
SUGAR TO TASTE
CINNAMON TO TASTE

Wash and quarter apples; remove any bruised spots. Place apples in Crockpot or heavy covered casserole. Add water, cover, and cook on low setting until soft and mushy. If using casserole, this can be done on stove top over low heat, or in 275° oven. Stir occasionally.

Press through food mill or sieve. Sweeten to taste with sugar. Sprinkle with cinnamon just before serving. Serve hot or cold with pork chops.

NOTE Some apples do not require sugar. As a rule of thumb, use ¼ cup sugar for each quart of applesauce. I keep a jar of unsweetened applesauce in the refrigerator and sweeten only if necessary for a specific dish.

MAKES APPROXIMATELY 1 QUART

Mom's Zesty Pork Chops

Mom developed this recipe for the May 1968 issue of the *Farm Journal,* when she was their guest cook. She gave food demonstrations as the home service director of an electric utility, Interstate Power Company, in Iowa and Minnesota.

She is an imaginative cook. In this recipe, "an apple slice steamed on top of each chop flavors the sauce and enhances the appearance. Fruit is so versatile. I use it in everything from meat to desserts . . . thus we rarely have a meal without fruit."

▪▪▪▪▪▪▪▪▪▪▪▪▪▪▪▪▪▪▪▪▪▪▪▪▪▪▪▪▪▪▪▪▪

Trim and score edges of meat. Wipe dry.

Heat oil in large skillet with lid or electric frying pan over medium high heat until hot. Brown chops on each side; drain off oil. Season with salt to taste.

6 LOIN CHOPS, ¾ INCH THICK
2 TABLESPOONS VEGETABLE OIL
½ TEASPOON SALT
½ CUP MAPLE SYRUP
½ CUP HICKORY-FLAVOR KETCHUP
2 TABLESPOONS LEMON JUICE
2 TEASPOONS WORCESTERSHIRE SAUCE
1 LARGE TART GREEN APPLE, CORED AND CUT INTO 6 THICK SLICES

1 TABLESPOON CORNSTARCH
⅓ CUP COLD WATER

In small bowl, combine syrup, ketchup, lemon juice, and Worcestershire sauce. Reserve ½ cup mixture; pour remaining mixture over chops.

Cover. Bring to a boil, reduce heat, and simmer over low heat 25 minutes.

Place an apple slice on each chop; top with reserved sauce. Cover and simmer 25 minutes longer. Remove chops to warm platter.

Blend cornstarch with water and stir into sauce in skillet. Cook, stirring constantly, until sauce comes to a boil. Boil 1 minute. Pour sauce over chops.

Serve with *Old-Fashioned Mashed Potatoes* (page 229) and *Fried Corn* (page 208).

S E R V E S   6

Barbecued Spareribs

◆

On special occasions, Mom made oven-barbecued ribs. Even though she did not grill any food outside (too many bugs and flies for her taste), they are perfect for an outdoor barbecue.

It was not only Mom who disliked outdoor dining, but Dad never thought doing so was "a big deal" because he worked in the elements all day and wanted shelter from the sun and wind while eating.

▪▪▪▪▪▪▪▪▪▪▪▪▪▪▪▪▪▪▪▪▪▪▪▪▪▪▪▪▪▪▪▪

Place ribs in large pot; cover with cold water. Add salt. Cover and bring to a boil. Reduce heat and simmer, partially covered, for 40 minutes. Drain.

TO MAKE BBQ SAUCE Mix ketchup, vinegar, sugar, mustards, Worcestershire sauce, ½ cup water, and spices together. Bring to a boil; reduce heat and simmer 15 minutes.

6 POUNDS SPARERIBS (2 RACKS, CUT INTO 4-RIB PORTIONS IF NECESSARY TO FIT IN THE POT)
1 TABLESPOON SALT

OLD-FASHIONED BBQ SAUCE

▪▪▪

1 CUP KETCHUP
2 TABLESPOONS APPLE CIDER VINEGAR
1 TABLESPOON BROWN SUGAR
1 TABLESPOON WHOLE-GRAIN MUSTARD
1 TABLESPOON DRY MUSTARD
2 TABLESPOONS WORCESTERSHIRE SAUCE
½ CUP WATER
½ TEASPOON RED PEPPER FLAKES
½ TEASPOON BLACK PEPPER, FRESHLY GROUND
1 TEASPOON PAPRIKA
1 TEASPOON CHILI POWDER

2 MEDIUM ONIONS, SLICED

"Boil the ribs, slather with a BBQ Sauce and bake in the oven until done." Mom

Can be done ahead. Store in glass jar in refrigerator up to 3 to 4 weeks.

Preheat oven to 350°. Cut cooked ribs into serving-sized portions. Make onion bed in large roasting pan and lay ribs on top. Coat ribs with BBQ sauce. Bake, partially covered, for 1 hour, then uncovered for 30 minutes (total baking time: 1½ hours). Remove ribs to large platter. Serve with *Vanishing Potato Salad* (page 308), *Baked Corn* (page 207), *Perfection Salad* (page 307), and, of course, the caramelized onions from the roaster!

SERVES 6

Sauerkraut, Ribs, and Potatoes

Great-Great-Grandmother Broadwater's influence is evident in this recipe. She was frugal, practical, and —at times—downright bossy. The short ribs and other pork bones were "boiled up," added to sauerkraut and potatoes, and cooked until done. The result: a complete meal for the family.

By browning the ribs first, adding apples, onions, carrots, and caraway seeds to the sauerkraut, and topping with a hot mustard sauce, the original plain peasant dish is transformed into a marvelous concoction fit for a king.

································

TO MAKE RIBS Preheat oven to 375°.

Cut bones into small portions. Mix flour, celery, salt, pepper, paprika, and garlic together in plastic bag.

Working in batches, shake ribs in flour mixture, until well coated. Place on rack inside large roasting pan and bake uncovered until brown and crisp, approximately 1½ hours.

TO MAKE SAUERKRAUT MIXTURE While ribs roast, melt butter in heavy casserole and sauté onions until soft and translucent.

RIBS
···

- **2 RACKS OF PORK RIBS (ABOUT 6 POUNDS OF MEATY RIBS AND BONES)**
- **½ CUP FLOUR**
- **1 TEASPOON CELERY SALT**
- **1 TEASPOON BLACK PEPPER, FRESHLY GROUND**
- **1 TEASPOON PAPRIKA**
- **1 CLOVE GARLIC, MINCED**

SAUERKRAUT MIXTURE
···

- **2 TABLESPOONS BUTTER**
- **3 MEDIUM ONIONS, PEELED AND CHOPPED**
- **2 CARROTS, PEELED AND CHOPPED**
- **2 STALKS CELERY, CHOPPED**
- **1 GREEN APPLE, PEELED AND CHOPPED**
- **1 QUART SAUERKRAUT, UNDRAINED**
- **1 TEASPOON BLACK PEPPER, FRESHLY GROUND**
- **1 TEASPOON CARAWAY SEEDS**
- **1 TABLESPOON BROWN SUGAR**

Add carrots and celery and sauté 3 to 4 minutes longer.

Add sauerkraut; cover and bring to a boil. Reduce heat and simmer 15 to 20 minutes. Season with pepper, caraway seeds, and sugar; taste and correct seasonings. Set aside off heat until meat is brown. This can be done ahead.

When browned, ribs should be added to sauerkraut mixture. Or, if desired, remove meat from bones, discard bones, and add meat to sauerkraut.

TO COOK POTATOES Place potatoes in and around sauerkraut and meat mixture. Add water (½ to 1

"Boil up your bones, take off the meat, put in a pot. Add your sauerkraut, as many potatoes as people plus one, enough broth to cook it. Cook until potatoes are done. Season with salt and pepper." Mom

cup) if necessary to keep moist; cover and bring to a boil. Reduce heat and simmer, partially covered, 20 to 25 minutes or until potatoes are cooked.

TO MAKE MUSTARD SAUCE Mix mustards together, adding a few drops of oil for proper consistency if

POTATOES
∎∎∎
7 MEDIUM POTATOES, PEELED AND QUARTERED

Hot Mustard Sauce
∎∎∎
½ CUP WHOLE-GRAIN MUSTARD
¼ CUP DIJON-STYLE MUSTARD
1 TABLESPOON DRY MUSTARD
FEW DROPS OLIVE OIL

necessary. Spoon small portion on top of whole affair or pass in bowl.

TO SERVE Bring casserole to table and ladle portions into soup bowls. Serve with hot mustard sauce, green salad, and crusty bread.

S E R V E S 6

Great-Grandmother and Grandfather Broadwater and Family (the little one is Granddad)

UNDRESSED SPRING CHICKEN

In early spring, Grams's old kitchen doubled as a hatchery for baby chicks. The 160-egg incubator with a kerosene lamp inside it sat next to the wood stove for auxiliary warmth. The unforgettable fumes were so unpleasant to Mom that she refused to eat eggs unless they were in an altered state—in cakes, puddings, or cookies. Every day each egg was checked and carefully turned until the baby chicks hatched. Crumbled hard-cooked eggs and hand-ground oatmeal was the first food for the baby chicks. Grams also made them cornbread (see Vintage recipe below) until commercial baby chick feed was available.

Dad, on the other hand, simply purchased our baby chicks on or about the first of April. After removing the backseat of our 1946 green two-door Plymouth, he covered the entire area with old muslin sheets to protect the upholstery and drove 45 miles to the hatchery in Rochester.

Fastidiously, Mom and Dad whitewashed the brooder house, a ten-by-twelve-foot rectangular Quonset hut–style coop with two small trap doors at the bottom for the chicks, a door for humans, and three or four windows in each end. In preparation for the newly hatched chicks, fresh peat moss was scattered on the floor and special care was taken to create as sterile as possible a living environment for them. After Mom sterilized the two-quart glass water dispensers that inverted onto a glass lip (the tiny chicks could drown in ordinary water troughs), we filled them with fresh

> *"Take 3 pints of sour milk or buttermilk, 2 large teaspoonfuls of soda dissolved in ½ cup hot water and 1 tablespoonful of salt. Stir well, then add 1½ pints of wheat bran, 3 pints of fine cornmeal and 4 tablespoonfuls of melted lard. Mix and pour into a dripping pan, bake 1 hour in a moderate oven. When fed (to chicks), moisten with hot sweet milk or water and sprinkle with black pepper."* <u>Ingelnook Cook Book, 1901</u>

water. An electrical cone-shaped hover hung from the ceiling to keep the wee birds warm.

The chicks, fifty to a box, arrived packaged in divided cardboard boxes with little round ventilation holes on the sides. What an exciting event! Three hundred tiny fuzzy yellow chicks chirping a tiny "peep" chorus. The four of us kids protectively stood watch over the brood.

As they grew, and with the onset of warmer weather, feed and water troughs replaced the glass water feeders, and a pan of crushed oyster shells (to insure good eggs) was added. The coops were well secured to protect the chicks from the farm cats, dogs, a red fox that lived in the back forty, and other predators who liked to eat chicks for lunch.

My chore was to open the small doors to let out the chicks to hunt and peck in the fenced-off area of the pasture. I signaled my arrival in the coop with careful quiet footsteps and either gentle words of assurance or a little cheerful whistle. Otherwise, the frightened chicks would run into one corner of the coop creating a heap or pile; those on bottom would not live.

As a young girl, Rubye had the same chore. One fateful day, the small door accidentally fell shut and locked on the outside of the coop. She was trapped inside with the chickens! In her absolute panic, Rubye broke one of the windows and climbed out to freedom. After reporting her mishap to Grams, she "received a bawling out in no uncertain terms!" for her "foolishness." I think it was a clever way to get out.

At the tender age of two months, fried spring chicken was on the family table. These are 2½-to-3-pound broiler size. After the chicks were four to five months old, now called "pullets," they began to lay small eggs, naturally named pullet eggs. They were just the right size for my breakfast.

Dad transferred the pullets from the brooder houses to the chicken coops in the farmyard. In the evening after they came home to roost (all chickens naturally roost in the same place every night), Dad, with Mom's help and a flashlight in hand, caught the pullets by their feet. They were transported in crates to the henhouse where they grew into hens. These birds were what we now call "free-range, natural chickens." They breathed farm-fresh air, ate nonchemically enhanced food, and exercised freely in the barnyard and around the chicken coops. (See breakfast chapter, pages 29–49, for more egg information.)

Chicken feed was packaged in fifty-pound cotton sacks. Mom and I stopped by the Preston feed store to pick out the prints that later would be transformed into curtains, a dress and matching apron for workdays, a pinafore for me, table napkins, and other items. She surveyed the whole warehouse, choosing ten bags with this print, six bags of that print, and so on. The printed feed sacks filled with chicken feed were hauled home. Once the bag was empty, Mom pulled the thread and unraveled the stitching, and shook out the excess feed. She soaked the bags in cold water to loosen any feed particles in the fabric. Nearly a yard and a half square, these pieces of cotton were then washed in hot soap and water. We hung the squares on the clothesline to dry in the sun. Grandma Schrock, using feed sack prints and other pieces of material, made me a patchwork quilt/bedspread that I used on my bed while I was at boarding school and college.

To kill and dress chickens, Grams heated salted water until very, very hot in a large copper boiler. Using a hatchet, Granddad chopped off their heads. The chickens were stuck into an old feed bucket to thrash around. This is where we get the phrase, "to go around like a chicken with its head cut off." Because Grams did not want dirty feathers, she did not allow the beheaded chickens to flop on the ground.

After the commotion stopped and the bucket was still, Grams, holding on to the feet, dunked the chickens into the near-boiling water a few times. She hung them upside down on a wire that stretched from side to side in the pump house. Lending a hand, Granddad helped her pluck off the feathers. Down from geese and ducks and chicken feathers were dried to be used in ticks and pillows. Grams singed off the tiny hairs by holding the chicken over a flaming torch of newspaper; Mom used a small can cover filled with rubbing alcohol. This process turned the feathers and hairs black, so they could be scraped off or pulled out with a sharp paring knife.

The plucked chickens were dressed and thoroughly washed in warm, then fresh cold well water, and chilled overnight in the pump house (pre-1920) or tank room. Grams called this "Saturday's work" in preparation for Sunday dinner.

Mom dressed one to two dozen chickens at a time using updated equipment for the same procedure. I marveled at her dexterity with a paring knife. My eyes were glued to her hands as she cleaned out the "grain sack" (lining) from the gizzard and detached the liver. My biology classes were a snap after this early education.

Clean white muslin sheets covered the inside of a flat box for the dressed fowl that—in the 1940's—she bartered for groceries at Read's grocery store. Ironically, Mom placed this box on the backseat of the same green Plymouth we had used to pick up the baby chicks at the beginning of this process. In anticipation of "Opal's chickens," the townspeople placed their orders with Mr. Read. The chickens were plump and delicious and very well dressed. Or "undressed" meant clean with no pin feathers, and so on.

Fresh-killed chickens for the table were immersed under cold water in a clean laundry tub, then chilled overnight in the tank room (in Grams's era), or refrigerated (in Mom's era). Any freshly killed chickens that were not cooked were either frozen in crocks covered with water, sealed, and left outside in the old days (now the winters are too warm)—or canned in glass jars (both Grams and Mom) and stored in the cool basement fruit room.

Now, Mom buys fresh-killed and dressed chickens from a young neighbor lady. The extra-fresh chickens are sealed in heavy plastic bags, frozen, and stored in the basement freezer. Mom purchased a Sears home freezer in 1949. Today, it still is overflowing with frozen foods, standing along the south wall in our basement.

ROAST CHICKEN A VARIETY OF WAYS

For this recipe, Grams always made a bread, onion, celery, and sage stuffing. After stuffing it into the chicken, she stitched up the cavity, placed it in a medium-sized blue enameled roasting pan or her large aluminum roasting pan (according to the size of the chicken), and roasted it. Mom prefers simply to stuff the chicken with onion, carrot, and a stalk of celery, then truss and roast the meat. She bakes the stuffing separately. I use both methods, depending on my personal whimsy at the moment.

"To Roast A Chicken: Dredge bottom of pan with flour. Place in hot oven and when flour is well browned reduce heat to moderate, then baste." Inglenook Cook Book, 1941

"Take a nice plump chicken, season with salt and pepper inside and out. Stuff with celery and onion and roast until done. Baste if needed (1/4 cup butter melted in 3/4 cup boiling water)." Mom

Great Uncle Rev. Glen Montz,
Aunt Iris, Delores, and David

Stuffing Rules

Never stuff fowl with warm stuffing. *Always* stuff the fowl with cool/cold dressing just before roasting.

Never stuff fowl the night, day, or even 1 hour before baking. These precautions are urged because conditions inside stuffed fowl are perfect for growing salmonella bacteria.

Basic Stuffed Roast Chicken

Preheat oven to 425°.

Wash chicken, then wipe dry with paper towels. Rub inside with cut side of lemon. (If desired, reserve neck and giblets for future stock. They can be wrapped separately and frozen.) Season with salt and pepper to taste.

Place half of chopped onion, carrots, and celery inside chicken; the rest, on bottom of roasting pan. Place roasting rack on top of vegetables.

Truss chicken: Cross legs, tie together with cotton kitchen string, and fold wings onto the back of the chicken. Stuff an onion in neck cavity and sew, pin, or tie shut.

Place chicken, breast side down, on roasting rack. Roast for 15 minutes, or until skin is crisp and brown. Turn bird over, roast 15 to 20 minutes, or until this side is brown. Reduce heat to 350° and continue to roast, basting with pan juices if necessary, for approximately 1 to 1½ hours.

Signs that chicken is fully cooked: Juices should run clear when fork is stuck into thigh, or thigh temperature should reach 190°. Total cooking time is approximately 2 hours.

Remove bird from oven. Rest on warm platter 15 to 20 minutes before carving.

TO MAKE GRAVY Strain vegetables from pan juices; discard if you like, but they taste great! Reserve

Ingredients

1 SIX-TO-EIGHT-POUND ROASTING CHICKEN
1 LEMON, CUT IN HALF
SALT
BLACK PEPPER, FRESHLY GROUND
1 LARGE ONION, CHOPPED
2 MEDIUM CARROTS, PEELED AND CHOPPED
2 STALKS CELERY, CHOPPED

1 MEDIUM ONION, PEELED

GRAVY (3 CUPS)

6 TABLESPOONS BUTTER OR PAN DRIPPINGS/OIL
6 TABLESPOONS FLOUR
3 CUPS HOT LIQUID—PAN JUICES, PLUS CHICKEN BROTH OR HOT WATER TO EQUAL 3 CUPS)
SALT, BLACK PEPPER, FRESHLY GROUND
DASH CELERY SALT (OPTIONAL)

juices, allowing fat to rise. I use a gravy strainer to skim off fat, then measure and add enough butter or oil to the fat to equal 6 tablespoons. Heat until melted in saucepan.

Stir flour into fat/oil. Cook over low heat, stirring constantly until mixture is smooth and color of brown paper bag. (Bubbles will cover entire bottom of pan.) Remove from heat.

Whisk in hot liquid; return mixture to heat and bring to a boil. Boil 2 minutes, stirring constantly.

Taste and season according to personal preference. If lumpy, strain through strainer into sauceboat.

NOTE Grams added top milk (similar to half-and-half) to the pan juices for a creamy rich gravy.

TO SERVE Carve chicken; garnish platter with bouquets of fresh herbs. Accompany with mashed potatoes and steamed vegetables.

VARIATIONS
Au Jus Sauce Add 1 to 2 cups chicken broth or 1 cup white wine and 1 cup chicken broth to roasting pan fat, juices, and vegetables. Bring to a boil; reduce by half. Taste and correct seasoning according to personal preference. Strain out vegetables to discard or eat. Pour into sauceboat and serve.
Carrot Roast Chicken Prepare roasting pan per recipe above. Rub inside cavity with lime instead of

lemon. Fill cavity with 8 small garden carrots (sliced), 1 bunch scallions (chopped), 3 sprigs fresh summer savory, and salt and pepper. Truss and roast according to recipe.

Fruit-Stuffed Roast Chicken TO PREPARE FRUIT STUFFING Plump 4 ounces dried apricots in ⅓ cup warm port for minimum of 30 minutes (or microwave 1½ minutes); peel and slice 2 medium tart green apples. Set aside. Melt ½ cup butter in skillet, add 2 medium onions (chopped), 3 stalks celery (sliced), and 6 shallots (minced), and sauté until soft and translucent. Add fruit to onion mixture and sauté 2 to 3 minutes. Season stuffing with 1½ teaspoons herbs de Pro-

vence or bottled poultry seasoning, and salt and pepper to taste. Add approximately ½ cup bread crumbs for drier consistency. Taste and correct seasonings. This part can be made ahead. Cover and refrigerate.

Stuff, truss, and roast chicken according to recipe, adding 30 minutes to total roasting time. When done, remove chicken to warm platter, and remove stuffing to bowl.

TO MAKE SAUCE Add ½ cup port and ½ cup chicken broth to pan juices; reduce by half. Strain out vegetables, then discard or eat. Taste and correct seasonings of sauce. Pour into sauceboat

Grams's Roast Chicken with Sage, Onion, and Celery Dressing

❖

Cube bread into 1-to-1½-inch squares and dry, uncovered, in mixing bowl overnight.

Melt butter in large skillet; add onion and celery, and sauté until vegetables are soft and translucent, about 7 to 8 minutes. Stir in parsley, sage, and pepper. Mix in half of the bread cubes and sauté until light brown. Place mixture in large mixing bowl. Toss in remaining bread cubes and mix well. Taste and correct seasonings.

Cool completely before stuffing. Can be done ahead and refrigerated

5 TO 6 CUPS DAY-OLD BREAD, CUBED
½ CUP BUTTER
1 MEDIUM ONION, CHOPPED
2 STALKS CELERY WITH LEAVES, CHOPPED
¼ CUP CHOPPED FRESH PARSLEY
1 TABLESPOON RUBBED SAGE
½ TEASPOON BLACK PEPPER, FRESHLY GROUND
½ TO ¾ CUP CHICKEN BROTH

MAKES 1½ TO 2 QUARTS ENOUGH FOR A 6 TO 8 POUND CHICKEN

1 to 2 days or kept frozen 1 to 2 weeks.

Just before stuffing, add enough chicken broth to moisten stuffing; mixture will hold its shape in your hand, but it will be neither soggy nor dry. Stuff, truss, and roast chicken according to basic recipe, adding 30 minutes to total roasting time. Remove stuffing immediately to serving bowl that can be kept warm in turned-off oven. Let chicken rest for about 10 minutes, then carve and serve.

and serve.

Garden Vegetable–Stuffed Roast Chicken
TO PREPARE VEGETABLE STUFFING Steam or parboil 2 carrots (sliced) and 1 fennel bulb (sliced) until barely crunch-tender.

Meanwhile, melt 1 tablespoon butter and sauté 5 shallots (minced), 5 medium mushrooms (sliced), and 1 stalk celery (sliced) for approximately 5 minutes. Add carrots and fennel to shallot mixture along with 1 cup fresh or defrosted green peas. Add ¼ cup chopped fresh parsley, ½ teaspoon celery salt, and ½ teaspoon black pepper, freshly ground. Toss well, taste, and correct seasonings. Can be made ahead; cover and refrigerate.

Stuff, truss, and roast chicken according to recipe, adding 30 minutes to total roasting time. When done, remove chicken to warm platter.

TO MAKE SAUCE Add ½ cup white wine and ½ cup chicken broth to pan juices; reduce by half. Strain out vegetables to discard or eat. Taste and correct seasonings. Pour into sauceboat and serve.

Garlic Roast Chicken Prepare chicken and roasting pan per recipe. Before roasting: Mix 6 large cloves garlic (minced), ⅓ cup chopped parsley, and ⅓ cup soft butter together to form a paste. Separate skin from breast and thigh meat. Place garlic "paste" on top of meat; draw skin back over paste. Rub excess butter on top of leg skin; truss and roast according to recipe.

Mustard Roast Chicken Prepare roasting pan per recipe. Rub inside cavity with lime instead of lemon. Soften ⅓ cup butter, add 1 large shallot (chopped), 1 teaspoon each of fresh marjoram and thyme, 1 tablespoon of fresh snipped chives, black pepper (freshly ground to taste), and ½ teaspoon celery salt. Mix well. Rub butter mixture inside cavity and underneath skin. Fill cavity with 1 onion (sliced). Truss, pat skin dry, mask entire skin with ½ to ¾ cup Dijon mustard, and roast according to recipe.

Rosemary Roast Chicken Prepare roasting pan per recipe. Chop 2 tablespoons fresh rosemary and 4 shallots together. Rub herb mixture inside cavity and under skin. Replace chopped onion, carrot, and celery with large onion studded with 2 cloves, truss, and roast according to basic recipe.

SERVES 6 GENEROUSLY

SUNDAY GO-TO-MEETIN' DINNER

"And God blessed the seventh day, and sanctified it: because that in

it he had rested from all his work which God created and made."

Genesis 2:3, King James Version

Generation after generation of my family, on both sides, observed the Sabbath. (Even the thought of work on Sunday was pushed out of mind.) Because of my family's devotion to their religious beliefs and their intuitive "common sense," these God-fearing, hard-working folks knew they needed a rest. It is no secret that, unless the preacher is a "real good talker," more often than not, over half of the men in the congregation "just rest their eyes" during the sermon.

The social aspect of the rural community was centered around the church as well. Our calendar was filled with "gatherings": Sundays after church services; Wednesday evening prayer meeting for cake and coffee; Thursday afternoon Ladies Aid meeting for sandwiches, cake, and coffee; Thursday night choir practice; Sunday evening youth group for games, devotions, and refreshments—plus numerous other "socials" held at church.

We went to church on Sunday morning at 10 A.M. for Sunday school and 11:00 A.M. for worship services, and returned Sunday evening for Church of the Brethren Youth Fellowship (C.B.Y.F.). We were not "so religious," but where else could we go? All our friends, their families, and everyone for miles around followed a similar schedule. I assumed that all able-bodied reasonable folks with the exception of the infirm and the sick socialized through their church.

As Grams would say, "That's just the way it was!" We were not stymied by this life-style. On the contrary, our family "lived what they believed." Thereby we were all nurtured, and—with the support of friends, neighbors, and fellow church people —given a steady "plumb line for life" for generations to come.

Grams began preparing for Sunday on Saturday. First on her unwritten but ingrained list was cleaning the house. This activity was followed by ironing Granddad's "good" suit (his "best bib 'n tucker"), and her daughters' and her own "Sunday" dresses and white gloves. Then shining Granddad's "good" black shoes. She generally performed a valet's job. Next in line came the food preparation for dinner guests "who came to eat more times than she cared to remember." This involved dressing chickens, baking buns, peeling potatoes and soaking them overnight in cold water, shucking peas, peeling carrots, slawing cabbage, preparing fruit compote, and churning butter—all completed in addition to her "regular" chores.

Meanwhile, in Indiana, Saturdays also meant that Grandmother Schrock traditionally baked a dozen pies. Her daughters thought she made too many, although not one piece was left by Monday. Grandfather Schrock, in his gregarious fashion, invited any "newcomer" or visitor home for dinner without the slightest worry that there would be enough to eat. Having a big family has its dividends, especially when distributing the labor. For example, Grandmother, using an Amish tradition, created a practical "game" for the ever-present, toddlers of the family. She poured heavy cream into a large canning jar, tightened the top, and handed it to the children. Sitting on the floor, with their feet touching to form a closed circle, the tykes rolled the jar from one to another, consequently churning the cream into butter while entertaining themselves.

After Saturday night supper, Grams filled (and then refilled) the galvanized tin washtub with hot water for baths that were taken in the kitchen near the stove. It is said that, in some families, every member bathed in the same bath water . . . starting with the youngest and ending with the father! Can you imagine that?

This was *definitely not the case* in our family. Grams insisted that all family members scrub themselves clean (according to the girls, "whether they needed it or not") every night. Mom maintained the same cleanliness standards, sometimes to an even greater extent. Once while I was staying with Grams, she asked me, "Why does your mother scrub you kids so hard?"!

Bright and early Sunday morning, after milking cows, Grams made oven-style fried chicken, baked two or three pies, and faithfully scrubbed the kitchen floor. Rubye said that was "part of her religion."

Following these preparations, the entire family, proudly dressed in their best Sunday Go-to-Meetin' duds, went to church via a horse and buggy. (The Schrock clan traveled by surrey, with two rows of benches on the side and a driver's seat in front, pulled by a team of horses.) About 1919, Granddad purchased a "Reo," his first open car with side curtains that snapped on in the event of rain. Traveling on a dirt road, with the vehicle stirring up dust, posed a problem for Grams's hat. She had a beautiful white hat—wide-brimmed, trimmed in white satin, with a large bow—covered with white netting. To prevent it from getting dirty, Grams wrapped a huge white linen towel around her head, hat and all, for the trip. Of course, as they approached the church, she removed the towel in order to arrive properly elegant and stylishly attired.

Grams's fashion statement didn't stop with one of her beautiful hats. She always slipped a pair of impeccable white gloves on her hands, carried a tiny package of "sen sens" and a clean handkerchief in her

EARLY 1900 TYPICAL SUNDAY DINNER MENU

Oven-Fried Chicken

Mashed Potatoes and Gravy

Buttered Peas and Carrots

Cabbage Salad

Homemade Buns with Butter and Strawberry Jam

Sweet Pickles, Apple Pickles, Beet Pickles

Fruit Compote

Raspberry Pie and Baked Custard Pie

Coffee

pocketbook, and wore a hint of Chanel #5 or Old English Lavender fragrance.

We grandchildren loved to sit next to her in church. But we knew that a stern scowl would soon appear on Granddad's face if we made "one peep" during the services. (That was the reason for "sin sins" in her pocketbook: She surreptitiously slipped a few into our hands when we got restless.)

After worship services, family and friends gathered at the back of the sanctuary to visit about the weather and the news from family members who had moved away. They reported who was sick or needed extra help, genuinely sharing the joys and the sorrows of every member of the congregation. This wholesome ritual still continues to embrace farm folk in many rural areas of this country today.

Once it was determined "who's eating where?" Grams rushed home and enlisted the help of Mom and Rubye to set the table. Preparation for Sunday dinner meant the best linen, and the Sunday china and flatware. Grams and the girls changed from their "good" clothes into their "nice-but-better-than-work" clothes. The pleasant aroma of fried chicken and freshly baked pies greeted the guests at the door while Grams put the final touches on the dinner. After dinner, the women and young girls washed the dishes while the men visited in the living room. Grams at last relaxed for the few remaining hours of the day of rest!

MOM'S TYPICAL SUNDAY DINNER MENU

Country Baked Pheasant with Creamy Sauce

Riced Potatoes

Buttered Cabbage with Green Peas

Mixed Green Garden Salad with Shallot Vinaigrette Dressing

Homemade Rolls

Butter and Strawberry Jam

Apple Pie and Gooseberry Pie

Coffee

Sundays for the next generation of my family were naturally more mobile and, from my perspective, full of surprises. After church, friends and relatives came for dinner by previous invitation, or we took an impromptu trip to the woods, or I went on a fishing trip with my friend Barbara Alexander. Her father, Kenneth, quite the fisherman, had more patience than most people, and helped me string a bamboo pole and bait the hook with an earthworm. I nearly fainted as I felt the tug of a nice-sized "sunny" on the hook— my first (and last) catch! I carried it home with great anticipation of a tasty supper. But to no avail—I did not have the heart to eat it.

For Sunday dinner, Mom served festive but not holiday foods. Although Dad did not hunt for game, in return for the many times he did favors and lent a helping hand, his friends often repaid him with a freshly dressed pheasant, a package of homemade sausages, or a side of venison. Marv and Jerry Rindels always shared their bounty with Dad even to this day.

Occasionally, while Dad napped and Mom read the Sunday paper (and "catnapped"), Joel and I baked. Sunday afternoon was the only time that Mom allowed us to practice on our own, with the stipulation that "you clean it up afterwards." One such day, Joel attempted to make brownies. When the recipe said, "Cream butter and sugar together," he added cream to the mixture. . . . Needless to say, that ended his baking career. However, he was very good at popping corn and an expert at scooping as much butter as he could onto each kernel of corn before eating it. (Twelve years later, Judy experienced the identical brownie baking result one Sunday afternoon. Undaunted, she has become an accomplished baker!)

Our Sunday night suppers, after such big dinners, were "pickups." I loved the fact that we were allowed to choose whatever available food that we felt like eating. If we ate two pieces of pie and an apple, Mom just let it pass with no comment. Unless of course we were sick; then, she supervised our diet very carefully.

The Fast Team, 1930s

Country Baked Pheasant

◆

One afternoon, as Mom and Aunt Marguerite (Dad's sister) were driving home from town, a pheasant happened to run across the road just north of the farm and was accidentally hit. Much to Mom's surprise, Aunt Marguerite insisted that Mom immediately stop the car. Marguerite ran back, picked up the pheasant, wrung its neck, carried it by the feet to the farm, and "dressed" it. Two days later, they feasted on pheasant. (Granted, this was an exceptional event. Usually we were given a hunter's catch.)

This recipe is fit for a feast, however you come by your pheasant.

▪▪▪▪▪▪▪▪▪▪▪▪▪▪▪▪▪▪▪▪▪▪▪▪▪

Preheat oven to 350°.

Cut pheasant into serving pieces, as you would chicken. Rinse, and pat dry with paper towels.

Mix flour, salt, pepper, and thyme in plastic bag; place pheasant pieces in bag and shake to coat with seasoned flour.

In large heavy skillet, heat oil and butter. Brown pieces of pheasant on both sides, approximately 5 to 6

**2 YOUNG PHEASANTS,
APPROXIMATELY
2½ POUNDS EACH
1 CUP FLOUR
½ TEASPOON SALT
2 TEASPOONS BLACK PEPPER,
FRESHLY GROUND
1 TEASPOON DRIED THYME
3 TABLESPOONS VEGETABLE
OIL
3 TABLESPOONS BUTTER
1½ TO 2 CUPS HEAVY CREAM

2 TABLESPOONS CORNSTARCH
2 TABLESPOONS COLD WATER**

Dad, Aunt Marguerite, 1920s

minutes per side. Remove browned pheasant to roasting pan; put dark meat pieces on bottom, white meat on top.

Discard excess oil. Slowly add cream to skillet and bring to a boil. Remove from heat. Pour enough hot cream in roasting pan to come ⅓ of way up side of meat, adding more if necessary; cover. Reduce oven to 325° and bake for 2 to 2½ hours, or until meat is tender to point of fork. Err on the side of a longer baking time for tender pheasant. Remove pheasant pieces to warm platter.

TO MAKE CREAMY SAUCE Blend 2 tablespoons cornstarch with 2 tablespoons cold water. Whisk into pan juices that have separated during baking process. Boil, stirring constantly, 3 to 4 minutes, or until thickened and smooth. Taste and correct seasonings. Pour into gravy boat and serve with riced potatoes. Garnish meat platter with watercress.

S E R V E S   6

Imagine a large china platter of fried chicken, covered with brown wrapping paper sitting on a woman's lap while she and her children traveled aboard a train from Aberdeen, South Dakota, to Foley, Minnesota. One of the children was Grams, then thirteen years old; she was with her brothers. The chicken was prepared by Grams's mom's mother-in-law, my great-great-grandmother. By the time they reached Minnesota, only the platter—the material symbol of my generation's connection to our maternal heritage—was left. Grams always served fried chicken on that heirloom platter.

Each of the 3½-to-4½-pound fryers (from chickens two to three months old) was cut into ten economical serving pieces. Grasping the thigh bone, Grams cut through the skin close to the body. By bending the leg back, the joint was separated and the drumsticks cut off at the joint. On either side of the wings, she cut the flesh toward the joint, separated the joint, and finished cutting the flesh. The breast was separated from the back by cutting through the skin just below the breastbone and following up the ribs to the shoulder, where it was disjointed. She inserted a knife between the wishbone and the breast and cut downward following the bone, making three pieces of white meat in total. The back was cut crosswise in two pieces.

The meat was seasoned with salt and pepper, rolled in flour, and fried

Country Fried Chicken

◆

2 CHICKENS, 3½ TO
    4½ POUNDS EACH
1 CUP FLOUR
1 TEASPOON SALT
2 TEASPOONS BLACK PEPPER,
    FRESHLY GROUND, OR MORE
    TO TASTE
⅔ TO 1 CUP VEGETABLE OIL,
    OR COMBINATION OF LARD
    AND BUTTER (¾ LARD,
    ¼ BUTTER)

GRAVY
(2½ TO 3 CUPS)
■ ■ ■

APPROXIMATELY
    2 TABLESPOONS
    VEGETABLE OIL
1 TABLESPOON BUTTER
6 TABLESPOONS FLOUR
2½ CUPS WATER, BOILING, OR
    HALF MILK AND WATER
1½ TEASPOONS SALT
¼ TEASPOON BLACK PEPPER,
    FRESHLY GROUND

in lard and butter in my Great-Great-Grandmother Crowe's Griswold black cast-iron skillet without the legs. This well-seasoned skillet was used only for frying. After the chicken was crisp brown, the excess oil was poured off and the flame lowered. She added some cold water, covered the pan, and continued to cook the meat until it was done. She thickened the pan juices with flour and added rich top milk for gravy.

Mom follows the same technique to cut up chicken into serving-size pieces before frying or broiling it.

■■■■■■■■■■■■■■■■■■■■■■■■■■■■■■■■

Cut chicken into serving-size pieces; rinse and pat dry with paper towels.

Mix flour, salt, and pepper in bag. Place no more than 2 pieces of chicken in bag at a time, shake to coat each piece with flour mixture; set them aside. Continue until all pieces are coated.

In large heavy skillet, heat oil until hot, about 3 to 4 minutes. Add chicken, a piece at a time, starting with dark meat, skin side down. Fry for 8 to 10 minutes or until golden brown. Turn; brown other side 8 to 10 minutes longer. Continue with white meat in same manner. Total browning time is approximately 20 minutes.

When all pieces are browned, pour off excess oil. Add ¼ cup cold water.

Reduce heat, cover, and cook until meat is tender and juices run clear when pricked with fork—another 15 to 25 minutes. Uncover pan for last 5 to 10 minutes to recrisp skin. Remove chicken and drain on brown paper bag. Place on warm platter.

TO MAKE GRAVY Measure pan drippings; add enough oil and butter to equal ¼ cup plus 1 teaspoon. Return to pan.

Stir flour into hot drippings. Cook 2 minutes or until mixture becomes color of brown paper bag. Whisk in hot water or milk and water; return to a boil. Stirring constantly, boil 2 minutes longer. Season; taste and correct seasonings. Pour into sauceboat immediately.

Serve chicken and gravy with riced potatoes and broccoli.

VARIATIONS
Broiled Garlic and Thyme Chicken Substitute 2 smaller chickens (2 to 2½ pounds) in recipe. Cut into quarters, breaking joints to keep flat. Drizzle juice of 1 lemon on inside and skin side. Season with 1 teaspoon dried or 1 tablespoon fresh thyme, ½ teaspoon celery salt, 1 clove garlic (minced), and 1 teaspoon black pepper (freshly ground), or more to taste. Place chicken on broiler pan (no rack). Brush with 3 teaspoons butter, melted and mixed with ¼ teaspoon paprika. Broil in preheated broiler 5 to 7 inches from heat, skin side down, for 10 minutes. Turn and brush with butter. Continue to broil 20 minutes longer,

"Coat with salt and pepper. Roll in flour. Slowly fry in hot lard ¼–½" deep until well browned. Make gravy with pan drippings." Mom

or until crisp and brown on outside and tender, with juices from thigh running clear when pricked with fork. This takes approximately 35 to 40 minutes in total. Serve with baked potatoes and steamed vegetables.

Deluxe Fried Chicken Combine ⅔ cup heavy cream and ⅔ cup milk together. Coat each piece of raw chicken well. Mix 2 cups flour, 1 tablespoon salt, 1 tablespoon black pepper (freshly ground), ¼ teaspoon celery salt, ½ teaspoon cinnamon, ½ teaspoon nutmeg, and 1 teaspoon ground cardamom together in plastic bag. Remove chicken from cream mixture and shake with flour mixture until well coated. Fry according to basic recipe.

Granddad's Favorite Fourth of July Fried Chicken Substitute 2 smaller chickens (2½ to 3 pounds) in recipe. Cut into 6 pieces each. Reduce frying time to 3 to 4 minutes on each side; reduce total cooking time as necessary. (Grams thought 2½-pound chickens did not have enough meat on their bones!)

Sunday Dinner Fried Chicken Fry chicken pieces as in basic recipe until brown. Place in roasting pan, cover, and bake in 300° oven 1½ to 2 hours or until tender and juices run clear. Remove chicken to warm platter; prepare gravy with pan drippings per original recipe.

S E R V E S   6

Great-Grandmother Broadwater's Chicken and Biscuits

This heirloom recipe brings forth various memories for each member of our family. Rubye remembers a March 29 birthday trip to Grandmother Broadwater's. Grams, Granddad, Mom, and she climbed into the horse-drawn sled. Because it was so cold, Grams heated a six-by-ten-inch square soapstone (the same stone she used to warm their bed) in the coals of the wood stove, and placed it on the floor of the buggy to keep their feet warm. Granddad covered the girls with a black horsehide throw to shield them from the snow and cold wind. Despite their precautions, the foursome arrived chilled to the bone, but the pleasant aroma of chicken and biscuits baking in the oven for Rubye's birthday dinner instantly warmed them.

Mom's less nostalgic image brings her back to her teens. Several cousins and Mom boarded at Grandmother Broadwater's house during the win-ter session of high school. Chicken and biscuits, because it was an economical dish, was served "all too often!" to her taste.

----

1 SIX-TO-SEVEN-POUND ROASTING CHICKEN WITH FAT AND NECK (NO GIBLETS)
2 TEASPOONS SALT
1 TEASPOON BLACK PEPPERCORNS
1 MEDIUM ONION, WASHED AND UNPEELED
2 CARROTS, PEELED AND CHOPPED
2 STALKS CELERY, CHOPPED

8 MEDIUM POTATOES, PEELED AND QUARTERED
6 MEDIUM CARROTS, PEELED AND CUT INTO 1-INCH LENGTHS
½ TEASPOON CELERY SALT
1 TEASPOON BLACK PEPPER, FRESHLY GROUND

Place chicken in large stockpot and cover with cold water. Add salt, peppercorns, onion, carrots, and celery. Cover and bring to a boil.

Reduce heat and simmer over low heat for approximately 2½ to 3 hours, or until tender and meat falls off bones. Remove from heat; cool until able to handle. Or do this ahead. Cool to room temperature and refrigerate until assembly time. Increase cooking time, if using cold broth. (Mom often uses home-canned chicken pieces.)

WHEN MEAT IS COOL Pour chicken, vegetables, and broth into strainer set over large bowl. Shake

On July 17, 1932, at the homecoming anniversary meeting of the Root River Church of the Brethren, guests from far and near dined on chicken and biscuits. Grandmother Broadwater called it chicken pie. Designated members of the Ladies Aid Society Food Committee prepared the food for this large gathering at home and brought it to church. They received the following handwritten specific instructions from Mary Drury Broadwater, preserved in Grams's Black Book

"Take one good size chicken. Those older and fatter chickens make richer broth. Cook in plenty of water until tender. Take out of broth and remove the bones and fatty pieces. Take a quart of potatoes, cut in fairly small pieces and cook in the broth. When the potatoes are done, return the chicken to the broth with the potatoes. Make a rich biscuit dough for the crust. (two cups of flour will be enough) Put the chicken, potatoes and part of the broth into a baking dish, season to taste. Cut the crust of biscuit dough into small biscuits, put on top and bake. When done, pour in the remainder of the broth. If you put broth all in at one time it will boil over. Have plenty of broth. Please use the above recipe so that the chicken pie will be uniform." Great-Grandmother Broadwater

off excess broth. Return broth to stockpot. Separate meat from skin, bones, and fat. Cut meat into pieces 2 to 3 inches in size and place in large baking/serving casserole dish. Discard skin, bones, connective tissue, fat, and vegetables.

Preheat oven to 350°.

Add quartered potatoes, then carrots, to dish with chicken. Season meat and vegetables with celery salt and pepper.

Taste chicken broth; correct seasonings. Pour enough hot broth over meat and vegetables to just barely cover the mixture. Cover casserole and bake until vegetables are done to fork tender, 30 to 40 minutes.

TO MAKE BISCUITS Sift flour, salt, baking powder, sugar, and baking soda together. Cut lard or butter into flour, as if for piecrust.

BAKING POWDER BISCUIT DOUGH

■ ■ ■

1¾ CUPS FLOUR
½ TEASPOON SALT
2 TEASPOONS BAKING POWDER
1 TEASPOON SUGAR
½ TEASPOON BAKING SODA
¼ CUP LARD OR
5 TABLESPOONS BUTTER
¾ CUP BUTTERMILK

Stir in buttermilk (Grams used heavy cream), until just mixed; dough will be sticky. Turn out onto floured board or pastry cloth. Knead a few times, keeping excess flour to a minimum. When dough becomes "bouncy," pat out to ¾ inch thick. Cut into 8 biscuits.

TO ASSEMBLE AND SERVE Remove chicken and vegetables from oven. Turn up temperature to 450°. Place biscuits on top of hot chicken, adding more broth if necessary (1 to 2 cups). Bake at 450°, uncovered, until biscuits are light and brown, 8 to 10 more minutes. Serve from casserole alongside green salad and relishes.

VARIATIONS
Chicken and Noodles Cook and cut chicken into serving-size pieces per recipe. Season and pour 2 to 2½ quarts of broth over chicken in large

saucepan on stove top. Omit potatoes and carrots. Bring whole affair to a boil. Stir in 8-ounce package of egg noodles or homemade noodles from recipe below. Cover and cook just at the boiling point, not a rolling boil, over moderate heat approximately 8 to 10 minutes or until noodles are cooked. Serve with green vegetables and salad.

HOMEMADE EGG NOODLES (APPROXIMATELY 1 POUND NOODLES) With fork, beat 2 egg yolks or 1 whole egg with 1 tablespoon water. Pour into well made in center of 1 to 1½ cups flour and ¼ teaspoon salt in bowl. Mix with hands to make smooth dough (as if for pasta). Knead until smooth, adding more flour only if necessary. Rest dough under pastry cloth 10 to 15

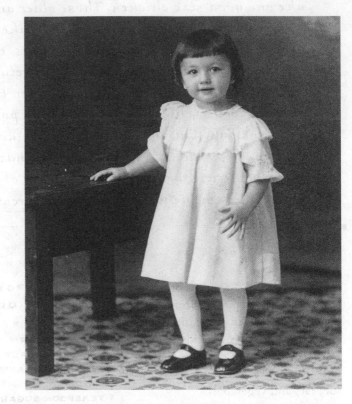

Mom, The Quintessential Prodigy, 1915

MOM'S VERSION

"Grandma B's Chicken pie—1 hen, fat and plump, (ha), cook in water. I add celery, carrot, onion, salt and pepper. Remove chicken cut in bite size pieces, cool broth. I strain off excess fat. Cut up chunks of white potatoes, add chicken and put in a casserole. Then pour on broth and cook till potatoes are done in hot 350° oven, covered. Remove cover, place baking powder biscuits made with flour, baking powder, salt and enough whipping cream to just stir it up; on top meat and potatoes. Bake until brown and light." *Mom*

minutes. Or wrap in plastic wrap and refrigerate 1 to 2 hours. Divide ball into 4 parts.

With rolling pin, roll each ball very thin on top of floured board or pastry cloth. Lay on floured tea towel until partially dry or easy to handle. Cut into desired widths (as thin as possible). Lay cut noodles on cake rack to dry thoroughly, or cook as directed above.

Chicken and Dumplings Prepare chicken and vegetables per recipe. Pour 2½ to 3 quarts of hot broth over chicken in casserole or saucepan with tight-fitting lid that can be used on top of stove. Substitute dumplings (see recipe below) for biscuit dough.

LIGHT DROP DUMPLINGS Sift 1 cup cake flour, 2 teaspoons baking powder, and ½ teaspoon salt together. Put 1 egg in measuring cup and add enough milk to fill 1 cup. Mix flour and egg mixtures well to form stiff dough. Bring broth to a boil and keep just at simmering temperature or dumplings will fall apart. Dip metal spoon into hot broth and then into dough. Drop spoonfuls of dough onto simmering broth until surface is covered but not crowded. Cover tightly and simmer for 10 minutes, or until dumplings are fluffy and wooden pick inserted into center comes out clean. Serve instantly.

For Cream Chicken:
Grams and Mom just mixed flour and cold milk together, stirred it into the hot mixture until it was the thickness of gravy. Mom

Creamed Chicken Cook chicken per basic recipe above. Put chicken pieces in baking casserole. Omit potatoes and carrots. Measure 1¾ quarts strained chicken broth and 1 cup cream, milk, or half-and-half into saucepan. Bring to a boil. In another saucepan, melt ½ cup butter; blend in ½ cup flour. Cook at a bubble 1 minute, stirring constantly. Remove from heat; whisk in hot broth mixture. Return to heat and bring to a boil, stirring constantly. Boil 2 minutes longer. Taste and correct seasoning according to personal preference. Pour cream sauce over cubed chicken.

Bake in 350° oven 15 minutes or until steaming hot. Can be reheated on top of stove. Serve with favorite rice, potatoes or baking powder biscuits, vegetables, and salad.

Creamed Chicken with Thimble Biscuits Prepare *Creamed Chicken* per above recipe. Raise oven temperature to 450°. Make biscuit dough per basic recipe; cut biscuits out with thimble. Place tiny biscuits on top of creamed chicken; bake in 450° oven 5 minutes or until biscuits are light and brown. (Everyone loves these tiny biscuits!) Serve with favorite vegetables.

SERVES 6 GENEROUSLY

175

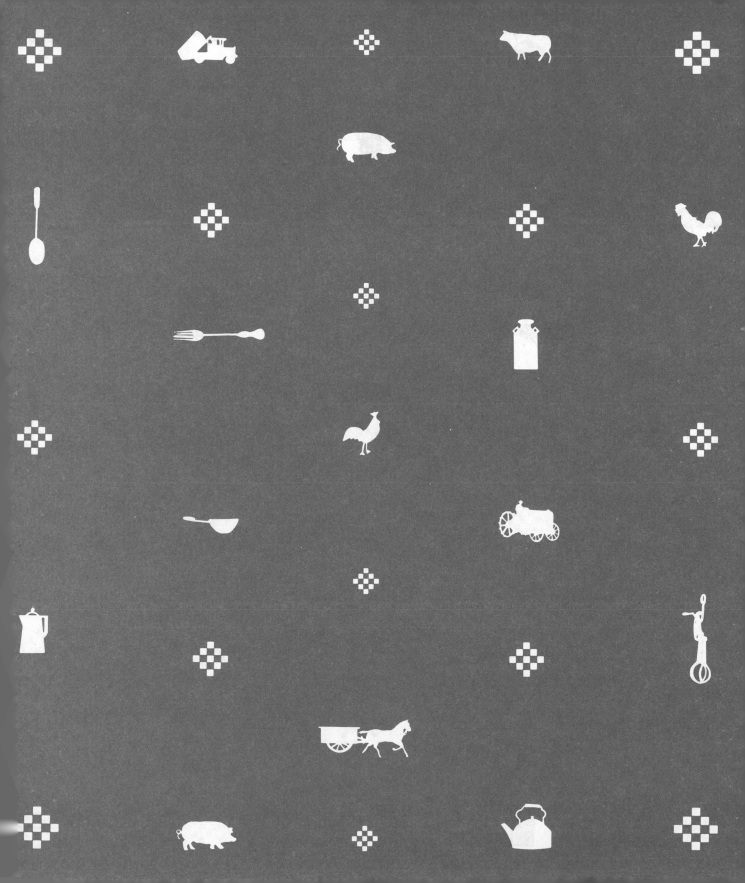

THE VEGETABLE TRUCK PATCH

Seed catalogs arrived during the cold, blustery month of January, giving the armchair gardener a brief escape from the subzero climate at hand. Thoughts of warm summer breezes and hot sunshine made the conditions outside bearable. With visions of marvelous-tasting vegetables, Mom and Dad ordered the seeds early. They met the arrival of each package from Burpee's and other seed companies with salivating palates in great anticipation of a good growing season.

Grams always saved the seeds from one *choice* tomato, the *best* pumpkin, the *largest* melon, and so on for next year's crop. But Mom ordered the majority of the seeds from catalogs. Her favorite tomato varieties are Celebrity, Fantastic, Jet Star, and Roma.

While the ground was still frozen, green pepper, tomato, celery, and other long-germinating seeds were planted in flats and placed next to the chimney in the kitchen. These seedlings were set out later in the spring. After there was no danger of frost and the ground was workable, Granddad plowed under the decomposed chicken manure that he had spread on the garden the previous fall. The exact time varied each year, depending on the weather. Using a walking plow and one horse, he turned over the soil. Afterwards, the furrows were smoothed out by a small, horse-drawn, one-section drag. Dad also used a walking plow and two horses for garden work until he purchased a small wide-wheeled front-end Ford tractor in 1951.

With conservation in mind, Dad spread on cow manure, and plowed the garden in the fall. Now this is referred to as organic compost material with less nitrogen content than chicken manure. The freshly plowed garden dirt exposed the soil-borne bacteria and insects to the sun and frost, thereby killing them so they could not eat the vegetables the next year. Winter rainfall and snow and then the spring rains effectively seeped into the fertile earth through the rough surface.

Granddad meticulously placed sticks on both sides of the prepared soil to mark the rows. String was strung between the stakes to form perfect, *absolutely perfect,* straight rows. Only Grams was allowed in the garden. She planted the seeds following his instructions exactly, after which she removed the string and stakes. They placed wood shingles around the seedlings to protect them from frost, wind, or sun damage. Once the plant was established and the evenings were warm, the protection was removed.

Mom and Dad made gardening a family affair, so we all planted seeds in the freshly dug rows or hills. Dad's instructions were encouraging and informative, spiced with a corny joke here and there. When planting lettuce, for example, he recited from the Bible (I John 4:7), "Beloved, *let us* love one another" —things like that. We protected the seedlings with hot caps—thin, white, paper triangle-shaped hats. Later recycled plastic jugs served as mini-greenhouses until the little plants were established.

Granddad's garden was untouched by chemical fertilizers and herbicides. However, Grams did use a "deadly poison," Paris Green, mixed with flour to take care of the cabbage loopers. Mom uses a minimum of pesticides for worm control on cabbages.

Dad, Wide-Wheeling It

"Our garden is as organic as possible without standing out there with two boards, killing the worms!" affirmed Mom. They use companion planting to discourage most of the pests—for instance, one row of marigolds next to all the cabbages, broccoli, and cauliflower.

After testing the soil, Dad will use a small amount of fertilizer to balance the nutrients. He always used and still uses alternative practices to enrich the land. Vegetables are rotated on a four-year basis to insure future productivity of the garden and for disease control. Sections of the garden are seeded with rye ("green manure") in the fall to add nutrients and to form tilth. This makes the soil soft, mellow, and tillable. Scarecrows and netting protected the berries and tomato plants from the hungry birds. Even extra lettuce is planted in anticipation of a rabbit or two helping himself to a fresh tender meal!

Both Mom and Grams weeded and tended to the garden as part of their many other farm-wife duties. Granddad assisted by hoeing early in the morning before working in the field. Dad enjoyed hoeing in the garden after the evening chores were done until it was dark. Grams used old newspapers for mulch while Dad used straw and other natural substances to spread between the rows of vegetables to limit weed growth and retain water. Nevertheless, Dad, with sharp hoe in hand, cut off any visible weed he could find. According to hearsay, Granddad's picturesque garden had no weeds at all. Dad said, "Frank was a very particular man!" Mom added, "A fanatic!"

Later, Granddad "retired" by spending every day except Sunday tilling, planting, hoeing, weeding, transplanting, pruning, and harvesting vegetables in his 1½-acre garden over at the "Eighty." He also puttered in their small garden (twelve square feet) in town every morning, while Grams cared for her flowerbeds.

With the proliferation of new vegetable plant varieties that were introduced to rural customers through volumes of seed catalogs in the 1940s, Mom and Dad's vegetable garden produced "every new vegetable that was available!" Despite the short growing season in Minnesota, Mom and Dad experimented with all species of vegetables.

Rows of every imaginable vegetable were planted. Each stage of maturation was carefully observed and lovingly attended to by the whole family. We could not wait for the first short stubby asparagus spike, tiny tender peas in the pod, and tart-yet-sweet crisp radishes.

They were (and still are) passionate gardeners, often growing enough vegetables for the family of twelve people that we never were! Bushels, pecks,

Mom, circa 1915

sacks, handmade berry carriers, and at times aprons, filled with fresh produce from the garden, were brought in to be prepared immediately for the table, frozen, canned, or dried for future gastronomic endeavors. "Say nothing of what was given away!"

We ate tiny baby carrots, budding sweet beets, small crisp green beans that snapped with the slightest bend, and juice-squirting ears of sweet corn, picked and hurried to the house just in time to husk and cook for dinner. Because Dad planted an abundance of every vegetable, Mom either canned or froze vegetables when they were at their peak. Frequently, she began processing the vegetables after supper and worked until late at night. The old adage —"Men work from sun to sun, but women's work is never done!"—was true for most farm families. In our family, Dad worked late into the night, too.

Before 1925, fresh potatoes, onions, squash, and some root vegetables were stored in the root cellar, but after Granddad built the "new house," produce-laden wooden crates were set on the floor of the basement vegetable room. Other vegetables were canned in jars and stored on the shelves. Both Grams and Mom stored carrots, cabbages, and apples in twenty- or fifty-gallon crock vessels in the basement vegetable room. The vegetables were brought in and the dirt shook off, then they were wrapped in layers of newspaper and placed in the crocks. These homegrown, nonchemical, natural vegetables were in what we now call "cold storage." Before it was fashionable, Grams preserved corn, apples, and tomatoes by naturally sun-drying them. With the advent of the home freezer, she discontinued the drying process. Too bad she's not alive now. She would have a good chuckle after hearing all the fuss about sun-dried tomatoes.

Whenever Mom had a "whole mess" of peas or corn to freeze, Grams drove out from town to lend a hand. Those two worked together quickly and efficiently—preparing, blanching, and packaging the vegetables. The "legwork" was mine. It was also my job to fit plastic bags inside either pint or quart boxes to be filled. Mom poured in the vegetables, and using a tiny rubber band, fastened the top. I ran the packages downstairs to the freezer in the basement. I wondered how in the world we would ever eat all that food. But by the next summer, most all the vegetables had been consumed at our table or given away to needy hungry people.

Grams simply cooked fresh vegetables in a large pot of boiling salted water until they were tender. Her definition of tender was softer than mine, but the colors were never faded, nor were the vegetables soft and mushy. No matter how she planned to serve them, she always added butter directly to the hot drained vegetables. If she wanted creamed vegetables, she poured heavy cream over them and thickened them with a bit of flour and water mixed together, seasoned with salt and pepper.

Mom the innovator cooked most vegetables in the timesaving pressure cooker, following the manufacturer's directions carefully. Now the microwave has replaced her pressure cooker. As a home service advisor and lecturer, she teaches microwave cooking throughout the tri-state area—southeastern Minnesota, northeastern Iowa, and northwestern Wisconsin—even now.

Ordinarily, I prefer the steaming method. My family has become accustomed to eating bright-colored and crunchy al dente vegetables; they say, "You cook them warm-raw!" When garden-fresh vegetables are properly prepared, they need no salt, pepper, sauce, or dressing. However, I have included the following vegetable recipes that were either recorded or remembered as being served in our family. Check with the master chart for the method most often used to cook your favorite garden-fresh vegetable.

Basic Method for Boiling Fresh Vegetables

Bring 7 to 8 quarts of cold water to a boil in large pot with 1 teaspoon salt. By handfuls, add prepared vegetables; return water to a boil. Boil as directed in each recipe or until just crunch tender, when vegetable gives slight firm resistance inside if stuck with point of knife. Drain in colander and immediately rinse with cold water to prevent overcooking. Drain well again and proceed according to recipe.

Basic Method for Steaming Fresh Vegetables

Bring 2 inches of cold water to a boil in bottom of steamer or saucepan with lid that will accommodate metal steamer or strainer. Add prepared vegetables in single layer, cover pan, and steam as directed in each recipe or until just crunch tender, when vegetable gives slight firm resistance inside if stuck with point of knife. Immediately rinse with cold water to prevent overcooking. Drain well again and proceed according to recipe.

TO STEAM IN MICROWAVE Place prepared vegetables in single layer on glass plate with 1 tablespoon water, cover with plastic wrap, and microwave according to manufacturer's directions or until just crunch tender. Rinse with cold water, drain well, and proceed according to recipe.

Preparing and Serving Vegetables

This chart shows the vegetables and herbs that were grown in the gardens of Grams and Granddad (1890–1930s) and Mom and Dad (1940–present), and how they were served:

Vegetables	Grams	Mom	Method of Preparation and Serving
ASPARAGUS	x	x	BOILED, CREAMED
BEANS, GREEN (KENTUCKY WONDER)	x	x	BOILED, CREAMED, BUTTERED
BEANS, LIMA	x	x	BOILED, CREAMED
BEANS, WAX/YELLOW	x	x	BOILED, BUTTERED
BEETS	x	x	BOILED, BUTTERED
BEET GREENS	x	x	BOILED, VINEGAR DRESSING
BROCCOLI		x	STEAMED, BUTTERED
BRUSSELS SPROUTS		x	BOILED, BUTTERED
CABBAGE (BOK CHOY, CELERY, GREEN, AND PURPLE)	x	x	BOILED, STEAMED, FRIED, CREAMED, RAW WITH VARIETY OF DRESSINGS
CARROTS	x	x	BOILED, BUTTERED, CREAMED, CANDIED, RAW
CAULIFLOWER		x	BOILED, BUTTERED, CREAMED, BAKED
CELERY	x	x	BOILED, CREAMED IN COMBINATION WITH OTHER VEGETABLES, RAW
CHARD	x		BOILED, DRESSED WITH VINEGAR AND BACON
CORN (ON COB)	x	x	BOILED, BUTTERED
CUT	x	x	BUTTERED, CREAMED, SCALLOPED
HOMINY	x	x	CREAMED, FRIED
CUCUMBERS	x	x	RAW, SALAD, PICKLED
DANDELION GREENS	x	x	BOILED, CREAMED
EGGPLANT	x	x	FRIED
GARLIC	x	x	USED FOR SEASONING
HERBS			USED FOR SEASONING
CHIVES	x	x	
DILL	x	x	
LAVENDER	x	x	SACHETS, MEDICINE
MINT	x	x	SEASONING, TEA
OREGANO		x	
PARSLEY	x	x	
ROSEMARY		x	
SAGE	x	x	
TARRAGON		x	
THYME		x	

Vegetables	Grams	Mom	Method of Preparation and Serving
HORSERADISH	X	X	RAW, CONDIMENTS
GREENS	X		BOILED, BUTTER AND VINEGAR
KALE	X	X	BOILED, BUTTERED
KOHLRABI		X	RAW, BOILED FOR SOUP
LETTUCE (EVERY KIND AVAILABLE FROM CATALOG)	X	X	RAW
ONIONS	X	X	RAW, BAKED, BOILED, CREAMED, FRIED, SCALLOPED
BERMUDA, WHITE	X	X	
MULTIPLIERS	X		
RED	X	X	
SCALLIONS	X	X	
YELLOW	X	X	
SHALLOTS		X	RAW, SAUTÉED, BAKED
PARSNIPS	X	X	BOILED, BROWNED, SOUPS
PEAS	X	X	BOILED, CREAMED, BUTTERED
SUGAR SNAP		X	RAW, STEAMED, SAUTÉED
PEPPERS GREEN, RED, YELLOW		X	RAW, FRIED, BAKED
POPCORN	X	X	POPPED
POTATOES (BAKING RUSSETS, EARLY REDS, SWEET, WHITE COBBLER)	X	X	BOILED, BAKED, FRIED, CREAMED
PUMPKIN	X	X	BOILED, MASHED FOR PIE
RADISHES	X	X	RAW
SPINACH		X	BOILED, STEAMED, BUTTERED, RAW
SQUASH (ACORN, BUTTERNUT, HUBBARD, SPAGHETTI, SUMMER—ZUCCHINI—TURBAN)		X	BAKED, FRIED, BOILED, BUTTERED
TOMATOES	X	X	RAW, BAKED, FRIED, STEWED, JUICED
CHERRY		X	
RED	X	X	
PEAR		X	
YELLOW	X	X	
TURNIPS, WHITE	X	X	BOILED, MASHED, SOUPS (EXCESS TURNIPS WERE CHOPPED AND FED TO THE COWS IN GRANDDAD'S ERA!)

Basic Cream Sauce for Vegetables

Both Grams and Mom creamed vegetables without a recipe. When asked, Mom replied, "Pour your cream over hot vegetables, thicken, season, and add a dollop of butter!" This recipe, also known as a basic thin white sauce or béchamel sauce, is my interpretation of the cream sauce that they used for vegetables. For those who can add a few calories without worrying about their weight, swirl another tablespoon of butter into the sauce at the end!

Melt butter in saucepan. Add flour after foam subsides; stir constantly and cook for 2 to 3 minutes, but do not brown. Off heat, whisk in hot milk all at once. Return to heat, stirring constantly, and cook 2 to 3 minutes longer.

Season with salt, peppers, and nutmeg; taste and correct seasoning according to personal preference. Swirl in butter, if desired, to finish sauce.

TO ASSEMBLE Add vegetables to cream sauce, then reheat until hot, but do not overcook! Taste and correct seasonings, and serve immediately.

2 TABLESPOONS BUTTER
2 TABLESPOONS FLOUR
2 CUPS MILK, BOILING
¼ TEASPOON SALT
½ TEASPOON WHITE PEPPER, FRESHLY GROUND
DASH CAYENNE PEPPER
¼ TEASPOON NUTMEG (OPTIONAL)
1 TABLESPOON BUTTER (OPTIONAL)

COOKED VEGETABLES, 4 TO 6 CUPS

VARIATIONS

Creamy Almond Sauce Stir ½ cup toasted sliced blanched almonds and ¼ teaspoon nutmeg into sauce before adding vegetables. Proceed according to recipe.

Creamy Cheddar Cheese Sauce Add ½ teaspoon dry mustard with seasonings. Blend in 1 cup grated sharp cheddar cheese before adding vegetables. Proceed according to recipe.

Creamy Mushroom Sauce Sauté 2 shallots (chopped) and ½ cup fresh mushrooms (sliced) in 2 tablespoons butter over high heat until cooked and liquid is evaporated. Season with ¼ teaspoon tarragon and ¼ teaspoon black pepper (freshly ground). Stir mixture into sauce just before adding other vegetables. Proceed according to recipe.

Creamy Parsley Sauce Stir ½ cup finely chopped parsley and ½ teaspoon paprika into sauce before adding vegetables. Proceed according to recipe.

MAKES 2 TO 2¼ CUPS; SERVES 6

ASPARAGUS

Surely asparagus is the first sign of spring. Dad cut off the first few short stubby spears from the bed west of the garden. His knowing smile signaled to me that he was looking forward to warm spring sunshine with the same eagerness he displayed for eating creamed asparagus.

Creamed asparagus was not the rest of the family's favorite vegetable. In fact, we pushed it aside when we could get by with it! However, now a convert, I always choose an asparagus dish at restaurants as well as at the greengrocer's.

At the market, I pick out asparagus with tightly closed heads on each spear. To store fresh asparagus: Cut about a half inch off the bottom of the stalks, stand them upright in two inches of cold water, invert a plastic bag over the top, and refrigerate until cooking time (overnight or up to three days). They magically refresh themselves.

TO COOK Peel asparagus from tips down to base of each stalk; cut off pithy bottom. Blanch, uncovered, in large skillet half filled with boiling salted water for about 3 to 4 minutes, or until just crunch tender. Do not overcook! Immediately plunge spears into cold water to prevent more cooking, drain well, and wrap in linen tea towel. This towel technique will keep the spears perfectly warm and not soggy for a few minutes until the sauce or final dinner preparations are done. If necessary, blanch asparagus ahead of time until barely tender or half done. Drain and wrap in tea towel. Five minutes before serving, place bundle, towel and all, in steamer or microwave and just reheat!

My favorite way to eat asparagus is simply dusted with freshly ground black pepper, undressed! My second choice is to dress it with melted butter. Dressed with *Mom's Shallot Vinaigrette* (page 297) is my third. But then I could go on and on about asparagus. See, I really am a convert!

DOUBLE SNAP BEANS

With great anticipation we watched the bean blossoms grow to a respectable size. We snapped them off long before they were mature according to the seed packet. Kentucky Wonder beans climbed up the strings that Dad strung between the poles along the rows. The baby beans—known as French *haricots verts* in the greengrocer's today—had skins slightly fuzzy from the leaves. I secretly snitched one or two, rubbed off the fuzz, and relished their essence of green bean.

There is a double snap in each fresh string bean. The first snap sound happens when the bean is picked, the second is when the end is snapped off just before cooking. If a garden is too far from your kitchen to experience the first snap, look for unblemished, slightly fuzzy, bright green, slim, uniform-size beans in your market.

TO COOK Wash beans, do not snap or cut off ends. Bring 8 to 10 quarts of cold water to a boil, add 2 teaspoons salt, and return to a boil. Drop beans, a handful at a time, into water. Cook uncovered until crunch tender or for about 2 minutes after water returns to a boil. Think warm-raw! Drain and immediately plunge into cold water to prevent further cooking and so they retain their color. Drain well, cut off stem end (leaving the tiny tip on the other end), and proceed with recipe. If necessary, cook beans ahead. Store in sealed plastic bag and refrigerate overnight.

Green beans are both versatile and universally liked. Mom liked buttered beans, Dad liked creamed beans (Mom says he just likes cream sauce!), and I like them every way.

Green Beans with Herbed Tomatoes

3 POUNDS GREEN BEANS, WASHED
2 TABLESPOONS OLIVE OIL
1 TABLESPOON BUTTER
1 LARGE CLOVE GARLIC, MINCED
1 LARGE TOMATO, PEELED, SEEDED, AND CHOPPED, OR 1 CAN OF PLUM TOMATOES (14½ OUNCES), DRAINED AND CHOPPED

1 TABLESPOON FRESH BASIL, CHOPPED
2 TABLESPOONS FRESH PARSLEY, CHOPPED
¼ TEASPOON SALT
PINCH SUGAR
½ TEASPOON BLACK PEPPER, FRESHLY GROUND

Cook beans—boiled—according to directions above. Reserve.

In skillet, heat oil and butter. Sauté garlic until soft. Do not brown. Add tomato, herbs, salt, sugar, and pepper; simmer 3 to 4 minutes. Taste and correct seasonings. Can be done ahead. Reserve until serving time.

Add reserved beans; shake pan to coat beans with tomato "sauce" and heat through. Serve immediately.

S E R V E S   6

Marcheta's
Green Beans

❖

**3 POUNDS GREEN BEANS,
   WASHED**
6 SLICES BACON
2 TABLESPOONS BUTTER
2 TABLESPOONS FLOUR
2 TEASPOONS SUGAR
1 CUP HOT CHICKEN BROTH
2 TEASPOONS CIDER VINEGAR
**BLACK PEPPER, FRESHLY
   GROUND**

After living in New York City for several years, I visited my college friend Marcheta Tate, who lives with her family on a veal farm in North Manchester, Indiana. One bright sunny morning, I followed her into their huge garden to pick green beans for supper. I explained to my good friend how I missed a garden, fresh air, and the simple pleasures of country living. With great anticipation of freshly picked beans, I was surprised when she said she needed to start cooking them right after dinner!

I suffered silently as I watched her fry bacon in the pressure cooker, stirred flour and sugar into the bacon drippings, added some water, and filled the cooker with the cut beans. After securing the lid, she cooked them for almost four hours! The results were a typical midwestern, soft, brownish bean dish with an interesting sweet-sour flavor.

After supper, I asked, "May I cook beans for tomorrow's dinner?" She replied, "I'd be delighted to have you in my kitchen!" After serving Marcheta and Roger beautiful green, crunch-tender beans, Roger exclaimed, "So this is what beans are supposed to taste like!"

This recipe has the same sweet-sour flavor, but the beans are green and crisp.

Cook beans—boiled—according to directions on page 188. Reserve.

In large skillet, fry bacon until crisp and brown. Remove bacon, and drain on paper towels. Discard excess fat, but do not wash skillet.

Melt butter in skillet. Stir in flour and cook 1 to 2 minutes, stirring constantly. Stir sugar into hot broth and whisk into skillet. Bring to a boil, stirring constantly; boil 1 minute.

Stir in vinegar, but do not boil. Season with pepper; taste and correct seasonings. Add reserved beans and reheat until hot, careful not to boil. Serve beans immediately, garnished with reserved crumbled bacon.

S E R V E S   6

BEETS AND BEET GREENS

Long before the beets themselves matured, Mom dressed the tender greens with either Dad's favorite hot bacon dressing or butter, or her choice, pepper and vinegar. If they had asked us kids about their taste as we endured them, we would have told our parents that beet tops were at the bottom of a popularity contest.

However, all of us devoured every last slice of those beautiful, dark red, cooked beet bulbs, topped with a hefty dollop of creamy yellow butter. The delicious memory of that sight makes me hungry for beets right now.

Buy beets with smooth, unblemished skins and crisp dark green leaves. Cut off the tops about two inches from the bulb. Soak the bulbs in cold water, while washing the greens in cool-warm water. Drain the greens well; store in a tightly sealed plastic bag.

Refrigerate the greens and reserve for salad, garnish, or cooking. With a vegetable brush, scrub beet bulbs, leaving the top two inches and root ends on.

TO COOK Place scrubbed beets in large saucepan filled with cold, unsalted water. Cover and bring to a boil. Reduce heat; simmer until tender. Here's the rub: about ½ to 1 hour for small, young ones; about 1 to 2 hours for older beets. Drain and plunge into cold running water. Cool until able to handle. Wearing rubber gloves, slip/rub off skins and cut off tops and roots; reserve.

You may also pressure-cook or microwave beets according to manufacturer's directions. Or to bake: Place washed beets in baking pan and bake in 350° oven until tender (about 1 to 2 hours, depending on size).

Country Beets with Beet Sauce

This sweet-sour snappy sauce adds up to a downright delicious dish.

Cook beets according to directions on page 190. Slice or dice beets as you prefer; reserve.

Melt butter and sauté onion until soft and translucent. Mix vinegar

3 POUNDS BEETS
3 TABLESPOONS BUTTER
½ CUP CHOPPED ONION
¼ CUP CIDER VINEGAR
2 TABLESPOONS SUGAR
1 ¼ CUPS WATER OR CANNED BEET JUICE
2 ½ TABLESPOONS CORNSTARCH
2 TABLESPOONS COLD WATER
½ TEASPOON BLACK PEPPER, FRESHLY GROUND, IF DESIRED

and sugar into water or beet juice. Pour mixture into onion and bring to a boil; boil 1 minute.

Mix cornstarch with cold water, then whisk into boiling liquid; boil 1 minute. Add reserved beets and simmer until heated through. Season to taste and serve immediately.

S E R V E S   6

Buttered Beets

Cook beets according to directions on page 190. Cut beets into ¼-inch dice; reserve.

Melt butter in skillet. Add onion and cook slowly until soft and translucent, 5 to 6 minutes. Toss reserved

3 POUNDS BEETS
4 TABLESPOONS BUTTER
**1 MEDIUM ONION, PEELED
AND DICED**
PINCH SALT
**½ TEASPOON BLACK PEPPER,
FRESHLY GROUND**
**1 TO 2 TABLESPOONS
CHOPPED PARSLEY**

beets with onion. Heat through.

Season to taste. Garnish with chopped parsley and serve immediately.

S E R V E S   6

Wilted Beet Greens

A close relative, Swiss chard, is a good substitute for beet greens in this recipe.

Place greens in large skillet with lid. Sprinkle water over tops, cover tightly, and steam until wilted, about 2 to 3 minutes. With chopsticks or tongs, stir and lift every so often. Drain off excess liquid and keep warm in colander.

In skillet, quickly brown butter, being careful not to burn it. Toss in greens. Season to taste with pepper and vinegar and serve immediately.

**WASHED BEET GREENS FROM
3 POUNDS OF BEETS**
1 TABLESPOON WATER
**3 TABLESPOONS BUTTER (OR
2 TABLESPOONS OLIVE OIL
AND 1 TABLESPOON
BUTTER)**
**1 TEASPOON BLACK PEPPER,
FRESHLY GROUND**
**1 TABLESPOON APPLE CIDER
VINEGAR**

NOTE Red wine vinegar, balsamic vinegar, or herbed vinegar are all good substitutes for the cider vinegar.

VARIATION
Hot Bacon Dressing Substitute 6 slices of bacon for butter. Fry until crisp and brown, then crumble bacon into drippings. Add 1 tablespoon vinegar and 2 teaspoons sugar; bring to a boil. Toss cooked beet greens in dressing, season, and serve according to recipe.

S E R V E S   6

TIGHT-BUDDED BROCCOLI

Handsome broccoli plants were not in Granddad's garden because the seeds were not yet available. Grams's old cookbooks had nary a mention of the colorful blue-green flowered heads. Fortunately for us, Dad planted ample amounts.

Buy small, budded, tight blue-green flowerets with firm tender stalks. I give broccoli the same storage treatment that I give asparagus. Remove the outer leaves, cut one inch off the bottom of the stems, stand them upright in two inches of cold water, invert a plastic bag over the top, and refrigerate until ready to cook.

TO COOK Boil 3 to 4 inches of water in bottom of steamer or saucepan with lid that will accommodate metal steamer or strainer. Holding broccoli upside down, peel stalks by inserting paring knife under skin at bottom of stalk; with down-ward motion, skin will easily pull off to floweret in one fell swoop. Separate head into flowerets and cut into uniform pieces. Slice stalks into bite sizes. Steam until crunch tender, one layer at a time, approximately 3 to 4 minutes for flowerets and 5 to 6 minutes for stalks. Immediately run under cold water to stop their cooking and then drain well. If necessary, cook broccoli ahead of time. Store in sealed plastic bag and refrigerate until needed.

If serving steamed broccoli naked is too crude for your palate, simply dress it with browned butter or lemon butter and trim it with black pepper, freshly ground. Of course, broccoli can be gussied up with every cream sauce imaginable, combined with any number of other vegetables, and woven into casseroles and soups.

Dad, 1960s

Broccoli with Broccoli Sauce

◆

Because this recipe is a hit with both the cook (it can be made ahead and reheated) and the diner (it is so tasty), make extra sauce. Seconds are a foregone conclusion!

Prepare broccoli and separate stalks from flowerets. Following directions on page 192, cook stalks for 9 to 10 minutes, or until completely soft when pierced with fork. Then cook flowerets and set them aside.

Puree stalks in food processor until coarsely chopped. Add butter through feeding tube and continue to puree until smooth. Season with peppers and nutmeg; taste and correct seasoning.

**2 TO 3 LARGE HEADS BROCCOLI
4 TO 6 TABLESPOONS SOFT BUTTER
1½ TEASPOONS BLACK PEPPER, FRESHLY GROUND
PINCH CAYENNE PEPPER
1 TEASPOON NUTMEG, FRESHLY GRATED**

This part of preparation can be done ahead. Cover sauce and flowerets and refrigerate for up to 12 hours or overnight.

TEN MINUTES BEFORE SERVING Reheat broccoli sauce in double boiler over boiling water until hot. Reheat flowerets in steamer, just until hot. Arrange flowerets around edges of warm platter and spoon hot sauce in center.

OR Arrange flowerets and sauce ahead of time on glass platter, cover with plastic wrap, and reserve. Microwave until hot, according to manufacturer's directions (about 2 to 3 minutes).

S E R V E S 6

BABY BRUSSELS SPROUTS

⬩

Like broccoli and cauliflower, brussels sprout seeds were not readily available, so Grams did not grow these "baby cabbages" with their hefty stalks. Brussels sprouts alway conjure up memories of dinner with roast goose, turkey, or duck—definitely something festive. And with good reason: They are late fall bloomers, just in time for the holiday season.

Look for firm, small, primary-green-colored, unspotted brussels sprouts. Store them in their containers or a plastic bag until cooking time.

TO COOK Peel off outer leaves from each sprout, rinse, and with paring knife cut cross in bottom. (They cook faster and keep on their leaves after this procedure.) Add brussels sprouts to 4 to 6 quarts of boiling salted water. Return to a boil, cook uncovered 5 to 6 minutes for barely tender sprouts or 7 to 8 minutes for crunch tender. Immediately run under cold water to prevent overcooking and drain well. If necessary, cook ahead of time. Store in sealed plastic bag and refrigerate.

OR TO STEAM Prepare brussels sprouts; cook in steamer until crunch tender, doubling boiling time. Immediately run under cold water to prevent overcooking and drain well.

Butter-Braised Brussels Sprouts

This is definitely my favorite brussels sprout recipe. It can be prepared ahead and simply popped into the oven thirty minutes before serving. My family obviously feels the same way I do, because I cook two 10-ounce containers (there are only four of us) per meal, and not one brussels sprout is left. Even if I made more, their fate would be the same.

⬩

2 QUARTS BRUSSELS SPROUTS OR 3 TEN-OUNCE CONTAINERS
4 TO 5 TABLESPOONS BUTTER OR OLIVE OIL
¼ TEASPOON BLACK PEPPER, FRESHLY GROUND
½ TEASPOON THYME OR SUMMER SAVORY

Preheat oven to 350°.

Prepare and cook brussels sprouts according to directions above. Cook until barely tender.

Melt butter in casserole or baking/serving dish; add pepper and thyme.

Arrange brussels sprouts on bottom of baking dish, heads up. Place buttered round of waxed paper or parchment paper directly over vegetables; cover. Can be done ahead to this point. Refrigerate for up to 24 hours.

Bake vegetables 30 to 45 minutes, or until vegetables are tender. Or heat vegetables and butter until sizzling on top of stove, then move to oven, and bake 20 minutes or until tender. (In case you need the oven space, reheat on top of the stove until tender.) Serve immediately.

S E R V E S 6

"SOME SORT OF" CABBAGE

Cabbage, the most economical and, in many cases, the only available source of a fresh green vegetable, was a staple winter item on the farm table. During the work on this book, whenever I queried Mom, "What vegetable did you eat with that meat?" she almost always answered, "Cabbage of some sort."

Had Grams purchased fresh green lettuce from Read's grocery, in Preston, it would have frozen on the way home. (Remember, she traveled via horse and buggy.) No matter, there were always firm, green, fresh cabbages from the garden at home: Unspoiled heads, snugly wrapped in newspaper, were stowed in a fifty-gallon crock vessel in the vegetable room of the basement. If you venture into the "cold storage" vegetable room during the winter, you will find luscious cabbages from Mom's garden stored in the same tried-and-true fashion.

When buying a cabbage, look for firm, tight-fitting, green leaves on the head. It should feel heavy for its size.

TO COOK Remove tough outer leaves, wash, and reserve for garnish. Quarter head, remove inner core, and slice into ½-inch slices, or chop according to each recipe. Arrange slices in single layer in steamer; steam approximately 5 minutes or until crunch tender. Run under cold water to prevent overcooking. Drain and proceed with recipe.

OR Prepare cabbage as directed above, then plunge into large nonaluminum pot of boiling salted water. Cook approximately 5 to 6 minutes or until crunch tender. Drain, run under cold water, re-drain, and proceed with recipe.

TO MICROWAVE Prepare cabbage for cooking as directed above. Microwave according to manufacturer's directions. Proceed with recipe.

When Grams cooked cabbage, she simply boiled it in a large pot of salted water until it was done! For extra flavor, she added a ham bone or a chunk of salt pork to the water before cooking the cabbage. To be sure, Grams slathered butter on top just before serving. The family helped themselves to the salt, pepper, and cider vinegar that had been placed in the center of the table.

Trim, core, and slice cabbage into ¼-inch slices.

In large nonaluminum saucepan, boil broth and 1 teaspoon butter. Add cabbage; cover and cook approximately 5 to 6 minutes or until

Buttered Cabbage

2 POUNDS CABBAGE
1 CUP CHICKEN BROTH
1 TEASPOON BUTTER

1 TABLESPOON BUTTER
SALT
BLACK PEPPER, FRESHLY GROUND

crunch tender. Remove cabbage to warm bowl.

Over high heat, reduce cooking liquid to 2 tablespoons. Swirl 1 tablespoon butter into reduction. Season to taste with salt and pepper. Dress cabbage with reduced pan juices and serve.

VARIATION
Grams's Creamed Cabbage Follow recipe above, adding ½ to 1 cup heavy cream to reduced cooking liquor. Bring to a boil; reduce until thickened. Return cabbage to pan and swirl in butter and seasonings. Cook 2 to 3 minutes longer, or until cabbage is coated with sauce, and serve.

S E R V E S   6

Buttered Cabbage with Peas

Trim, core, and slice cabbage into ¼-inch slices.

Prepare and cook cabbage according to directions on page 195, undercooking slightly. Reserve.

Blanch peas in boiling salted water for 1 minute. Run under cold water, drain, and reserve.

In large skillet, melt butter until foam subsides and gives off nutty

2 POUNDS CABBAGE
2 CUPS FRESHLY SHELLED PEAS (1¼ POUNDS), OR
1 TEN-OUNCE PACKAGE OF TINY TENDER PEAS (DEFROSTED)
5 TABLESPOONS BUTTER
PINCH SALT
½ TEASPOON BLACK PEPPER, FRESHLY GROUND
2 TABLESPOONS FRESH PARSLEY, FRESH MINT, THYME, OR SUMMER SAVORY, CHOPPED (OPTIONAL)

aroma. Add the drained vegetables; lightly toss until completely coated with butter.

Season with salt and pepper (and optional herbs, if desired) to taste. Line serving bowl with reserved cabbage leaves; fill with hot vegetables and serve.

S E R V E S   6

Belonging to a 4-H club meant giving project-demonstrations before an audience of peers and adult advisors. When I was about ten or eleven, my demonstration was "How to Make Scalloped Cabbage." My poor family tolerated multiple home practice sessions. They ate scalloped cabbage nearly every day for two weeks. My efforts were rewarded with a blue ribbon and my family received a welcome rest.

Don't worry, this easy recipe does not warrant weeks of practice on your part—I was just a perfectionist. Mom's instructions were: "Shred cabbage, wilt it, make a custard

> *"Scalloped Cabbage: ¹/₂ head of cabbage, (cook), 3 Tbls of butter, milk and cream, salt and pepper, 2 eggs."* Grams's Black Book

Cook cabbage per *Scalloped Cabbage* recipe (above). Replace eggs and milk with this sauce: Melt 3 tablespoons butter, add 3 tablespoons flour, and cook 2 to 3 minutes. Remove from heat, whisk in 2 cups hot half-and-half, return to heat, and cook 2 to 3 minutes longer, stirring constantly.

Season with ¼ teaspoon celery salt, ½ teaspoon black pepper, and

Scalloped Cabbage

❖

2 POUNDS CABBAGE
2 TABLESPOONS BUTTER
3 EGGS
Approximately 2 cups MILK, OR HALF-AND-HALF
¼ TEASPOON SALT
½ TEASPOON BLACK PEPPER, FRESHLY GROUND

Cheddar-Dressed Cabbage

❖

with eggs, milk, butter, salt, and pepper like you do for a custard pie. Bake at 350°."

Preheat oven to 350°.

Prepare and cook cabbage according to directions on page 195. Place cabbage in buttered 3-quart baking dish; dot top with 2 tablespoons butter.

Whisk eggs together with milk; season with salt and pepper. Pour mixture over cabbage. Add more milk or half-and-half if necessary to barely cover cabbage. Bake 35 to 45 minutes, or until knife inserted into center comes out clean.

VARIATIONS

1 Add ½ teaspoon caraway seeds along with salt and pepper.
2 Sprinkle ½ cup buttered bread crumbs or crushed potato chips over cabbage before baking; proceed according to recipe.

S E R V E S 6

¼ teaspoon nutmeg (freshly grated). Taste and correct seasonings. Arrange half of cabbage in prepared baking dish, pour half of sauce over, and top with ¼ cup shredded cheddar cheese. Repeat process, ending with ¼ cup cheese. Bake 25 to 30 minutes or until sauce bubbles and top is brown.

S E R V E S 6

Sweet-Smelling Sauerkraut

I clearly recall watching Grams, wearing a freshly ironed floral cotton house dress and matching apron, a hair net over her neatly finger-waved gray hair, as she bent over the wooden kraut cutter. The fragrance of Old English Lavender Toilet Water mingled with the smell of fresh cabbage. Grams shredded what seemed to me bushels and bushels of cabbage into a fifty-gallon crock, salting each layer as she worked. Due to the rather strong smell, later —when the cabbage fermented— the whole sauerkraut business was performed outside on the north side of the house. After using a wooden kraut-stamper to bruise each layer of cabbage, she covered the crock with a snug-fitting, hand-carved wooden lid that was weighted down by a heavy stone. Every so often, during the four-week curing process, Mom spooned out a bit of the half-done cabbage for a taste test. Oddly enough, it tasted much better than it smelled! When the fermentation was complete, the kraut was packed into sterilized quart jars and processed for twenty minutes in a hot water bath. These jars were added to the already groaning basement larder.

1 THREE-POUND HEAD CABBAGE (APPROXIMATELY 2½ POUNDS AFTER SHREDDING)
5 TO 6 TABLESPOONS KOSHER SALT (USE 2 TEASPOONS KOSHER SALT FOR EACH POUND OF SLAW—NOT CABBAGE BEFORE CORING)

"Shred cabbage on kraut cutter. Put cut cabbage in vessel to fit. Salt and stamp down each layer until full. Place clean cabbage leaves over top, weight down to ferment." (50 lbs cabbage = 1 lb coarse salt) Grams's Black Book

In my unbiased opinion, the flavor of homemade sauerkraut is unmatched by any processed commercial brand. You too can enjoy this taste. But keep those nosey homefolks out of the bowl to prevent exposure to the air during the fermentation process.

Trim, wash, and halve cabbage. Core and cut into wedges that will fit into food processor. Using light pressure, shred wedges with slicing blade.

Place layer of cabbage in bottom of clean 4-quart glass bowl. Sprinkle salt on top and continue to layer cabbage and salt until bowl is full. Mix well and press down firmly with potato masher or wooden spoon until drawn juices nearly cover cabbage. Cover with plastic wrap.

Fill gallon seal-lock plastic bag with cold water. Place full bag on top of cabbage. It should fit snugly against cabbage and sides of bowl to prevent exposure to air.

Set bowl aside on kitchen counter or tucked away in cabinet. Do not disturb for 4 weeks. After that, check for full-fermented flavor. It has a good crunch to the tooth, probably unlike any you've ever tasted before at this point, and yet it is reminiscent of store-bought sauerkraut. After 4 to 5 weeks' fermentation, freeze as directed below.

TO STORE Place sauerkraut in heavy-duty plastic pint bags or freezer containers and seal; freeze until ready to use. Can be kept frozen 2 to 3 months.

Defrost overnight in refrigerator or bring to a boil in saucepan on top of stove. Or microwave according to manufacturer's directions.

Use in the recipe for *Sauerkraut, Ribs, and Potatoes* (page 156), or as a side dish at a wiener roast.

MAKES 2 TO 2½ QUARTS

Fried Cabbage

❖

2 POUNDS CABBAGE
3 TABLESPOONS BUTTER
1 TABLESPOON OLIVE OIL
½ TO ¾ CUP HEAVY CREAM
1 TO 1½ TABLESPOONS
    APPLE CIDER VINEGAR
    (OPTIONAL)
¼ TEASPOON SALT
½ TEASPOON BLACK
    PEPPER, FRESHLY
    GROUND
2 TABLESPOONS CHOPPED
    PARSLEY

This German-influenced recipe is from Great-Great-Grandmother Broadwater. It was her custom to serve a large bowl of boiled potatoes as a companion dish because "folks mashed their potatoes on their plate and spooned this creamy cabbage on top, like gravy." I have substituted butter and olive oil for the bacon drippings. Grams used to fry the cabbage until it was very brown. She used "top milk" or heavy cream that thickened on its own when cooked. If desired, add ¼ teaspoonful of cornstarch to cold milk as a replacement for heavy cream.

Trim, core, and slice cabbage into ¼-inch slices.

Melt butter and oil in large skillet. Add slawed cabbage and stir-fry until tender and brown on edges; watch carefully. Add heavy cream; continue to cook until thickened. Add vinegar, if desired.

Season with salt and pepper; taste and correct seasoning. Garnish with parsley. Serve with boiled potatoes and roast pork.

SERVES 6

Red Cabbage with Apples

Traditionally, this dish accompanied a roast pork, mashed potatoes, and gravy, plus a green vegetable. However, it is simply delicious when featured as the main attraction for lunch. Serve it with crusty rye or French bread, and Vermont cheddar or Wisconsin longhorn cheese, topped off with a frosty glass of ice cold beer.

·································

Trim, wash, and slaw cabbage ¼ inch thick. Reserve.

In large skillet, fry bacon until crisp. Remove meat, drain on brown paper bag until cooled, crumble, and

2 POUNDS RED CABBAGE
2 SLICES BACON
2 TABLESPOONS BUTTER
2 TABLESPOONS SUGAR
1 LARGE ONION, CHOPPED
2 GREEN APPLES, PEELED, CORED, AND SLICED
1 TABLESPOON CIDER VINEGAR
½ CUP APPLE JUICE OR CIDER
¼ TEASPOON CARAWAY SEEDS
¼ TEASPOON SALT
½ TEASPOON BLACK PEPPER, FRESHLY GROUND

reserve. Discard excess fat, but do not wash pan. In same skillet, melt butter, stir in sugar, and cook 2 minutes.

Add onion. Cook over low heat until soft and translucent, 4 to 5 minutes. Add reserved cabbage and apples and stir-fry 3 to 4 minutes. Add vinegar, apple juice, caraway seeds, salt, and pepper.

Cover; cook over low heat 10 minutes or until cabbage is tender. Remove lid; raise heat. Continue to cook 10 to 15 minutes or until liquid is reduced to a glaze.

Serve hot or cold.

S E R V E S   6

BEJEWELED CARROTS

Dad thinned out the carrot row to allow the remaining carrots to mature, then wiped the dirt off the baby carrots onto his overalls. Almost magician-like, he appeared at the house with a handful of these tiny tender treasures. After cutting off the tops and scrubbing the little jewels, Mom parceled out the treat to us.

Late in fall we dug up the mature carrots with a pitchfork. After shaking off the dirt and cutting off the tops, we layered them between old newspapers in a crock. Their final storage place was of course the basement tank room.

Our family ate carrots from the smallest, slender baby size to large, fat, mature ones. Mom shredded, pared, cut, diced, cubed, sliced, boiled, mashed, buttered, stewed, creamed, candied, and baked them. Carrots are one of the most versatile vegetables in the garden. Whether carved into botanical or geometric shapes (then simply boiled and used for a garnish), or transformed and served anytime from the first course to dessert, they are without a doubt worth their weight in gold.

A freshly plucked carrot is a crisp, succulent, and sweet morsel. But if the closest garden is the grocery store, buy carrots with their tops still a fresh bright green.(I use the tops as garnish or in the compost heap.) If bagged carrots are all that is available, sneak a look where the bag is not colored orange to find out their color and relative smoothness—watch out for "whiskers."

TO COOK Peel carrots and cut off tops and root ends. Cut into odd-shaped ovals, slice, or chop according to recipe. Drop into boiling salted water and cook until crunch tender. (A carrot will give slight firm resistance inside when stuck with the point of a knife.) Drain in colander and immediately rinse with cold water to prevent overcooking. Drain again well and proceed according to recipe, or cook ahead and store well sealed in refrigerator for up to 24 hours.

Or to steam: When cooking several vegetables, place carrots in water at bottom of steamer and steam other vegetables on top. Reserve cooking water for soup stock or for cooking pasta or rice.

Being an inventive person, Mom presented ordinary vegetables in an extraordinary fashion. Mashed carrots were seasoned with "whatever I had on hand or felt like eating at that moment"! This recipe will entice even the most stubborn vegetable-hater to have a bite.

■■■■■■■■■■■■■■■■■■■■■■■■■■■■■■■■

Preheat oven to 350°.

Peel carrots, then leave whole or cut into chunks. Cook in boiling salted water until tender; drain well. Puree, batch by batch, in food processor until smooth. Or partially mash by hand and beat with electric mixer until smooth.

> *"Mash cooked carrots, add some onion, grated fine for flavor, season with salt and pepper to taste. Beat 2–3 eggs into carrots and add enough cream to just bind mixture. Pour into buttered 1 quart ring mold. Bake in oven until eggs are cooked. Unmold onto platter, fill the center with creamed peas and serve."* Mom

Baked Carrot Ring with Creamed Peas

◆

1½ TO 2 POUNDS CARROTS
2 EGGS, BEATEN
¼ CUP HALF-AND-HALF, OR MORE IF NECESSARY TO BIND
2 TABLESPOONS GRATED ONION
¼ TEASPOON SALT
½ TEASPOON BLACK PEPPER, FRESHLY GROUND

Mix eggs with half-and-half. Gradually beat egg mixture into carrots, adding more half-and-half if necessary. Mixture should be thick and hold its shape when mounded in spoon. Add onion and mix well.

Season with salt and pepper; taste and correct seasoning. Press into generously buttered 1-quart ring mold. Bake 30 to 40 minutes, or until top is brown and eggs are set. Remove from oven; place plate or platter on top of mold. Immediately invert with hefty jerk or shake. Fill enter with creamed peas (see page 186) and serve.

VARIATION

Carrot and Rutabaga Ring Rutabaga, otherwise known as yellow turnip, was one of the few vegetables Mom purchased from the grocery store. She and Dad tried to grow them, but the fertile soil and weather conditions were not favorable. Because we were not fond of turnips, Mom disguised them with carrots and this became a family favorite.

Cook and mash 1 pound carrots according to first part of recipe. Peel and cube 1 pound rutabaga; cook in boiling salted water until tender. Drain well. Puree in food processor, adding ½ tablespoon butter to each batch. Remove to large bowl. Add pureed carrots to rutabaga and mix well. Proceed according to recipe. Garnish with raw carrot curls just before serving.

S E R V E S   6

Shredded Carrot Ring Mold

As Mom's young "apprentice," grating or shredding the carrots for her was my job. I am ever-so-grateful for the food processor; no need for nicked knuckles nowadays.

■■■■■■■■■■■■■■■■■■■■■■■■■■■■■■

Preheat oven to 350°.

Generously butter 1-quart ring mold or baking dish.

Peel, wash, and cut carrots into lengths that will fit in food processor feeding tube, food mill, or hand grater, and shred.

Melt butter in skillet. Add onion; sauté 3 to 4 minutes, or until soft and translucent. Add carrots and water. Cover and cook, stirring every so often, for about 5 to 7 minutes, or until carrots are tender. If necessary, remove lid, raise heat, and reduce liquid. Set aside.

Beat egg with milk and add to carrot mixture; blend well. Melt butter and sauté bread crumbs until lightly browned; stir into carrot mixture. Add more milk if necessary to bind. Mixture should hold its shape when mounded in spoon. Season with celery salt, pepper, and thyme; taste and correct seasonings.

Press into prepared mold; bake 30 to 40 minutes, or until lightly browned on top and eggs are set.

Place plate or platter (large enough to hold it) on top of mold. Immediately invert with hefty jerk or shake. Fill center with buttered peas or broccoli flowerets and serve.

1½ TO 2 POUNDS CARROTS, SHREDDED (APPROXIMATELY 6 CUPS, FIRMLY PACKED)
3 TABLESPOONS BUTTER
1 MEDIUM ONION, MINCED (½ CUP)
APPROXIMATELY ½ CUP WATER
1 EGG
¼ CUP MILK
2 TABLESPOONS BUTTER
½ CUP WHOLE WHEAT BREAD CRUMBS
¼ TEASPOON CELERY SALT
½ TEASPOON BLACK PEPPER, FRESHLY GROUND
½ TEASPOON DRIED THYME

S E R V E S   6

Stolen Buttered Carrots

Like most farm youngsters, Joel and I played in a treehouse that Dad built for us in an old maple tree in the northwest grove. We imagined various episodes and happenings in normal childlike fashion. Together, we decided to weed out some baby carrots and cook them. While Joel decided which carrots were large enough to pull out, I quietly stole into the basement to scavenge around for a clean coffee tin and butter. After washing the carrots at the windmill—clearly away from Mom's watchful eye—we boiled them in a pound of butter over our campfire.

Seeing smoke curling up through the trees, Mom ran from the house to investigate. She found the two of us with our fingers in the tin, digging out lukewarm carrots with the butter dripping down our arms! She was aghast at our audacity! Needless to say, we neither built a fire nor filched another pound of butter after that.

CAULIFLOWER

Beautiful white heads of cauliflower flourished in Mom and Dad's garden with tender care and a watchful eye. Even though she cooked cauliflower for the family, Mom preferred eating it raw.

Buy cauliflower that is heavy for its size, with a tightly flowered white head. It should not be brown or crumbly, although certain varieties have a tinge of pale purple on the head.

TO COOK Trim off outer leaves, hollow out core, and cook whole, in large pot of boiling salted water. Cook 10 to 12 minutes or until crunch tender. There should be slight resistance when stuck with point of knife. Exact time depends on the size of head. Drain and plunge into cold water to prevent overcooking. Drain well and proceed according to recipe.

Cauliflower au Gratin

I f my family handed out prizes for best vegetable dish, surely this recipe would have a blue ribbon. No matter how much cauliflower I cook, the casserole is completely empty after the meal.

1 LARGE HEAD CAULIFLOWER, APPROXIMATELY 2 TO 2½ POUNDS

SAUCE

3 TABLESPOONS BUTTER
3 TABLESPOONS FLOUR
2½ CUPS HOT MILK
1 CUP SHREDDED CHEDDAR CHEESE, PLUS ¼ CUP SHREDDED SWISS CHEESE
¼ TEASPOON CAYENNE PEPPER
¼ TEASPOON WHITE PEPPER
½ TEASPOON DRY MUSTARD
¼ TEASPOON CELERY SALT
¼ CUP DRY BREAD CRUMBS

Preheat oven to 350°.

Butter baking/serving dish.

Trim and cook cauliflower according to directions above. Separate head into flowerets. Arrange in prepared baking dish.

TO MAKE SAUCE Melt butter in heavy saucepan. Add flour after foam subsides; stir constantly and cook for 2 to 3 minutes. Do not brown.

Off heat, add hot milk all at once, stirring constantly. Return to heat and cook 2 to 3 minutes longer. Stir in both cheeses; continue to cook until cheeses are melted and sauce is smooth.

Season with peppers, mustard, and celery salt; mix well. Taste and correct seasonings.

TO BAKE Pour sauce over cauliflower. Sprinkle bread crumbs on top. Bake 10 to 15 minutes, or until sauce bubbles and bread crumbs are brown.

S E R V E S   6

EYE-HIGH CORN

Luckily for my ancestors, the area of southern Minnesota where they farmed was covered with a topsoil rich and thick enough to produce corn that grew "as high as an elephant's eye!"

In August, the peak of the season, fresh sweet corn was served nearly every day until the family tired of eating it. At that point, much in the same way our forefathers preserved the precious golden gift of corn from the Indians, Grams sun-dried a portion of the flavor-rich nuggets to be eaten during the cold months ahead. The remaining corn was canned in quart jars that set the larder shelves ablaze with a bright yellow color.

Mom put up corn for the freezer as opposed to canning it like Grams. She simply blanched the ears in boiling water for about two minutes or until they turned color, cut off the kernels, packaged them in plastic bags, and stored the bags in the freezer.

Dad heightened our anticipation of eating the first-of-the season corn on the cob by announcing, "I believe the corn will be ready by tomorrow!"

Mysteriously, Mom boiled a large pot of water that was waiting for the just-picked corn that Dad brought in. By the time he washed up, the steaming golden yellow ears were on the table. We delved into the platter with great gusto.

No one will dispute the fact that the best corn is just-picked, only a few minutes from the field. It should be perfectly cooked—whether that means boiling, steaming, baking, or grilling—slathered with oodles of fresh creamery butter, and immediately eaten. However, do not despair, very few people have a nearby cornfield. In the market, look for ears with light, golden silks peeking out from the green, slightly moist husks, that have a tinge of fuzzy feeling about them. If a local farm stand is near you, casually ask the farmer when he picks the corn. Upon hearing the answer, arrive at the stand as close to picking time as possible. Once home, refrigerate the corn until dinner time and cook just before serving.

Corn
on the
Cob

✦

TO GRILL (SEASHORE OR BACK-YARD METHOD) Light grill; have ready clean bucket of saltwater from ocean. After pulling back husks from corn, remove silk, replace husks, and soak ears in water 10 to 15 minutes. Salted tap water will do just fine. Place ears directly on grill and cook until husks are brown but kernels are moist and succulent (approximately 15 to 20 minutes, depending on the heat of the fire).

To test: Pull back husks, cut kernel with point of knife. Juices should run clear, not cloudy. Remove immediately. Use pulled back husks to hold on to ear, slather with butter, and eat.

TO MICROWAVE Pull back husks and remove silk, then run tap water over "bare ear," replace husks, and wrap in paper towel. Microwave for 2 minutes, or according to manufacturer's directions. Allow 2 minutes' resting time before peeling and buttering.

TO BOIL Fill large enamel or stainless steel stockpot with cold water. Add 2 tablespoons sugar and splash of milk to water; bring to a boil. Add husked and desilked ears; cook approximately 3 to 5 minutes, or until tender and juice runs clear, not milky, when kernel is cut with point of knife.

OR Cover ears with cold, unsalted water and cook, covered, just until water boils; drain. Serve immediately with plenty of fresh unsalted butter.

Cut
Corn
and
Relatives

✦

Grams sat on a wooden kitchen chair with a large white enamel pan (originally used for washing clothes) secured between her knees to catch the golden kernels of corn. After each cob was expertly stripped of its corn with a small razor-sharp paring knife, she scraped off the remaining pulp with the back of the knife, thereby adding the "milk" and the hand-grated corn to the kernels. There are corn scrapers, strippers, and all sorts of gadgets to perform this task, but Grams's age-old technique is still the best.

"1 pint canned corn or grated fresh corn, 1/2 cup cream, 1 egg well beaten, 1 cup cracker crumbs. Put corn in dish, season with salt and sugar; add cream, egg and cracker crumbs and beat thoroughly. Lay chunks of butter over the top and bake 1/2 hour in hot oven."
Grams's Black Book

Baked Corn

Whenever available, use fresh corn scraped off the cob for this recipe. But the middle of the winter, frozen cut corn will substitute just fine. Be creative by adding one or a combination of vegetables (I use red, green, and hot peppers) to the dish. Or choose an herb bouquet that complements the meat on the menu.

━━━━━━━━━━━━━━━━━━━━━━━━━━━

Preheat oven to 350°.

Butter 1½-to-2 quart baking/serving dish.

Cut kernels from cob with sharp knife; scrape pulp and "milk" directly into bowl. Beat eggs with milk; season with sugar and pepper. Stir mixture into corn.

8 EARS FRESH CORN (ENOUGH FOR ABOUT 4 TO 5 CUPS OF KERNELS)
2 EGGS, BEATEN
1½ CUPS MILK
PINCH SUGAR
¼ TEASPOON BLACK PEPPER, FRESHLY GROUND
1½ CUPS SODA CRACKER CRUMBS (ABOUT 20 TO 24 CRACKERS, SMALL SQUARES)
1 TABLESPOON BUTTER, CUT INTO SMALL CUBES

Crumble soda crackers by hand. Or process with 3 to 4 pulses in food processor. Alternate layers of corn mixture with cracker crumbs, beginning with corn and ending with crumbs. Dot top with butter.

Bake uncovered, for 35 to 40 minutes, or until corn is tender, custard is set, and top is brown.

VARIATION
Cheese-Topped Corn Bake Add 2 cups shredded cheddar cheese (about 6 ounces). When layering corn and cracker crumbs, sprinkle cheese on top of corn. Proceed according to recipe.

S E R V E S   6

Dad with Knee-High Corn

Fried Corn

Grams and Mom used this recipe for fresh corn that was past its peak. Once tasted, you may prefer it to corn on the cob!

∙∙∙∙∙∙∙∙∙∙∙∙∙∙∙∙∙∙∙∙∙∙∙∙∙∙∙∙∙∙∙

Cut kernels from cob with sharp knife. Scrape pulp and "milk" directly into bowl; it should measure 4 to 5 cups.

Sauté bacon in large skillet until crisp. Remove and drain on brown paper bag or paper towels.

Heat butter with pan drippings. Sauté onion 2 to 3 minutes. Add

> "Cut corn off the cob, heat bacon and ham drippings, the size of an egg; when hot add corn and fry not too hard. Season with salt and pepper." Grams

8 EARS FRESH CORN
3 SLICES BACON
1 TABLESPOON BUTTER
1 SMALL ONION, CHOPPED (ABOUT ⅓ CUP)
PINCH SUGAR
PINCH SALT
½ TEASPOON BLACK PEPPER, FRESHLY GROUND
½ TEASPOON FRESH THYME (OPTIONAL)
1 TEASPOON FRESH CHOPPED BASIL (OPTIONAL)
2 TEASPOONS FRESH CHOPPED PARSLEY (OPTIONAL)

corn and continue to stir-fry 8 to 10 minutes, or until corn is tender. Season with sugar, salt, and pepper (and optional herbs, if desired); taste and correct seasonings.

Crumble bacon on top and serve.

VARIATIONS

Bean and Corn Sauté Add 1 cup fresh cut green beans (blanched 2 to 3 minutes) to onion; proceed according to recipe.

Creamed Corn Sauté Omit bacon. Melt 4 tablespoons butter; sauté corn 4 to 5 minutes. Pour 1 cup heavy cream over corn and continue to sauté, stirring constantly, until corn is tender and mixture is thickened (10 to 15 minutes). Season to taste according to recipe and serve.

Corn and Pepper Sauté Add 1 cup chopped green or red pepper to corn; proceed according to recipe.

Corn and Tomato Sauté Add 1 large tomato (peeled, seeded, and chopped) to onion, proceed according to recipe.

S E R V E S   6

Corn Fritters

Fritters made with either vegetables or fruit were a delicious alternative to an ordinary supper dish. Thin slices of cold baked ham or roast beef along with Wisconsin cheddar cheese were on the menu for those who wanted protein. Eschewing the meat, Dad and I generously poured hot maple syrup, *Old-Fashioned Griddle Cake Syrup* (page 36), or my favorite—sorghum syrup—over the fritters and polished off a platter full. (Sorghum is a rich-flavored syrup made from a grain, a cornlike grassy plant; the consistency and color of the rich-flavored sorghum syrup is similar to dark karo syrup.)

Show me a host of corn fritter recipes and I'll show you as many hostesses preparing them. Each recipe contains corn, milk, eggs, flour, and sugar and spices; "oysters" (see variation below) differ from fritters because the eggs are separated and the stiffly beaten whites are folded into the batter at the end of the ingredients list just before frying.

:::::::::::::::::::::::::::::::::

Cut kernels from cob with sharp knife. Scrape pulp and "milk" di-

8 EARS FRESH CORN
4 EGGS
1½ CUPS MILK
1½ CUPS FLOUR
1 TEASPOON BAKING POWDER
1 TABLESPOON SUGAR
¼ TEASPOON SALT
½ TEASPOON BLACK PEPPER, FRESHLY GROUND
¼ TEASPOON RED PEPPER FLAKES
½ TEASPOON WHITE PEPPER
¼ TEASPOON THYME
2 TO 4 TABLESPOONS CORN OIL

SERVES 6 (3 TO 4 DOZEN 3-INCH FRITTERS)

rectly into bowl; it should measure about 4 cups.

Beat eggs in large bowl. Add milk, flour, baking powder, sugar, salt, peppers, and thyme; mix well. Stir in corn.

Heat heavy griddle/skillet or electric fry pan until hot. Using 1 teaspoon of oil at a time, grease pan. Drop batter by tablespoonfuls onto griddle; fry approximately 1 minute on each side, or until golden brown. Transfer fritters to baking sheet and keep warm in low (250°) oven until all are fried.

VARIATION
Corn Oysters (or "Sham Oysters," as they were called in the *Inglenook Cook Book,* 1901): Separate eggs; beat egg yolks. Add milk, flour, sugar, salt, pepper, thyme, and corn (omitting baking powder). Mix well. Beat egg whites until stiff; fold into batter. Proceed to fry. Or increase oil to approximately 4 cups; preheat oil in electric skillet to 370° or until cube of white bread browns in 60 seconds. Drop batter by tablespoonfuls into hot oil. Deep-fry approximately 1 minute on each side or until evenly golden brown. Drain on brown paper lined baking sheet and keep warm in low (250°) oven until ready to serve.

Hull-Less
Hominy

❖

Field corn, primarily consumed by farmyard animals, was transformed into "people food" or hominy. The conversion method removed the outside hull and the black tip (seed germ) from the kernels. These "scrubbed" kernels were sun-dried whole, flaked, or ground into grits. However, both Grams and Mom processed quart jars of the plumped-up corn in a hot water bath and stored them with the other vegetables.

Do not worry, serving hominy is no trouble at all today because it is found in the ethnic food section of the grocery store. Simply open the can, drain, and rinse the white or pale yellow kernels. This down-home, creamy, stick-to-your-ribs recipe is a great side dish for pork chops or chicken.

2 ONE-POUND CANS HOMINY
3 TO 4 TABLESPOONS BUTTER
½ TO ¾ CUP HEAVY CREAM
½ TEASPOON SALT
½ TEASPOON BLACK PEPPER, FRESHLY GROUND
SNIPPED FRESH PARSLEY OR CHIVES

"Take 1½–2 gallons of water and 1 quart lye, bring to a boil. Add 1 gallon clean corn, boil 30 minutes, stirring every so often. Drain in colander. Wash and wash. Put corn back in kettle, cover with fresh water, boil and stir, draining off water 3–4 times. Fill kettle with fresh water, return corn and simmer all day. Rub off any remaining black ends." Grams's Black Book

Drain hominy in colander. Rinse well and drain completely. Melt butter in saucepan; add hominy and sauté 2 to 3 minutes. Pour cream over hominy. Continue to cook over moderate heat 5 to 10 minutes or

"Take a quart of hominy, add butter and heavy cream, salt and pepper. Cook until thick." Mom

until cream is thick and reduced. Season with salt and pepper; taste and correct.

Garnish top with parsley or chives and serve.

S E R V E S 6

Minnesota
Succotash

❖

One of my childhood favorite vegetable combinations was lima beans and corn marvelously married with top milk and butter. The rough sounding name, *succotash,* seems inappropriate for such a smooth creamy comfort food. John Mariani, in *The Dictionary of American Food and Drink,* reveals the root of succotash: "The term first made its appearance in print in 1751, an Americanism formed from the Narraganset Indian word misickquatash (and other Indian words, for example, sukquttahas and msakwitash) referring to various ingredients in a stew pot, and more specifically in the Narra-

3 TO 4 TABLESPOONS BUTTER
2 CUPS COOKED CORN AND 2
CUPS COOKED LIMA BEANS
(CAN BE FRESH COOKED; OR
1 TEN-OUNCE PACKAGE OF
EACH FROZEN, DEFROSTED,
AND DRAINED)
½ CUP HEAVY CREAM
¼ TEASPOON SALT
½ TEASPOON PEPPER

ganset, to an ear of corn." Hence, other recipes use green beans, tomatoes, onions, beef, or bacon.

Melt butter in medium saucepan. Add corn and lima beans; sauté 3 to 4 minutes. Pour cream over vegetables; bring to a boil. Reduce heat and simmer 6 to 8 minutes, or until cream is thick and reduced. Season with salt and pepper; taste and correct seasoning.

Serve with cubed steak or fried ham slice.

VARIATIONS

1   Add 1 cup chopped onion to butter and sauté until soft and translucent. Continue according to recipe.
2   Add 1 cup chopped onion to butter and sauté 3 to 4 minutes. Add ½ cup chopped, peeled, and seeded tomato to corn and beans. Add pinch of sugar and cayenne pepper to seasonings. Proceed according to recipe.

"Take cooked equal amounts of cooked corn and lima beans, pour cream on top and thicken. Season with salt and pepper." Mom

S E R V E S   6

GARDEN GREENS

When the first little sprigs of green dandelions poked their heads through the ground, Grams's nimble fingers plucked them up and tenderly washed them for dinner. Truly warm weather was on its way and she craved fresh greens. We ate fresh lettuce year-round, but, unfortunately for us kids, Dad loved those tangy, tart, sharply notched dandelion leaves, too. Mom served them wilted in a creamy bacon dressing for dinner. Dreading this dastardly dish, I wished there was a hungry dog under the table to feed.

Ironically enough, each spring I now look for these tasty bitter greens at the greengrocer's to tantalize sluggish winter tastebuds.

HORSERADISH GREENS

Grams greeted pale young horseradish greens with the same glee that she bestowed on the first dandelion shoots. Luckily for us, Mom had no desire to cook or eat them! I mention this easy preparation for those die-hard lovers of greens and for nostalgic reasons: Simply boil the horseradish greens in salted water five to ten minutes or until just tender; drain well. Proceed according to the basic beet-tops recipe on page 191.

Dandelion
Greens

Wash greens, dry, and reserve.

In stainless steel or enamel skillet, fry bacon until crisp. Remove bacon; drain on brown paper bag or towels and reserve. Stir flour into pan drippings, adding a bit of butter if necessary; cook until brown.

Whisk in water, stirring constantly; boil 3 to 4 minutes. Add sugar, vinegar, salt, and pepper; taste and correct seasonings. Add cream, as needed, to dress greens.

2 QUARTS DANDELION GREENS
3 SLICES BACON
1 TABLESPOON FLOUR
1 CUP HOT WATER
1 TABLESPOON SUGAR
1½ TEASPOONS CIDER VINEGAR
¼ TEASPOON SALT
¼ TEASPOON BLACK PEPPER, FRESHLY GROUND
¼ TO ½ CUP HEAVY CREAM

Stir in greens and cook 4 to 5 minutes or until wilted. Taste and correct seasonings.

Crumble reserved bacon and sprinkle on top. Serve with fried chicken and boiled or mashed potatoes. Or garnish the top, if you like, with 2 hard-boiled eggs, chopped; serve over toast.

S E R V E S 6

EGGPLANT

❖

If I judged one vegetable to be the beauty queen of the garden, a purple eggplant would be crowned. The brilliant deep blue-red "eggs," hanging on a stalk underneath a big green leaf, brings spectacular contrast to the whole garden scene. We all took delight in watching the baby eggs grow into magnificent regal globes.

Look for an umblemished, smooth-firm, even-colored skin. It should feel slightly heavy for its size when lifted. A greengrocer friend told me to look for an oval-shaped indent at the bottom. Supposedly it is a female plant, with fewer and smaller seeds. Beware, this guideline may start a hilarious discussion over the greengrocer's counter with a fellow food lover.

Some recipes call for the eggplant to be peeled, others do not. Salting the flesh and letting it sit extracts excess moisture and any bitterness. Then, after patting the slices dry, they absorb less fat during cooking. Neither Mom nor Grams peeled off the skin, they simply rinsed off the dirt, then thinly sliced and salted the eggplant.

Fried Eggplant

❖

1 LARGE EGGPLANT (1 TO 2 POUNDS)
1 TO 2 TABLESPOONS SALT
½ CUP FLOUR
¼ TEASPOON BLACK PEPPER, FRESHLY GROUND
2 EGGS, BEATEN
3 TABLESPOONS MILK
1 CUP CRACKER CRUMBS, FINELY CRUSHED (20 TO 24 SODA CRACKERS)
5 TO 6 TABLESPOONS VEGETABLE OIL OR LARD AND BUTTER

Wash eggplant and cut off stem. Slice into ¼-inch slices. Sprinkle each slice with salt, place in colander, and weight down with plate. Let stand 20 to 30 minutes; Wipe off salt and pat dry with paper towels.

In small bowl, season flour with pepper. In another small bowl, beat eggs with milk. Crush crackers with hands or roll in plastic bag with rolling pin; place in shallow bowl or plate.

Heat oil in skillet until hot. Dust eggplant with flour, dip in egg-milk mixture, and roll in cracker crumbs. Fry until golden brown on both sides, then drain on brown paper bag.

Serve immediately with roast chicken. Or with salad, bread, and cheese for supper.

VARIATIONS

1 Add 1 teaspoon dried basil or thyme to cracker crumbs. Proceed according to recipe.

2 Omit flour; instead, roll slices in 1 cup finely grated Parmesan cheese, egg, and cracker crumbs. Sauté 2 whole garlic cloves in olive oil until brown, remove with slotted spoon, and proceed according to recipe.

> *"Slice eggplant, place in bowl, cover with salted water. Weight down and let stand for a while. When ready to fry, drain, pat dry with towel, dip in flour, then egg and milk and roll in cracker crumbs. Fry until done."* Mom

S E R V E S   6

ONIONS IN A PETUNIA PATCH

✦

". . . a lonely little petunia in an onion patch, an onion patch, an onion patch." We hummed this tune as we planted the onions. Down-to-earth, easy to grow and store, these root vegetables were as basic to food from the farm as eggs, butter, and cream. Starting as a base for soup, onions wind their way through the entire meal hidden, obvious, alone, together, dressed, and undressed in almost every dish except dessert.

At the edge of Grams's garden grew a bed of old-fashioned green onions, called multipliers. The perennial, green, scallion-like onion clumps flourished, bloomed, and seeded themselves every year. Grams and Granddad partook of them raw, ate them with bread and butter as a sandwich, made relish, tossed them in salads, or used some for seasoning.

Early spring—as soon as the frost was out of the ground—we planted rows and rows of onion sets, hoping the fresh rain would soak deep into the soil to ensure sweet and mild onions. In addition to moisture, the length of the growing season also determines the quality and size of each year's onion crop.

Yellow onions have dry and relatively thick, light brown skins that allow them to be stored for a longer period of time than most of their relatives. For this reason, they are the most readily available at the market. They are delicious baked, boiled, creamed, fried, scalloped, steamed, stewed, or just sliced.

Bermuda onions differ from yellow onions by having a thinner skin and creamy white-colored centers. They taste great raw, sliced on a juicy hamburger, or in almost any sandwich or salad. I learned this garnish trick from a French fellow we all know and love, Jacques Pépin: He suggests keeping chopped onions white by thoroughly rinsing them under cold running water, draining well in a stainless steel or plastic strainer, wringing dry in a tea towel, and storing in the refrigerator until ready to use. The water washes off the onion juices that turn black (oxidize) when exposed to the air.

Unfortunately, red onions lose their bright color when cooked, but do not despair: Raw, purple, paper-thin slices are marvelous in salads and on sandwiches.

Thin sweet scallions on homemade buttered bread comprised one of my all-time favorite school lunch sandwiches. Look for perky, slender, and unblemished greens atop the small white bulbs. If the green stalk is thick, it will be tough and have a strong flavor.

Grams's garden lacked shallots, those marvelous small melt-in-your-mouth sweethearts of the onion family. Luckily, Mom and Dad grew them.

Every gardener should grow at least one form of onion, whether it is a tiny chive plant in a pot on the windowsill or an acre of large Bermuda onions. If you haven't laid eyes on a field of blooming onions, try to imagine each blue-gray-green stalk looming above a bulb, topped with a round purple blossom. A chive plant grows in every flowerbox on my deck, ready to be snipped each spring as soon as the sun awakens them from their winter nap. I allow one plant to bloom, giving me the loveliest purple posies.

Buy onions that have dry smooth skins with no signs of green sprouting from the top. If they are bagged, sniff and carefully inspect all sides for any telltale signs of spoilage. Once home, remove the onions from the plastic bag. Store onions in an open basket in a cool, dry, dark place.

Peel onions from the top, leaving the root end intact because that is where the strongest juices are. If the onion is big, cut the unpeeled onion in half lengthwise (through root and all), remove the skin with the tip of a knife or fingernail, lay flat, and cut the side of the onion on a cutting board. Slice or mince, while firmly holding the root end to steady the onion. Wearing glasses helps to keep the strong onion vapors from your tear ducts.

Cutting-
Edge
Onions

❖

After "putting an edge" on her paring knife by pulling it across the rough bottom of a teacup, Grams carefully sliced a couple of onions to "fry up." If cholesterol is not a problem, use leaf lard (fat from around the pork kidneys) with a tad of butter to re-create the authentic version. The flavor is incomparable.

She often served this honest dish with steak or hamburgers. However, high honors go to these onions when they are served heaped on top of a crusty roll, and sprinkled with Parmesan cheese for lunch.

▪▪▪▪▪▪▪▪▪▪▪▪▪▪▪▪▪▪▪▪▪▪▪▪▪

6 MEDIUM YELLOW ONIONS, SLICED
1 TABLESPOON BUTTER
3 TABLESPOONS VEGETABLE OIL
3 TABLESPOONS FLOUR
2 TABLESPOONS CIDER VINEGAR
1 TEASPOON SALT
1 TEASPOON BLACK PEPPER, FRESHLY GROUND

Peel and thinly slice onions. Over medium heat, melt butter and oil in large skillet that has lid. Add sliced onions; sauté until soft and translucent, stirring frequently, about 10 minutes.

Sprinkle flour over onions; mix well. Add vinegar; mix well and cook, partially covered, approximately 10 minutes, or until onions are brown. Season with salt and pepper; taste and correct seasoning.

Serve as side dish or as main dish.

S E R V E S   6

Upon entering Grams's back porch in Preston, I was greeted by the aroma of her Old English Lavender hand soap blended with freshly cut onion. The unpeeled onions were stored in a basket on the cool floor while the cut side of a half-peeled onion was resting on a small salad plate, ready to be added to anything.

Christmas and New Year's Day dinner would not be the same without baked onions. Of course we ate them other times of the year, but Grams's glass dish filled with onions and cream were symbols of our celebrations.

Use onions of any size you have on hand: A uniform size facilitates the baking process; small ones are just as tasty as the large ones.

Preheat oven to 350°.

Peel onions and cut X in root end of each one. Cook onions in boiling salted water for 10 minutes or until tender but firm; drain well. Arrange them root end down in buttered glass or enamel baking/serving dish large enough to hold onions in one layer. Dot top of each onion with 1 teaspoon butter.

Bring cream to a boil on top of stove; pour over onions. Season onions with salt and peppers. Sprinkle bread crumbs, then paprika, over onions. Bake approximately 30 minutes, or until all bubbly and brown.

VARIATIONS
Herb-Topped Baked Onions

Nostalgic Baked Onions

**6 UNIFORM MEDIUM-LARGE
YELLOW OR WHITE ONIONS
(OR 12 SMALL-MEDIUM)
2 TABLESPOONS BUTTER
½ CUP HEAVY CREAM
PINCH SALT
¼ TEASPOON BLACK PEPPER,
FRESHLY GROUND
PINCH CAYENNE PEPPER
½ CUP BUTTERED BREAD
CRUMBS
DASH PAPRIKA**

Add ½ cup chopped fresh green herbs (parsley, thyme, savory, rosemary, etc.) to bread crumbs. Omit paprika; proceed according to recipe. *Mom's Cheddar-Baked Holiday Onions* Prepare onions according to recipe. Omit butter and heavy cream. Meanwhile, melt 4 tablespoons butter and 4 tablespoons flour in saucepan. Cook for 3 minutes but do not brown. Remove from heat; add 2 cups boiling milk and beat until smooth. Return to heat and cook 2 minutes longer, stirring constantly. Remove from heat; beat in 1 teaspoon Dijon mustard, ½ teaspoon black pepper (freshly ground), dash cayenne pepper, ¼ teaspoon celery salt, and 1 cup shredded cheddar cheese. Taste and correct seasonings. Pour sauce over onions. Bake according to recipe.

S E R V E S   6

"*Onions are delicate and delicious cooked thus: Cover 6 large ones with boiling water; boil 10 minutes, drain and cover again with boiling water; add ½ teaspoonful of salt and boil till tender but firm. Drain, put in a baking dish, sprinkle with salt, put a lump of butter on each and cover with rich milk; give a hearty sprinkling with bread crumbs and bake till a light brown. The milk can be heated before put in the baker, requiring less heat in the baker than if put in cold.*" Inglenook Cook Book, 1901

French-Fried Onion Rings

When Mom brought a platter heaped high with salted French-fried onion rings, we all grabbed as many as we dared.

After filling the high-sided, black cast-iron skillet with lard, Grams French-fried the onion rings. Mom continued in the same fashion until she received a deep-fat fryer as a gift. A thermostat controlled the heat, making the whole process easier. I use an electric skillet or wok filled with vegetable or safflower oil for deep frying.

We placed several layers of newspaper on a baking sheet and topped them with a brown paper bag to absorb the grease. I carry on the same tradition today.

■■■■■■■■■■■■■■■■■■■■■■■■■■■■■

4 LARGE SWEET ONIONS
2 CUPS MILK
4 TO 6 CUPS VEGETABLE OIL
½ TO ¾ CUP FLOUR
1 TEASPOON SALT
¼ TEASPOON NUTMEG, FRESHLY GRATED

Preheat fryer to 370°.

Line baking sheet with newspaper and top with brown paper bag.

Peel onions and cut into ¼-inch slices; separate into rings and place in shallow glass dish. Pour milk over onions and soak for 30 minutes, turning once or twice.

Heat oil in deep skillet or wok (until a cube of white bread browns in 60 seconds), or electric fryer. Season flour with salt and nutmeg; dip onions into mixture, coating well.

Deep-fry rings, several at a time, until golden on both sides. Drain on prepared baking sheet. Place in warm oven while frying rest. Sprinkle with salt; serve immediately.

VARIATION
Batter-Fried Onion Rings Mix ½ cup flour, ¼ teaspoon salt, ½ teaspoon baking powder, 1 lightly beaten egg, 2 tablespoons vegetable oil, and ¼ cup milk together. Dip onions into batter and deep-fry according to recipe.

S E R V E S   6

> *"Peel and cut onions in ¼" slices and separate into circles. Salt and pepper; dip into milk, then into flour or bread crumbs. Fry in pre-heated fat until golden brown; 4–6 minutes. Shake onto sheet of brown paper to absorb any fat." Inglenook Cook Book, 1911*

Gussied-Up
Onions

Typical of farm cooking, every vegetable gets scalloped at one time or another. Mom said, "Sometimes you gussied up whatever you had, just to make do!"

▪▪▪▪▪▪▪▪▪▪▪▪▪▪▪▪▪▪▪▪▪▪▪▪▪▪

Preheat oven to 350°.

Peel and slice onions. Drop into boiling salted water for 5 to 7 minutes. Drain well, pat dry, and reserve.

Sprinkle layer of cracker crumbs on bottom of buttered 9-by-13-inch baking/serving dish. Melt butter and reserve.

Place layer of onions on top of crumbs, drizzle top with 1 to 2 tablespoons melted butter, and season with pepper. Continue to layer, ending with crumbs.

**6 MEDIUM-LARGE ONIONS
(ABOUT 2½ QUARTS)
1 QUART CRUSHED SODA
CRACKERS
8 TABLESPOONS BUTTER
½ TO 1 TEASPOON BLACK
PEPPER, FRESHLY GROUND
2 CUPS HALF-AND-HALF**

S E R V E S   6

"Parboil 12 sliced onions. Prepare cracker crumbs or bread crumbs enough to make a layer of crumbs and a layer of onions, putting crumbs first, and on the top adding butter, salt and pepper to season. And last pour over 1 pint of milk and bake." Inglenook Cook Book, 1901

Pour half-and-half over whole affair. Bake for 35 to 40 minutes, or until onions are tender, bubbly, and brown.

SNOWBANK PARSNIPS

Because parsnips grow best in loose sandy soil, our fertile black Minnesota earth did not produce blue-ribbon specimens. Nevertheless, Mom liked to serve them, so Dad planted parsnips at the edge of the garden along with the radish seeds in the same row. By the time the parsnips were mature, the radishes were long since eaten.

Parsnips have a long growing season, so they were left in the ground at least until after a good hard frost, sometimes even until spring. There is a special flavor, along with a degree of satisfaction, derived from eating parsnips freshly dug out from under a snowbank.

Buy uniform-sized, unblemished, and relatively smooth-skinned parsnips. A first cousin to a carrot, they can be prepared in the same manner as carrots and/or in tandem with them. (See pages 201–203.) But their own unique flavor sets them apart. Mashed parsnips impart a sweet flavor to plain old mashed potatoes, and no self-respecting country cook would even think of making soup without at least one or two parsnips in the pot.

Browned Parsnips

This grandmother-classic preparation of parsnips was unrecorded in *Grams's Black Book,* but re-created by memory because of its simplicity. The result is a truly delicious dish.

Peel parsnips and halve lengthwise. Cook in boiling salted water 5 to 8 minutes or until barely tender; drain well.

1½ POUNDS PARSNIPS
½ CUP FLOUR
¼ TEASPOON BLACK PEPPER,
FRESHLY GROUND
4 TO 5 TABLESPOONS BUTTER

Season flour with pepper. Roll parsnips in flour. Melt butter in large skillet over medium heat; add parsnips and fry until brown on both sides. Serve immediately.

VARIATION
Replace flour with finely rolled cracker crumbs. Proceed according to recipe.

S E R V E S   6

Parsnips, Carrots, and New Peas

This friendly combination suits a holiday dinner just fine. It's decorative, delicious, and done ahead (most of the work).

Preheat oven to 350°.

Trim ends of vegetables. Wash carrots and parsnips; leave whole.

Melt butter in large casserole fitted with a lid. Sauté vegetables uncovered until coated with flavor seal. Add sugar; cook 2 minutes longer to glaze.

Add enough broth to cover bottom of casserole. Cover with lid and bring to a boil. Braise in oven for 20 to 25 minutes, or until vegetables are barely tender to point of knife. Remove vegetables from casserole to baking/serving dish.

Over high heat, reduce braising liquid to thick syrup. Pour reduction over vegetables and reserve. This dish can be done ahead to this point; refrigerate. (A few hours before serving, remove dish from refrigera-

6 MEDIUM CARROTS, PEELED
6 MEDIUM PARSNIPS, PEELED
2 TO 3 TABLESPOONS BUTTER
PINCH SUGAR
¼ TO ½ CUP CHICKEN BROTH

1 TEN-OUNCE BOX TINY
  GREEN PEAS
2 TABLESPOONS BUTTER

tor to bring to room temperature.)

Preheat oven to 375°.

Return vegetables to oven (now 375°), cover, and bake approximately 15 to 20 minutes, or until hot.

Meanwhile, plunge peas into large pot of boiling, salted water. After they rise to top, drain and immediately plunge into cold water to prevent overcooking. Drain well.

Melt butter in skillet; add peas. When ready to serve, cover skillet and reheat 3 to 4 minutes. Arrange peas on top of hot carrots and parsnips. Serve.

TO MICROWAVE Place carrots and parsnips in glass serving dish that will fit in microwave. Reheat 2 to 3 minutes, or according to manufacturer's directions until hot. Cook peas according to recipe, arrange peas on top of carrots and parsnips, and reheat if necessary.

S E R V E S   6

"PITCHER" PEAS

Both Granddad and Dad prided themselves on planting peas and potatoes early enough to eat on the Fourth of July. This particular tradition has been kept alive throughout my lifetime.

We kids snitched a few preview peas before they were near the proper size. We were just checking to see if they were ready for dinner dishes. They are mighty good directly from the vine to the tummy.

Near Harmony, a few farmers contracted their land to Libby's canning company for growing peas. When the peas were ripe, they were picked and shelled right in the field. Truckloads of peas traveled directly to the processing plant, arriving within a few hours after harvesting. The vines were pitched by hand onto stacks that were later hauled away and used for cattle fodder. Joel, one of several sturdy teenage farmboys in the area, was a "Pea Pitcher." This exhausting summer job was grueling because, when acres and acres of ripe peas were ready, the crew worked around the clock to harvest the complete crop quickly.

Buy smooth, unblemished fresh green pods that are pregnant with peas and with a little top leaf that looks very perky. If dreary-looking peas are all that's available, I head for the freezer section and buy extra-fancy *petits pois,* or tiny peas that are sold in foil-wrapped boxes. This is one of only three vegetables that I purchase frozen. The other two are chopped spinach and baby lima beans. A word to the wise: Forget the directions on the side of the box. Simply defrost them and proceed according to the recipe.

TO COOK Fresh new green peas need only to be blanched in a large pot of boiling salted water. Drop by handfuls into hot water and, once they have risen to top—even before water boils—they are done. Drain and immediately plunge peas into cold water to prevent overcooking. Drain well and reserve for whatever final preparation.

PLANTING PEPPERS

Between the refrigerator and the chimney in our kitchen was a niche with a countertop, a shelf, and an open space for a stool, extra bags, or whatever. This continuously warm spot doubled as Mom's sprouting shed once a year. On or about April 1, Mom meticulously spread rich dirt onto a baking pan and sterilized it in the oven in preparation for planting seeds. She was ever-so-careful to measure just the right amount of water, dirt, and fertilizer in proportion to the seeds. Some seeds were sprouted in a damp tea towel and then planted, but the pepper seeds were planted directly into the dirt-filled seedling trays. We covered the soil with clean muslin material that was then dampened daily with water. The whole family marveled, once again, at the mystery of life, when little heads of the pepper plants poked up through the soil. They flourished under Mom's tender care. They were set in the sun during the middle of the day, rotated for even growth, and the whole shebang! Before you knew it, they grew into seedlings. The seedlings were set out in the garden to continue growing once the weather was moderate enough for the plants to survive.

It took as much patience as one could muster to leave the small green bells on the plant long enough to mature. The crisp, clean, green peppery taste of a fresh-from-the-vine pepper is unmatched by any store-bought pepper I have ever eaten.

We ate the first-of-the-season green peppers raw, cut into strips, and savored each bite until the last piece was gone. After we'd had our fill of plain raw ones, Mom added peppers to salads, fried them, made relish, and prepared them stuffed and baked.

When shopping for peppers, look for unblemished, firm, bright-colored globes. Each should be heavy for its size. Green peppers turn red as they ripen on the vine. This is the reason red peppers are sweeter and have a shorter storage life than green peppers. Store peppers in the vegetable compartment of the refrigerator and wait to wash them until just before eating or cooking.

Paige's Stuffed Peppers

Our family includes a vegetarian. This recipe is not only meatless, but it's delicious, too—even if you're not a vegetarian.

▪▪▪▪▪▪▪▪▪▪▪▪▪▪▪▪▪▪▪▪▪▪▪▪▪▪▪▪▪▪▪

Preheat oven to 350°.

Blanch peppers in boiling salted water for 3 minutes; drain. Trim off tops, core, and seed; invert to drain again. Reserve. Can be done ahead.

In large skillet, sauté croutons in oil until golden brown. Add garlic; sauté 2 to 3 minutes more. Stir in pine nuts, currants, parsley, and basil; mix well. Season with pepper.

6 MEDIUM GREEN PEPPERS
2 TO 2½ CUPS FRESH CROUTONS
¼ TO ½ CUP OLIVE OIL
2 LARGE CLOVES GARLIC, MINCED
½ CUP PINE NUTS
½ CUP CURRANTS
½ CUP CHOPPED FRESH PARSLEY
¼ CUP CHOPPED FRESH BASIL
¼ TO ½ TEASPOON BLACK PEPPER, FRESHLY GROUND
3 TO 4 TABLESPOONS WHITE WINE

ASSEMBLY
■ ■ ■

⅓ CUP CUBED MOZZARELLA
¼ CUP MELTED BUTTER

Taste and correct seasonings.

Moisten with enough wine until mixture holds its shape when mounded in spoon. Set off heat; cool slightly. This can be done ahead to this point. Refrigerate.

TO ASSEMBLE Toss cheese into mixture. Arrange peppers in buttered baking dish large enough to hold peppers in one layer. Fill each pepper with stuffing. Drizzle a bit of butter over top of each. Bake for 30 to 40 minutes, or until peppers are tender, yet hold their shape.

S E R V E S 6

SPINACH

✦

We kids put spinach in the same category as medicine: "It should be taken only when absolutely necessary!" Because Dad liked it fixed with a creamy sweet-sour dressing and Mom ate it wilted and seasoned with pure cider vinegar and black pepper, we were pushed to be members of the Clean-Plate Club though neither preparation was agreeable to us. Right then and there, I unashamedly vowed never to eat it again. Despite my well-intentioned vow, I now frequently prepare and enjoy eating all forms of spinach.

Look for loose, unpackaged, unblemished, dark green leaves. If packaged spinach is all that's available, I head straight for the freezer section and choose frozen chopped spinach for cooking. (I substitute romaine or escarole if the recipe needs fresh leaves.)

To wash fresh spinach, soak the leaves in lukewarm water to dislodge the sand, ten to fifteen minutes. Pick up the leaves from the water with your hands, shake off any excess water, dump the sandy water out, rinse the bowl, and refill with cool water. Allow the greens to soak as long and with as many changes as necessary, until the water is no longer sandy and the spinach is clean. It is a bothersome travail, and for me not worth the effort if you plan to cook and chop it afterwards. For a sandless salad, however, it is essential.

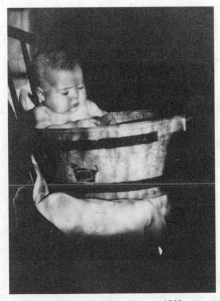

Baby Doreen Broadwater, 1923

Buttered
Spinach

The traditional farm method of boiling spinach in water is wasteful unless the water is saved for soup stock. However, wilting fresh spinach with a few drops of water in a tightly covered skillet happens as fast as a cat can wink its eye and it is palatable too. Aluminum pans and spinach are not good partners . . . the spinach becomes bitter (one reason most kids hate it). Use stainless steel or enameled cookware for the job.

∷∷∷∷∷∷∷∷∷∷∷∷∷∷∷∷∷∷∷∷∷∷∷∷∷

Wash fresh spinach according to directions on page 225 and pull tough stems from spinach. Leaving some water drops on leaves, place spinach in large stainless steel skillet. Set over high heat, cover, and cook/ steam/wilt for 1 to 2 minutes, or until spinach is limp. Stir every so often if necessary. Remove lid and evaporate excess moisture. Remove from heat.

Dress with butter. Season with pepper and nutmeg according to taste.

4 TO 6 POUNDS FRESH SPINACH, OR 2 TEN-OUNCE BOXES FROZEN (DEFROSTED AND WRUNG DRY IN TEA TOWEL)
2 TO 3 TABLESPOONS BUTTER
½ TEASPOON BLACK PEPPER, FRESHLY GROUND
¼ TEASPOON NUTMEG

VARIATIONS

Mom's Dressing Drizzle 1 to 2 tablespoons apple cider vinegar instead of butter over cooked spinach and serve.

Dad's Dressing Add 2 tablespoons apple cider vinegar, mixed with 2 heaping tablespoons sugar and 2 tablespoons cream, to butter. Stir into spinach and cook 2 to 3 minutes and serve.

Paige's Dressing Use frozen spinach, defrosted and wrung dry in towel. Increase butter to 8 tablespoons; brown, nearly burning butter in skillet. Add wrung-out spinach to butter. Stirring constantly, cook spinach 4 to 5 minutes over high heat. Season with 1 teaspoon black pepper (freshly ground) and 1 teaspoon freshly grated nutmeg.

Creamed Spinach Stir ¼ to ½ cup heavy cream into buttered wilted spinach. Stirring constantly, cook spinach 5 to 6 minutes over high heat, or until thickened. Butter and season according to recipe.

S E R V E S 6

SPUDS

◈

Every self-respecting farmer plants at least a few hills of potatoes in his garden. Both Granddad and Dad planted potatoes by Good Friday, anticipating creamed peas and new potatoes on July Fourth. They started by cutting out two or three eyes from last year's leftover potatoes. Continuing, Dad spaded a 6-to-8-inch deep hole every 18 inches along the row, and instructed us how to plant the potato "eye side up" in each dip. After which, we "hilled up" the eyes with dirt to keep the spuds underground until midsummer, and hoped for the best. (The plants need about twelve weeks of good growing weather for the little new potatoes to set on.) Every so often during the rest of the summer, we dug up a hill or two, if necessary, for the family to eat.

With a pitchfork in hand at summer's end, Dad dug up each mound of potatoes and shook off the excess dirt. We kids piled the spuds into open wooden crates that were carted back to the house and stored in the basement vegetable room. It seemed to me that we had enough potatoes for the whole community, but Dad reassured me, "We'll use them all before next year." He was always right!

I left out one very important addendum to the potato story. Without fail, one or two mice crawled into the crate of potatoes in the field and got transported to the basement by our own doing! Sooner or later, telltale signs were on the basement floor. If we

were lucky, we caught the mice before they bore a litter, but on more than one occasion, we fought the continuous battle with cheese-laden mousetraps. One winter's morning, a mouse crawled up into the coat closet under the stairs in the dining room. After seeking refuge behind the refrigerator in the kitchen, our breakfast scene became riotous. Both Dad and Joel, the macho-men with brooms in hand, tried to catch the little devil. Meanwhile, Judy (then a whopping 1½ years old) was totally amused by the commotion. Standing near the table, she merely stepped on its tail and caught the mouse.

Look for potatoes that are firm and heavy for their size, without any hint of green or a sprout. All-purpose potatoes are just what the name implies, all-purpose, but especially good for boiling. Generally, I buy baking potatoes, whether they are from Idaho, Maine, Minnesota, or Long Island. The best new potatoes are those freshly dug, but if the grocery store is your nearest potato source, again, look for shiny, unblemished thin-skinned little beauties. Store potatoes, out of plastic bags, in a cool, dry, dark, well-ventilated place.

We ate potatoes almost every day, in one form or another, at one of the three meals. They possess double goodness—good for you and good to eat. The only fattening part are the trimmings.

Baked Potatoes

❖

Every time I think of the best baked potato, I remember my early grade-school lunches. I trudged along the gravel country road to school on cold winter mornings with as large a potato as I could find tucked into my lunchbox. Upon my arrival, I poked the spud into the glowing coals of the black stove in the center of the room. By the time 12 noon arrived, the delightful aroma of charred baked potatoes permeated the room. My stomach was growling by the time we were excused for lunch.

To re-create that hard outer crust on baked potatoes, bake them about 1 hour in a very hot oven (475°). One word of caution, be sure to prick the skins a few times before baking. Otherwise the potatoes explode and the oven is a royal baked-on mess! Bake until soft in the middle and top with your favorite dressing.

Potato Skins

❖

The "craze" of serving potato skins at fast-food chains and other burger-type restaurants is a curious turn of events for us folks raised on the farm. We have relished eating potato skins ever since I can remember.

We scooped out and fork-mashed the insides and dressed them with pan gravy. The skins were set aside to dry off a bit while we ate the other food on our plates. Then we slathered them with butter, seasoned them with salt and pepper, and savored every little bite.

TO MAKE POTATO SKINS EN MASSE Bake as many potatoes as needed. Scoop out insides; reserve for mashing, ricing, or salad. Place skins on baking sheet. Sprinkle with freshly grated Parmesan cheese and Hungarian paprika or whatever strikes your fancy. Return dressed skins to 425° oven and bake until cheese melts. Great for after-school snacks!

Old-Fashioned Mashed Potatoes

◆

10 LARGE BOILING POTATOES
1 TABLESPOON SALT
6 TO 8 TABLESPOONS BUTTER
½ CUP MILK OR MORE

SALT
BLACK PEPPER, FRESHLY
** GROUND**
1 TABLESPOON BUTTER

For this farm favorite classic dish, be sure to add two or three extra potatoes "for the pot" because some of the most unlikely little people can consume big amounts.

- -

Peel and quarter potatoes. Place them in large pot; cover with cold water. Bring to a boil. Add salt and continue to cook, uncovered, until tender to point of knife. Cooking time will vary. Drain, reserving water for another use. While potatoes are still hot, rice in potato ricer set over large mixing bowl.

Meanwhile, melt butter in milk. Gradually add hot liquid while beating potatoes until creamy, light, and rather fluffy. Season according to taste. Spoon into warmed serving bowl. Dip back of serving spoon into hot water, shake off excess, and press an "indent" in center. Fill indent with butter and serve.

NOTE Simply riced potatoes are perfectly fine "as is" for both family and "company" dinners. Serve generous amounts of butter or gravy for the potato lovers.

VARIATIONS
"Dressy" Mashed Potatoes Season riced potatoes with ¼ teaspoon white pepper and ½ teaspoon nutmeg (freshly grated). (Salt is optional.) Beat 2 whole eggs plus 2 egg yolks and 2 tablespoons milk together until light and foamy. Grad-

ually add mixture while beating potatoes until well mixed and fluffy. Fill pastry bag fitted with large star tip, then pipe potatoes into serving-size portions onto greased baking sheet. Brush tops with melted butter and run under broiler or bake in 425° oven until light brown. Or, "plank" glazed ham or meat loaf with potatoes and brown as directed. *Potato Balls* Add 2 beaten egg yolks, ⅛ teaspoon cayenne pepper, and ⅛ teaspoon dry mustard to old-fashioned mashed potatoes; mix well. Cool slightly. Dust hands with flour and shape potatoes into 2-to-2½-inch balls. Brush potato balls with milk, roll in 1 to 2 cups fine dry bread crumbs, and place on greased baking sheet. Bake in 425° oven 6 to 8 minutes, or until hot and evenly brown. Serve immediately. *Potato Cakes* Add 2 well-beaten eggs to each 2 cups of cold old-fashioned mashed potatoes. Season with dash of salt, ¼ teaspoon black pepper (freshly ground), and ⅛ teaspoon freshly grated nutmeg. Mix well. Dust hands with flour, shape potatoes into "cakes," 1 inch thick and 2½ inches round. Roll in flour. Melt 2 to 3 tablespoons butter with 2 to 3 tablespoons vegetable oil in skillet; fry "cakes," turning carefully, until brown on both sides. These crisp on the outside and soft on the inside "cakes" were a family supper favorite dish.

S E R V E S   6

Fried Potatoes

In my kitchen equipment drawer is an old Calumet Baking Powder tin. One end is cut out and it measures about three inches in diameter and stands five to six inches high. It fits as comfortably in my hand as it did in Grams's. That tin chopped many boiling potatoes into small dice for frying in lard and butter in the by-now-famous black cast-iron skillet. Truthfully, I have yet to become deft at wielding this tin, so I use my trusty chef knife to cut the potatoes before frying. But I keep the tin "just-in-case" I master the technique.

According to any farm wife, fried potatoes are easy to prepare. To ensure crisp fried potatoes, drop raw potatoes immediately into cold water after cutting. Keep in cold water until just before frying.

▪▪▪▪▪▪▪▪▪▪▪▪▪▪▪▪▪▪▪▪▪▪▪▪▪▪▪▪▪▪▪▪

Pare potatoes and cut into uniform slices or dice; immediately drop into cold water. Reserve until ready to fry.

7 LARGE BAKING POTATOES
4 TO 5 TABLESPOONS BUTTER
2 TO 3 TABLESPOONS VEGETABLE OIL (MOM AND GRAMS USED LARD)
SALT
BLACK PEPPER, FRESHLY GROUND

Heat butter and oil in heavy cast-iron skillet until hot. After draining potatoes and patting dry with paper toweling, add them to hot skillet. Allow crust to form on bottom, turn over, and shake pan to seal potatoes. Lower heat and cover. Fry about 15 minutes, or until tender and dark brown. Remove cover for last 5 minutes of frying. Season to taste.

VARIATIONS

Lattice Fried Potatoes Cut potatoes with a corrugated slicer with a wavy edge by making one slice, rotating potato ½ turn, and slicing again. Make slices thin enough to form tiny holes in each slice. Drop in ice water and proceed according to recipe.

Grams's Fried Boiled Potatoes Grams used the old tin to cube boiled potatoes as they were frying. To re-create that recipe, cube boiled potatoes by hand. Replace raw potatoes with cubes and proceed according to recipe.

S E R V E S   6

French Fries

❖

The laborious part of making crisp French fries is cutting them. For easier cutting, slice each peeled potato in half, lengthwise. Place cut side down on a cutting board. With a sharp knife, slice each half into ¼-inch-thick slices. Again, lay the flat side of 3 or 4 slices on the board and cut ¼-inch-thick strips. Immediately drop into cold water. Continue until all the potatoes are cut and keep in the water until ready for frying.

Peel and cut potatoes into ¼-inch-thick French fries. Drop into cold water.

Heat oil to 330° in deep-fat fryer, wok, or skillet. It should be about 3 inches deep. Batch by batch, remove potatoes from water; pat completely dry with paper toweling. Dip slotted spoon into hot oil. With that spoon, slowly lower cut potatoes into hot oil. Fry 3 to 4 minutes, or until potatoes are soft and cooked, but not brown.

**6 LARGE BAKING POTATOES
1 TO 1 ½ QUARTS VEGETABLE
OIL**

Remove from oil and drain on brown paper bag–lined baking sheet. Reserve. They can be done ahead to this point. Set aside or refrigerate for up to 2 to 3 hours.

Just before serving, reheat oil to 400°. Repeat above procedure, this time frying potatoes 4 to 5 minutes, or until crispy brown.

Serve immediately. Salt if desired.

VARIATION
Potato Chips Thinly slice potatoes across grain on kraut cutter or with very sharp knife. Following procedure above, fry only once in 375° oil until light brown. Drain on paper bag, then lightly salt each batch while hot. When cool, place waxed paper between each lightly resalted layer and store in large earthenware crock. Tightly cover and keep in dry place.

S E R V E S   6

Scalloped Potatoes

A dish of scalloped potatoes is the most widely known, best-loved "potato casserole." It is no wonder that farm women created variations on the same theme, to free up their time for chores and obligations apart from cooking.

Before homogenization, top milk or cream on the milk pail became so thick that Mom used a knife to "cut" it off. It melted and soaked right into the sliced potatoes while they baked.

Not having top milk, I prepare scalloped potatoes in the same fashion as Julia Child's original Gratin Dauphinois. My family has been known to eat the leftovers, cold, in the middle of the night, with the refrigerator door left open. I suggest making a large batch.

:::::::::::::::::::::::::::::::::

Preheat oven to 350°.

Peel and thinly slice potatoes. (This may be done in food processor.) Place potatoes in large heavy saucepan. Pour cream and half-and-half over potatoes, adding more if necessary to nearly cover. Season with salt and pepper.

Over moderate heat, stirring every so often to keep them from sticking to bottom of pan, cook potatoes, uncovered, for 20 minutes,

8 TO 10 LARGE BAKING POTATOES
2 CUPS HEAVY CREAM
½ CUP HALF-AND-HALF
1 TEASPOON SALT
1 TEASPOON BLACK PEPPER, FRESHLY GROUND
2 TABLESPOONS BUTTER, CUT INTO SMALL PIECES

"Pare as many potatoes as you need. Slice them. Take a large pan and put in enough potatoes to cover the bottom. Sprinkle with salt, pepper and a little flour. Place another layer of potatoes, salt, pepper and flour and so on, until all the potatoes are in the pan. Cover with top milk and bake 'til done."
<u>Mom</u>

or until mixture starts to thicken. Pour hot potatoes into large, generously buttered baking/serving dish. Dot top with butter and bake approximately 45 minutes, or until potatoes are tender to point of fork, and top is brown.

Let stand 10 minutes before serving. This dish can be done ahead. Refrigerate, then reheat in oven until hot and bubbly.

VARIATIONS
Au Gratin Scalloped Potatoes Sprinkle ¾ to 1 cup shredded Swiss, cheddar, or American cheese over potatoes jut before baking. Proceed according to recipe.
Garlic Scalloped Potatoes Add 3 cloves garlic (chopped) to raw potatoes, either in au gratin or basic preparation. Proceed according to recipe.
Appetizer Garlic Scalloped Potatoes Follow *Garlic Scalloped Potatoes* recipe. Pour potatoes into two generously buttered jelly roll pans. Sprinkle ¾ cup shredded Swiss cheese over each pan of potatoes; top with ¼ cup grated Parmesan cheese (also for each pan). Reduce baking time to 20 to 25 minutes. Proceed according to recipe. Cool in pan, then cut into bite-sized pieces. Reheat at 350° for approximately 8 to 10 minutes. Garnish with parsley sprig and serve.

Peppered Scalloped Potatoes Stir ½ cup chopped green peppers, ¼ cup chopped red peppers, and 1 tablespoon chopped hot peppers (jalapeño) into hot potatoes just before baking. Proceed according to recipe.
Scalloped Potatoes with Ham or Hot Dogs Omit salt. Stir 2 cups baked/boiled ham or beef frankfurters, cut into ½-inch cubes, into hot potatoes just before baking. Proceed according to recipe.

S E R V E S   6

Boiled New Potatoes

❖

3 POUNDS NEW POTATOES
3 TO 4 TABLESPOONS MELTED BUTTER
SALT
BLACK PEPPER, FRESHLY GROUND

I t makes no difference if new potatoes are red or white, these tasty totters need only to have the dirt scrubbed off and then be boiled. Grocery-store new potatoes were "new" some time ago, making their skin thicker than the home-dug variety. Therefore, I peel a ring around the middle of the spuds to allow them to split their skins attractively while they are being cooked.

Wash and scrub potatoes, and peel ring around center of each. Drop into large pot of boiling salted water; cook 20 to 25 minutes, or until tender to point of fork. Drain well.

Serve as is or with butter. Season according to taste.

VARIATIONS
Browned New Potatoes In large skillet, melt 4 to 5 tablespoons butter with 2 tablespoons vegetable oil. Roll boiled potatoes into mixture, coating each one. Sauté over moderate heat, turning and/or shaking pan, until they are crisp and brown. Serve immediately. Season according to taste.
Minted New Potatoes Top *Browned New Potatoes* with ½ cup chopped fresh mint.
Parsleyed New Potatoes Top *Browned New Potatoes* with ½ cup chopped fresh parsley.

S E R V E S   6

Pommes à la Crowe

This recipe has been in our family for years; I coined the name after Grams died about fifteen years ago. Previously, we simply called them "shredded potatoes." Use *only* a solid vegetable shortening or lard for frying these potatoes, in order to obtain the end result of a crisp, dark, golden-brown outside crust and magically a soft, almost-creamy inside.

Peel potatoes; immediately drop in cold water until ready to shred. Reserve.

Heat shortening in large black cast-iron skillet until sizzling. Drain potatoes, then, using shredder blade, shred potatoes. Empty bowl immediately into skillet. Press potatoes flat; fry 6 to 8 minutes on one side, or until dark brown. Carefully lifting with 2 pancake turners, flip

**7 LARGE BAKING POTATOES
½ TO ¾ CUP SOLID
VEGETABLE SHORTENING
(GRAMS USED LARD)**

Arlone Aletta Crowe
(Soon to become Broadwater), 1912

"cake" over. If it seems impossible, cut in half and turn each half. Continue to fry until dark brown on other side. Should be crusty on outside, tender on inside.

Cut into wedges. Garnish with fresh watercress. Season according to personal taste at the table.

VARIATIONS

Potato Pancakes Add 2 beaten eggs, ½ teaspoon salt, and ½ teaspoon black pepper (freshly ground) to shredded potatoes. Reduce shortening to ¼ to ½ cup. Drop ¼ cup potatoes into hot skillet. Fry until crispy brown on both sides. Remove to brown paper bag–lined baking sheet. Keep hot in warm 300° oven while frying remaining cakes.

Potato Pancakes with Onion Add 1 grated medium onion (½ cup) to raw potatoes. Proceed according to *Potato Pancake* recipe.

S E R V E S 6

NO-TROUBLE SQUASH

The sweet aroma of acorn squash baking is reminiscent of a clear, beautiful crisp October Saturday afternoon. Because we had lots of trees around the house, raking leaves was the perfect task to "keep those kids out of trouble"! After sticking the squash into the oven, Mom joined us in the yard. She said she needed the exercise, but we thought it was to keep an eye on our progress.

Luckily, we don't need to wait until the leaves fall to prepare squash. Many varieties are available year-round at the grocery store, ready to be baked and dressed for dinner. Look for unblemished hard outer skins with colors that are characteristic for the variety you are choosing. Size is merely a matter of taste and necessity, because in a winter squash's case, small does not mean more tender or sweeter.

Baked Acorn Squash

Preheat oven to 350°.

Wash skins, halve squash lengthwise, and scoop out seeds. Place cut side up on baking sheet large enough to hold squash in one layer. Fill each center with 1 tablespoon butter. Bake for 1 hour, or until soft to point of fork.

Season according to personal preference.

3 LARGE ACORN SQUASH
6 TABLESPOONS BUTTER
SALT
BLACK PEPPER, FRESHLY
 GROUND

VARIATIONS
Bare Baked Squash Omit butter, bake "bare," season with pepper, and top with dollop of yogurt.
Sweet Baked Squash Add 1 tablespoon brown sugar, maple syrup, or honey to butter. Proceed according to recipe.

S E R V E S 6

Butternut
Squash
Moons

❖

Being a particular housekeeper, Mom washed all forty-eight windows from top to bottom, inside and out, before hanging the storm windows on the hooks secured to the outside window sashes. It goes without saying that the storm windows were also scrubbed shiny clean.

Frosty designs formed on the storm window as the temperature dropped, leaving the inside window clear and dry. In real ice-cold weather, these intricate natural "paintings" remained stuck to the outer window all day long but the air pocket between window and storm window was insulation from the cold.

When the time came to hang the storm windows, before the cold frosty wind blew in from the north, the color of the harvest moon was as rich yellow gold as the insides of a butternut squash.

Peel the butternut squash with a vegetable peeler. Slice the neck into

1 LARGE BUTTERNUT SQUASH (4 TO 5 POUNDS)
APPROXIMATELY ½ CUP FLOUR
½ TEASPOON DRIED THYME
PINCH SALT
¼ TEASPOON BLACK PEPPER, FRESHLY GROUND
3 TABLESPOONS VEGETABLE OIL
2 TABLESPOONS BUTTER

¼-inch-thick round slices. The "bulb" portion contains the seeds; scoop out the seeds and slice the outer portion into crescent moon shapes.

Peel, clean, and slice squash into moon shapes ¼ inch thick. Season flour with thyme, salt, and pepper. Roll squash in seasoned flour.

Heat oil and butter in large skillet until foam subsides. Add squash in one layer. Fry 4 to 5 minutes, or until brown on one side. Turn. Continue to fry until tender inside and crisp brown outside. Drain on brown paper bag–lined baking sheet. Keep warm in 300° oven until all are fried.

Top with maple syrup or powdered sugar if desired, or serve savory as is.

S E R V E S 6

TOMATOES

◆

Granddad took great pride in growing prizewinning tomatoes. Grams served them for dinner and supper daily throughout the season. Neither Grams nor Mom thought it proper to serve cooked tomatoes during their prime. Grams carefully peeled the gorgeous fresh fruit with a small paring knife before slicing them for Granddad's dinner. Religiously he sprinkled salt, ¼ teaspoon sugar, and a dash of pepper on each slice before eating it. We ate the rosy red succulent slices—skin and all—seasoned with salt and pepper, no sugar. Many quarts were canned whole or juiced for winter dining.

Look for smooth, unblemished, even-colored, ruby red–skinned tomatoes that feel heavy for their size. August and September are the boon months for tomatoes in Minnesota as well as New York. "Eat your fill now," Mom would say to us, "the season is soon over!" I shun those dreadful, cardboard-tasting, poor excuses for tomatoes available during the winter.

TO PREPARE Drop tomatoes into boiling water for a few seconds or until skins start to slip under pressure from your thumb. Immediately remove them from water, slip off skins, cut in half, and squeeze pulp slightly between hands above strainer set over bowl to remove excess seeds. Place pulp on chopping board set in jelly roll pan to catch juices. Chop according to desired size. Proceed according to recipe. Remember to use only stainless steel or enamel pans for cooking tomatoes, because of their acid.

Stewed Tomatoes

◆

Make this recipe with the "culls" towards the end of the season. I cook up a large batch, fill plastic containers, and freeze them for a taste of summer in the winter.

▪▪▪▪▪▪▪▪▪▪▪▪▪▪▪▪▪▪▪▪▪▪

Melt butter in large nonreactive saucepan; add chopped onion. Sauté over moderate heat 6 to 8 minutes, or until soft and translucent. Stir in flour; continue to cook 2 to 3 minutes longer.

2½ TABLESPOONS BUTTER
1 LARGE YELLOW ONION, COARSELY CHOPPED (¾ CUP)
1 TABLESPOON FLOUR
2 QUARTS CHOPPED FRESH TOMATOES WITH JUICES
¼ TEASPOON SALT
½ TEASPOON BLACK PEPPER, FRESHLY GROUND
PINCH SUGAR

Peel, seed, and chop tomatoes, saving juices, according to directions on page 237. Add to pan. Season with salt, pepper, and sugar. Continue to cook until tomatoes are soft and juices are slightly thickened. Taste and correct seasonings.

VARIATION

Add 1 medium green pepper (chopped) to onion; proceed with recipe.

S E R V E S 6

TURNIPS

◆

Although turnips grow best in sandy loam, the family garden produced rather fine, firm white turnips with a clear purple ring around the top. Grams boiled and mashed them with tons of creamy butter. Adding their pungent taste to soups was Mom's favorite way of fixing turnips. But the most interesting treatment happened outside the house. Granddad chopped the extra or leftover turnips (not eaten by humans) for cow feed. I wonder what the milk tasted like after that.

Once again, look for unblemished white bottoms with clear purple-topped, hard round spheres. They too should be heavy for their size and have smooth skins. Store them as you would carrots.

Butter-Braised Turnips

◆

Braising turnips with what seems to be an enormous amount of garlic is the secret to this recipe. Guests have asked me "What is this marvelous vegetable?" My reply—"Turnips!"—is always met with total disbelief.

·······························

Preheat oven to 350°.

Peel and cut turnips into uniform-sized quarters or sixths; set aside. Peel garlic and cut off end to leave cloves whole; reserve.

In heavy ovenproof casserole, melt butter and oil until sizzling. Add

2 POUNDS WHITE TURNIPS
2 WHOLE HEADS GARLIC
3 TABLESPOONS BUTTER
1 TABLESPOON OLIVE OIL
½ CUP CHICKEN BROTH
¼ CUP CHOPPED FRESH PARSLEY

garlic cloves, reduce heat, and sauté 4 to 5 minutes, stirring often. Add turnips and sauté 2 to 3 minutes to coat with butter seal. Add broth, cover, and bring to a boil.

Bake for 20 to 25 minutes, or until turnips are tender. Remove from oven. With slotted spoon, place vegetables in serving dish; cover and reserve.

On top of stove, reduce cooking liquid to a glaze; this will take about 4 to 5 minutes. Pour reduction over vegetables and garnish with parsley.

S E R V E S   6

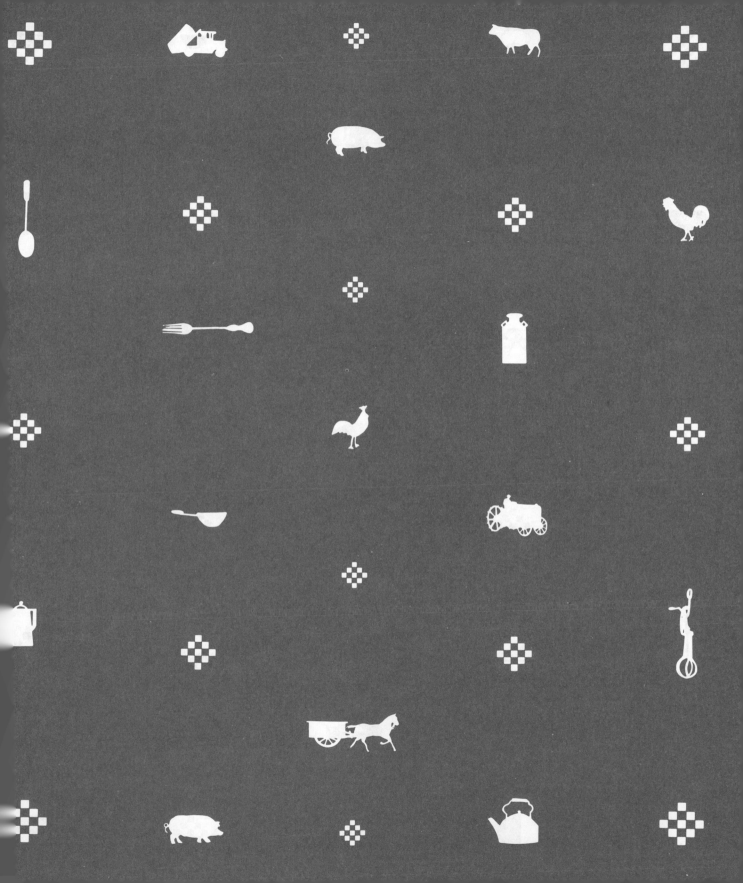

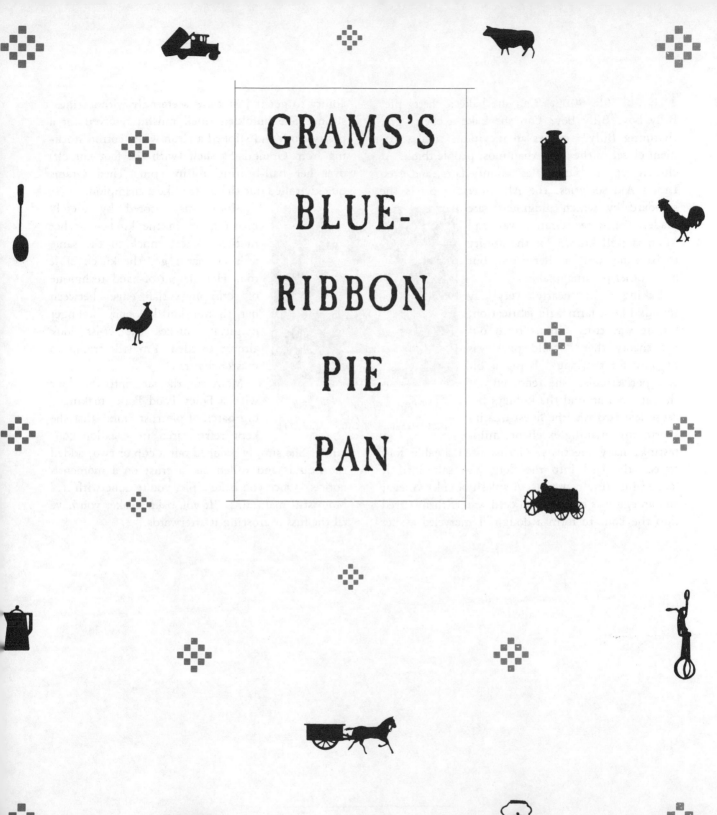

GRAMS'S BLUE-RIBBON PIE PAN

That old folk song, "Can she bake a cherry pie, Billy boy, Billy boy? Can she bake a cherry pie, charming Billy?" carries an inevitable rural sentiment closer to the truth than most people think. At church suppers, farm sales, county fairs, and even Ladies Aid societies, the All-American pie is the standard by which judgments are made. For sure, Grams was and Mom is well known for the ability to bake not only a cherry pie, but every other pie imaginable.

Baking a pie nearly every day sounds like a farm-wife fabrication, but it was true. Grams lived out the theory that day-old pie "was fit only for the dog!" Being a bit of a perfectionist, she rendered out the fat from around the kidneys because leaf lard was the finest quality shortening, making excellent, mild-tasting, flaky piecrusts. Grams used a table fork to cut the lard into the flour and salt until it looked like tiny new peas. A splash of cider vinegar and an egg was beaten with cold water, then stirred into the flour to form a dough. I marveled at her

Our Family's Favorite Old Folk
Great-Grandmother Crowe, circa 1900

ability to get it just right seemingly without measuring. She unfolded thick muslin reserved for a pastry cloth and slipped a clean white cotton stocking from Granddad's shelf (with the foot cut off) over her ball-bearing rolling pin. Then Grams quickly rolled out the pastry like a champion.

Mom was tutored by merely growing up in the kitchen at her mother's knee, much in the same fashion that I got the knack of it too. Her sleight-of-hand technique of crimping the edge between her thumb knuckle and forefinger magically makes the crust look almost braided. I'm still trying to master that trick.

Mom cut the lard into the flour with a Foley Food Fork, making a big batch of piecrust "mix" that she kept refrigerated in a gallon container. She simply scooped out a cup or two, added the liquid, and rolled out a crust on a moment's notice. "Once you bake a pie, you're done with it," Mom still maintains. "If you bake a cake, you have all the fuss of frosting it afterwards."

Basic Pie-crust

A lard crust is so flaky that it melts in your mouth almost before you chew it. If for some dietary reason lard is not allowed, unsalted butter (Land O Lakes is my choice) is the best substitute. Omit the vinegar when using butter.

To eliminate the possibility of a tough crust, do not overwork the dough. Using a light touch is an appropriate approach to pie baking.

3 CUPS FLOUR, UNSIFTED
1 TEASPOON SALT
1 CUP LARD OR SWEET BUTTER
1 EGG, BEATEN
1 TABLESPOON CIDER VINEGAR
4 TO 5 TABLESPOONS ICE WATER

Measure flour and salt into mixing bowl. With pastry blender or 2 table knives, cut lard into flour until mixture resembles coarse meal with lumps the size of small peas. Dough can be done ahead to this point. Refrigerate in airtight container.

With table fork, mix egg, vinegar, and 3 tablespoons water together. Make well in flour mixture and pour in liquid. Pull liquid through flour, bit by bit, adding water by tablespoonfuls until mixture forms ball. Wrap dough in plastic wrap; chill at least ½ hour.

TO PROCESS DOUGH IN FOOD PROCESSOR Use chopping blade, keep lard very cold, and process 4 or 5 pulses, or until mixture of flour, salt, and lard resembles coarse meal. Turn into mixing bowl and add liquids by hand.

TO ROLL Divide dough into quarters. Place one-quarter of dough on floured pastry cloth or board. Flatten ball with hand or rolling pin. Roll from center out, lifting rolling pin up as you move toward edge. Rotate dough as you work to keep thickness even. Roll into circle large enough for pie pan, leaving ½ to 1 inch extra. Fold circle in half or quarters to pick up, then unfold dough as you fit it into pan. (I reroll the pastry back onto the rolling pin, holding my thumb on the end of the pin to keep it from unrolling while I move the pastry to the pie pan, then I unroll it directly over the pan and proceed.)

FOR SINGLE-CRUST PIE With scissors, trim off excess dough; roll or tuck overhanging dough under crust on lip-edge of pie pan. Crimp in decorative manner. Proceed according to recipe.

TO BAKE Prick bottom of crust with fork in several places. Line crust with aluminum foil and weight

MAKES ENOUGH FOR 2 NINE-INCH, DOUBLE-CRUST PIES OR FOR 1 TEN-INCH, DOUBLE-CRUST PIE PLUS 1 NINE-TO-TEN-INCH SINGLE-CRUST PIE

with beans. Freeze whole affair for ½ hour. Can be done ahead, sealed in plastic bag, and kept frozen 1 to 2 weeks.

Bake in preheated 425° oven for 8 minutes. Remove beans and foil; continue to bake 5 to 6 minutes longer, or until crust is baked with an even brown color. Cool on rack. Reserve. Fill according to recipe.

FOR DOUBLE-CRUST PIE With knife or scissors, trim off overhanging dough from bottom crust. Fill with fruit according to recipe. Roll out another quarter of dough for top crust in manner described in recipe. With knife, cut decorative design in dough to vent out steam. Wet two fingers with cold water "glue" and dampen top of crust on lip-edge of pan. Carefully lay top crust over filled crust. Trim off excess dough, leaving approximately ½ inch overhang. Tuck overhanging dough under dampened crust on lip-edge of pan; crimp with your fingers in decorative manner. Bake according to recipe.

NOTE I dust the scraps of dough left from trimming with cinnamon and sugar (according to my sweet tooth), place them on a baking sheet, and bake in a 425° oven for 5 to 6 minutes, or until brown on edges. My children call these scraps "crumpets"; however, I call them "peace offerings" because they keep peace in the family and the family out of my pie!

Graham Cracker Crust

❖

1 ½ CUPS GRAHAM CRACKER CRUMBS (1 INNER PACKAGE FROM A 1-POUND BOX)
3 TABLESPOONS SUGAR
⅓ CUP MELTED BUTTER

As soon as I could wield a rolling pin, my job was to crush the graham crackers between two sheets of waxed paper. It was no mean trick to keep those pesky little crumbs confined to a sheet of waxed paper. The advent of plastic bags made my work much easier to manage, while the food processor makes crumbs in an instant. Progress!

Preheat oven to 350°.

Roll crackers evenly into fine crumbs or process in food processor. Add sugar. Add butter and mix well.

Reserve ¼ cup for top of pie. Evenly press remaining crumbs into pie pan. Bake for 10 minutes, then cool on rack. Fill according to recipe.

VARIATIONS
Chocolate Graham Crust Add 3 tablespoons unsweetened cocoa with sugar and increase butter to ½ cup. Proceed according to recipe.
Cookie Crumb Crust Substitute vanilla or chocolate wafers or gingersnap cookies for graham crackers. Omit sugar. Proceed according to recipe.
Nut Crumb Crust Add ¼ cup finely chopped nuts to crumbs. Proceed according to recipe.

MAKES 1 NINE-INCH PIE CRUST

Mom's
Nut
Crust

❖

Every spring, my high school gave a mother/daughter tea. We students planned and prepared the food for the event. We served individual tarts, as Mom did at Christmas (see page 115). Our variation added crunchy chopped pecans to the crust for the tangy lemon tarts. Mom thought it was a splendid addition. Thereafter, she included nuts in her crusts.

When making a banana cream pie, she uses Spanish peanuts; pecans are the perfect counterpoint for citrus filling, hazelnuts for chocolate flavors, and almonds for everything else.

Because nuts are naturally rich, three tablespoons of butter in the recipe are replaced with vegetable shortening. The crust will remain flaky, with a delicious crunch.

2/3 CUP LESS 3 TABLESPOONS BUTTER
3 TABLESPOONS SOLID VEGETABLE SHORTENING
2 CUPS FLOUR
1/4 CUP SPANISH PEANUTS, CHOPPED FINE
1 EGG, BEATEN
3 TABLESPOONS ICE WATER

∎∎∎∎∎∎∎∎∎∎∎∎∎∎∎∎∎∎∎∎∎∎∎∎∎∎∎∎∎∎

Preheat oven to 425°.

Cut butter and shortening into flour until it resembles coarse meal.

Stir chopped peanuts into dough. With table fork, mix egg and 1 tablespoon water together. Pull liquid through flour. Add water by tablespoonfuls until mixture forms ball. Wrap dough in plastic wrap; chill at least ½ hour.

NOTE When substituting pecans or other nuts for peanuts, add ½ teaspoon salt to flour. Proceed according to recipe.

TO BAKE Roll out dough according to directions for *Basic Piecrust* recipe on page 243. Prick bottom of crust with fork in several places. Line crust with aluminum foil and weight with beans. Freeze whole affair for ½ hour. Can be done ahead, sealed in plastic bag, and kept frozen 1 to 2 weeks.

Bake for 8 minutes. Remove beans and foil. Continue to bake 5 to 6 minutes longer, or until crust is baked with an even brown color. Cool on rack and reserve. Fill according to recipe.

**MAKES 1 NINE-INCH
SINGLE PIECRUST**

Mom's Soda Cracker Piecrust

✦

Although this is actually a torte shell, we considered it to be a fancy piecrust that was prepared when company was coming. Egg whites, both economical and plentiful, are the basic ingredient needed for this melt-in-your-mouth, confection-like, dry-on-the-outside, moist-and-crunchy-on-the-inside, crust. Allow your creative taste buds to blossom when adding the optional ingredients.

With all due respect to Grams's a-crust-a-day theory, this crust can be baked ahead and sealed in an airtight plastic bag, then kept in a cool dry place for several days or frozen up to 1 to 2 weeks. Simply defrost, fill, and serve. The crust becomes "chewy" but still delectable if eaten partially frozen.

3 EGG WHITES
1 CUP SUGAR
⅔ CUP FINE SODA CRACKER
  CRUMBS (SALTINE)
2 TEASPOONS BAKING
  POWDER

OPTIONAL INGREDIENTS

■ ■ ■

½ CUP COCONUT
½ CUP RAISINS
½ CUP CHOPPED NUTS
¼ CUP CHOCOLATE,
  UNSWEETENED AND GRATED
½ CUP GRANOLA
½ CUP OATMEAL

Preheat oven to 350°.

Beat egg whites until frothy; add sugar. Continue beating until stiff but not dry. They should have dull, smooth satin shine on top. Fold cracker crumbs and baking powder into meringue.

Fold one, any, or all optional ingredients (totaling 1 cup) into egg whites. Work quickly. Spread into 9-inch buttered pie tin, making shell of uniform thickness.

Bake for 30 minutes, or until toothpick comes out clean when inserted into center. Cool on rack and reserve. Can be done ahead. Store in cold oven overnight, or seal in plastic bag and freeze for 1 to 2 weeks.

Fill with fresh fruit topped with whipped cream, ice cream, mousse, or custard filling.

MAKES 1 NINE-INCH PIE CRUST

246

Butterscotch Pie

❖

Although the original recipe from *Grams's Black Book* called for a meringue, I prefer to serve unsweetened whipped cream and shaved unsweetened chocolate curls atop this divine, buttery, caramel-flavored cream pie.

In spite of using only 1½ cups milk, this recipe provides an ample amount of filling for a nine-inch pie. Make this dessert for the "sweet tooth" members of your family.

▪▪▪▪▪▪▪▪▪▪▪▪▪▪▪▪▪▪▪▪▪▪▪▪▪▪▪▪▪▪

Bake *Basic Piecrust* for one-crust pie according to recipe on page 243.

In heavy saucepan, combine sugar, cornstarch, and salt together until well mixed. With wire whisk, stir in milk. Cook over moderate heat, mixing constantly, until mixture comes to a boil. Boil 1 minute; it will be thick. Remove from heat.

Gradually whisk half of hot milk into beaten yolks. Stirring constantly, return tempered yolks to milk in saucepan. Continue to whisk

¾ CUP DARK BROWN SUGAR
2 TABLESPOONS CORNSTARCH
PINCH SALT
1½ CUPS COLD MILK
2 EGG YOLKS, BEATEN
1 TABLESPOON BUTTER
1 TEASPOON VANILLA

1 CUP HEAVY WHIPPING CREAM
½ TEASPOON VANILLA
½ SQUARE UNSWEETENED CHOCOLATE

until well combined. Return pan to heat. Boil 1 minute longer, stirring constantly.

Remove from heat; mix in butter and vanilla. Pour into baked pie shell. Cool completely. Can be done head. Refrigerate 3 to 4 hours before topping.

Whip cream until stiff. Fold in vanilla. Pipe or spoon whipped cream on top of cold filling. Refrigerate until serving time. With vegetable peeler, slice a few shavings of unsweetened chocolate over whipped cream for garnish.

MAKES 1 NINE-INCH PIE

"Butter Scotch Pie: 1½ cups milk, 2 Tbsp corn starch, 1 cup med. brown sugar (scant), 2 egg yolks, 1 Tbsp butter, 1 tsp vanilla extract. Mix ingredients well and stir over fire until it thickens and comes to boiling point. Pour into a baked pie shell. Cover with meringue of the two egg whites beaten stiffly with 2 Tbsp sugar. Set the whole in oven and lightly brown." Grams's Black Book

Banana Cream Pie

If faced with the difficult decision —a slice of banana cream pie with a peanut crust or coconut cream pie— Dad probably would have a slice of each. The salty crunch of Spanish peanuts is a good addition to the soft texture of bananas and the buttery filling.

Skim milk produces a smooth, less "rich" but equally delicious creamy-cream pie.

Bake *Mom's Nut Crust,* with peanuts, according to recipe on page 245.

In heavy saucepan, mix sugar, cornstarch, and salt together. With wire whisk, stir in milk. Cook over moderate heat, stirring constantly, until mixture comes to a boil. Boil 1 minute, while stirring to prevent scorching. Soon it will be thick; remove from heat.

In small bowl, beat egg yolks. Gradually whisk half of hot milk into beaten egg yolks. Stirring constantly, return tempered yolks to milk in saucepan. Continue to whisk until well combined. Return pan to heat; boil 1 minute longer, stirring constantly. Remove from heat, and stir in butter and vanilla, then cool for 10 to 15 minutes.

⅔ CUP SUGAR
3 TABLESPOONS CORNSTARCH
¼ TEASPOON SALT
3 CUPS COLD MILK
3 EGGS, SEPARATED
1 TABLESPOON BUTTER
2 TEASPOONS VANILLA

PINCH SALT
6 TABLESPOONS SUGAR
½ TEASPOON VANILLA

3 LARGE BANANAS, SLICED

Meanwhile, preheat oven to 400°.

Beat egg whites in medium bowl with salt until frothy; gradually add sugar. Beat until stiff and glossy; do not underbeat. Fold in vanilla.

Layer sliced bananas on bottom of baked pie shell. Pour half of custard over and repeat. Spread remaining custard evenly over top.

A spoonful at a time, place meringue around edges over filling. Move toward center last. "Seal" custard completely with meringue. Swirl into decorative shapes with back of spoon.

Bake 8 to 10 minutes or until light brown. Cool on rack away from drafts.

VARIATIONS
Whipped Cream Topping Omit meringue. After filling is cold, top with whipped cream: Whip 1 cup whipping cream with ¼ cup powdered sugar until stiff; mix in ½ teaspoon vanilla. Spread on *completely cold* cream filling and refrigerate until serving time.

Coconut Cream Pie Bake *Basic Piecrust* for one-crust pie according to recipe on page 243. Toast 1 cup shredded or flaked coconut (sweetened or unsweetened, according to personal preference) in 350° oven for 8 to 10 minutes or until brown.

Omit bananas; fold ¾ cup toasted coconut into cooked custard. Pour directly into baked pie shell. Top with meringue or whipped cream according to recipe.

Chocolate Cream Pie Bake *Basic Piecrust* for one-crust pie according to recipe on page 243. Increase sugar to 1 cup. Add 2½ squares unsweetened chocolate (grated) to milk. Omit bananas. Proceed according to recipe. Top with meringue or whipped cream, garnished with shaved chocolate.

MAKES 1 NINE-INCH PIE

S'Mores
Pie

30 LARGE MARSHMALLOWS
½ CUP MILK
1 CUP HEAVY CREAM
2 SQUARES UNSWEETENED CHOCOLATE, SHAVED OR GRATED

Uncle Lee Burrous, a medical doctor married to Dad's next-to-oldest sister, Aunt Viola, proclaimed at one of the family reunions that "a piece of pie and a cup of coffee is a complete nutritional meal!" Thereby he gave the rest of the family a doctor's permission to eat pie—not that they needed it! No friendly encouragement is necessary when this 1930s popular pie is served. The combination of marshmallows, graham crackers, and chocolate is reminiscent of the campfire classic, "S'mores." And it's a "snap" to make.

Bake *Graham Cracker Crust* according to recipe on page 244.

In heavy saucepan, over low heat, melt marshmallows with milk, stirring often until smooth. Remove from heat. Cool to room temperature, stirring occasionally. When cool, beat until light and fluffy.

Whip cream until stiff. With wire whisk, fold cream into cold marshmallow mixture. Fold chocolate into filling. Pour into baked and cooled graham cracker crust.

Garnish top with reserved ¼ cup leftover graham cracker mixture (as instructed in recipe for crust). Chill until serving time.

MAKES 1 NINE-INCH PIE

Grams's Sour Cream–Raisin Pie

This all-time great recipe of Grams's catches every raisin fancier's eye. If you like rice pudding with raisins, you'll love this pie; it is one of Dad's favorites. Even though it was served rather frequently at family meals, raisin cream pie was always added to the overflowing dessert board at Thanksgiving, Christmas, and even Easter dinners too.

"Cook 1½ cup raisins in 1 cup water until plump. Add ⅔ cup white sugar, 2–3 beaten egg yolks, 2 Tbsp cornstarch, 3 Tbsp water, vanilla and butter. Cook thick. Cool a bit. Stir in 1 cup sour cream. Pour into pre-baked crust. Meanwhile cook 1 Tbsp cornstarch, 2 Tbsp water added to ½ cup boiling water until thick. Chill. Add starch to 2–3 egg whites beaten very stiff with 6 Tbsp sugar and vanilla. Then, when stiff add cooled starch and beat until stiff. Put on pie and bake 375°."
Grams's Black Book

1½ CUPS RAISINS
1 CUP WATER
⅔ CUP SUGAR

2 TABLESPOONS CORNSTARCH
3 TABLESPOONS COLD WATER
3 EGGS, SEPARATED (WITH YOLKS BEATEN)
1 TABLESPOON BUTTER
2 TEASPOONS VANILLA
1 CUP SOUR CREAM

1 TABLESPOON CORNSTARCH
2 TABLESPOONS COLD WATER

6 TABLESPOONS SUGAR
1 TEASPOON VANILLA

Bake *Basic Piecrust* for one-crust pie according to recipe on page 243.

In heavy saucepan, cook raisins in 1 cup water until plumped and hot. Add ⅔ cup sugar and continue to cook until sugar is dissolved.

Mix 2 tablespoons cornstarch in 3 tablespoons cold water; stir mixture into raisins. Boil 2 minutes, stirring constantly. Remove from heat.

Gradually whisk half of hot raisin mixture into beaten egg yolks. Stirring constantly, return tempered eggs to remaining hot raisin mixture in saucepan. Continue to whisk until well combined. Return pan to heat. Boil 1 minute longer, stirring constantly.

Remove from heat; mix in butter and vanilla. Cool slightly. Fold in sour cream and pour mixture into baked pie shell.

Meanwhile, mix 1 tablespoon cornstarch with 2 tablespoons cold water. Boil ½ cup water in heavy saucepan; whisk in softened cornstarch. Bring to a boil; boil 2 to 3 minutes, or until thick and clear. Set aside and cool to room temperature.

Preheat oven to 375°.

Beat egg whites in electric mixer until frothy. Gradually add 6 tablespoons sugar; beat until stiff and glossy, but not dry. Fold in 1 teaspoon vanilla and cooled starch; continue to beat until stiff.

Using a spoonful at a time, place meringue around edges over filling, moving toward center last. "Seal" filling completely with meringue. Swirl into decorative shapes with back of spoon.

Bake 8 to 10 minutes, or until light brown. Cool on rack, away from drafts; refrigerate until serving time.

MAKES 1 NINE-INCH PIE

Classic Lemon Meringue Pie

❖

1½ CUPS SUGAR
⅓ CUP CORNSTARCH
1½ CUPS COLD WATER
3 EGGS, SEPARATED
3 TABLESPOONS BUTTER
6 TABLESPOONS LEMON
  JUICE, FRESHLY
  SQUEEZED
GRATED RIND OF
  1 LARGE LEMON
PINCH CREAM OF TARTAR
6 TABLESPOONS SUGAR FOR
  MERINGUE
¼ TEASPOON LEMON JUICE
  FOR MERINGUE

Grams, like other farm wives, traditionally baked a lemon pie for dessert when she served fried spring chicken for a Sunday dinner. Mom shared Grams's love of lemon, although she served this pie (with lightly browned peaks of meringue that reminded me of the top of a large circus tent) whenever fellow-lemon-infatuated folks came for dinner no matter what was on the menu.

Bake *Basic Piecrust* for one-crust pie according to recipe on page 243.

Preheat oven to 400°.

In heavy saucepan, thoroughly

"Lemon Pie, Take 2 eggs, 2 teacups of white sugar, 2 teacups boiling water, 3 Tablespoonfuls of cornstarch, butter the size of an egg, and 2 lemons. Cook on top of the stove and pour into baked crust." Grams's Black Book

mix sugar and cornstarch together and gradually whisk in water. Cook over moderate heat, stirring constantly until it thickens and comes to a boil. Boil 2 minutes.

With wire whisk, beat egg yolks until frothy. Gradually whisk half of hot mixture into egg yolks. Return tempered egg yolks to saucepan. Return to heat and boil 2 minutes longer, stirring constantly. Remove from heat.

Blend in butter, lemon juice, and rind. Pour into baked piecrust and set aside.

Beat egg whites with cream of tartar until frothy. Gradually add sugar and continue to beat until stiff and glossy. Fold in lemon juice.

Using a spoonful at a time, place meringue around edges over filling. Moving toward center last, "seal" filling completely with meringue. Swirl into peaks with back of soupspoon.

Bake 8 to 10 minutes or until light brown, being careful not to burn. Cool on rack away from drafts.

MAKES 1 NINE-INCH PIE

Matchless Mincemeat Pie

MINCEMEAT (6 TO 8 QUARTS)

∎∎∎

3 TO 5 POUNDS BEEF CHUCK WITH BONES OR NECK BONES, OR VENISON

1 QUART CHOPPED TART APPLES (PEELED, CORED, AND CHOPPED)
2 POUNDS RAISINS, WASHED
1 POUND CURRANTS, WASHED
½ POUND CITRON, CHOPPED, OR CANDIED PINEAPPLE, CHOPPED
1 POUND SOUR CHERRIES, PITTED (OPTIONAL)
¼ POUND DRIED PEACHES (OPTIONAL)
1 POUND MIXED CANDIED FRUITS (OPTIONAL)
4 CUPS APPLE CIDER
6 CUPS SUGAR
½ CUP CIDER VINEGAR
2 TEASPOONS CINNAMON
¼ TEASPOON ALLSPICE
½ TEASPOON GINGER
½ TEASPOON NUTMEG, FRESHLY GRATED
1 TEASPOON SALT (OPTIONAL)
JUICE AND ZEST OF 1 LEMON

Soon after a beef steer was butchered, both Grams and Mom cooked up a big batch of mincemeat that was "saved for special occasions" throughout the year. (Christmas Day, first on the list, followed by Thanksgiving, and then whenever Mom "had a yen for it.") Had I spent the time necessary to prepare the mincemeat, I would save it for celebrations, too.

While Grams simmered the mincemeat over a slow fire, Mom and Rubye (as little girls) meticulously covered English walnuts with "recycled" tin-foil wrap from packages of tea leaves, which they carefully removed and saved in a special bag in the cupboard during the year. Though black walnuts grew in the backyard, English walnuts in the shell were a precious speciality purchased from the grocery store. Their nimble fingers wrapped the nuts with foil and joyfully tied red satin ribbon around each one, transforming the pale nuts into bright Christmas tree ornaments.

Nowadays most people buy their Christmas ornaments, but, though it may seem overwhelming at first glance, making mincemeat is well worth the effort. Prepare a large batch, can it in pint jars, and process it the length of time recommended by the manufacturer—or freeze it up to one year. It is a great holiday gift idea.

Although some aficionados deem that hard sauce belongs on mincemeat pie, we *never* served or ate it. The homemade mincemeat stood on its own very well.

■■■■■■■■■■■■■■■■■■■■■■■■■■■■■■■■

TO MAKE MINCEMEAT In large heavy saucepan, cover meat with cold water. Bring to a boil, reduce heat, and simmer partially covered for 1 hour, or until meat is tender and falls off bone. Drain off broth and reserve for soup. Remove bones. Grind or coarsely chop meat. It should yield approximately 5 to 6 cups coarsely chopped meat. Reserve.

In large heavy saucepan, bring ground meat, apples, raisins, currants, citron, sour cherries, dried peaches, mixed candied fruits, and cider to a boil. Add sugar, vinegar, spices, salt, if desired, and lemon juice and zest. Mix well. Reduce heat to low and simmer, stirring occasionally, for 1 hour, or until thick. Taste and correct seasonings.

Store in clean glass jars in refrigerator for 2 to 3 weeks, or freeze for 1 year in plastic containers.

PIE
■ ■ ■

2½ CUPS COLD MINCEMEAT
1 TABLESPOON FRUIT BRANDY
1 TEASPOON BUTTER
1 TEASPOON SUGAR

NOTE The essence of this recipe is apples, raisins, currants, meat, and flavoring. If available, Mom replaces sour cherries and dried peaches with 4 cups of fresh or canned plums.

TO MAKE PIE Make *Basic Piecrust* for double-crust pie according to recipe on page 243 and pre-bake in 425° oven for 5 minutes, as described on page 254.

Preheat oven to 425°.

Flavor mincemeat with brandy. Fill prepared bottom crust with mincemeat. Dot top with butter. Place top crust over filling and sprinkle with sugar. Bake for 30 minutes, or until an even brown. Cool on rack.

NOTE If time is limited, heat the mincemeat in the microwave until hot, then fill the crust. Bake in a 425° oven for 10 to 15 minutes, or until brown.

MAKES 1 NINE-INCH PIE

Nostalgic Baked Custard Pie

◆

Mom whipped up this pie, what I call "nursery food," on a moment's notice. Baked custard is reminiscent of almost everyone's early childhood and the nurturing care that went right along with it.

If sprinkling nutmeg on the bottom of the pie seems odd, do not worry. As the custard bakes, the nutmeg gently rises to the top, flavoring the milk and eggs as it passes through, and eventually decorates the top!

Make *Basic Piecrust* for one-crust pie according to recipe on page 243. Pre-bake at 425° for 5 minutes, or

"Scald milk, beat up egg yolks, sugar and vanilla. Sprinkle nutmeg in bottom of raw crust. Beat egg whites separately. Pour into crust and bake. Sometimes richer than others, depending on the milk." *Mom*

2⅔ CUPS MILK
4 EGGS, SEPARATED
⅔ CUP SUGAR
PINCH SALT (OPTIONAL)
1 TEASPOON VANILLA
¼ TEASPOON NUTMEG, FRESHLY GRATED (SEE NOTE)

until crust looks dry in a few places, not shiny; reserve.

In saucepan or microwave, scald milk until it forms crust on top; set aside.

Beat egg whites until stiff but not dry; set aside.

In mixing bowl, gradually add sugar to egg yolks, beating constantly; mix well. Add salt, if desired. Whisk in hot milk and vanilla; continue to whisk until well combined. Fold in beaten whites until only small bits are visible. Sprinkle nutmeg on partially cooked crust; pour custard into crust.

Bake in 425° oven for 10 minutes. Reduce heat to 350°; continue to bake 20 minutes, or until table knife inserted 1 inch from side comes out clean.

Cool on rack. Serve warm or cold.

NOTE Hanging on the pegboard in my kitchen is Grams's nutmeg grater. Following in her tradition, for every recipe that uses nutmeg, I grate the whole oval "nut (meg)" on that grater directly into a measuring spoon. Its fresh taste is unmatched. Whole nutmeg is available in the spice section of the supermarket.

MAKES 1 NINE-INCH PIE

Pecan
Pie

Every family in America that I know serves pecan pie at least once a year, on Thanksgiving. Our family tradition included a pecan pie for Christmas, Easter, and any other reasonably festive occasion as well. Being a nut-lover, Dad relished every sweet morsel of this tempting pie. On the other hand, I used to pick off the pecans and eat the gooey portion with the crust. Mom thought the whole notion was too sweet, although she made many of them. She ate a mere sliver of it "just to be sociable!"

To give this easy-to-make classic pie a "gourmet look," use only unbroken pecan halves, adding ¼ cup more. To gild a lily, serve with vanilla whipped cream or homemade ice cream. (I serve it unadorned.)

3 EGGS
⅔ CUP SUGAR
½ TEASPOON SALT
⅓ CUP BUTTER, MELTED
1 CUP DARK CORN SYRUP
1¼ CUPS PECAN HALVES OR
1 CUP BROKEN PECANS

Thanksgiving Day, California-Style
Grams, Granddad, and Relatives

Make *Basic Piecrust* for one-crust pie according to recipe on page 243. Do not bake.

Preheat oven to 375°.

With hand beater, beat eggs until frothy. Add sugar, salt, melted butter, and syrup; mix thoroughly. Mix in nuts, then pour into prepared pie shell.

Bake approximately 40 to 45 minutes, or until knife inserted halfway between edge and center comes out clean and pastry is brown. Cool on rack. This pie can be made ahead; seal in plastic bag and freeze 2 to 3 weeks. Serve warm or at room temperature.

MAKES 1 NINE-INCH PIE

Unequaled
Pumpkin
Pie

❖

"If a pumpkin pie is shiny smooth on top," warned Grams, "don't eat it!" It was her firm belief that the proper proportions of ingredients would render a pumpkin pie flavorful, rich, creamy on the tongue (custard style), and light enough to be able to eat another piece in peace. One day she lamented, "The last time Joel was here, he ate only *one* piece of pumpkin pie." (At home he ate two or three at one sitting.)

----

3 EGGS, SEPARATED INTO 2 BATCHES (1 BATCH INCLUDES ALL YOLKS AND 1 WHITE; OTHER BATCH CONTAINS 2 WHITES)
1 CUP SUGAR
2 CUPS PUMPKIN, CANNED (SEE NOTE)
½ TEASPOON SALT
1½ TEASPOONS CINNAMON
½ TEASPOON GINGER
1 TEASPOON ALLSPICE
¼ TEASPOON NUTMEG, FRESHLY GRATED
1 CUP HALF-AND-HALF OR EVAPORATED MILK

"Pumpkin Pie; 1 cup pumpkin, 1 egg, a good Tbsp flour, butter the size of hickory nut, ¾ cup sugar, 1 teas cinnamon, allspice and cloves, ½ teas ginger, pinch salt. 2 cup milk, very good." Grams's Black Book

Mom's editorial comment: "She probably used some cream, but I find evaporated milk rich enough."

Make *Basic Piecrust* for one-crust pie according to recipe on page 243. Do not bake.

Preheat oven to 425°.

Beat 3 egg yolks, plus one white, until frothy. Gradually add sugar and pumpkin. Add salt and spices; mix thoroughly. Stir in half-and-half.

Beat 2 remaining egg whites until soft peaks; fold into custard. Pour into prepared pie shell. Bake for 10 minutes. Reduce heat to 375°; continue to bake for 25 minutes, or until table knife inserted 1 inch from side comes out clean. Cool on rack. Serve warm or cold; top with whipped cream.

NOTE   Add 1 tablespoon flour and 1 tablespoon light molasses if using homemade pumpkin.

VARIATION
Sweet Potato or Winter Squash Pie Substitute mashed sweet potato or winter squash for pumpkin. Add 1 tablespoon flour and 1 tablespoon light molasses. Proceed according to recipe.

MAKES 1 NINE-INCH PIE

Un-Peckable Rhubarb- Cream Pie

❖

ollowing their forefathers' tradition, Grams and Granddad established a rhubarb bed that produced an abundant crop annually. Although pie was—and is—the most common use of the bright red, tart-flavored stalks, Grams also "brewed and stewed" it. Beware, if eaten by humans, the luscious-looking leaves are poisonous.

Somehow, at least once every spring, our old hens wandered through the back gate to "hunt and peck" (for bugs and worms) in the rhubarb bed. Being a nuisance, those darn chickens pecked at the plants (including the leaves), dug out tender new shoots, and "fowled up" the garden. "Keep that gate closed," Mom commanded, "if you want any rhubarb pie."

Mom's addition of grated orange rind accentuates the unique clean flavor of rhubarb in this recipe for cream pie.

3 EGGS
3 TABLESPOONS MILK
2 CUPS SUGAR
¼ CUP FLOUR
GRATED RIND OF ½ ORANGE
PINCH SALT
½ TEASPOON VANILLA
4 CUPS PINK RHUBARB, CUT INTO ¼-TO-½-INCH CUBES

Archibald and Elizabeth Frisby

Make *Basic Piecrust* for one-crust pie according to recipe on page 243. Pre-bake in 400° oven for 5 to 6 minutes. Cut dough scraps (see page 243) into 1-inch-wide strips for lattice if desired. Set aside.

Preheat oven to 400°.

With fork, beat eggs slightly. Add milk and stir well. Mix sugar, flour, orange rind, and salt together; stir into milk mixture. Flavor with vanilla.

Fold rhubarb into "custard" and pour into pie shell. Place lattice strips over filling if desired. Bake for 15 minutes. Reduce heat to 350° and bake 25 minutes longer, or until table knife inserted in center comes out clean. Cool on rack. Serve warm or cold.

VARIATION
Strawberry Rhubarb Cream Pie
Substitute fresh strawberries for half of rhubarb. Reduce sugar to 1⅔ cups. Proceed according to recipe.

MAKES 1 NINE-INCH PIE

Fresh
Strawberry
Pie

❖

**1 CUP FRESH STRAWBERRIES
AND 1½ CUPS WATER
OR, 1 TEN-OUNCE PACKAGE
FROZEN UNSWEETENED
STRAWBERRIES (WITH
THEIR JUICE OR WATER TO
EQUAL 2½ CUPS IN TOTAL)
1⅓ CUPS SUGAR
½ CUP CORNSTARCH
5 TO 6 DROPS RED FOOD
COLORING (OPTIONAL)
3 TABLESPOONS LEMON JUICE**

**2 CUPS WHOLE,
UNSWEETENED
STRAWBERRIES (FRESH OR
FROZEN)**

Generation after generation of our family rejoiced at the onset of June because it brought the welcome warm weather and ambrosial red ripe strawberries. We ate strawberries every meal during "berry time." Great-Grandfather Broadwater, Granddad, and Dad alike cultivated a small strawberry bed for the family's consumption. But then in preparation for "his retirement project," Dad planted three acres of strawberries to establish the beds in 1975. The next year, his "patch" bore thousands of perfect (with only a few not-so-perfect) berries. Some retirement! Dad still rose before sunrise, pruned, transplanted, weeded, mulched, took stock of the fruit, and then came into the house for breakfast.

Over the next twelve years, people came from near and far to pick "Troy Schrock's Strawberries." The bed was as "clean as a whistle" because Dad placed a chopped corn-fodder mulch between each row, that, in turn, held the moisture around the plants, retarded weed growth, and most important, cushioned the knees of the pickers. Every person, young and old alike, filled their six-quart handmade cedar carriers until they overflowed. At times, as many as five hundred to six hundred quarts were picked in one day!

Before the pickers settled their bill, Dad heaped each quart, making it a bargain. "Grandpa, why do you give away all those extra berries?" Scott queried during one of his month-long summer visits to Minnesota. "You could sell them and make more money!" Dad could always justify his goodwill: "I like to give good value for the money. Besides which, they'll be back for more berries next week."

And he was right. Every Monday, Wednesday, and Friday were "picking days." (Dad rested on Sunday.) More often than not, there were more pickers than berries. But on a rare occasion, Dad stayed in the patch until he picked all the remaining berries. After supper, with a freshly sharpened hoe in hand, he returned to the patch to "catch those pesky little weeds" that he noticed during the day.

In 1988, at the young age of seventy-eight, Dad plowed the berry beds under and planted soybeans in that space because his knees and hips were "too tired" from all the stooping and bending. Customers, neighbors, and friends all felt saddened at the loss of "Troy's Strawberries."

They were the best—the in-patch comaraderie, and Dad's generosity of fruit and kindness.

Even if the closest berry patch is a grocery store, you can prepare and serve this magnificent strawberry pie with the confidence of a veteran berry-picker/lover. The stiff filling is necessary to keep the whole berries suspended throughout the pie. When sliced with a knife, each berry is not only evident but a toothsome treat.

Janeen, Dad, Joel, and Mom

Bake *Basic Piecrust* for one-crust pie according to recipe on page 243. Cool on rack. Soften 1½ tablespoons cream cheese with ¼ teaspoon milk. Spread smooth mixture evenly over baked crust to form "protective seal" from fruit juices. Reserve.

In heavy saucepan, bring 1 cup fresh berries and 1½ cups water (or frozen berries equivalent, partially thawed) to a boil. Mix sugar and cornstarch together; gradually stir into hot berries. Continue to boil, stirring constantly, for 3 to 4 minutes, or until very thick and clear. Stir in red coloring if desired, until bright red; stir in lemon juice and mix well.

Fold 2 cups whole berries into hot mixture and pour into prepared pie shell; refrigerate until serving time. Serve with dollop of whipped cream on each piece.

VARIATION
Fresh Raspberry Pie Substitute raspberries for strawberries; increase sugar to 1½ cups. Proceed according to recipe.

**MAKES 1 GENEROUS
9-INCH PIE**

TWO-CRUST FRUIT PIES

Great-Grandmother Broadwater added a dash of salt —no butter—to the filling of each fruit pie. She claimed, "It brings out the flavor." On the other hand, Grams added a generous tablespoonful of butter—no salt—"to bring out the flavor." Using her own good judgment, Mom eliminated both salt and butter, allowing the flavor of the fruit to stand alone.

Almost any fruit or combination of fruits can be made into a pie. Use the following chart for the amount of fruit, sugar, flour, and flavorings necessary to fill a nine-inch pie pan. (See recipe for pie crust, page 243.) Before filling, pre-bake the lining crust at 425° for five minutes, or until the crust looks dry in a few places, not shiny. Then fill the crust with the fruit mixture and cover with the top crust. Bake in a 425° oven for the recommended time. If the top crust is browning too fast, reduce the heat and lengthen the baking time until the fruit is soft to the point of a table fork stuck into the vent near the center of the pie and the juices are bubbly around the edge. The crust should be an even brown color. Plan on an hour of baking time.

Cool the pie on a rack until ready to serve.

"To eliminate fruit juice 'boil-overs' in the bottom of the oven or edge of crust browning too fast: Tear 3 aluminum foil strips 3 inches by 12 inches, using a drugstore wrap [page 65], connect the strips together (3 inches by 36 inches). Place 'dull side' next to the edge of the pie pan, form a collar approximately 1½" above the rim and 1½" below the rim of the pan. Securely press foil to pan and connect the extra rim. This rim catches the boiled over juices and allows the crust to brown uniformly . . . keeping the oven clean, Eureka!" Mom

Two-Crust Fresh Fruit Pie Chart

Wash, pare, peel, core, and slice fruit as necessary; drain well. Generously fill glass measuring cup with fruit in specified amounts below. Use rounded tablespoon for flour measurements. All other measurements are exact.

Mix flour, sugar, and dry spices together. Fill 9-inch piecrust with prepared fruit; sprinkle flour mixture over top. If directed, add water or lemon juice. Place top crust over whole affair, crimp, and bake for time indicated.

Fruit	Cups	Sugar	Flour	Water	Other	Baking Time
Apples, thinly sliced	4 cups	1¼ cups	3 tbsps.	none	1 tsp. cinnamon	50–60 min.
Apricots	3 cups	1½ cups	3 tbsps.	3 tbsps.	2 tbsps. lemon juice	45–50 min.
Blueberries	3 cups	1 cup	3 tbsps.	3 tbsps.	1 tbsp. lemon juice	45–50 min.
Cherries, sweet and unpitted	3 cups	¾–1 cup	3 tbsps.	2 tbsps.	none	50–60 min.
Cherries, sour and unpitted	2 cups	1½ cups	3 tbsps.	1 tbsp.	4 drops food coloring (optional)	40–50 min.
Gooseberries	2 cups	1½–1¾ cups	3 tbsps.	3 tbsps.	none	60–70 min.
Ground-cherries	3½ cups	1½ cups	3 tbsps.	3 tbsps.	1 tbsp. lemon juice	60–65 min.
Elderberries with sliced apples	(2 cups each)	1½–1¾ cups	3 tbsps.	3 tbsps.	2 tbsps. lemon juice	50–60 min.
Peaches	3½ cups	1 cup	3 tbsps.	none	1 tbsp. lemon juice	50–60 min.
Plums, pitted and tart	3 cups	1½ cups	3 tbsps.	none	none	60–65 min.
Raspberries	3 cups	1¼ cups	3 tbsps.	none	none	50–60 min.
Rhubarb	3½ cups	1½–1¾ cups	3 tbsps.	none	Grated rind of ½ orange	50–60 min.
Strawberries	4 cups	1¼ cups	3 tbsps.	none	3–4 drops red food coloring	50–60 min.
Raisins, plumped in 1 cup water	2 cups	1 cup	3 tbsps.	none	2 tbsps. lemon juice	50–60 min.

Note For fruit combinations, follow the longest baking time and add water or juice as desired.

THE MILK-MAID'S SUPPER HOUR

Granddad, a punctual man, came into the house for supper at six o'clock during the summer, and five o'clock in the winter. Not only was his body clock ready for food, but the cows with their bags full of milk were in the barnyard ready to be fed and milked. After Grams, Granddad, Rubye, and Mom ate supper, Rubye washed the dishes while the others went about the milking process.

Before electricity came in 1928, the milking was done by hand. Gas lanterns dimly illuminated the barn. The hungry cows pushed and shoved their way into stanchions where their big black tongues curled around to lick up the fortified ground cornmeal feed. As a rule, Granddad tied each cow's hind legs and swishy tail together with a rope to keep her from kicking the bucket. Mom elaborated, "Or so they didn't kick the daylights out of you!" The threesome —Grams, Granddad, and Mom—performed this chore balanced on one-legged stools fashioned out of 2 two-by-fours: It looked like they were sitting on the top of a capital letter T. With five-gallon metal milk pails nestled between their legs, they milked twenty to thirty cows twice a day. Granddad milked the "kickers" while "the milkmaids" Grams and Mom milked the other cows. When Mom married Dad, she vowed never to milk cows again, and she hasn't.

After being strained through a metal strainer lined with linen cloth, the milk was separated via a separator. The raw skimmed milk was fed to the little pigs, calves, dogs, and cats, while the cream was poured into cream cans, carried to the pump house, and chilled in water tanks. The cream was later transported to the Granger Creamery and made into butter or cheese. One gallon of whole milk was saved from the "best" cow, for family consumption, but the remaining milk was given to the animals. Milk-fed pork—they raised it years ago!

Splish, Splash Janeen and Joel by the Pump House, 1942

In the 1950s a much less quaint ritual took place at milking time. Dad used electric milkers and cooled the milk in a large electric cooler in the milk room section of the barn. Eventually a pipeline led to the bulk tank and so on. Nonetheless, we continued to eat supper before the cows were milked. After the milking was done, Dad worked in the field or garden until the sun set. Now, he hoes by hand in the soybeans, garden, or flower bed. Sometimes he mows the lawn. Mom dons a healthy film of mosquito repellent before fetching her razor-sharp hoe to work in the rose bed until dark.

Supper was considered as important a meal as dinner because we needed sustenance to continue our work until dark. But supper always seemed a bit less hectic. Farmers, a healthy-tired lot at day's end, pondered tomorrow's good weather—sun or rain, whatever was needed for a bountiful crop yield—and lingered for a spell over the last cup of coffee.

Most farm supper menus were a mirror image of that day's dinner. But Mom cleverly whipped up a complete new menu, taking extra care not to serve the same meat or accompaniments. From planting through harvest time, we had meat, vegetables and fruit, potatoes or noodles, milk, and dessert—similar to dinner. Mom watched our daily diet, which meant keeping us healthy by balanced meals, whether we liked it or not. I don't remember any supper without a bowl of seasonal fresh fruit on the table, along with the usual bread, butter, and jam. However, our suppers were definitely not run-of-the-mill variety. (A young hired hand and neighbor lad, Arlen Heusinkveld, once asked, "Is *this* supper?" He thought his eyes were deceiving him as he sat down to a strawberry shortcake supper.)

Mom fixed *Apple Fritters* (page 280) or waffles with bacon in the fall; *Fresh Peach Cobbler* (page 286) —or plum—with a thick top crust, the juices spooned up from underneath it and heavy cream poured over the whole affair, in summer; rice cereal–style pudding topped with home-canned sour cherries in the winter; and *Fried Cornmeal Mush* (page 33) with sausages and syrup or *Corned Beef and Cabbage* (page 284) in the spring. An all-time-favorite-supper dish for us kids was *Successful Hamburger Gravy* (page 287) on homemade white bread. We also ate hearty soups, salads, and sandwiches for supper, in the same fashion that many people eat lunch now. During strawberry season, supper con-

sisted of piping-hot, baking powder biscuits made with cream, topped with crushed fresh berry sauce, plus whole strawberries and more cream. We ate our fill and felt totally satisfied. The winter rendition of this menu consisted of graham muffins, baked in an old black cast-iron muffin tin, slathered with butter, topped with home-canned strawberries and their juices plus a splash of heavy cream or a dollop of whipped cream. What a feast!

Dad's favorite supper dish (that he makes for himself if he eats alone) is bread and milk or crackers and milk. He simply crumbles the bread or crackers into a bowl, generously sprinkles sugar over the top, and pours on the milk. The whole Schrock clan grew up on this basic dish. So, we Sarlins still carry on the tradition. He likes saltine-style crackers, but my family and I prefer graham crackers.

The absolute rule of all our other meals applied at our family supper table as well: "Clean your plate!"

Economical and nutrition-minded, Grams and Mom saved the vegetable and meat cooking liquids to be transformed eventually into a delicious soup. Oftentimes, soup was the main dish for supper along with a large basket of crackers. "Soup without crackers is like cake without frosting," according to Dad, as he crumbled the saltines in his hands held over his flat, plate-style soup bowl. Mom nibbled on plain wheat crackers between each bite of soup with the piping-hot steam curling out of her deep, round soup bowl. We kids ate buttered crackers on the side, trying desperately not to slurp our soup. Mom was adamant about that!

Just because we ate these foods for supper does not mean they can't be eaten at any meal. Most likely included in a dinner, lunch, or late supper menu, these foods are sure to enhance as well as expand both your palate and your girth—unless you work off the calories with chores before sunset.

FROM GRAMS'S "WHATNOT" STOCKPOT

The age-old story of the poor hungry peddler who made the magical Stone Soup with the reluctant help from local villagers brings to mind Mom's amazing ability to make something out of (seemingly) nothing. "Good heavens, everyone knows how to make soup!" Mom scoffed when I asked her about the recipes from Grams. "I use whatever I have on hand, incorporating leftovers and whatnot." Does this sound familiar? No wonder the Stone Soup story lives on.

To soup lovers, bowl size and shape, spoon size and shape, and the optimum temperature are crucial individual issues. My family prefers to eat their soup from a mug. Suit yourself about the container, but for sure, cook up a big pot of soup and savor the aroma as it simmers. Then grab the best dish around and sip—but do not slurp—your soup. When no one is looking, pick up the bowl, and drink the last drop. (Ye gads!)

Indiana Truck Patch Harvest

Beef
Broth

◆

Traditionally, Grams used meaty soup bones plus a "good piece of chuck" to make beef broth. She simply placed them in a large kettle, filled it with cold water, and boiled them. After simmering the bones and meat all day, she poured off the broth, removed the bits and pieces of meat, fed the bones and the fat to the dog, and chilled the liquid overnight in the tank room. The broth was degreased and made into soup the next day.

I follow Mom's technique outlined in the following recipe. The rich beef flavor can be strengthened if the broth is reduced by half. Actually, if it is reduced by three-quarters, you will become the proud owner of boullion.

3 TO 4 POUNDS RAW BEEF BONES, OR 3 POUNDS BEEF CHUCK WITH BONES INTACT
2 CARROTS, CHOPPED
2 STALKS CELERY, CHOPPED
1 MEDIUM ONION, CHOPPED
6 TO 8 QUARTS WATER
2 TABLESPOONS BLACK PEPPERCORNS
½ BAY LEAF
3 CLOVES GARLIC, WHOLE
5 TO 6 PARSLEY STEMS, WHOLE
SALT TO TASTE

Sear bones or meat over high heat, turning often to brown evenly, for about 10 minutes. *Or,* brown bones and meat in 450° oven until dark brown (30 minutes).

Add chopped carrots, celery, and onion to meat; brown briefly. Add enough cold water (6 to 8 quarts) to cover meat and vegetables by 2 inches. Add peppercorns, bay leaf, garlic, and parsley stems.

Cover and bring to a boil. Reduce heat. Simmer, partially covered, skimming off gray foam every so often, over low heat for 3 to 4 hours, or until bones and meat are completely separated. Add boiling water if necessary to keep meat covered.

Remove from heat; cool slightly. Taste; add salt according to personal preference.

TO STRAIN Pour meat, vegetables, and broth into strainer set over large bowl. Shake off excess liquid. Return broth to stockpot. Separate meat from skin, bones, and fat. Cut meat into small pieces and reserve. Discard skin, bones, connective tissue, fat, and vegetables.

If using right away, pour broth into gravy strainer; rest for 5 to 10 minutes, or until fat comes to top. Gradually pour broth into clean bowl or saucepan. Continue working in batches until all broth is degreased. (Aunt Rubye runs an ice cube over the top of the broth to collect some of the fat if she is in a hurry to use the broth.)

If time allows, chill broth in refrigerator overnight. Next day, remove and discard fat formed on top of broth. After fat is removed, bring broth to a boil. Simmer approximately 45 minutes, or until broth develops full flavor and reduces. Remove from heat.

Place dampened clean white linen napkin or tea towel inside strainer set over clean large bowl; pour broth through lined strainer. Reserve broth for soup. Can be done ahead. Refrigerate 2 to 3 days or freeze 2 to 3 months.

TO CLARIFY Bring broth to a boil; meanwhile break washed egg shells and white of 2 eggs into small bowl. (Reserve yolks for another use.) Whisk until frothy. Gradually whisk 1 cup hot broth into egg whites, then reverse the process by whisking the egg white–broth mixture into the stockpot. (It will look absolutely awful at this point—a glob!) Continue whisking to distribute egg mixture throughout liquid until broth comes to a boil. Stop whisking; reduce heat to barely simmering and simmer 5 to 10 minutes. Remove from heat and cool slightly. Place dampened clean white linen napkin or tea towel inside strainer set over clean large bowl. Pour broth–egg white mixture through lined strainer. Discard "goop." Reserve clear broth for consommé or aspics.

VARIATIONS
Quick Beef Broth Over high heat, brown ½ pound ground beef in large saucepan. Add ½ cup each of chopped carrot, celery, and onion. Sauté 1 to 2 minutes. Add 3 cans (10½ ounces each) of beef broth, plus 1 can water, and splash of white wine. Cover and bring to a boil. Reduce heat and simmer with lid

ajar for 30 minutes. Strain out meat and vegetables. Proceed according to recipe.

Chicken Broth Follow *Great-Grandmother Broadwater's Chicken and Biscuit* recipe for cooking chicken (page 172) to the point before assembly. Use meat for soup, hot dishes, or salad. Degrease or clarify broth as directed in *Beef Broth* recipe. Reserve clear broth for soup.

Quick Chicken Broth Bring 3 cans (10½ ounces each) of chicken broth, plus 1 can water, to a boil. Add 1 whole chicken breast or a few chicken bones, along with ½ cup each of chopped carrots, celery, and onion. Cover and bring to a boil. Reduce heat and simmer with lid ajar for 30 minutes. Strain out meat and vegetables. Proceed according to recipe.

Can be done ahead. Refrigerate 2 to 3 days or freeze 2 to 3 months.

MAKES ABOUT 6 QUARTS BROTH

Vegetable Soup Base

❖

2 TABLESPOONS BUTTER
1 TABLESPOON OIL
1 LARGE ONION, CHOPPED
4 MEDIUM CARROTS, PEELED AND CHOPPED
3 STALKS CELERY, CHOPPED
1 TO 2 TEASPOONS HERBS, CHOPPED
1 TEASPOON BLACK PEPPER, FRESHLY GROUND
SALT TO TASTE
3 TO 4 CUPS MEAT/ VEGETABLES
2 TO 2½ QUARTS BEEF OR CHICKEN BROTH (SEE PAGES 269—270)

Once a good beef or chicken broth has been prepared or quickly "doctored up," a full-bodied, rich-flavored vegetable soup commences. Lightly sauté some carrot, celery, and onion in butter to impart a "flavor seal." After this base is established, add vegetables you enjoy. Sauté a bit first and then pour in broth, along with prepared meat, noodles, pasta, barley, or whatever suits your fancy.

Here then is the base. Chop the vegetables into uniform size to facilitate even cooking time and also for the sake of appearance. Whet your taste buds and create your own variations, using this recipe merely as a guide.

Melt butter and oil in large stockpot or saucepan. Over moderate heat, sauté onion for 4 to 5 minutes. Add carrots and celery and continue to sauté for 6 to 8 minutes longer, or until onion is soft and translucent. Season with herbs, pepper, and salt to taste.

Stir in prepared meat and/or vegetables. Sauté 2 to 3 minutes more. Add prepared broth; cover and bring to a boil. Reduce heat and simmer, partially covered, over low heat for 15 to 20 minutes, or until vegetables are tender. Taste and correct seasonings. The soup can be made ahead. Cool uncovered. Then cover and refrigerate 1 to 2 days or freeze 1 to 2 weeks.

VARIATIONS

Beef Barley Soup Prepare beef stock for soup base. Rinse 1 cup pearl barley under running water. In saucepan, cover barley with cold water; bring to a boil, and boil 2 minutes. Remove from heat and soak barley 1 hour. Meanwhile, wash ½ pound mushrooms; slice and add to sautéing soup base vegetables. Season with ½ teaspoon each of thyme and tarragon. Raise heat and sauté 4 to 5 minutes, adding a bit more butter if necessary.

Add 1 cup cooked beef (cut into ½-inch dice); sauté 2 minutes. Pour 2 quarts broth over vegetables. Cover, bring to a boil, and simmer 15 minutes. Drain barley; add to soup along with 1 cup additional broth if necessary. Simmer 20 to 30 minutes longer, or until barley is tender. Taste and correct seasonings.

Beef Noodle Soup Prepare beef broth. Add 2 cups cubed beef to sautéing soup base vegetables. Season with ¼ teaspoon thyme, ½ teaspoon rosemary, and pepper to taste. Add 2 quarts broth; simmer 10 to 15 minutes. Add 4 ounces (about 3 cups) fine egg noodles with 1 cup additional broth if necessary. Bring to a boil. Simmer 20 to 30 minutes longer, or until noodles are tender. Taste and correct seasonings.

Beef Vegetable Soup Prepare beef broth. To base vegetables, add 2 leeks (cleaned and chopped), ½ cup rutabaga (cubed), 1 large cubed potato, and 1 cup each of chopped carrots, beans, peas, and corn. Season with ½ teaspoon thyme, ½ teaspoon bouquet garni, 1 clove garlic (minced), and pepper to taste. Sauté along with 1½ cups cubed beef for 2 to 3 minutes. Add 2 quarts broth. Proceed according to basic recipe.

Beef Vegetable Soup with Tomatoes Add 1 can (28 ounces) of whole tomatoes with thick tomato puree—or 2 large fresh tomatoes (peeled, seeded, and chopped) and 2 tablespoons tomato paste—plus 1 bay leaf before beef broth. Proceed according to beef vegetable recipe. Remove bay leaf before serving.

Hamburger Soup (This was a favorite of us kids when we were little, because no strange, unlikeable vegetables were included.) Prepare beef broth. Brown 2 pounds ground beef in skillet over high heat. Season with 1 teaspoon rosemary, ½ teaspoon thyme, 1 clove garlic (minced), 1 tablespoon tomato paste, and 2 teaspoons black pepper (freshly ground). Add browned meat plus 2 cups sliced carrots, 2 cups peas, and 2 large potatoes (diced) to sautéing soup base vegetables. Add 2 quarts broth. Proceed according to recipe.

Chicken Noodle or Chicken Vegetable Soup Substitute chicken broth for beef broth and diced cooked chicken for meat, and proceed according to beef soup recipes.

MAKES 2½ TO 3 QUARTS (SERVES 6)

"What-Ever" Potato Soup

◆

The French call it *Potage Parmentier,* and served cold it's called *Vichyssoise.* Farm families call it Potato Soup and call for it often. Not one soul that I know would turn down a bowl of this heart-warming comfort food. The simplicity is as appealing to the cook as it is to the diner. There are as many variations as you can imagine. "It just depends," Mom stated. "On what?" I asked. "On whatever one feels like!" she answered.

∙∙∙∙∙∙∙∙∙∙∙∙∙∙∙∙∙∙∙∙∙∙∙∙∙∙∙∙∙∙∙∙∙

Sauté onions in butter over moderate heat until soft, 4 to 5 minutes. Add potatoes; sauté 2 to 3 minutes. Add enough water to cover vegetables by

"Cook your potatoes in a little bit of water, just enough to cook them without burning. Once they are cooked, add as much milk as you want, bring to a boil, season with salt, pepper and a dab of butter." Mom

3 CUPS CHOPPED ONIONS
2 TABLESPOONS BUTTER
4 CUPS PEELED AND DICED POTATOES
6 TO 7 CUPS WATER OR CHICKEN BROTH (SEE PAGE 270)
1 TO 2 TEASPOONS SALT
½ TEASPOON WHITE PEPPER

at least 1 inch. Season with salt and pepper.

Cover and bring to a boil. Reduce heat; simmer, partially covered, 20 to 25 minutes, or until potatoes are tender. Taste and correct seasonings.

NOTE Substitute leeks for onions for a traditional favorite flavor. Or use half leek, half onion, if desired.

VARIATIONS
Creamy Potato Soup Add 1 cup heavy cream after potatoes are tender. Bring to a boil, taste, and correct seasonings.
Spicy Creamy Potato Soup Add 1 teaspoon nutmeg and 1 teaspoon black pepper (both freshly grated), pinch of crushed red pepper flakes (or more to taste), plus ½ teaspoon celery salt to *Creamy Potato Soup* above. Proceed according to recipe.
Embellished Potato Soup Add 1 carrot (finely diced) and 1 stalk celery (finely diced) to leeks and onions. Season with ¼ teaspoon thyme and ½ teaspoon black pepper (freshly ground). Substitute chicken broth for water. Proceed according to *Creamy Potato Soup* recipe.
Thickened Embellished Potato Soup Puree 2 cups of finished soup in food processor or Foley food mill. Add puree to remaining soup and proceed according to recipe.

MAKES 2½ TO 3 QUARTS (SERVES 6)

Grams's Rivel Soup

❖

Great-Grandmother Broadwater served Rivel Soup nearly every night for supper. (Rivels are an economical extender of the food dollar, a mixture of flour, salt, and egg, formed into pea-sized lumps, and added to hot liquid—most generally, potato soup.) Her family ate it because they had no choice but to Mom it was just plain monotonous. Remember, she boarded there for four years. She hoped never to eat it again, but we begged her to make it for us. Our memories of Grams's Rivel Soup were tasty indeed.

Serve it with a green salad, fresh fruit, and crusty herb bread and butter on a cold winter night. Not boring at all.

5 MEDIUM POTATOES, PEELED AND DICED
2 TABLESPOONS BUTTER
APPROXIMATELY 2 CUPS WATER
1 CUP FLOUR
½ TEASPOON SALT
1 EGG
1 QUART MILK
½ TEASPOON CELERY SALT
½ TO 1 TEASPOON BLACK PEPPER, FRESHLY GROUND
1 MEDIUM ONION, CHOPPED

"Put 2 quarts of milk, with a pinch of salt, on the stove over an asbestos mat to boil. Take 2 teacups of flour, break into it 1 egg, mix with the hand and rub into rivels; Stir into boiling milk and let boil a few minutes." Great-Grandmother Broadwater

Sauté potatoes in butter to form "seal." Pour enough cold water over potatoes to barely cover. Cover pan and bring to a boil. Reduce heat; simmer 15 to 20 minutes or until potatoes are soft.

Meanwhile, make rivels. Mix flour and salt together. Add egg to flour; stir with fork to form lumps the size of peas and lima beans. Set aside.

Add milk to cooked potatoes; season with celery salt and pepper. Bring to a boil. Immediately add rivels and excess flour to soup. Once hot, simmer 15 to 20 minutes longer, or until rivels are completely cooked. Taste and correct seasoning; top soup with chopped onion.

MAKES 2½ QUARTS (SERVES 6)

Christmas
Eve
Oyster
Soup

Oyster soup was a delicacy in our family. Grams placed her oyster order with the Preston Locker in October for our annual holiday oyster soup supper. The white, round, waxed cardboard quart container held the big, fat, juicy, shucked oysters and their liquor. Either Grams or Rubye invited the family for the oyster feast because Mom hated fish in any form.

This simply wonderful, true-blue, true-to-form soup can be a standard on your menu as opposed to a specialty item.

Pick over oysters and rinse with cold water. Strain liquor through fine mesh sieve to catch a random piece of shell.

In large soup pot, bring milk to a full boil. Just before milk reaches top of pot, pour in oysters; add liquor if desired. Cook only until edges of oysters begin to curl, *only* 1 minute.

1½ PINTS FRESHLY SHUCKED OYSTERS WITH LIQUOR
2 QUARTS WHOLE MILK
4 TABLESPOONS BUTTER
½ TEASPOON SALT
1 TEASPOON BLACK PEPPER, FRESHLY GROUND

CROUTONS

8 SLICES WHITE BREAD, CUBED
1 LARGE CLOVE GARLIC
4 TO 5 TABLESPOONS VEGETABLE OIL

Granddad and Grams

Add butter, salt, and pepper; mix well. Serve immediately, with croutons if desired.

TO MAKE CROUTONS Cube bread; arrange on baking sheet. Dry out in 325° oven for 20 to 30 minutes.

Sauté garlic clove in oil until evenly brown; remove garlic. Add dry bread cubes; fry over moderately high heat until light brown. Remove with slotted spoon onto folded brown paper bag to drain.

MAKES 2 TO 2½ QUARTS (SERVES 6)

RED, WHITE, AND BLUE CREAM SOUP

"Start with a basic cream sauce, then add the vegetables or other ingredients," Mom said. "Just remember the colors of the flag: red, white, and blue. Add the red to the white and you'll never be blue!" This rhyming rule for adding ingredients so a soup won't curdle on you is specifically applicable to cream of tomato soup. However, it works equally well when preparing other cream soups, too.

This recipe, the foundation on which to build your favorite cream soup, will not be rock solid but rather tasty smooth as an underpinning to ensure successful soup creations. Choose any vegetable or combination of vegetables; add cheese, meat, or whatever suits your menu. Let the produce from your garden be your guide.

Cream Soup Base

Melt butter; sauté onion until soft and translucent. Add flour; stirring constantly, cook for 2 to 3 minutes. Do not brown.

Off heat, add hot milk all at once, stirring constantly. Return to heat, whisk in rest of liquid, and bring to a boil. Reduce heat; stirring constantly, simmer 6 to 8 minutes, or until smooth and lightly coats spoon.

Season with salt and pepper according to personal taste and suitable for vegetables planned for inclusion. Base can be done ahead to this point. Place plastic wrap directly on top of base so no air pockets or skin forms on top. Refrig-

4 TABLESPOONS BUTTER
1 MEDIUM ONION, FINELY CHOPPED (APPROXIMATELY ¾ CUP)
¼ CUP FLOUR
4 CUPS MILK, BOILING
2½ CUPS MILK OR CHICKEN BROTH (SEE PAGE 270), ROOM TEMPERATURE
½ TEASPOON SALT
1 TEASPOON WHITE PEPPER

3 TO 4 CUPS VEGETABLES, COOKED AND SEASONED ACCORDING TO PERSONAL PREFERENCE (OR SEE VARIATIONS BELOW FOR SUGGESTIONS)

erate overnight or until ready to finish cooking. However, it does not freeze well.

Add prepared vegetables. Bring to a boil. Reduce heat; simmer 8 to 10 minutes or until vegetables are tender. Taste and correct seasonings.

VARIATIONS
Cream of Broccoli Soup Peel outer portion from stalks of 2 heads of broccoli. Remove flowerets; divide into bite-sized portions. Coarsely chop stalks. Steam until crunch tender; drain. Season cream soup base with 1½ to 2 teaspoons Dijon mustard; use 4 cups milk and 3 cups chicken broth. Add vegetables, sea-

son to taste, and proceed according to recipe.

Cream of Cauliflower Soup with Cheese Break 1 head of cauliflower into bite-sized portions. Steam or cook until crunch tender. Drain. Season cream soup base with 3 teaspoons Dijon mustard; use 4 cups milk and 3 cups chicken broth. Add ½ to ¾ cup shredded American cheese (cheddar or Swiss is good, too) and vegetables to base. Season to taste and proceed according to recipe.

Cream of Mushroom Soup Sauté ½ pound sliced or chopped fresh mushrooms in 2 tablespoons butter and 1 teaspoon oil over high heat 3 to 4 minutes. Season with 1½ teaspoons tarragon, ¼ teaspoon white pepper, and ½ teaspoon lemon juice. Add mushrooms to base. Season to taste and proceed according to recipe.

Cream of Tomato Soup Sauté 2 celery stalks with leaves (minced) in 1 tablespoon butter until soft and translucent. Add 1 cup canned tomato puree (not paste) plus 1 cup tomato juice; season with pinch of sugar and pinch of cayenne pepper. If using fresh tomatoes, cook 8 to 10 minutes before proceeding. Whisk tomato mixture ("add the red . . .") into hot base (". . . to the white"). Season to taste and proceed according to recipe.

**MAKES 2 TO 2½ QUARTS
(SERVES 6)**

Aunt Bets's Minnesota Wild Rice Soup

◆

½ CUP WILD RICE
2 CUPS COLD WATER
¼ CUP BUTTER
½ CUP FINELY DICED ONION
½ CUP FINELY DICED CELERY
½ CUP FINELY DICED CARROT
½ CUP SLIVERED ALMONDS
4 CUPS CHICKEN BROTH (SEE PAGE 270)
2 CUPS HALF-AND-HALF
3 TABLESPOONS CORNSTARCH
¼ CUP COLD MILK
DASH SALT
DASH BLACK PEPPER

Mom's youngest sister, Betty Gene—Aunt Bets to me—lives in Wells, Minnesota, about a hundred miles due west of the farm as the crow flies. Although Mom and Rubye thought she "had it easy" (growing up in Preston as opposed to the farm), I'm sure Bets would not confirm that assumption.

When Judd, their second son, was born, I (then fourteen) spent a month as a "mother's helper" to Aunt Bets and Uncle Buzz. My experience with two younger sisters came in handy with the baby, and the adults loved my cooking. Uncle Buzz complained that his trousers got too tight during my stay. (They must have shrunk.) Putting all that aside, Aunt Bets is an inventive good cook and a marvelous hostess.

Her recipe uses a well-known Minnesota product that is really a berry or seed, not a grain. It grows in fresh water lakes and swamps in northern Minnesota. The harvesting is done by two Native Americans in a canoe. One paddles through the stalks while the other "shakes" off the seeds into the bottom of the canoe.

Later, the rice is cured over smoke fires, dehulled, sifted, and then graded for packaging. All this is done by hand. No wonder it is expensive.

Though it is a luxury, the unmatched unique rich flavor is worth the price. The fact that ½ cup of raw rice makes 2½ cups cooked rice makes buying it easier.

Soak wild rice in cold water a few hours or overnight. Drain well and set aside.

Melt butter in heavy saucepan. Add onion, celery, and carrot. Sauté over moderate heat, 2 to 3 minutes. Stir in rice and almonds; sauté 4 to 5 minutes longer.

Add chicken broth. Cover; bring to a boil. Reduce heat; simmer 1 hour and 15 minutes. Skim occasionally if scum forms. Rice and vegetables should be tender. Gradually add half-and-half to hot soup; mix thoroughly.

Dissolve cornstarch in cold milk. Whisking constantly, gradually add cornstarch to thicken soup. Bring to a boil, then reduce heat; simmer 4 to 5 minutes longer. Taste and correct seasonings.

Janeen, Jeff, Aunt Bets, Judy, Joany, 1954

VARIATION

Wild Rice, Bacon, and Cheese Soup Rinse unprepared wild rice thoroughly with cold water. Place in heavy saucepan; cover with 2 cups fresh cold water. Cover pan and bring to a boil. Add ½ teaspoon salt, reduce heat, and simmer 45 minutes.

Meanwhile, sauté ½ pound bacon until crisp, drain well, and dice; reserve. Melt 4 tablespoons butter, add 1 large onion (diced), ½ cup celery (diced), and 3 large potatoes (diced), and sauté 4 to 5 minutes. Add 2 cups chicken broth and 1½ cups water. Cover; bring to a boil and cook about 15 to 20 minutes, or until potatoes are tender.

To assemble, drain excess liquid from rice. Add cooked vegetable mixture, reserved diced bacon, 2 cups half-and-half plus 2 cups milk, and 1 pound longhorn or cheddar cheese (shredded); mix well. Simmer together, stirring often, until cheese is melted and soup is hot. Serve immediately.

MAKES 2 QUARTS (SERVES 6)

Mom's Swedish Fruit Soup

This surprisingly refreshing soup can also be served either as a first course (when serving game later) or as dessert. Mom's favorite version began with a large can of purple plums drained of the syrup. To the syrup, add tapioca "enough to thicken," sugar, and lemon juice and/or rind "to taste." Cook until thick. When cool, return the plums to the soup and chill thoroughly. Serve with a dollop of sour cream or yogurt.

■■■■■■■■■■■■■■■■■■■■■■■■■■■■■■■

Cover dried fruits with cold water. Soak 1 to 2 hours, or until tender.

In heavy saucepan, simmer fruits over low heat until tender, but so

**1 POUND MIXED DRIED FRUIT
—APPLES, PEARS,
PEACHES, APRICOTS,
PRUNES, ETC.
2 TO 3 CUPS COLD WATER
½ CUP SUGAR
¼ TEASPOON SALT
½ CUP RAISINS
¼ CUP TAPIOCA
2 WHOLE CLOVES
2-INCH STICK CINNAMON**

pieces retain their shape. Add sugar and salt; simmer 10 minutes longer. Drain off 2 cups of juice into another pan. Set aside rest with cooked fruit.

Add raisins, tapioca, cloves, and cinnamon to 2 cups of juice. Slowly simmer until tapioca is cooked, approximately 8 minutes. Add reserved cooked fruit and juices.

Remove from heat, cover, and cool to room temperature; remove cloves and cinnamon stick. Chill 3 to 4 hours or overnight. Serve with dollop of whipped cream for dessert, sour cream for presentation as a first course.

MAKES 2 QUARTS (SERVES 6)

Easter Monday Ham and Pea Soup

❖

After a delicious Easter Sunday ham dinner, we just knew that soon we would be eating split pea soup made with the ham bone. Mom made it other times, too, but this post-Easter ritual was a given.

No need to wait until after Easter for this soup. Add sliced hot dogs or knockwurst to the pea soup for an attractive as well as tasty variation.

Cover split peas with 3 quarts water and soak overnight in large kettle. Drain and return peas to pot.

The next day, in skillet, sauté onion, celery, and carrots in butter 3 to 4 minutes. Add garlic and sauté 2 to 3 minutes.

Add vegetables to kettle with soaked peas. Then add ham bone, broth, 1 quart water, and clove-studded onion. Cover; bring to a boil. Reduce heat. Simmer, stirring occasionally, for approximately 1½ hours, or until peas are tender and soup is thickened.

Remove ham bone and whole onion. Chop any meat from bone fine; return to soup. (Discard bone and onion.) Bring soup to a boil. Add pepper; taste and correct seasoning.

1 POUND DRIED SPLIT PEAS (2 CUPS)
1 LARGE ONION, MINCED
4 STALKS CELERY, MINCED
2 CARROTS, MINCED
2 TABLESPOONS BUTTER
1 LARGE CLOVE GARLIC, MINCED
1 HAM BONE, OR ½ POUND BAKED HAM PIECES
1½ QUARTS CHICKEN BROTH (SEE PAGE 270)

1 MEDIUM ONION, PEELED, LEFT WHOLE, AND STUDDED WITH 3 WHOLE CLOVES
1 TO 1½ TEASPOONS BLACK PEPPER, FRESHLY GROUND

VARIATIONS

Ham and Pea Pureed Soup For smooth soup, puree cooked vegetables in food processor. Then add chopped ham, heat through, and serve.

Pea Soup with Hot Dogs or Knockwurst Omit ham bone or ham. Cook vegetables in broth and water. Thinly slice 1½ hot dogs or 1 knockwurst per person; add sliced meat to cooked soup. Bring to a boil, reduce heat, and simmer 10 to 15 minutes. Taste, correct seasonings, and serve.

Ham and Bean Soup Substitute 1 pound of navy beans, northern beans, or other dried beans for split peas. Proceed according to recipe.

Mom's Stoplight Soup Substitute red kidney beans for split peas. After the kidney beans are tender, add 2 cups fresh or frozen whole kernel corn and 1 cup fresh or frozen cut green beans to soup. Proceed according to recipe.

MAKES 2 TO 2½ QUARTS (SERVES 6 TO 8)

NO-HOLDS-BARRED MAIN DISHES

✦

Because Mom approached the supper menu with a "no-holds-barred" attitude, the following recipes are as varied as her creativity and the availability of resources allowed. However, she always adhered to one rule, "The meal must be nutritionally balanced for a growing family." Calories were included in the mix (thank goodness) and we looked forward to every supper with spoon and fork in hand to taste her creations.

Apple Fritters

✦

As a little girl, I played for hours on the cement steps of the front porch on the east side of our house. Because the porch was facing the road, I thought Mom was not within earshot of the fictitious conversations that I shared with my imagined "customers" who came to my "drugstore, soda fountain, and short-order counter restaurant." In my fabricated restaurant (without a single prop, I might add), I served a million cups of coffee, a reasonable number of chocolate milk shakes and ice cream sodas, along with grilled cheese sandwiches, BLTs, and hamburgers. From time to time, Mom appeared at the front door of the house, inquiring, "Why are you frittering away all your time with this nonsense?" I don't recall any specific answer on my part. However,

2 EGGS, SEPARATED
1 ½ CUPS MILK
1 TABLESPOON MELTED BUTTER
1 ¼ CUPS FLOUR, SIFTED
PINCH SALT
1 TO 1 ½ QUARTS VEGETABLE OIL
6 TO 7 MEDIUM APPLES, PEELED, CORED, AND SLICED ¼ INCH THICK (SOAKED IN JUICE OF HALF LEMON TO PREVENT BROWNING)

the minute she left, I offered Apple Fritters to my next imaginary customer.

In spite of my "nonsense," the following recipe is not an illusion nor is eating it a waste of time. When Dad brought a bushel of freshly picked firm apples home, we were certain that Mom would be serving Apple Fritters for supper. Our individual taste preferences for the topping made the setup for pancake supper fixings look sparse. Sitting on our table were pitchers of maple syrup, sorghum, homemade sugar syrup, dark and light karo syrup, plus a bowl of powdered sugar. The menu was complete with the addition of crisp bacon strips or a platter of cold cuts, plus carrot and celery sticks and milk for the family to drink.

Beat egg yolks until light and lemon-colored. Beat in milk and butter. Mix in flour and salt; set aside.

Beat egg whites until stiff. Set aside.

Heat oil to 370°, or until cube of bread dropped into oil browns in 1 minute.

Fold stiff whites into batter, just before frying.

TO FRY Dip apples into batter. Deep-fry until golden brown, turning over at least once with long fork. Apples should be tender to the point of fork. (Judge cooking time for the remainder after the first fritter is done.) Drain fritters on rack placed over baking sheet lined with brown paper bag.

Serve hot with syrup or powdered sugar.

S E R V E S   6

LUCKY FELLOWSHIP DISHES

❖

"First the fellowship and then the food" was the motto of our church suppers. We called them potluck. Casserole dishes were not only a popular contribution, but a convenience as well. It was always a mystery to me that, though no one dictated the number or types of dishes necessary for each supper, somehow, not only was there superb variety, but also the desired ratio of casseroles to salads to desserts always managed to materialize.

Imagine a six-foot-long table lined with umpty-ump casseroles: One dish contained chicken pieces and rice plus a vegetable or two smothered in a creamy sauce that thickened while it baked. Another held beef and cabbage dressed in a fine tomato sauce, topped with crunchy bread crumbs. Yet another was

a delicious combination of ground beef, onions, celery, and green pepper—laced with herbs and tomatoes, layered between creamy noodles, and finished with cheddar cheese.

The notion that these casseroles—more often called "hot dishes"—were made with a warmed-up conglomeration of leftovers could not have been further from the truth! Mom always started from scratch, using fresh quality ingredients combined with a rich creamy white sauce, cheese sauce, or tomato sauce to create a tasty supper dish, whether for church or for us.

No luck is needed for the following recipe, but a covered baking dish is a must.

Use the following typical hot dish recipe as a guide for other combinations, too. Wild rice, a Minnesota specialty (see page 276), adds a rich, one-of-a-kind, nutty flavor to this dish. If wild rice is not in your cupboard, use brown rice instead.

▪▪▪▪▪▪▪▪▪▪▪▪▪▪▪▪▪▪▪▪▪▪▪▪▪▪▪▪▪▪▪▪▪▪

TO MAKE BEEF/RICE FILLING
Rinse rice under cold running water. In saucepan, cover rice with cold water; bring to a boil. Cover, reduce heat, and cook 20 to 30 minutes, or until tender. Drain off any excess liquid; reserve.

Meanwhile, in large skillet, brown meat over moderately high heat. Add onion, celery, mushrooms, and parsley to meat; sauté until onion is soft and translucent.

Add garlic, reduce heat, and continue to sauté, stirring often, 4 to 5 minutes longer. Season with thyme, rosemary, and pepper. Mix drained wild rice into meat mixture; reserve.

Preheat oven to 350°.

TO MAKE SAUCE Melt butter in saucepan and sauté onion until soft and translucent. Add flour, stirring constantly, and cook for 2 to 3 minutes; do not brown.

Off heat, add hot broth combination all at once, stirring constantly. Return to heat, whisking con-

Beef and Wild Rice Casserole

BEEF/RICE MIXTURE
▪ ▪ ▪

1 CUP WILD RICE
2 TO 3 CUPS COLD WATER
2½ POUNDS GROUND CHUCK
1 LARGE ONION, CHOPPED (1 HEAPING CUP)
4 STALKS CELERY, WITH TOPS, CHOPPED
½ POUND MUSHROOMS, SLICED
1 SMALL BUNCH PARSLEY, CHOPPED
1 CLOVE GARLIC, MINCED
1 TEASPOON THYME
½ TO 1 TEASPOON ROSEMARY
1 TEASPOON BLACK PEPPER, FRESHLY GROUND

SAUCE
▪ ▪ ▪

4 TABLESPOONS BUTTER
¼ CUP CHOPPED ONIONS
4 TABLESPOONS FLOUR
1½ CUPS CHICKEN BROTH PLUS 1½ CUPS BEEF BROTH, BOILING (SEE PAGES 269–270)
ABOUT 1 CUP WARM MILK

½ CUP CRUSHED POTATO CHIPS (OPTIONAL)

stantly, and bring to a boil. Simmer 5 to 6 minutes or until smooth. Whisk in enough milk for desired consistency; it should be thick enough to hold casserole together.

TO ASSEMBLE CASSEROLE Pour creamy sauce over meat and rice mixture. Add more milk or broth, if necessary, to thin sauce. Mix well; taste and correct seasonings. Spoon into 10-cup covered casserole and top with crushed potato chips, if desired.

Bake in 350° oven 50 to 60 minutes, or until top is brown and sauce is bubbly.

NOTE Whenever possible, I make a double amount. After the ingredients are combined and at room temperature, line a baking/serving casserole with plastic wrap. Spoon in the mixture, cover with plastic wrap, and freeze overnight. When frozen solid, remove the wrapped ingredients from the casserole, double-wrap in a plastic bag, and close with an airtight seal. Replace in the freezer. (This allows other uses for the casserole dish.) When ready to bake/serve, remove the casserole from the freezer, unwrap, replace it in the casserole dish, and defrost. Cover, bake, and serve.

S E R V E S   6

Aunt Rubye's Famous Mushroom Hot Dish

When friends and family gathered at Aunt Rubye's for a birthday dinner (or other dinners like Easter), often she served this dish. Grams, Mom, and Aunt Bets also prepared this casserole, but it never tasted quite the same as it did at Rubye's. Though we did not think of it as a vegetarian dish at the time, it is easy to prepare, practically on demand, for any non—meat eaters coming for dinner.

This recipe will guarantee that the end result will be as close to eating it at Rubye's as you can get.

■■■■■■■■■■■■■■■■■■■■■■■■■■■■■■■

Preheat oven to 350°. Butter a 3-quart baking/serving dish or large casserole dish.

Spread bread cubes in one layer on baking sheet; drizzle melted butter over cubes. Bake for 20 to 25 minutes, or until light brown and dry. Set aside.

Meanwhile, in saucepan, cover eggs with cold water. Add salt and bring to a boil; reduce heat and simmer 11 minutes. Drain off hot water, and immediately plunge eggs into cold water. Crack shells, peel, and drain eggs; chill in refrigerator.

TO MAKE SAUCE Melt butter in large saucepan. Add flour and cook 2 to 3 minutes, stirring constantly. Off heat, whisk in hot milk all at

6 CUPS WHITE BREAD, STALE OR DAY OLD, CUBED INTO 2-INCH SQUARES
4 TO 5 TABLESPOONS BUTTER, MELTED

4 LARGE EGGS IN SHELL
1 TEASPOON SALT

SAUCE
■ ■ ■

6 TABLESPOONS BUTTER
6 TABLESPOONS FLOUR
3 CUPS HOT MILK
1½ TEASPOONS CELERY SEED
¼ TEASPOON BLACK PEPPER, FRESHLY GROUND
1½ CUPS CHEDDAR, LONGHORN, OR AMERICAN CHEESE, "CHUNKED" INTO ½-INCH CUBES

1½ TO 2 POUNDS MEDIUM FRESH MUSHROOM CAPS, RINSED, OR 1 CAN (14 OUNCES) LARGE BUTTON MUSHROOMS, DRAINED
2 TABLESPOONS BUTTER
1 TABLESPOON VEGETABLE OIL

½ TO 1 CUP BREAD CUBES (¼ TO ½ INCH IN SIZE), SAUTÉED IN 1 TABLESPOON BUTTER (FOR TOPPING)

> "1 can mushrooms, 3 boiled eggs, cheese grated, celery seed, buttered bread crumbs, white sauce made with 2 Tbsp butter and flour to 1 cup milk." Aunt Rubye

once. Return to heat, stirring constantly, and bring to a boil. Cook 5 to 6 minutes or until smooth. Season with celery seed and pepper. Mix in cheese and take off heat. (Cheese will melt as sauce cools.)

If using fresh mushrooms, melt butter and oil in large skillet. Add mushrooms and sauté over high heat, stirring or shaking pan frequently, 6 to 8 minutes. Continue cooking until juices have evaporated. Cool slightly before assembly.

TO ASSEMBLE Combine mushrooms, large toasted bread cubes (reserved), and sliced cooked eggs with white sauce; mix lightly. Pour into prepared baking/serving dish; bake 30 minutes. Remove dish, sprinkle small sautéed bread cubes over top, and return to oven. Bake until crusty brown on top. (Rubye runs the whole affair under the broiler to brown the top bread cubes.)

S E R V E S   6

Corned Beef
and
Cabbage

Although no Irish blood ran through Grams's veins, she cured a mean corned beef. Not only Grams, but other farm women preserved a portion of the freshly killed beef in the same fashion. The meat was "relatively safe" in this brine for up to three months when kept cool.

After rubbing coarse salt into the raw beef (usually a piece of about 100 pounds), Grams placed it in a large crock to "stand" overnight. Meanwhile, she "brewed" a brine consisting of 8 pounds of salt, 2 ounces of saltpeter, 2 pounds of brown sugar, 1 ounce of baking soda, and 4 gallons of water. After this concoction boiled and the scum was skimmed off the top, she let it cool; the next day she rinsed the salt off the meat, poured the brine over it, and repacked it into the earthenware crock. Much in the same fashion as making sauerkraut, the wooden lid was weighted down with a heavy stone until the brine completely covered the meat. However, the corned-beef curing process took place in the tank room. Two weeks after Grams

started this business, she removed a portion of the meat and asked Granddad to take it up to Dave Ogg's smokehouse where it was made into dried beef. The remaining meat continued to cure for two to four weeks before it was ready to cook.

To cook corned beef and cabbage, Grams simply removed the meat from the brine, cut off what she needed, and placed the rest back in the crock. Before the warm weather set in, Grams canned any meat left in the crock to preserve it. Although Mom often followed Grams's example in food preparation, corned beef was one exception. Mom and Dad took their meat into Austin's Locker to be cured and dried under conditions according to the USDA safety standards.

Lucky for us, corned beef is available at butcher shops and grocery stores, ready to be cooked without six weeks' preparation.

1 CORNED BEEF, 4 TO 6 POUNDS (AVAILABLE AT THE BUTCHER OR FOOD MARKET)
4 SMALL WHOLE ONIONS, PEELED, EACH STUDDED WITH 3 CLOVES
4 LARGE CLOVES GARLIC, PEELED AND LEFT WHOLE

1 MEDIUM HEAD GREEN CABBAGE, WASHED AND OUTER LEAVES REMOVED

HORSERADISH SAUCE

⅓ CUP GRATED FRESH HORSERADISH
1 TABLESPOON SUGAR, OR MORE TO TASTE
1 TO 1½ TABLESPOONS HEAVY CREAM
SPLASH CIDER VINEGAR

Rinse brine from meat and place in heavy casserole. Add onions around meat. Add garlic and cover whole affair with enough cold water to cover by 1 inch.

Cover and bring to a boil. Reduce heat and simmer 3 to 3½ hours, or until meat is tender to point of fork.

> "Take corned beef out of the brine, wash it well. Cook it in a pot with onion and enough cold water to cover until tender. Skim off fat. Add cabbage, continue cooking until the cabbage is done." Mom

Remove meat to warm platter. Skim fat from broth. Or pour into gravy strainer, let rest 4 to 5 minutes, and return strained broth to casserole.

Cut cabbage into 2-inch wedges. Add to broth; cover and bring to a boil. Reduce heat and simmer uncovered about 15 minutes, or until cabbage is tender.

Slice meat against the grain. Place meat in center of large platter; arrange cabbage around meat. Serve with boiled potatoes and horseradish sauce.

TO MAKE SAUCE Mix horseradish, sugar, cream, and vinegar until smooth. Taste and correct seasoning.

VARIATION
Roasted Corned Beef Follow initial cooking procedure. Allow meat to cool in broth; refrigerate overnight. Next day, remove brisket from liquid; place meat on roasting rack set over roasting pan. Stud corned beef with cloves (score first for a diamond design like a ham). Press ¾ cup light brown sugar over top of meat. Roast in 325° oven approximately 1½ to 2 hours, or until crisp brown crust is formed. Slice meat against the grain. Serve with *Scalloped Cabbage* (page 197) and *Kidney Bean Salad* (page 305).

SERVES 6 GENEROUSLY

Farm-Style Hash

❖

3 TO 4 TABLESPOONS BUTTER
3 LARGE ONIONS, CHOPPED
3 LARGE RAW POTATOES, PEELED AND CUBED (OR LEFTOVER, BOILED)
2 TO 3 TABLESPOONS VEGETABLE OIL, IF NECESSARY
LEFTOVER CORNED BEEF, BEEF, CHICKEN, OR TURKEY (CUBED) (APPROXIMATELY 3 TO 4 CUPS)
½ TEASPOON THYME
½ TEASPOON ROSEMARY
1 TEASPOON BLACK PEPPER, FRESHLY GROUND
SALT TO TASTE
¼ CUP CHOPPED FRESH PARSLEY
1 CUP MILK

"Mother made hash to extend the meat. More often than not, she used the leftover (from dinner) meat and boiled potatoes for supper." Mom

285

Although *Grams's Black Book* did not include a recipe for hash, Mom recalls eating it often for supper. Grams gussied up the hash by adding fried onions to the potatoes and then the meat. Grandma Schrock used more potatoes than meat, and Mom does not "bother with eating it at all." However, I prefer equal parts of meat, raw potatoes, and onions, seasoned with herbs and topped with an egg for each person.

Preheat oven to 350°.

Melt butter in heavy, ovenproof skillet; add onions and sauté 2 to 3 minutes. Add cubed potatoes (and oil if necessary) and fry until half done and brown, stirring often.

Add cubed meat. Sauté 4 to 5 minutes longer, turning often. Season with herbs, pepper, and salt; taste and correct seasonings.

Pour milk over whole affair. Bring to a boil, stirring up once or twice. Bake, uncovered, 25 to 30 minutes, or until potatoes are soft and dish browns.

VARIATION
Hash and Eggs Allow 1 egg per person. When hash is brown, remove from oven. With back of large spoon, make indent. Break egg into each nest and return to hot oven. Bake 5 to 8 minutes longer, or until eggs are baked.

Or, in separate skillet, fry eggs according to personal preference. Remove hash from oven, place an egg in each nest, and serve.

SERVES 6

Fresh
Peach
Cobbler

❖

1 ½ CUPS SUGAR
2 TABLESPOONS CORNSTARCH
2 TABLESPOONS LEMON JUICE
½ CUP WATER
**2 QUARTS FRESH PEACHES,
PEELED, PITTED, AND
SLICED**
**½ TEASPOON ALMOND
EXTRACT**
½ TEASPOON CINNAMON
**1 TABLESPOON BUTTER, CUT
INTO SMALL PIECES**

CRUST
∎∎∎

2 CUPS FLOUR
1 TABLESPOON SUGAR
**1 TABLESPOON BAKING
POWDER**
PINCH SALT
6 TABLESPOONS BUTTER
**1 CUP MILK OR HALF-AND-
HALF**

1 TO 2 PINTS HEAVY CREAM

"Cobble up" means to put together roughly or hastily. In peach season, I am reminded of peach cobbler, a typical country dish that every mother in our family tree quickly fixed for supper. We gladly heaped our plates full by spooning the steaming sweetened juices from the bottom over the thick biscuit crust and generously poured on the heavy cream. Yummmm . . . We all licked our plates clean before pushing our stuffed bellies away from the table.

▪▪▪▪▪▪▪▪▪▪▪▪▪▪▪▪▪▪▪▪▪▪▪▪▪▪▪▪▪▪▪

Preheat oven to 400°. Butter 3-quart baking/serving dish or large casserole dish.

Mix sugar and cornstarch in saucepan; add lemon juice and water. Bring to a boil, and boil 1 minute, stirring constantly. Mix in sliced peaches and almond extract and pour into prepared baking dish. Sprinkle cinnamon on peaches; dot with butter, and set aside.

TO MAKE CRUST Mix flour, sugar, baking powder, and salt together in bowl. Cut butter into flour mixture until it looks like coarse meal. (This can be done in a food processor.) Add milk and stir until it forms soft dough.

Drop dough by spoonfuls onto hot fruit in even pattern. Bake 20 to 25 minutes, or until top is golden brown.

For supper, serve hot cobbler in flat soup bowls, and pass pitcher of cream for pouring over cobbler. For company dessert, cut cobbler into squares or spoon onto dessert plates, and top with whipped cream.

SERVES 6 FOR SUPPER,
8 AS DESSERT

Successful Hamburger Gravy

◆

Though they lived and worked on a farm, Grandfather Schrock, an ordained minister in the Church of the Brethren, took turns preaching (for free of course) on Sunday mornings, along with three other ministers. Because of his own education at both Manchester College and Mt. Morris Bible School, he provided for and encouraged all of his thirteen children to have the education that they needed. He gave each one seventy-five dollars upon their graduation from high school. Thereafter, they worked hard to pay their own way through school. Grandfather Schrock's motto was: "I can only measure my success by the success of my children!" Being slightly prejudiced, his grandchildren (all sixty-two of us) would agree that he was extremely successful.

2 POUNDS GROUND CHUCK
1 MEDIUM ONION, CHOPPED
1 CLOVE GARLIC, MINCED
¼ TEASPOON SALT
½ TEASPOON BLACK PEPPER, FRESHLY GROUND
½ TEASPOON CELERY SEED
6 TABLESPOONS FLOUR
3 TO 4 CUPS MILK
¼ CUP FRESH PARSLEY, CHOPPED

Lest we forget: Feeding these thirteen children was an important link to the success and general health of the family. All that credit goes to Grandmother Schrock. She skillfully managed this feat on a shoestring budget, economizing without sacrificing the quality and quantity of the food.

This recipe, reminiscent of Grandmother Schrock's style of cooking, always triggered a happy storytelling time from Dad during supper. We kids asked for hamburger gravy often.

In large stainless steel skillet, brown meat over moderately high heat; add some vegetable oil if the meat sticks. Add onion and garlic. Continue to cook until onion is soft and translucent and meat is well done.

Season with salt, pepper, and celery seed. Stir in flour and cook over moderate heat until flour is brown, but not burned, stirring constantly.

Whisk in milk, stirring up brown bits. Boil for 4 to 5 minutes, stirring constantly until sauce is smooth and thick. Add more milk if necessary to obtain a gravy consistency. Taste and correct seasoning.

Serve over toast; garnish with chopped parsley.

NOTE The Schrocks "successfully" ladled this gravy over plain white bread or pancakes.

Grandfather and Grandmother Schrock

S E R V E S   6

Saturday night suppers during the busy strawberry season consisted of light-as-a-feather biscuits (shortcakes), fresh, whole strawberries sweetened with a fresh crushed strawberry sauce, and cream either whipped or poured on top.

When I was little, the winter rendition of this supper—graham muffins with homemade canned strawberries—was met with the same enthusiasm. Nowadays, Mom uses frozen strawberries only when fresh ones are unavailable.

Grams's biscuit cutter, measuring 2¾ inches in diameter, is a recycled baking powder can with the outer rim removed. (I cut out biscuits with it today.) On the other hand, Mom fancies a recycled tunafish or tomato paste can for this task. You need not run to the store for a biscuit cutter before making this recipe.

- -

TO MAKE SHORTCAKE Preheat oven to 450°. Mix flour, baking powder, salt, and sugar together. Add enough cream to make dough. Knead dough on floured board until smooth, or for about 2 minutes. With rolling pin, roll ¾ to 1 inch thick. Cut dough into biscuits 2½ to 3 inches in diameter.

Place on greased baking sheet and bake for 10 to 12 minutes, or until golden brown.

TO MAKE BERRY SAUCE Wash, hull, and drain berries. Measure 5 cups berries into bowl, reserving perfect ones. With Foley food fork

Saturday Night Special Strawberry Shortcake

❖

CREAM BISCUIT SHORTCAKE
∎ ∎ ∎

2 CUPS FLOUR
2½ TEASPOONS BAKING POWDER
½ TEASPOON SALT
½ TEASPOON SUGAR
¾ TO 1 CUP HEAVY CREAM

BERRY SAUCE
∎ ∎ ∎

6 TO 7 CUPS STRAWBERRIES
¾ TO 1½ CUPS SUGAR

1½ CUPS HEAVY CREAM

or potato masher, crush/smush the not-perfect berries until juices run. It is a lumpy sauce, not a puree. Sweeten to taste with sugar and set aside.

Just before serving, mix in whole berries.

TO ASSEMBLE Serve biscuits directly from oven. Halve horizontally and spoon crushed sauce in middle. Place top half on and spoon whole berries and more sauce on top. Pass heavy cream in pitcher or top biscuits with generous dollop of whipped cream (made by whipping 1½ cups heavy cream with 1 tablespoon sugar and 1 teaspoon vanilla).

VARIATION
Winter Version Substitute graham muffins for shortcake: Preheat oven to 400° and generously grease 12 muffin tins. Beat 1 egg with 1 cup milk and ¼ cup melted butter or vegetable oil (Mom used melted lard). Mix 1 cup white flour, 1 cup whole wheat (graham) flour, ¼ cup brown sugar, 2½ teaspoons baking powder, and ½ teaspoon salt together in mixing bowl. Add egg mixture to dry ingredients. Quickly stir until just mixed; batter will be lumpy.

Immediately spoon into prepared muffin tins. Bake 20 to 25 minutes, or until toothpick inserted into center comes out clean and top is brown. Immediately tip out of tins, split, and serve with strawberries and cream.

S E R V E S 6

Pan-Fried Fish

❖

After Granddad moved to town he had more time to fish. He'd head for a favorite undivulged (according to rumor) "fishing hole" with his paraphernalia and prospective luck. Of course Grams knew where he went, so now I know that he fished along the Mississippi, at a lake "up north"—where he caught northern pike and walleyes, and also went ice fishing in the winter, at the Root River, and in a trout stream near Preston. When he returned, he would proudly and carefully empty his green fish pack, bulging with scaled and cleaned best-of-the-catch, into a basin filled with cold fresh water. From this point, Grams took over.

Effortlessly, she heated butter in a black cast-iron skillet, large enough to hold the fish in one piece, until it stopped sizzling. She rolled the fish in flour, fried it until it was perfectly done, sprinkled on a little salt and pepper, and garnished the plate with lemon wedges and one sprig of parsley. Simply the best. Grams always served *Parsleyed New Potatoes* (page 232) (or browned "old" potatoes using the same recipe) with fish.

Though this recipe uses a whole trout, the same procedure also applies to fish in the form of fillets, steaks, or other pieces. Remember, fresh fish has a delicate flavor and needs very little embellishment. However, fine, dry bread crumbs flavored with chopped fresh parsley can be substituted for the flour.

6 WHOLE TROUT, ½ POUND EACH, CLEANED, WASHED, AND PATTED DRY (OR ANY OTHER SMALL FISH IS FINE)
6 TO 8 TABLESPOONS CLARIFIED BUTTER (SEE NOTE)
½ CUP FLOUR
½ CUP FRESH PARSLEY, CHOPPED
FRESH LEMON, CUT IN WEDGES

Sprinkle cavities of fish with salt and pepper. Heat butter until very hot in heavy skillet.

Roll fish in flour, tap off excess, and fry in hot butter. (If using fillets, place skin side down first.) Fry 5 minutes, carefully turn over with flat spatula, and fry other side 5 minutes, or until flesh separates from backbone, is firm to the touch of a finger, and nicely brown. Remove immediately to warm plate.

Sprinkle a bit of parsley in hot skillet; sauté a few seconds. Pour butter and parsley over fish. Garnish with bunch of uncooked fresh parsley and lemon wedges.

NOTE To clarify butter: Melt ½ pound butter slowly in saucepan or in microwave according to manufacturer's directions. Allow butter to settle on counter 10 to 15 minutes. Skim off foamy top, leaving clear yellow liquid butter (with some milky residue at the bottom). Spoon out only clear yellow liquid (pure butter fat). The milk solids in the foam and residue burn at a lower temperature than the butter fat, which is why you don't want to use them here.

S E R V E S   6

Welsh Rarebit Romance

❖

Rural farm communities observed Sundays by attending the church of personal choice and by "visiting" friends and family. The younger generation followed the same tradition. Young men traveled by horse and buggy when they "came to call" on the young ladies whom they fancied. Sunday was the only day of the week that farm youth—both girls and boys—were not expected to be "lending a hand" with the work at hand.

According to family lore, Mom's beaux were invited to stay for Sunday supper. Aunt Bets, thirteen years younger than Mom and rather impressionable, associated Welsh Rarebit with romance, because Grams served Mom and her beau Welsh Rarebit at a round table in the sewing room while the rest of the family ate in the kitchen. No wonder it has a special aura about it.

With or without a romantic caller, this dish is well suited for a late-night supper after the theater or as a luncheon dish.

Grams (and Mom, too) purchased five-pound blocks of Land O Lakes processed American cheese from the Preston Creamery. This cheese, wrapped in cheesecloth and packaged in a wooden box, was used for sandwiches, casseroles, salads, and sauces, as well. (It is now available in a plastic vac-pack inside a cardboard carton in the dairy case at the market.)

CHEESE SAUCE
▪ ▪ ▪

6 TABLESPOONS BUTTER
6 TABLESPOONS FLOUR
3 CUPS HOT MILK
¼ TEASPOON WHITE OR BLACK PEPPER
½ TEASPOON ONION POWDER
1 TEASPOON PREPARED MUSTARD
2 CUPS CHEDDAR, SWISS, OR LONGHORN CHEESE, CHUNKED (OR MORE, IF DESIRED)

6 TO 8 SLICES BREAD, TOASTED

TO MAKE SAUCE Melt butter in 3-quart saucepan; add flour. Stirring constantly, cook 2 to 3 minutes; do not brown.

Off heat, whisk in hot milk all at once. Return to heat. Stirring constantly, bring to a boil and cook 5 to 6 minutes, or until smooth. Stir in pepper, onion powder, and mustard; mix well.

Add cheese and stir until melted. Sauce should be smooth and thick but pourable, with rich cheese flavor. Taste and correct seasonings.

TO ASSEMBLE Place toast on heated plate; pour cheese sauce over. Garnish with sprig of parsley or watercress. Serve Canadian bacon on the side.

S E R V E S 6

EAT YOUR GREENS

Unlike Grams, who was limited to her own seasonal vegetables for winter green salads, Mom traveled to Rochester to market for fresh herbs and salad greens. Then she added our homegrown root vegetables to stretch our winter green salad bowl. However, as soon as the first tiny green leaf was "pickable," we dined on countless numbers of salads built around homegrown vegetables. The possibilities were not limited to only what we planted in the garden. We also picked cress and wild greens from along the riverbank near Granger, the stream at Big Springs, or the Root River. Picking fresh greens (and flowers) was one of our favorite Sunday afternoon pastimes in the spring.

After staying a week at Mom and Dad's, my cousin Julie remarked, "At Auntie Opal's you have to 'eat your greens' breakfast, lunch, and dinner!" She was absolutely right! Mom served fresh fruit and/or vegetables at every meal.

Cabbage and carrots—both "good keepers"—were the backbone of a fresh winter salad in Grams's horse-and-buggy days. Home-canned beans, beets, corn, peas, and fruits ingeniously found their way into salad-dom as well. Potato salad was relegated to the summer months because Grams believed that only hot potatoes should be eaten in cold weather. She served macaroni with fruits for a dessert salad. (Of course, Mom expanded on Grams's salad repertoire.) We devoured a zillion fruit salads—from fresh fruits held together with sweetened whipped cream to a Waldorf-style matchstick salad. Not to mention the various molded salads that were quite the rage at one time. Green, orange, and red shimmering bowls of sweet concoctions lined the salad and dessert tables at every potluck supper.

Here are some of my favorites.

Janeen and Joel, 1944

SALAD DRESSINGS

Classic Boiled Dressing

3 TABLESPOONS SUGAR
½ TEASPOON SALT
1½ TABLESPOONS FLOUR
2 TEASPOONS DRY MUSTARD
½ CUP MILK
¼ CUP CIDER VINEGAR
4 EGG YOLKS OR 2 WHOLE
EGGS
2 TABLESPOONS BUTTER

Partially because of prolific chickens and partially because of prudence, farm women—Grams and Mom no exception—transformed the leftover egg yolks from baking into cooked salad dressing. This dressing was used as a substitute for classic mayonnaise and as the base for a variety of other dressings.

■■■■■■■■■■■■■■■■■■■■■■

In heavy saucepan, mix sugar, salt, flour, mustard, milk, and ¼ cup water with wire whisk. Cook over moderate heat, stirring constantly, until mixture comes to a boil. Boil 2 minutes. Add vinegar; continue beating.

In small bowl, beat eggs. Gradually whisk half of hot mixture into beaten eggs. Stirring constantly, return tempered eggs to remaining hot liquid in saucepan. Continue to whisk until well combined. Return pan to heat, boil 3 minutes longer, or until thick and smooth, stirring constantly. Remove from heat, and stir in butter, then cool to room temperature. Refrigerate in glass jar up to 3 weeks.

Cook 1 cup sugar, 1 cup cider vinegar, 1 egg, 1 tablespoon lemon juice and 1 teaspoon prepared mustard together until thick, beat well. Thin with sweet cream (heavy cream, whipped) just before serving.
Grams's Black Book

USES

1   Thin dressing with a bit of milk or cream, and dress potato, cabbage, or lettuce salad; or use as substitute for mayonnaise.

2   Whip 1 cup heavy cream until stiff, add ½ cup boiled salad dressing, mix well, and dress fruit salads.

MAKES APPROXIMATELY 1½ CUPS

Aunt Rubye's Celery Seed Dressing

❖

This savory-sweet dressing from Norma Lingen—a contemporary of Aunt Rubye's—tastes particularly great on a mixture of bitter and tender greens tossed with slices of fresh tart apples and red onion.

----

1 ¼ CUPS WHITE SUGAR
⅔ CUP CIDER VINEGAR
2 CUPS VEGETABLE OIL
1 SMALL ONION, GRATED
1 TEASPOON DRY MUSTARD
1 ½ TEASPOONS BLACK PEPPER, FRESHLY GROUND
1 ½ TEASPOONS CELERY SEED
1 TEASPOON SALT (OPTIONAL)

Mix sugar, ⅓ cup vinegar, oil, onion, mustard, pepper, celery seed, and salt; beat well with rotary beater or whisk. Add ⅓ cup more vinegar; beat again. Taste and correct seasonings; refrigerate up to 3 weeks. Shake well before serving.

MAKES APPROXIMATELY 3 CUPS

Dad's Creamy Salad Dressing

❖

Dress soft greens, such as red leaf, Boston, or lamb's lettuce, with this sweeter-than-sour favorite dressing of Dad's.

½ CUP HEAVY CREAM
⅓ CUP WHITE SUGAR
2 TABLESPOONS CIDER VINEGAR

Mix cream, sugar, and vinegar together until smooth. Refrigerate up to 2 weeks. Shake well before serving.

MAKES ⅔ CUP

French Dressing

✦

This spicy-sweet salad dressing has a good, old-fashioned taste that nearly everyone craves at one time or another. Mom put all the ingredients in a recycled peanut butter jar and "gave it a good shaking." (After Campbell soups were available, many farm wives made French dressing with equal parts tomato soup, oil, sugar, and vinegar.)

Use this dressing for a countryfied mixed green salad made with greens,

½ CUP VEGETABLE OIL
½ CUP FRESH LEMON JUICE
1 TABLESPOON SUGAR
¼ TEASPOON BLACK PEPPER, FRESHLY GROUND
½ TEASPOON PAPRIKA
¼ TEASPOON DRY MUSTARD
1 TABLESPOON GRATED OR FINELY CHOPPED ONION

carrots, cucumber, radishes, and onion.

Whisk or beat together all ingredients—oil, fresh lemon juice, sugar, pepper, paprika, mustard, and onion—until combined. Taste and correct seasonings. Refrigerate up to 2 weeks. Shake well before serving.

MAKES ABOUT 1 CUP

Mom's Shallot Vinaigrette

✦

Mom's repertoire of dressings includes this versatile recipe that can be made in quantity, ahead of time. Refrigeration does not affect its quality. Use it on numerous vegetables, pasta salads, or green salads, or as a sauce for dunking bread into. It is *that* good!

4 SHALLOTS, PEELED
⅔ CUP OLIVE OIL
⅓ CUP RED WINE VINEGAR
2 TABLESPOONS DIJON MUSTARD
2 TABLESPOONS FRESH PARSLEY
½ TEASPOON COARSE SALT
½ TEASPOON BLACK PEPPER, FRESHLY GROUND
¼ TEASPOON SUGAR

Place shallots in food processor and process 2 to 3 pulses. Add oil, vinegar, mustard, parsley, salt, pepper, and sugar. Process 6 to 8 pulses or until shallots are chopped. Seal in glass jar. Refrigerate for 3 to 4 weeks. Shake well before using.

MAKES 1½ CUPS

Mom's Carrot Salad

✦

The classic salad with raisins is part of every family's food heritage, including ours. Though this old original recipe is unlike others, it remains fresh and healthful—no oil, no salt, and if desired, no sugar. Plus, shredding the carrots in a food processor is a darn sight better than nicking my knuckles on Grams's old Rapid grater set!

■■■■■■■■■■■■■■■■■■■■■■■■■■■■■■

In food processor fitted with shredding blade, shred carrots to make 6 cups. Turn into glass or stainless steel mixing bowl. Add sugar and

10 TO 12 WHOLE MEDIUM CARROTS (TO MAKE 6 CUPS SHREDDED), PEELED
½ CUP SUGAR (SEE NOTE)
⅓ CUP FRESH LEMON JUICE
¼ TEASPOON BLACK PEPPER, FRESHLY GROUND

enough lemon juice to just moisten, or until carrots glisten.

Season to taste with pepper; mix well. Should be made at least 6 hours ahead. Can be refrigerated up to 2 weeks. Remove carrots from liquid with slotted spoon and serve on lettuce leaf.

NOTE Use more sugar to taste or replace sugar with artificial sweetener. After setting overnight, the flavored carrots ooze some of their own juice, so do not add extra lemon juice.

S E R V E S 6

Old-Fashioned Coleslaw

❖

Grams, a veteran cabbage lover, shredded bushels of cabbage in her lifetime. The dressing varied according to the rest of the menu. Grams was fond of the unique flavor of Chinese cabbage and, at times, she simply added a splash of vinegar, salt, and pepper with a pinch of sugar before serving it. Both Mom and Grams secreted a bowl of slawed cabbage direct from the brewing kraut crock on busy days. Often, chopped onion and shredded carrots were partnered with green cabbage, then they were dressed with *Classic Boiled Dressing* (page 295). However, this uncooked coleslaw remains my favorite.

Trim, core, and slice cabbage into 2-inch wedges. Use food processor fitted with slicing blade. Fit into processor tube and shred. Turn into large mixing bowl.

TO MAKE DRESSING Place chopping blade in food processor. Add chunked onion and pulse 3 to 4 times. Add parsley to bowl; pulse 3 to 4 more times.

2 POUNDS GREEN OR RED CABBAGE (1 LARGE HEAD), OR 1 POUND OF EACH

DRESSING

...

1 LARGE ONION, PEELED AND CHUNKED
½ CUP PARSLEY LEAVES, NO STEMS, LOOSELY PACKED
½ CUP MAYONNAISE (SEE NOTE)
2 TABLESPOONS PREPARED MUSTARD
1 TABLESPOON CIDER VINEGAR
1 TEASPOON SUGAR
1 TEASPOON BLACK PEPPER, FRESHLY GROUND
½ TEASPOON CELERY SEED

Add mayonnaise, mustard, vinegar, sugar, pepper, and celery seed. Process 8 to 9 pulses or until onion and parsley are chopped. Do not overprocess.

Pour dressing over cabbage. Add optional ingredients suggested in Variations and mix well with table fork. Taste and correct seasonings. Refrigerate up to 3 to 4 days. Slaw tastes better after 12 hours, when flavors develop.

NOTE Add more mayonnaise if necessary to dress the cabbage. It's best to be skimpy rather than too generous.

VARIATIONS

1   Add 2 to 3 carrots, shredded, and proceed.
2   Add 1 green pepper (chopped) and 2 carrots (shredded); add more mayonnaise if necessary to bind.
3   Using half red and half green cabbage, toss in 2 red apples (cored, sliced, and chopped) *just before serving.*

SERVES 6 TO 8

Bets's Stressless Coleslaw

❖

My uncle Buzz (Maynard to others) and his father owned the funeral home in Preston and later moved to Wells, Minnesota. Being a funeral director in a small town also meant owning and operating the area's only ambulance. More often than not, their family dinner hour was interrupted with a phone call and Uncle Buzz would be off. Aunt Bets, both flexible and prepared, smartly collected recipes that tasted as delicious after multiple temperature changes as they did at first making. Such is the case with this recipe. In fact, it improves with stress and age!

▪▪▪▪▪▪▪▪▪▪▪▪▪▪▪▪▪▪▪▪▪▪▪▪▪▪▪▪▪▪▪▪

Trim, core, and slice cabbage into 2-inch wedges. Use food processor fitted with slicing blade; fit cabbage into tube horizontally to slaw. Or shred by hand. Turn into large mixing bowl.

2 POUNDS GREEN CABBAGE (1 LARGE HEAD)
4 MEDIUM CARROTS, PEELED
1 GREEN PEPPER, CORED
1 TEASPOON SALT

DRESSING
▪▪▪

1 CUP CIDER VINEGAR
¼ CUP WATER
2 CUPS SUGAR
1 TABLESPOON MUSTARD SEEDS
1 TABLESPOON CELERY SEEDS

Place shredding blade in food processor; shred carrots. Or grate them by hand. Add to cabbage.

Thinly slice pepper. Add to other vegetables, along with salt. Let stand 1 to 2 hours at room temperature. Drain off liquid. Squeeze dry in linen tea towel.

TO MAKE DRESSING In saucepan, bring vinegar, water, sugar, mustard, and celery seeds to a boil. Boil 1 minute or until sugar is dissolved. Remove from heat. Cool to room temperature.

After vegetables are squeezed dry and dressing cooled, mix everything together. Serve at any temperature. Store for later by packing slaw into containers that are suitable for one serving. Refrigerate 1 to 2 months or freeze 5 to 6 months.

SERVES 6 TO 8 GENEROUSLY

Corn Salad Relish

❖

The original recipe requires a huge kettle and a host of children or menfolk to eat it. But similar to *Bets's Stressless Coleslaw* (page 300), it freezes very well. The lingering memory of fresh corn-on-the-cob is not lost after tasting this multi-colored summer bouquet of a salad in the middle of winter.

"*18 ears corn, 5 green or red peppers, 4 large onions, 1 large cabbage or 2 small ones, 1/4 lb mustard, 1/2 cup salt, 3.3/4 cups sugar, 1 1/2 quarts vinegar . . . chop all fine, boil 20 mins, cool and serve.*" Grams's Black Book

6 EARS OF CORN
1 GREEN PEPPER, CHOPPED
1 RED PEPPER, CHOPPED
1 LARGE ONION, CHOPPED
½ SMALL GREEN CABBAGE
1 TABLESPOON DRY MUSTARD
2 TEASPOONS SALT
1 CUP SUGAR
1½ CUPS CIDER VINEGAR

Husk, silk, and cut corn off cob; set aside.

Wash, core, and slice peppers. Peel and chop onion. Wash, core, and cut cabbage into wedges; slice with slicing blade of processor or by hand. Fit processor with chopping blade; working in batches, process peppers, onion, and cabbage until evenly chopped. Remove to mixing bowl. Add reserved corn. Toss well.

In large stockpot, bring mustard, salt, sugar, and vinegar to a boil. Add vegetables, bring to a boil, reduce heat, and cook 20 minutes. Remove from heat. Cool to room temperature. Serve as desired or divide into small meal-size containers, seal, and refrigerate 2 to 3 weeks or freeze 3 to 4 months.

SERVES 6 TO 8 GENEROUSLY

The first of the season's cucumbers were the best. Grams used well water for this salad but Mom used ice water. I was especially impressed when Aunt Marguerite, a missionary in Africa for nearly thirty years, reported that mashed raw cucumber was the first solid food the native mothers fed to their babies.

Peel cucumbers or score their skins with dinner fork. Slice thinly. Soak in bowl of ice water, seasoned with sugar and vinegar for ½ to 1 hour. Drain and pat dry with paper towels.

Cucumber Salad

12 KIRBY CUCUMBERS
½ TEASPOON SUGAR
1 TABLESPOON WHITE WINE
   VINEGAR
1 ONION, SLICED THINLY
   (SEE NOTE)

SERVES 6

Toss onion with cucumbers; season to taste with your favorite dressing or one of the following.

NOTE Substitute a red onion, 1 to 2 bunches of scallions, or ¼ cup snipped chives for the onion.

TO STORE CUCUMBER SALAD Invert salad plate on bottom of container, so that excess juices run under plate, thereby keeping salad from getting soggy. Add cucumbers, seal with airtight cover, and refrigerate. With slotted spoon, remove cucumbers and serve.

Creamy Dill Dressing

½ CUP SOUR CREAM
2 TABLESPOONS
   MAYONNAISE
¼ CUP CHOPPED DILL
½ TEASPOON BLACK PEPPER,
   FRESHLY GROUND

Whisk sour cream, mayonnaise, dill, and pepper together. Dress cucumbers and refrigerate until serving time.

Old-Fashioned Cream Dressing

¼ TO ½ CUP HEAVY CREAM
   (AMOUNT DEPENDS ON SIZE OF
   CUCUMBERS)
1 TO 2 TABLESPOONS CIDER
   VINEGAR, OR MORE TO TASTE
¼ TEASPOON SALT, OR MORE TO
   TASTE
¼ TEASPOON BLACK PEPPER,
   FRESHLY GROUND, OR MORE TO
   TASTE

Whisk ingredients together. Dress cucumbers; add chopped parsley if desired. Refrigerate until serving time.

PRIME SPECIMEN FRUIT SALADS

"I chose the best of the season's fresh fruit from the market," says Mom. "Then I added the prime specimens that I reserved from the past season's berry picking and stuffed dates or figs with marzipan or nuts, or, whatever I had on hand, for a holiday fruit platter."

Despite the countless other dishes that she served, we always ate every morsel on that platter.

The following trio of unadulterated timeless recipes from *Grams's Black Book* date back to 1900, although they are suitable for use now and into the next century.

APPLE SALAD

1 DOZEN BANANAS
1 DOZEN APPLES

Cut up bananas and apples; sprinkle a little salt over the apples.

Thin the following dressing with whipped cream. Put this on the apples and bananas and serve.

Mix 1 cup sugar and 1 tablespoon cornstarch together. Beat 2 eggs until fluffy. Stir the beaten eggs into the sugar and cornstarch. Add juice of 2 lemons and 1 cup water. Put on stove and cook like other dressing [until thick].

BEST FRUIT SALAD

Cut up 1 pineapple, ½ dozen bananas, 1 cup English walnut meats, chopped, and marshmallows—15 cents [1 cup, snipped marshmallows]. Toss with pineapple juice that has been reduced, thickened, and to which sweet cream has been added. Mix well and serve.

HEAVENLY HASH

Dice 1 pineapple and 4 oranges. Sweeten well. Roll 1 box of strawberries first in nuts, minced fine; pressing nuts gently into berries, and then roll in sugar. Place pineapple and oranges in layers, as a ring, leaving open, a place in the center for berries. Chill. Just before serving, fill the center with the coated berries. Cover [the whole affair] with heavy whipped cream. Border plates with lettuce, dotted with grapes and candied cherries.

Hot

Wilted

Salad

Long before the current hot goat cheese or warmed chicken breast salad, Grams served a Hot Wilted Salad. The hot dressing wilted the greens. Sliced slab bacon and crisp stale bread cubes topped it all. She used horseradish, dandelion, and/or garden cress. Mom and I use curly chicory or an assortment of tart salad greens.

◼◻◼
◻◼◻
◼◻◼

2 CUPS STALE BREAD CUBES

1 HEAD CURLY CHICORY, WASHED AND DRAINED
½ POUND SLAB BACON
3 TABLESPOONS OLIVE OIL
1 ½ TEASPOONS FLOUR
⅓ CUP RED WINE VINEGAR
½ TEASPOON BLACK PEPPER, FRESHLY GROUND

Cut bread into 1-inch cubes and toast in warm oven until dry. Or heat 3 to 4 tablespoons oil in skillet, add bread cubes, and sauté until dark brown. Be careful not to burn. Drain on brown paper bag and reserve.

Tear greens into salad bowl; set aside.

Cut bacon into small dice. Drop into pot of boiling water and blanch for 1 minute. Drain and pat dry with toweling. Sauté bacon in olive oil until crisp and brown. Add flour to pan; cook, stirring constantly, 3 to 4 minutes, or until flour is color of brown paper bag.

Whisk vinegar and ⅓ cup water into hot skillet; continue to cook until smooth and dressing consistency. Season with pepper. Immediately toss greens with hot dressing.

Top with reserved bread cubes and serve.

S E R V E S 6

Kidney
Bean
Salad

❖

Red kidney beans, with their meaty-rich flavor, were an inexpensive source of protein, providing an excellent substitute—though not necessarily for farmers like our family—for meat during the Great Depression. (Under any circumstances, even now, they carry the same virtue.) My great-aunt Isla created a meatless meat loaf using these versatile beans to extend her food dollar. The dried beans, available in bulk from the grocery store, were soaked in cold water overnight, drained the next morning, and then cooked until tender in preparation for every dish that she used them for. Both Grams and Mom added them to succotash and various hot vegetable combinations. But this salad, in my opinion, was the best of the lot.

Canned red kidney beans simplify the whole process for this recipe. (Mom no longer soaks red kidney beans, either!)

2 ONE-POUND CANS RED KIDNEY BEANS, OR 4 CUPS COOKED DRIED BEANS
3 TO 4 STALKS CELERY, WITH LEAVES, WASHED (1 CUP)
1 MEDIUM YELLOW ONION, PEELED (ABOUT 1 CUP)
1½ CUPS LONGHORN CHEESE, CUBED TO APPROXIMATELY THE SAME SIZE AS THE BEANS

¼ CUP CHOPPED SWEET PICKLES
¼ CUP CHOPPED FRESH PARSLEY, OR MORE TO TASTE

½ CUP MAYONNAISE, OR MORE IF NECESSARY (OR USE *CLASSIC BOILED DRESSING*, PAGE 295)
1 TEASPOON PREPARED MUSTARD
½ TEASPOON BLACK PEPPER, FRESHLY GROUND

Drain and rinse beans. Set aside.

Dice celery including leaves; place in mixing bowl. Dice onion; add to celery. Add cheese to vegetables.

Finely chop pickles; place in small mixing bowl. Add chopped parsley to pickles. Stir mayonnaise, mustard, and pepper into pickle mixture.

Add kidney beans to vegetable/cheese bowl. Stir in mayonnaise and pickle mixture. Mix well, adding more mayonnaise only if necessary to bind. Taste and correct seasonings. Cover and refrigerate until serving time. This salad may be made 1 day ahead.

Serve in lettuce-lined bowl or individual lettuce cups.

S E R V E S   6

Company's Coming Frozen Fruit Salad

When Grams and Granddad moved into town, the kitchen there included a refrigerator (what luxury)! Ice cubes and frozen desserts were fascinating to her. Grams favored making this salad "when company came" because it was done ahead. Though it contains rich farm food like heavy cream and mayonnaise, this salad is surprisingly refreshing.

▪▪▪▪▪▪▪▪▪▪▪▪▪▪▪▪▪▪▪▪▪▪▪▪▪▪

Soften gelatin in water and lemon juice in cup or glass dish. Place in pan of simmering water and heat until gelatin is dissolved. Add fruit juices to dissolved gelatin and mix well; set aside.

Cut pineapple into smaller pieces; place in mixing bowl. Add bananas to pineapple. Mix oranges, cranber-

1 ENVELOPE UNFLAVORED
   GELATIN
¼ CUP COLD WATER
¼ CUP LEMON JUICE
¼ CUP PINEAPPLE JUICE
¼ CUP ORANGE JUICE

1 CUP PINEAPPLE CHUNKS
   (FRESH OR CANNED)
1 CUP SLICED BANANAS
½ CUP DICED ORANGES
½ CUP COARSELY CHOPPED,
   RAW CRANBERRIES
½ CUP DICED PEACHES
½ CUP CHOPPED PECANS

1 CUP HEAVY CREAM
½ CUP MAYONNAISE

ries, peaches, and nuts into fruits.

Whip cream until stiff; fold in mayonnaise and dissolved gelatin. Mix well; fold in fruit and nut mixture. Spoon into cylinder-shaped freezer containers, seal, and freeze overnight. This salad may be frozen 2 to 3 months.

TO SERVE Remove from freezer; place hot towel, wrung dry, around container for 1 to 2 minutes. "Slip" salad out of container, slice into 1-inch slices, and place on lettuce leaf.

NOTE Substitute fresh berries or homemade canned fruits for the pineapple or peaches.

SERVES 6 TO 8 GENEROUSLY

Perfection
Salad

Admittedly, I am not a fan of Jell-O salads. However, this recipe relic from *Grams's Black Book* is on top of a long list of jellied salads. You remember them: shredded carrots and pineapple in lemon Jell-O; cottage cheese and bing cherries in lime Jell-O; fruit cocktail and marshmallows in cherry Jell-O; raspberries in raspberry Jell-O; cream cheese, celery, and pecans in orange Jell-O—and the similar combinations of vegetables, fruits, and whatnot.

For guests, Grams filled individual ring or round molds that were later unmolded onto lettuce leaves and topped with a dollop of *Classic Boiled Dressing* (page 295).

2 PACKAGES UNFLAVORED GELATIN
½ CUP CIDER VINEGAR
2 TABLESPOONS LEMON JUICE
½ CUP SUGAR
DASH SALT

1½ CUPS FINELY SHREDDED CABBAGE
1 CUP FINELY CHOPPED CELERY
1 CUP FINELY SHREDDED CARROT
2 TABLESPOONS GRATED ONION
¼ CUP CHOPPED PIMIENTO
¼ CUP STUFFED GREEN OLIVES
½ CUP CHOPPED GREEN PEPPER

Use either 9-by-13-inch glass dish, or eight to ten ½-cup ring or round molds set on baking sheet.

Soften gelatin in vinegar and lemon juice. Bring 2½ cups water to a boil, add sugar, and stir to dissolve. Add softened gelatin and salt; stir until completely dissolved.

Mix cabbage, celery, carrot, onion, pimiento, olives, and green pepper together. Add vegetables to flavored gelatin. Pour into dish or molds and refrigerate until firm. Can be made 1 to 3 days ahead.

TO SERVE Unmold or cut into squares, place on lettuce leaf, and top with dollop of unsweetened mayonnaise.

SERVES 8 TO 10 GENEROUSLY

Left to right: Joany, Judy, Esther Lee, Janeen, Grams   Background: Aunt Gebe, Mom

Vanishing
Potato
Salad

❖

Potato salad was, and still is, a classic dish served at every picnic, family reunion, summer festival, and supper. Some folks made a meal of potato salad alone. After tasting this salad, you will understand their obvious rate of consumption. Though the amounts suggested here seem oversized, never fear: The left-overs will disappear as quick as a cat can wink her eye.

∙∙∙∙∙∙∙∙∙∙∙∙∙∙∙∙∙∙∙∙∙∙∙∙∙∙∙∙∙∙∙∙∙∙

Boil potatoes in large pot of salted water (page 229); cook until tender. Pour off water, and save for other uses. Drain potatoes. Using pot holders or two-prong fork, place hot potatoes on cutting board; slice or chop. Remove to large mixing bowl. Immediately toss vinegar and oil onto hot potatoes.

Chop onions and parsley; add to warm potatoes. Stir in mustard and mayonnaise (or salad dressing), celery salt, and pepper; mix well. Taste and correct seasonings. Cool to room

5 POUNDS ALL-PURPOSE POTATOES, SCRUBBED AND PEELED
SALT
3 TABLESPOONS CIDER OR WHITE WINE VINEGAR
1 TO 1½ TABLESPOONS VEGETABLE OIL
2½ TO 3 POUNDS ONIONS, CHOPPED
½ CUP CHOPPED, FRESH PARSLEY
1 GENEROUS TABLESPOON PREPARED MUSTARD
1 TO 2 CUPS MAYONNAISE OR *CLASSIC BOILED DRESSING* (PAGE 295)
1 TEASPOON CELERY SALT, OR MORE TO TASTE
1½ TEASPOONS BLACK PEPPER, FRESHLY GROUND

6 TO 8 EGGS
2 TEASPOONS SALT

¼ TO ½ CUP MAYONNAISE
¼ TO ½ TEASPOON SALT
¼ TO ½ TEASPOON BLACK PEPPER, FRESHLY GROUND

temperature; refrigerate until cold or overnight.

Meanwhile, in saucepan, cover eggs with cold water. Add salt and bring to a boil. Reduce heat and simmer 11 minutes. Drain off hot water and immediately plunge eggs into cold water. Crack shells, peel, and drain eggs; chill in refrigerator.

TO ASSEMBLE A few hours before serving, chop cold cooked eggs. Add to potato salad. Season with more mayonnaise, salt, and pepper; mix thoroughly. Taste and correct seasonings. Cover and keep refrigerated until serving time.

NOTE To transport to a picnic, place the salad in the bottom of a cooler and put an ice pack *on top* of the bowl. Keep in the cooler until serving time.

VARIATION
Add 1 cup whole large green stuffed olives just before serving.

SERVES 6 TO 8 GENEROUSLY

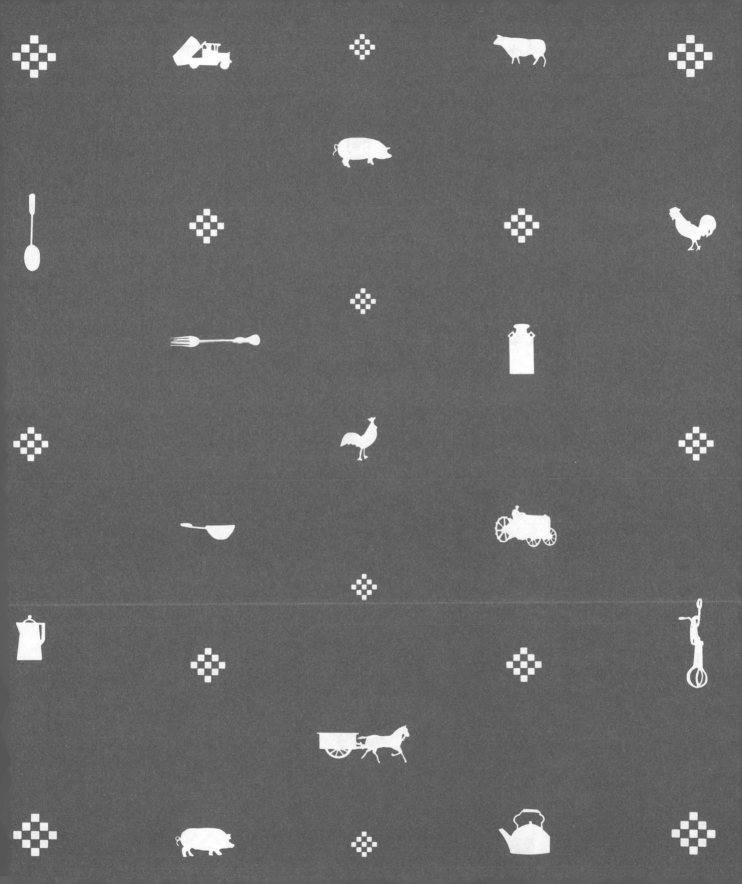

A
COLLECTION
OF
HEIRLOOM
CAKES

As soon as Mom was old enough—about eight or nine—Grams assigned the cake-baking department to her. She would "rather bake a pie or a batch of bread, any day." Rubye claims that Mom, in turn, assigned the task of washing the dishes to her. Whether or not the two girls kept to their own departments is not really as important as the multitude of delectable cakes that were produced from that kitchen. Just think: All they had was a wood-burning stove without a thermometer. They had no electric mixers or food processors, no dishwasher or hot water heater. And no how-to books or videotapes.

Like cookies, a cake was a farm wife's vehicle for her personal expression and creativity. Most farm cooking was "just plain food." However, after a special cake was well received by the family and applauded by her neighbors and friends, it became a woman's "signature cake"—an edible art form. The batter was sprinkled with a competitive spirit. Incomplete recipes were often passed to wanting friends, thereby ensuring that their cakes would not measure up to the original.

Here's an example from my mother: "RED DEVILS FOOD CAKE: ⅔ cup brown sugar, ⅔ cup shaved chocolate, ¼ cup sweet milk and 1 spoon vanilla. Put chocolate on stove and melt. Add milk slowly, cook until smooth. Let cool. Then to ½ cup butter add 1 cup brown sugar, 2 eggs, beat till light. Then add cooled chocolate and ½ cup milk, 1 teaspoonful soda and 2 cups sifted flour, beat hard." This recipe "leaves a lot to the imagination," says Mom.

The original owners of most of the following recipes are long since gone, but their cakes live on. Between Mom and myself, we have baked, tasted, and served them many times over, so that none of you need rely on your imagination.

Starting with an angel food, and continuing with all the variations of butter, chocolate, spice, and white cakes, I have chosen a farm-dozen collection of fifteen recipes. After asking for favorite recipes from the mothers of my grade-school classmates and testing them, then uncovering some family heirloom 100+-year-old cake recipes and adding the accumulation of my own, it was a hard choice to make. Narrowing that tall stack of cake recipes to a precious few was a tough task.

Unless otherwise stated, the following recipes use sweet, unsalted butter (I prefer Land O Lakes), all-purpose white flour, granulated sugar, whole milk, and "packable" light brown sugar.

Two Generations of Sisters Celebrating Birthdays

Mom, Bets, Rubye, 1930

Joanny, Janeen, Judy, 1953

Angel Food Cake

1 CUP SIFTED CAKE FLOUR
1½ CUPS POWDERED SUGAR
¼ TEASPOON SALT

1½ CUPS EGG WHITES (12 TO 13)
1½ TEASPOONS CREAM OF TARTAR
¼ TEASPOON SALT
1 CUP WHITE SUGAR
1½ TEASPOONS VANILLA
1 TEASPOON ALMOND EXTRACT

Weather dictates when to bake this cake. If it is raining, wait until tomorrow because the barometric pressure affects the stiffness of the egg whites. If they are not beaten to stiff peaks, the cake becomes rubbery and absolutely dreadful. The second rule is to use a bowl, beaters, utensils, and a cake pan that are impeccably clean. If one itsy-bitsy smudge of grease is in the bowl, the egg whites will not increase to their full volume.

That said, baking a perfect angel food is actually a simple task. I do not agree with all the "experts" about the necessity of egg whites at room temperature. Mom and I find that cold egg whites whip up just as fast as those more tepid. However, do not allow even a tiny portion of the yolk to spill into the whites or you will beat until kingdom come and they will not get stiff enough.

Preheat oven to 400°. Position oven rack on lowest level; remove other rack. Wash and thoroughly dry 10-by-4-inch tube pan with removable bottom. Reserve, ungreased.

Measure flour, powdered sugar, and salt; sift together 3 times onto waxed paper and set aside.

In *clean* mixer bowl, place egg whites, cream of tartar, and salt; beat until frothy. With beaters running, gradually add sugar, 2 tablespoons at a time, to egg whites.

Once sugar is incorporated, continue to beat until very stiff peaks; do not underbeat. Beat in vanilla and almond flavoring.

Reduce mixer speed. Gradually add reserved flour mixture a little at a time into meringue. Carefully fold after each addition; mix only until flour disappears.

With large spoonfuls, place batter in prepared tube pan. With table knife, pull/cut through batter to remove air pockets.

Place on bottom oven rack. Reduce oven to 375° and bake 50 to 55 minutes, or until top is brown. Cake is done when it springs back when pressed with finger. Do not underbake.

Remove from oven. Immediately invert pan to "hang" on funnel or small-necked bottle. Let hang until cold. Store baked cake *in* pan, wrapped in airtight plastic bag. Can be kept 1 to 2 days at room temperature or frozen 1 to 2 months.

TO SERVE Use a long-bladed knife to remove cake from pan. Place sharp edge against pan and cut around outside of cake pan and center tube, thereby separating cake from pan. Holding on to center tube, pull cake out of pan. Invert cake onto cake plate that is large enough to hold it. With knife, cut between cake and bottom of pan. Cake will drop onto plate. Dust off crumbs. Serve unadorned or dust top with powdered sugar. Use *serrated* knife to slice cake.

VARIATIONS

Chocolate Angel Food Cake
After sifting, remove 3 tablespoons of flour from cup. Add 3 tablespoons unsweetened cocoa to flour-powdered sugar mixture and resift. Proceed according to recipe.

Glorified Angel Food Cake
Velda Mandelko, our next-door neighbor "up the road a piece," served this cake to the ladies attending Homemakers Club and caused quite a stir because of the spectacular results.

TO MAKE FILLING Whip 2 cups heavy cream with 2 tablespoons sugar until stiff; divide whipped cream into thirds. Add 1 cup well-drained, crushed pineapple to one third; 1 cup well-drained, crushed fresh strawberries to second third; 1 teaspoon vanilla to remaining cream, reserving last vanilla-cream third for frosting.

TO ASSEMBLE Slice cake horizontally into thirds. On large cake plate, place 1 layer (originally the top of the cake, as it baked) on plate. Spread pineapple cream evenly over layer. Place center cake layer on top of pineapple cream; spread strawberry cream evenly over this layer. Top with last third of cake (originally the bottom of the cake, in the pan) and dust off excess crumbs. Frost with reserved vanilla whipped cream. Use back of soup spoon to create thumbnail or swirl effect. Refrigerate 2 to 3 hours before serving.

Devilish Double Chocolate Angel Food Cake Bake *Chocolate Angel Food Cake* according to recipe above.

TO MAKE FILLING Melt 4 ounces semisweet chocolate together with 40 marshmallows and ½ cup milk over low flame. Add 2 teaspoons vanilla and mix well; cool to room temperature.

Whip 2 cups heavy cream until stiff. Fold into *cool* chocolate mixture and continue to mix until smooth. Mix in ½ cup chopped, toasted almonds.

TO ASSEMBLE Cut 1½ inches from top of cake horizontally; place "lid" on counter. With scissors or table fork, remove "insides" of cake, leaving approximately 1¼-inch "case" to hold filling. Stuff a spoonful of cake "insides" on bottom of center hole (from tube pan). Fill "case" and center hole with chocolate cream; replace "lid." Add a few pieces of "insides" to level top of cake and nibble on rest. Frost whole affair with remaining chocolate cream. Sprinkle toasted ground almonds over top. Or just before serving, dust with unsweetened cocoa. Or arrange sliced almonds around base of cake in pattern and then again around outside of top of cake.

Definitely not a cake for the fainthearted!

**SERVES 10 TO 12
(ONE 10-INCH TUBE CAKE)**

Angelic
Sponge
Cake

◆

This twin sister to Angel Food Cake comes from real twin sister Doris Nagel. Doris, her husband Norris, and their children frolicked with our family for two generations, all the way from grammar school to 4-H Club to piano lessons with Mrs. Larsen in Preston to singing in the Men's Chorus. And Doris was a fine baker.

The abundant farm-fresh egg yolks are transformed into a beautiful golden yellow airy and moist creation. The basic "clean bowl" rule applies here again. But do not worry so much about getting the egg yolks in the whites.

▪▪▪▪▪▪▪▪▪▪▪▪▪▪▪▪▪▪▪▪▪▪▪▪▪▪▪▪▪

Preheat oven to 400°. Position oven rack on lowest level; remove other rack. Wash and thoroughly dry 10-by-4-inch tube pan with removable bottom. Reserve, ungreased.

Beat egg yolks and whole egg in clean bowl until frothy. Gradually add sugar, beating constantly. Continue to beat approximately 10 minutes, or until mixture is thick and lemon-colored.

Meanwhile, sift flour, baking powder, and salt together twice onto waxed paper.

**8 OR 9 EGG YOLKS, PLUS
1 WHOLE EGG
1¼ CUPS WHITE SUGAR**

**1⅓ CUPS SIFTED CAKE FLOUR
2 TEASPOONS BAKING
POWDER
½ TEASPOON SALT
9 TABLESPOONS WARM
WATER
½ TEASPOON LEMON ZEST
1 TEASPOON LEMON EXTRACT
OR JUICE**

Reduce mixer speed. Gradually fold flour mixture into egg mixture. Mix just until flour disappears. Add warm water a tablespoonful at a time, mixing well after each addition. Fold in lemon zest and extract or juice.

With large spoonfuls, place batter in prepared tube pan. With table knife, pull/cut through batter to remove air pockets.

Place on bottom oven rack. Reduce oven to 375° and bake 50 to 55 minutes, or until top is brown and cake is done when it springs back when pressed with finger. Do not underbake.

Remove from oven. Immediately invert pan to "hang" on funnel or small-necked bottle. Let hang until cold. Store baked cake *in* pan, wrapped in airtight plastic bag. Can be kept 1 to 2 days at room temperature or frozen 1 to 2 months.

NOTE Orange or lime zest and juice can be substituted for that of the lemon.

TO SERVE Dust with powdered sugar or leave unadorned. Slice with serrated knife.

**SERVES 10 TO 12
(ONE 10-INCH TUBE CAKE)**

Heavenly Lemon Roll

◆

This first cousin to both angel food and angelic sponge cakes was merely one of many divine cakes that made Mom famous. Our community practiced a variation on the romantic May first and second tradition of hanging a basket of sweets on the doorknob of a loved one. We kids hung "May baskets" on the doors of our friends with no romantic strings attached. For this occasion, Mom baked this luscious lemon roll. We wrapped each slice in waxed paper and carefully tucked it into a pretty paper basket and filled the top with a few freshly picked violets.

Do not overlook this down-to-earth but heavenly cake. It is the perfect ending to almost every dinner party because of the tart/sweet taste. If a shower or ladies' luncheon is planned, use this creation, decorated with fresh flowers, for an edible centerpiece.

- -

Preheat oven to 375°. Grease 15½-by-10½-by-1-inch jelly roll pan with solid vegetable shortening and line with waxed paper; trim and grease paper.

CAKE
∎∎∎

6 EGGS, SEPARATED
1 CUP SUGAR
2 TABLESPOONS WARM WATER

1 CUP SIFTED FLOUR
1 TEASPOON BAKING POWDER
½ TEASPOON SALT
1 TABLESPOON LEMON ZEST

LEMON FILLING
∎∎∎

1 CUP SUGAR
1¼ CUPS WATER
1 TABLESPOON BUTTER
¼ CUP CORNSTARCH
3 TABLESPOONS COLD WATER
3 EGG YOLKS
2 TABLESPOONS MILK
⅓ CUP FRESH LEMON JUICE
ZEST OF 1 LEMON

TO MAKE CAKE Beat egg yolks until frothy; gradually add ½ cup sugar. Continue to beat until thick and lemon-colored. Mixture should form ribbon when beaters are lifted. Add water; beat until smooth.

Meanwhile, sift flour, baking powder, and salt together. Fold flour mixture and lemon zest into batter; mix until flour disappears.

Beat egg whites until frothy. Gradually add remaining ½ cup sugar; continue to beat until stiff but not dry. Carefully fold egg whites into batter.

Spread into prepared pan. Bake for 15 to 20 minutes, or until toothpick inserted into center comes out clean and cake springs back when pressed with finger.

Remove from oven. Invert pan directly onto linen tea towel dusted with powdered sugar. Carefully peel off waxed paper. Roll lengthwise in tea towel; cool on rack.

TO MAKE LEMON FILLING In heavy saucepan, combine sugar, water, and butter; bring to a boil. Blend cornstarch in cold water; whisk liquid cornstarch into hot sugar mixture. Boil, stirring constantly, for 8 minutes, or until it is clear and thick.

In small bowl, beat egg yolks slightly; add milk. Gradually whisk half hot mixture into beaten egg yolks. Stirring constantly, return tempered yolks to liquid in saucepan. Continue to whisk until well combined. Return pan to heat; boil 2 minutes longer, stirring constantly.

Remove from heat, and stir in lemon juice and zest; mix thoroughly. Cool slightly. If done ahead, place plastic wrap directly on top of filling.

TO ASSEMBLE Unroll cake. Evenly spread lemon filling on cake. Reroll lengthwise, using towel as guide. "Cradle" roll in towel and lift/transfer onto board or long platter. Refrigerate until serving time.

TO SERVE Dust top with powdered sugar, or garnish with fresh berries, fresh flowers, and/or washed lemon leaves.

VARIATIONS
Celestial Chocolate Roll with Vanilla Filling or Mocha Chocolate Filling This was my idea of the ultimate birthday cake . . . my

request was always "vanilla filling" fulfilled.

TO MAKE CHOCOLATE ROLL Reduce flour to ¾ cup. Add ¼ cup unsweetened cocoa to dry ingredients. Eliminate lemon zest. Add 2 teaspoons vanilla to egg yolk mixture. Proceed according to lemon roll recipe. Cool completely before assembling with either vanilla or mocha chocolate filling.

TO MAKE VANILLA FILLING Whip 1½ cups heavy whipping cream with ½ cup powdered sugar until stiff. Whisk in 2 teaspoons vanilla. Unroll chocolate roll. Evenly spread whipped cream on cake. Reroll, cradle in towel, and transfer to serving platter. Refrigerate until serving time. Garnish with chocolate shavings or fresh flowers just before serving.

TO MAKE MOCHA CHOCOLATE FILLING Mix 1½ cups heavy whipping cream with ½ cup powdered sugar, 2 tablespoons cocoa, and 1 tablespoon instant coffee. Refrigerate 2 to 3 hours or overnight. Just before assembly with chocolate roll, whip until stiff. Proceed according to vanilla filling recipe.

SERVES 10 TO 12 (ONE 10½-INCH-LONG CAKE ROLL)

As youngsters, Mom and Rubye set up an elaborate play house in the old corncrib. Together, they saved odd bottles that Grams did not need, broken dishes, sturdy wooden fruit boxes from the grocery store, tin syrup pails, and chipped tea cups. As soon as the last ear of corn was fed to the cows, the two moved in. Scraps of materials and pieces of rugs covered the floor. Wooden boxes became the kitchen cupboard and table. Following their real-life roles, Mom did the baking and cooking; Rubye cleaned the house and washed the dishes.

While Mom created cakes from mud, Rubye picked wild daisies and flowering weeds for decoration. She pressed a perfectly formed leaf into the bottom of a tin, Mom "tamped" mud down in the "mold." The next day, it was magically transformed into a beautiful mud cake. An early pastry business!

Aunt Rubye's Peerless Apple Cake proves that she knew how to bake as well as Mom. Her neighbors and friends will be thrilled to learn the secret to her famous signature cake!

Preheat oven to 375°. Grease and flour two 12¾-by-4½-by-2⅜-inch loaf pans or two 9-by-5-by-3-inch loaf pans.

Aunt Rubye's Peerless Apple Cake

TART APPLES (ENOUGH TO MAKE 4 CUPS SLICED)
2 CUPS WHITE SUGAR
1 CUP BROWN SUGAR
ZEST OF 1 LEMON
2 EGGS, SLIGHTLY BEATEN
½ CUP VEGETABLE OIL
2 TEASPOONS VANILLA
3 CUPS SIFTED FLOUR
2 TEASPOONS BAKING SODA
2 TEASPOONS CINNAMON
½ TEASPOON NUTMEG, FRESHLY GRATED
½ TEASPOON SALT

½ CUP CHOPPED NUTS (OPTIONAL)
½ CUP GROUND RAISINS (OPTIONAL)

SERVES 8 TO 10 PER CAKE (2 LOAF CAKES)

Peel, core, and thinly slice apples; place in large bowl. Add sugars and lemon zest. Let stand approximately 20 minutes, or until apples become moist.

Meanwhile, with rotary beater or whisk, beat eggs; add oil and vanilla. When apples are moist, add egg mixture to apples.

Sift flour, baking soda, cinnamon, nutmeg, and salt together. With wooden spoon, stir in dry ingredients, add optional ingredients if desired, and mix thoroughly.

Pour into prepared pans. Reduce oven to 350°, and bake 55 to 60 minutes, in 12¾-by-4½-by-2⅜-inch pans, or 60 to 70 minutes in 9-by-5-by-3-inch pans (or until toothpick inserted into center comes out clean).

Remove from oven; cool in pan 10 minutes. Remove from pan, and finish cooling on rack.

TO STORE Wrap in plastic wrap; keep on counter 1 to 2 days or freeze 1 to 2 months.

TO SERVE
- Slice unfrosted cake; top with dollop of cinnamon-flavored whipped cream or vanilla ice cream.
- Dust top with powdered sugar.
- Frost with *Vanilla Powdered Sugar Frosting* (prepare according to following recipe) or other favorite frosting.

Vanilla Powdered Sugar Frosting

❖

1 CUP BUTTER (2 STICKS)
1 POUND POWDERED
  SUGAR
2 TEASPOONS VANILLA
APPROXIMATELY
  3 TABLESPOONS CREAM

Place butter and sugar in food processor; process until well blended. Through feeding tube, add vanilla and enough heavy cream until mixture becomes spreadable. Dust crumbs off cake; evenly spread frosting on top.

Moonstruck Applesauce Cake

❖

½ CUP BUTTER
1 CUP SUGAR
1 CUP THICK UNSWEETENED
  APPLESAUCE, PREFERABLY
  HOMEMADE (SEE NOTE)
1 EGG, BEATEN
1 TEASPOON VANILLA
1½ CUPS SIFTED FLOUR
1 TEASPOON CINNAMON
½ TEASPOON NUTMEG
¼ TEASPOON CLOVES
¼ TEASPOON ALLSPICE
½ TEASPOON SALT
2 TEASPOONS BAKING
  POWDER
½ CUP CHOPPED WALNUTS
  (OR CHOPPED RAISINS OR
  PECANS)

I n the late 1940s, after the new cattle-shed addition to the barn was finished, we threw a large Halloween party. Costumed guests—from students at Prairie Queen School and their parents to assorted friends and neighbors—were invited.

The chill in the air was dispelled as soon as we were inside the spanking-new shed. Dad arranged hay bales in various clusters for seating; two-by-four planks laid on top of sawhorses became tables; apples bobbed in water-filled washtubs; and jack-o'-lanterns glowed in the dark. The costumes ranged from the ridiculous to the sublime. Once the party was in full swing and after Mom brought out the food, the masks immediately disappeared.

On the menu were *C.B.Y.F. Barbecued Beef Buns* (page 63), garlic dill pickles, carrot sticks, popcorn balls, cookies, and applesauce cake, along with fresh-pressed apple cider, hot cocoa, and coffee for the grownups. Even the full moon contributed to the festive mood that evening.

Do not wait for Halloween or a full moon to bake this ambrosial old-fashioned apple-flavored favorite.

Preheat oven to 375°. Grease and flour 9-by-5-by-3-inch loaf pan.

Cream butter and sugar together until light and fluffy; add applesauce, egg, and vanilla, and mix thoroughly.

Sift flour, spices, salt, and baking powder together. Add nuts to flour mixture. With wooden spoon, stir flour mixture into applesauce mixture; mix thoroughly.

Pour into prepared pan and bake in preheated oven approximately 50 minutes, or until toothpick inserted into center comes out clean.

Remove from oven; cool in pan 10 minutes. Remove from pan and finish cooling on rack.

TO STORE Wrap in plastic wrap and refrigerate 1 to 2 days or freeze 1 to 2 months.

TO SERVE

- Serve unfrosted (my favorite).
- Dust top with powdered sugar (Mom's favorite).
- Frost with *Brown Bag Butter Frosting,* prepared according to following recipe (Dad's favorite).

P.S.: Just like the three bears, but not in costume!

NOTE To make 1 cup unsweetened applesauce: Wash 6 medium unpeeled apples, quartered; place in saucepan with ¼ cup water. Cover and bring to a boil. Cook, uncovered, until tender and water is evaporated. Push through Foley food mill and discard skins and seeds.

SERVES 8 TO 10 (1 LOAF CAKE)

Brown Bag Butter Frosting

½ CUP BUTTER (1 STICK)
APPROXIMATELY 1 POUND
  POWDERED SUGAR
APPROXIMATELY 1 TO 2
  TABLESPOONS HEAVY
  CREAM
1 TEASPOON VANILLA

In small saucepan or skillet, melt butter until foam subsides; continue to heat until butter becomes color of brown paper bag, but not burned. Remove from heat. Add powdered sugar, 1 cupful at a time, beating well after each addition. Add enough sugar until it becomes spreadable consistency; add cream if necessary. Flavor with vanilla.

Trick or Treat, 1920s Style   Mom's Grade-School Chums

rams (and other farm women, too) marketed for food once or, if lucky, twice a month. She bought "precious" green bananas whenever they were available. Around 1890, Grams stored and ripened fruits in the unlighted root cellar with one door to the outside. Rubye and Mom thought they were so clever sneaking a banana or a bunch of grapes, but Grams knew all along. As you can guess, after two or three weeks, a few bananas were not in prime condition for eating as is. "Waste not, want not" in mind, Grams whisked those blemished bananas into a spicy batter, then baked and converted them into a tasty cake.

Preheat oven to 350°. Grease and flour two 9-inch round cake pans.

Cream butter and sugars together until light and fluffy. Add eggs, one by one, beating well after each addition.

Sift flour, baking powder, soda, salt, cinnamon, and nutmeg together. (Reserve ½ cup and dust the nuts with it; set aside.) Stir mixed dry ingredients into butter-egg mixture; mix thoroughly.

Add lemon juice to milk; allow to "clabber" (curdle) 5 minutes. Stir milk into bananas, then add vanilla. Stir all banana-milk mixture into batter; mix thoroughly. Fold in dusted nuts set aside above. (To prepare in food processor, add ingredients in order given; process 2 to 3 pulses after each addition.)

Pour into prepared pans. Bake for 25 to 30 minutes, or until toothpick

Saved Banana Cake

½ CUP BUTTER
1 CUP SUGAR
½ CUP BROWN SUGAR
2 EGGS
2½ CUPS SIFTED FLOUR
2 TEASPOONS BAKING POWDER
½ TEASPOON BAKING SODA
½ TEASPOON SALT
½ TEASPOON CINNAMON
¼ TEASPOON NUTMEG
½ CUP CHOPPED WALNUTS (OR OTHER FAVORITE NUTS OR COCONUT)
¼ CUP MILK PLUS 1 TEASPOON LEMON JUICE (OR USE ¼ CUP BUTTERMILK)
1½ CUPS MASHED BANANAS (3 TO 4 RIPE)
2 TEASPOONS VANILLA

SERVES 10 TO 12 (ONE 2-LAYER CAKE)

inserted into center comes out clean.

Remove from oven. Cool in pans 10 minutes. Remove from pans, and finish cooling on rack.

TO STORE Wrap in plastic wrap and refrigerate 1 to 2 days or freeze for 2 to 3 weeks.

TO FROST Dust crumbs off cake. Evenly spread *Caramel Frosting* (page 98) between layers. Frost sides and top of cake. After frosting is set, store under cake plate cover, in cool place.

VARIATIONS
Unfrosted Banana Loaf Cake Grease and flour two 9-by-5-by-3-inch loaf pans. Pour batter into prepared pans and bake in 350° oven 45 to 50 minutes, or until toothpick inserted into center comes out clean. Center crack is characteristic. Store according to recipe. Serve unfrosted, sliced as if bread.
Whipped Cream Frosting Dust crumbs off cake. Two to three hours before serving: Whip 2 cups heavy cream together with ½ cup powdered sugar until stiff. Fold in 2 teaspoons vanilla. Spread ⅓ of cream mixture on first cake layer; top with ½ banana thinly sliced and rolled in lemon juice to prevent discoloring.

Top with next layer, then spread remaining whipped cream on sides and top. Refrigerate until serving time. Just before serving, arrange pieces of ½ banana, thinly sliced and rolled in lemon juice to prevent discoloring, around bottom edge of cake and sprinkle top with ½ cup finely chopped walnuts.

A sour cream cake was more the rule than the exception in Grams's era, as a result of no refrigeration. (Remember that sour cream was just cream that went sour.) Whenever Grams carried the old green-and-white speckled cream pitcher into the kitchen, the girls ran in the other direction. (One hundred years later, this recipe uses commercial sour cream.)

Preheat oven to 350°. Grease and flour two 8-inch round cake pans.

Sift flour, baking soda, and salt together 2 times; reserve.

Cream butter until fluffy. Gradually add sugar and continue to beat until light and fluffy. Add egg and vanilla; mix thoroughly.

In a double boiler, melt chocolate and cool to room temperature. Add to batter; mix thoroughly. Add flour, sour cream, and milk alternately to batter, starting and ending with flour. Mix well after each addition.

"Hands-Down" Chocolate—Sour Cream Cake

❖

2 CUPS FLOUR
1 TEASPOON BAKING SODA
½ TEASPOON SALT
⅓ CUP BUTTER
1¼ CUPS SUGAR
1 EGG
1 TEASPOON VANILLA
3 SQUARES UNSWEETENED CHOCOLATE
½ CUP SOUR CREAM
¾ CUP MILK

Pour into prepared pans. Bake 30 to 40 minutes, or until toothpick inserted comes out clean.

Remove from oven. Cool in pans 10 minutes. Remove from pans, and finish cooling on rack. To store, wrap in plastic wrap and keep on counter 1 to 2 days or freeze 2 to 3 months.

TO FROST Traditionally Grams frosted this cake with *Brown Bag Butter Frosting* (page 320) or *Vanilla Powdered Sugar Frosting* (page 319). Or try the frosting recipes below.

Dust crumbs off cake. Evenly spread frosting between layers. Frost sides and top of cake. Use back of soup spoon dipped into hot water to create thumbnail effect. After frosting is "set," store under cake plate cover at room temperature.

SERVES 10 TO 12 (ONE 2-LAYER CAKE)

Old-Fashioned Fluffy Marbled Frosting

❖

Prepare *Old-Fashioned Fluffy Frosting* then shave 1 square unsweetened or semisweet chocolate onto waxed paper. Fold shavings into frosting after it becomes satiny.

Old-Fashioned Fluffy Frosting

❖

This is my absolute favorite frosting for this chocolate cake. Mom calls it "7-minute frosting."

In top of double boiler, beat 1 egg white with ¾ cup sugar, 2½ tablespoons cold water, and pinch of cream of tartar (1/16 teaspoon). Bring water to a boil, place double boiler 1 inch over simmering water, *not touching the water*. Continuously beat with hand-held electric mixer for 7 minutes. Mixture will be stiff and glossy. Remove from heat; continue to beat until mixture becomes satiny, approximately 5 minutes longer.

High Seas Chocolate Loaf Cake

My great-uncle Glen was the pastor of the Church of the Brethren when Mom was little. He and Aunt Iris lived only a mile east of the farm. After the ice was off the sink-hole pond across from their house (on Ed Huesinkveld's farm), Mom and Aunt Rubye walked over "to visit." They carefully carried their home-made paper boats, coated with secreted paraffin on the bottom for waterproofing, and their dreams of putting out to sea. Aunt Iris and her youngest sister, Violet, accompanied them on their sail. Although Mom and Rubye's humble boats had more casualties than successes, the girls returned home with renewed vigor and elaborate ideas for bigger and better boats rigged with billowing colored sails and ready for winsome experiences.

No experience—winsome or otherwise—happened in the country without a "little something to eat." This uncomplicated chocolate loaf (from another century-old recipe) is the perfect sweet not only for a voyage, but for an afternoon tea in the parlor. It is reminiscent of a chocolate pound cake.

▪▪▪▪▪▪▪▪▪▪▪▪▪▪▪▪▪▪▪▪▪▪▪▪

Preheat oven to 350°. Grease and

1½ SQUARES UNSWEETENED CHOCOLATE
6 TABLESPOONS HOT WATER
½ CUP BUTTER
1½ CUPS SUGAR
4 EGGS, SEPARATED
1½ TEASPOONS VANILLA
1¾ CUPS FLOUR, SIFTED
2¼ TEASPOONS BAKING POWDER
PINCH SALT
½ CUP MILK

Great Aunt Iris, circa 1900

flour 9-by-5-by-3-inch loaf pan or 12¾-by-4½-by-2⅜-inch loaf pan.

Dissolve chocolate in hot water; mix thoroughly, then cool.

Cream butter until fluffy. Add sugar and continue to beat until light and fluffy. Beat egg yolks into batter. Add cooled chocolate and vanilla; mix thoroughly.

Sift flour, baking powder, and salt together. Add flour and milk alternately to batter, starting and ending with flour; mix well after each addition. Beat egg whites until stiff but not dry. Stir one whisk-full of whites into batter. Carefully fold remaining whites into batter.

Pour into prepared pan. Bake 45 to 50 minutes, or until toothpick inserted into center comes out clean. Remove from oven and cool in pan 10 minutes. Remove from pan and finish cooling on rack.

TO STORE Wrap in plastic wrap and keep on counter 1 to 2 days or freeze 1 to 2 months.

TO SERVE Dust top with powdered sugar or frost with your favorite frosting.

SERVES 8 TO 10
(1 LOAF CAKE)

Cold Water–Chocolate Cake

This recipe comes from Irene Nagel, an old family friend. "By far the *best* chocolate cake I have ever eaten!" says Mom.

Originally, our family's cakes were baked in a serviceable twelve-by-seventeen-inch black baking tin. Because we had only one oven, the cakes were baked alongside the meat. A large "sheet" cake saved time, and every minute counted.

Every chocolate-sweet-tooth dream will come true if you bake this light-textured, yet rich-tasting, cake in layers, add *Date Cream Filling,* and frost it with *Rubye's Chocolate Frosting* (page 97).

½ CUP BUTTER
1 CUP SUGAR
⅛ TEASPOON SALT
1 TEASPOON VANILLA
½ CUP UNSWEETENED COCOA
⅓ CUP COLD WATER
2½ CUPS SIFTED CAKE FLOUR
1 CUP COLD WATER
3 EGG WHITES
¾ CUP SUGAR
1⅓ TEASPOONS BAKING SODA
2 TABLESPOONS HOT WATER

Preheat oven to 350°. Grease and flour two 8-inch square cake pans.

Cream butter until fluffy. Add 1 cup sugar and continue to beat until light and fluffy. Beat in salt and vanilla.

Stir cocoa into ⅓ cup cold water and mix until smooth; add to butter mixture and mix thoroughly. Add flour and 1 cup cold water alternately to batter, starting and ending with flour; mix thoroughly.

In separate bowl, beat egg whites until frothy. Gradually add sugar and continue to beat until stiff and glossy. Carefully fold stiff whites into batter.

Dissolve soda in hot water; fold into batter using 50 strokes. Pour into prepared pans. Bake 35 minutes, or until toothpick inserted in center comes out clean. Remove from oven and cool in pans 10 minutes. Remove from pans and finish cooling on rack.

TO ASSEMBLE Dust crumbs off cake. Evenly spread *Date Cream Filling* (below) between layers of cake. Reserve excess filling for another cake.

Prepare *Rubye's Chocolate Frosting* (page 97). Frost sides and top of filled cake. After frosting is set, store under cake plate cover in cool place.

SERVES 10 TO 12 (ONE 2-LAYER CAKE)

Date Cream Filling

Over simmering water, in double boiler, combine ½ cup chopped dates and 1 cup milk. In separate bowl, mix 1 tablespoon flour, ¼ cup sugar, and 1 beaten egg together; gradually add egg mixture to hot milk mixture, stirring constantly. Continue to cook over moderate heat, stirring constantly, approximately 6 to 8 minutes, or until thick. Remove from heat. Add ½ cup chopped nuts and 1 teaspoon vanilla; mix thoroughly. *Cool* before filling cake. Can be made ahead and refrigerated.

"Pistol" Peach Marmalade—Coconut Cake

According to our family heirloom chronicles, Mary Bestor, first cousin to Granddad, was a first-rate gifted baker and "she was a pistol!" with a crackerjack sense of humor. Lucky for me, her daughter Veva not only treasured her mother's recipes, but carries on the legacy of Mary's wit by performing a few shenanigans of her own. Peaches do not fall far from the tree.

To make peach marmalade in the 1990s, follow Mary's vintage recipe, using half the amounts given. Peel, pit, and slice 7¼ pounds peaches into a large mixing bowl. Stir in 4 pounds sugar, ½ cup orange juice, and ¼ cup maraschino cherries, chopped fine. Cover with plastic wrap and let set overnight on the counter.

Add the juice of 1 lemon to macerated peach mixture, and cook in a large enameled or stainless steel saucepan. Bring to a boil, reduce the heat, simmer 2 to 2½ hours, or until the marmalade reaches 218° to 220° on a candy thermometer.

Remove from the heat, ladle the marmalade into sterilized jars, and seal according to the manufacturer's directions for shelf storage. Can be refrigerated 2 to 3 months or frozen indefinitely. Great for gift-giving.

Substitute a quality brand of store-bought peach marmalade if fresh peaches are not available to make your own.

1 CUP BUTTER
1½ CUPS SUGAR
3 EGGS, SEPARATED
3 CUPS SIFTED FLOUR
1 TEASPOON BAKING SODA
1 TEASPOON GROUND NUTMEG
1 TEASPOON GROUND CINNAMON
½ TEASPOON GROUND CLOVES
½ TEASPOON SALT
1 CUP BUTTERMILK
1 CUP RAISINS
1 CUP COCONUT, SHREDDED
1 CUP WALNUTS
½ CUP MARASCHINO CHERRIES, DRAINED
1 CUP PEACH MARMALADE
½ CUP SUGAR

Preheat oven to 350°. Grease and flour two 9-inch-square cake pans or one 9-by-13-inch cake pan.

Cream butter until fluffy. Add 1½ cups sugar and continue to beat until light and fluffy. Beat egg yolks, then beat into batter, mixing thoroughly.

Sift flour, baking soda, nutmeg, cinnamon, cloves, and salt together twice; set aside. Add flour mixture and buttermilk alternately to batter, starting and ending with flour; mix well after each addition.

Chop raisins, coconut, nuts, and cherries until evenly chopped. Place in separate bowl and add marmalade to nut mixture. Fold fruit and nut mixture into batter; mix thoroughly.

Beat egg whites until frothy. Gradually add ½ cup sugar and continue to beat until stiff, but not dry. Carefully fold stiff whites into batter.

Pour into prepared pans. Bake 60 minutes, or until toothpick inserted in center comes out clean.

PEACH MARMALADE

"15 lbs peaches, 8 lbs sugar, juice of 2 oranges and 1 small can cherries (maraschino), cut fine. Stir well, let set overnight. Add lemon juice. Cook next morning until thick. Can and seal. Makes 15 cups." Mary Bestor

Remove from oven. Cool in pans 10 minutes. Remove from pans, and finish cooling on rack.

TO FROST Prepare *Caramel Frosting* (page 98) or *Vanilla Powdered Sugar Frosting* (page 319).

SERVES 10 TO 12 (ONE 2-LAYER CAKE)

PEACH MARMALADE COCONUT CAKE

"Cream together 1 cup butter and 2 cup white sugar. 3 eggs beaten stiff, 3 cups sifted flour, 1 tsp soda, 1 tsp nutmeg, cinnamon and cloves, 1/2 tsp salt, 1 cup raisins, coconut, nuts (chop all these), 1 cup sour milk, 1 cup peach marmalade, 1/2 cup cherries chopped. Use brown or white frosting." <u>Mary Bestor</u>

Great-Great-Great-Grandmother Rebecca's Raisin-Spice Cake

3 CUPS GROUND PORK FAT, ABOUT 1½ POUNDS (SEE NOTE)
2 CUPS BOILING WATER

1 POUND CURRANTS
1 POUND RAISINS (6 LOOSELY PACKED CUPS, AFTER GRINDING)
1 CUP WALNUTS, CHOPPED

3 EGGS, SEPARATED
1 CUP SUGAR, SEPARATED INTO TWO ½-CUP BATCHES
1 CUP DARK MOLASSES
6 CUPS SIFTED FLOUR, SEPARATED INTO
    2 BATCHES OF 1 CUP AND 5 CUPS
2 TEASPOONS CINNAMON
1 TEASPOON SALT
2 TEASPOONS BAKING SODA

Here is another recipe from that witty wonderful Mary Bestor, who lived ninety-nine years and eleven months to its fullest. The cake recipe was actually handed down from her grandmother (my great-great-great-grandmother). Much like Grams's cakes, it was originally baked in an oversized, heavy, black-tinned baking pan. There is no doubt in my mind that this cake traveled by covered wagon from Maryland to South Dakota, sustaining the family for the trip.

Do not be daunted by pork fat; this is a lighter-than-you'd-guess, enticingly spicy old-fashioned cake with a long shelf life. One bite warms the cockles of your nostalgic heart. And it's a great cake to have on hand in the larder. The batch is big, so you can freeze a cake for later.

Preheat oven to 350°. Grease and flour two 9-by-13-inch cake pans, or one 9-by-13-inch and two 8-inch-square pans. Line with parchment or waxed paper; grease and flour paper.

From butcher, order fresh pork fat, ground. Place fat in large mixing bowl; pour boiling water over and mix well. Cool to room temperature. The boiling water will soften the fat to the consistency of oatmeal.

Meanwhile, in food processor, grind dried currants and raisins until chopped; remove to clean bowl. Add nuts to raisin-currant mixture.

In clean mixer bowl, beat egg whites until frothy. Gradually add ½ cup sugar and continue to beat until stiff and glossy. Remove to another clean bowl.

In same mixer bowl, beat egg yolks until frothy; add ½ cup sugar and continue to beat until thick and lemon-colored. Beat molasses into egg yolks and mix thoroughly.

Thoroughly mix 1 cup flour into egg yolk mixture. Slowly add cooled and softened fat to egg mixture; mix thoroughly. Pour batter over raisin-nut mixture; with wooden spoon, mix thoroughly.

Add cinnamon, salt, and baking soda to last 5 cups flour; sift over batter. Mix thoroughly with wooden spoon.

**SERVES 12 TO 15
(2 OR 3 LARGE CAKES)**

Fold beaten egg whites from above into batter; spoon into prepared pans.

Bake in 8-by-8-inch pans for 60 minutes; allow 75 to 80 minutes for 9-by-13-inch pan. Toothpick inserted into center should come out clean when cake is done.

Remove from oven and cool in pans 10 minutes. Remove from pans and peel off paper; finish cooling on rack.

TO STORE Wrap in plastic wrap and keep on counter 1 to 2 weeks or freeze indefinitely.

TO SERVE
- Serve unfrosted.
- Serve with whipped cream or ice cream.
- Frost with *Vanilla Powdered Sugar Frosting* (page 319).

NOTE There is really no substitute for the pork fat.

"PORK CAKE"

"3 cup ground fat pork (fine), pour 1 pint boiling water over this. Add: 1 lb currants, 3 cups sugar, 2 tsp cinnamon, 1 tsp salt, 6 cups flour, 1 cup nuts, 1 cup molasses, 2 tsp soda, 3 eggs, beaten well and 1 lb raisins. Combine all ingredients, mix well. Line baking pans with brown paper. Grease and flour. Bake at 350° for 1 hour, depending on size of the pans." Mary Bestor

Veva, her daughter, added this footnote to the recipe: "Mother's mother (Rebecca) made this when she was young."

"Un-Trickable" Rhubarb Cake

❖

Barbara Alexander, my best friend and constant companion during our preschool days, lived a half mile down the road, down a *big* hill from the farm. I tramped along the road nearly every day to play, until I finally learned how to ride my bike. ("Whew!" talk about a million falls on the bumpy grass yard.) Along with her younger brother Klaren, we co-conspired and masterminded as much mischief as we could get by with.

Her parents—the totally "untrickable" Rebecca, who was my "other mother," and Kenneth— grew the most picture-perfect vegetable garden. The weeds did not stand a prayer at their house. A bountiful bed of red rhubarb grew at one end; from its produce she baked a rhubarb cake that was as much springtime as the tulips and irises at the other end of the garden.

▪▪▪▪▪▪▪▪▪▪▪▪▪▪▪▪▪▪▪▪▪▪▪▪▪▪

Preheat oven to 350°. Grease and flour 9-by-13-inch cake pan.

½ CUP BUTTER
1½ CUPS BROWN SUGAR
1 EGG, BEATEN
1 TEASPOON VANILLA
2 CUPS SIFTED FLOUR
¼ TEASPOON SALT
1 TEASPOON BAKING SODA
1 CUP BUTTERMILK (SEE NOTE)
1⅓ CUPS DICED FRESH RHUBARB
½ CUP SUGAR
1 TEASPOON CINNAMON

Cream butter; add sugar and continue to beat until light and fluffy. Add egg and vanila; mix thoroughly.

Sift flour, salt, and baking soda together. Add flour mixture and buttermilk alternately to batter; starting and ending with flour; mix well after each addition.

Chop rhubarb into small dice; fold into batter. Pour batter into prepared pan. Mix sugar and cinnamon together and sprinkle mixture on top of batter.

Bake 35 to 40 minutes, or until toothpick inserted into center comes out clean. Remove from oven and cool in pan set on rack.

TO SERVE Cut into squares, then serve unadorned or top with cinnamon-flavored whipped cream or ice cream.

NOTE To substitute altered sweet milk for the buttermilk, add 1 tablespoon lemon juice and 1 teaspoon baking powder (omit the baking soda).

SERVES 8 TO 10 (1 LARGE CAKE)

Antique Turtle Cake

◆

Great-Great-Grandmother Broadwater's signature cake for a birthday or a special occasion dinner was Turtle Cake. After layering two 8-inch-square spice cakes with a vanilla custard, she "dug holes out" of the sides of the cake with a teaspoon in random fashion—each hole big enough to hold a muscat raisin (a very plump, black, and juicy one), representing a turtle in its nest. Clever lady.

She frosted the top with a vanilla powdered sugar frosting and stuck on the candles. It is reported that family members and friends alike requested a birthday celebration more often than once a year.

If Turtle Cake strikes your fancy, use the following spice cake recipe and create a new tradition for your family.

▪▪▪▪▪▪▪▪▪▪▪▪▪▪▪▪▪▪▪▪▪▪▪▪▪▪▪▪▪

Preheat oven to 375°. Grease and flour two 8-inch round cake pans. Line them with waxed paper; grease and flour paper.

Cream butter until fluffy; add sugar and continue to beat until light and fluffy. Add eggs and continue to beat until thoroughly mixed.

Sift flour, baking soda, spices, and salt together. Add flour mixture and buttermilk alternately to batter, starting and ending with flour and mixing well after each addition.

SPICE CAKE

▪ ▪ ▪

½ CUP BUTTER
2 CUPS BROWN SUGAR
2 EGGS, BEATEN
2¼ CUPS SIFTED CAKE FLOUR
1 TEASPOON BAKING SODA
1 TEASPOON GROUND CINNAMON
¼ TEASPOON GROUND CLOVES
½ TEASPOON GROUND NUTMEG
½ TEASPOON GROUND ALLSPICE
½ TEASPOON SALT
1 CUP BUTTERMILK

RAISIN FILLING

▪ ▪ ▪

1¼ CUPS RAISINS, PACKED
¾ CUP COLD WATER
1 CUP SUGAR
5 TABLESPOONS CORNSTARCH
2½ TABLESPOONS COLD WATER
1 TABLESPOON VANILLA
1 TABLESPOON BUTTER
GRATED ZEST OF ½ LARGE ORANGE

Pour into prepared pans and bake 30 minutes, or until toothpick inserted in center comes out clean.

Remove from oven; cool in pan 10 minutes. Remove from pan; peel off paper and finish cooling on rack.

This is Mom's twentieth-century rendition of *Antique Turtle Cake*. First, bake spice cake according to recipe. Then fill and frost cake as follows.

TO PREPARE RAISIN FILLING In food processor, grind raisins with ¾ cup cold water until fine grind; pour into saucepan. Stir in sugar and bring to a boil.

Blend cornstarch with 2½ tablespoons cold water. Stir into raisin mixture. Continue to cook, stirring constantly 3 to 4 minutes or until thick and clear. Remove from heat. Blend in vanilla, butter, and orange zest. Cool to warm before proceeding.

TO ASSEMBLE Dust crumbs off cake. Evenly spread raisin filling between layers.

Prepare Aunt Rubye's *Caramel Frosting* (page 98). Frost sides and top of filled cake. Dip metal spatula in hot water to create swirl effect. After frosting is "set," store under cake plate cover at room temperature.

SERVES 10 TO 12 (ONE 2-LAYER CAKE)

Cerebral White Cake

❖

This light-as-a-feather creation from Paradise is another legacy from the by-now-famous Mary Bestor. (She called it a Lady Baltimore Cake.) Her kitchen was the hottest place around. These cakes were also baked in a wood-burning stove with a "wet-hand" temperature gauge.

Combine this no-fail heavenly white cake with a *Fabulous Figgy Filling* and frost the combo with *Old-Fashioned Fluffy Frosting* (page 322).

Preheat oven to 375°. Grease and flour two 8-inch-square cake pans.

Cream butter until fluffy; gradually add sugar and continue to beat until light and fluffy. Add vanilla; mix thoroughly.

Sift flour, baking powder, and salt together. Add flour mixture, ½ cup water, and milk alternately to batter, starting and ending with flour and mixing well after each addition.

Beat egg whites until frothy. Gradually add sugar and continue to beat until stiff. Fold into batter; do not overmix.

½ CUP BUTTER
1 CUP SUGAR
1½ TEASPOONS VANILLA
3 CUPS SIFTED CAKE FLOUR
3 TEASPOONS BAKING POWDER
¼ TEASPOON SALT
½ CUP MILK
4 EGG WHITES
½ CUP SUGAR

FABULOUS FIGGY FILLING

■ ■ ■

½ POUND DRIED FIGS (GOLDEN OR BROWN)
⅔ CUP SUGAR
DASH SALT
1½ TABLESPOONS CORNSTARCH
1 TEASPOON VANILLA
GRATED ZEST OF ½ LEMON AND 1 TABLESPOON BUTTER (OPTIONAL)

Pour into prepared pans. Bake 25 to 30 minutes, or until toothpick inserted in center comes out clean. Remove from oven and cool in pan 10 minutes. Remove from pans, and finish cooling on rack.

TO MAKE FILLING In food processor, process figs with ½ cup tap water until coarsely chopped. Pour into saucepan and add another ½ cup tap water. Stir in sugar and salt; bring to a boil.

Blend cornstarch with 1 tablespoon cold water and stir into fig mixture. Continue to cook, stirring constantly, 3 to 4 minutes, or until thick and clear. Remove from heat. Blend in vanilla, and lemon and butter if desired. Cool to warm before filling layers.

TO FROST After filling, spread *Old-Fashioned Fluffy Frosting* (page 322) over top and sides of stacked layers.

SERVES 10 TO 12 (ONE 2-LAYER CAKE)

Beguiling Burnt Sugar Cake

The deception here is the "burnt" sugar. The sugar is caramelized but not burned. However, be careful not to burn yourself with the hot sugar and the steam that rushes off the skillet when water is added.

Preheat oven to 375°. Grease and flour two 8-inch-square baking pans.

In heavy skillet, over moderate heat, melt 1 cup sugar until clear and color of brown paper bag. Shake pan gently to keep from burning.

Remove skillet from heat. Using long-handled spoon or whisk, gradually stir in boiling water. Return sugar and water to heat. Stir until lumps are dissolved. Off heat, pour "caramel" liquid into measuring cup. Add more cool water to make 1 cup total. Cool to room temperature and reserve.

Cream butter until fluffy. Add 1 cup sugar and continue to beat until light and fluffy. Beat egg yolks until frothy; add to creamed butter. Add vanilla; mix thoroughly.

Sift flour, baking powder, and salt together. Add flour mixture and room-temperature "caramel" liquid alternately to batter, starting and ending with flour. Mix well after each addition.

Beat egg whites until stiff, but not dry. Carefully fold egg whites into batter. Pour into prepared pans; bake for 25 to 30 minutes, or until toothpick inserted into center comes out clean.

Remove from oven. Cool in pan 10 minutes. Remove from pans, and finish cooling on rack.

TO FROST Prepare *Fluffy "Burnt Sugar" Frosting* according to following recipe. Dust crumbs off cake. Evenly spread spoonful of frosting for filling between layers (or fill with fruit filling). Frost sides and top of cake. Use back of soup spoon dipped into hot water to create thumbnail effect. After frosting is "set," store under cake plate cover at room temperature.

SERVES 8 TO 10 (ONE 2-LAYER CAKE)

BURNT SUGAR SYRUP

2 CUPS SUGAR
½ CUP BOILING WATER
½ CUP BUTTER
3 EGGS, SEPARATED
1 TEASPOON VANILLA
2½ CUPS SIFTED FLOUR
2½ TEASPOONS BAKING POWDER
¼ TEASPOON SALT

Fluffy "Burnt Sugar" Frosting

Brown sugar gives this fluffy frosting the burnt sugar taste.

In top of double boiler, beat 1 egg white with ¾ cup brown sugar, 2½ tablespoons cold water, and pinch of cream of tartar. Bring water to a boil; place double boiler 1 inch over simmering water, *not touching water*. Continuously beat with hand-held electric mixer for 7 minutes. Mixture will be stiff and glossy. Remove from heat and continue to beat until mixture becomes satiny (approximately 5 minutes longer). Flavor with vanilla if desired.

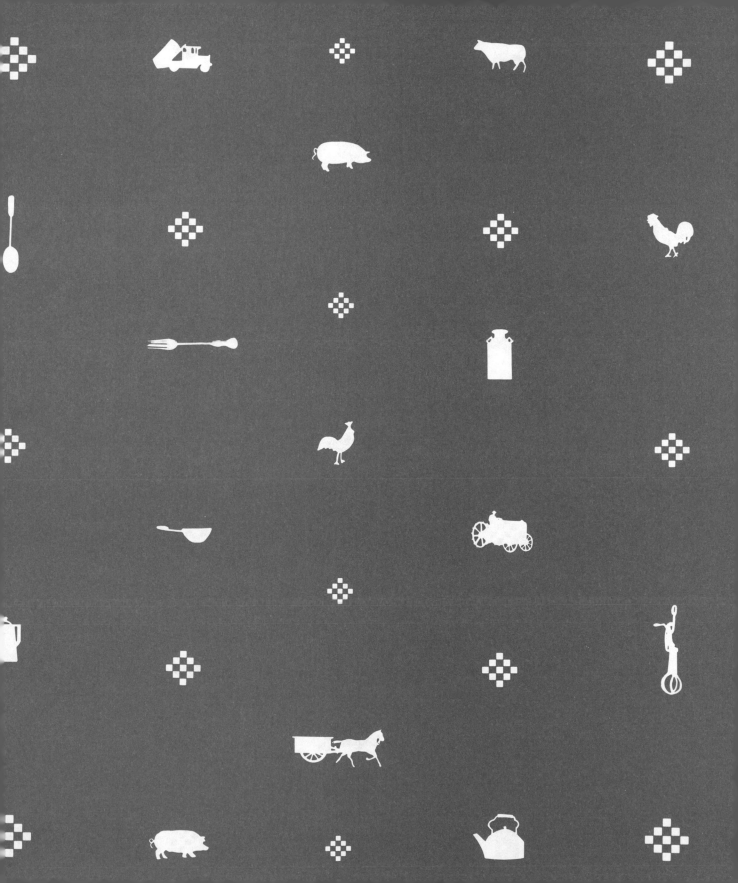

THE FAMILY'S SECRET RECIPE FILE

Every family keeps privileged information, hush-hush shenanigans, mystical rituals, and clandestine affairs along with the-black-sheep-of-the-family stories under wraps. However, after I reveal the following secret recipes and remedies, you'll have a glimpse of the real scoop!

Nothing Hush-Hush Here
Great-Grandmother Crowe, standing, with
Granddad sitting on porch, circa 1900

The Broadwaters' Caramel Corn

❖

Both Granddad and Dad raised popcorn for their family's consumption. After the corn was harvested, the husks were pulled back, and the corn was hung to dry in the basement. Once the corn was dried, Dad's strong thumbs shelled the kernels off the cob directly into a pan. ('Twas a good winter evening's project.) To clean or "winnow" the corn, Dad (or Mom) stood outside in the blowing wind, holding one pan over the second, pouring corn from one into the other and reversing the process until the chaff was gone. The cleaned corn was either popped that evening or stored in metal gallon syrup pails or other clean, airtight containers.

Believe it or not, Granddad popped corn nearly every night in the winter for the family. This was his culinary contribution. During the ritual, he gathered dry popcorn cobs and stoked the fire in the wood-burning stove to "get it good and hot." Then, with careful deliberation, he melted lard in a round-bottomed, cast-iron kettle that fit directly into the hole on the top of the stove, over the hot coals.

Pouring the corn into the hot grease, he vigorously shook the kettle until a big batch of corn was popped. They munched on the popcorn as they sat around the living room coal heater. Picture this: Granddad in his rocking chair, reading his newspaper, with Grams sewing in her chair on the other side of the kerosene lamp, while Mom and Rubye read, did their homework, or played a cardgame on the floor. Granddad preferred his popcorn plain, with salt and butter. However, for at least two generations before him, the Broadwater women made caramel corn in that same pot.

The secret, long guarded, is now revealed below.

¼ CUP VEGETABLE OIL (THEY USED LARD)
¼ CUP WHITE SUGAR
¼ CUP WINNOWED POPCORN

Over high heat, heat oil in 3-to-4-quart heavy saucepan with tight-fitting lid until it shimmers. Add sugar, swirling pan as you pour. Quickly pour in popcorn, top with lid, and "shake like the devil!"

Keep heat high. Alternate, using first a vigorous shaking motion, then letting pan sit on heat for a moment. Repeat shaking motion, then rest on heat. Continue, following "shake and sit" routine until all corn is popped and caramelized.

Corn is done when popping sound is silent. Remove from heat, *but keep on shaking pan!* Immediately pour into bowl or baking tin. Be careful, it will burn your tongue. Allow caramel corn to cool before eating.

If more corn is needed, and it probably will be, start whole affair over again, using same proportions.

MAKES 1 QUART
CARAMEL CORN

Aunt Gladys's Light Doughnuts

with an Enlightened Introduction

◆

From the time I was a small child until recently it was my understanding that Uncle Paul—Dad's brother-in-law—was killed by a bolt of lightning. Having a vivid imagination and a yen for the dramatic, I perpetuated this story up to this date, and included it in the first version of this introduction.

Upon checking other family birth and death dates with Aunt Mabel Snider, who keeps the "Schrock Family Black Book" up to date, I asked if this tale was true. "We always liked a good story, so we won't deny it, especially if it makes good reading!" said she. Now enlightened, I will share with you what really happened:

A thunder and lightning storm once caught Grandpa Schrock and his brother working in the field. Being too far from the house, they ran into a nearby grove of trees for shelter. Much to their amazement, lightning struck close to the tree where they stood. In fact, their feet felt the effects of the bolt. "The earth moved! And I bet they had to send their trousers to the cleaners after that!" chuckled Aunt Mabel.

If she had heard my first story, Aunt Gladys, Uncle Paul's wife, a kind-hearted soul who always wore the most pleasant smile imaginable, would be laughing. Her delicate, lighter-than-usual, sugared doughnuts were always piled high under a glass dome sitting on her kitchen table. As a matter of fact, the doughnuts disappeared with the speed of light.

▪▪▪▪▪▪▪▪▪▪▪▪▪▪▪▪▪▪▪▪▪▪▪▪▪

NOTE *The real secret is to keep all ingredients as cold as possible.*

Melt butter, then cool to room temperature.

Beat eggs until frothy. Gradually add sugar and mix until light and lemon-colored. Add lemon extract; mix well.

Sift 3½ cups flour, then sift again with baking powder, baking soda, salt, nutmeg, mace, and cardamom into bowl. Add beaten egg mixture, melted butter, and buttermilk to flour. Mix thoroughly. Keep dough as soft as you can and yet be able to handle it. Add an additional sprinkle of flour if needed to bind dough.

Using pastry cloth or board, spread remaining 1 cup flour from above over area. Place dough on flour. With rolling pin, roll dough out to about ⅓ inch thick. Dip 2½-inch doughnut cutter into excess flour and cut out doughnuts. With cake spatula, lift raw doughnuts onto dry baking sheet. Refrigerate

Ingredients

2 EGGS

1 CUP SUGAR

1 TEASPOON LEMON EXTRACT

4½ CUPS FLOUR, PLUS ABOUT ½ CUP FLOUR FOR DIPPING THE CUTTER INTO

1½ TEASPOONS BAKING POWDER

½ TEASPOON BAKING SODA

PINCH SALT

¼ TEASPOON NUTMEG

PINCH MACE

PINCH CARDAMOM

2 TABLESPOONS LARD OR BUTTER, MELTED

1 CUP BUTTERMILK

1 TO 1½ QUARTS VEGETABLE OIL

1 TO 2 CUPS GRANULATED OR POWDERED SUGAR FOR SUGARING DOUGHNUTS

until frying time. This can be done a day ahead.

TO FRY   Fill deep-fat fryer, electric skillet, or wok with vegetable oil. (Gladys, Mom, and Grams used freshly rendered lard.)

Heat oil to 370°. When hot, fry one test doughnut. Break open to check for doneness. Taste. Judging by degree of golden color, fry remaining dough accordingly. Slide one doughnut at a time into hot oil from side of pan; do not crowd. Fry until golden brown on underside. Using long-pronged fork, turn over and fry other side likewise. Remove from oil, drain on rack, set over brown paper bag–lined baking sheet. Continue until all are fried.

TO SUGAR   Pour 1 to 2 cups sugar into brown paper bag. Shake one or two hot doughnuts at a time. Set aside and cool until all are fried.

TO FROST   Mix *Vanilla Powdered Sugar Frosting* (page 319) with a bit more heavy cream than called for to thin. Dip, glaze, or frost doughnuts just before serving.

TO STORE   Do not roll in sugar. Freeze in airtight plastic bags 2 to 3 weeks. Just before serving, reheat in warm oven, roll in sugar, and serve.

MAKES 3 DOZEN DOUGHNUTS

Homemade Ice Cream

2 QUARTS WHOLE MILK
2 CUPS WHITE SUGAR
1 CUP BROWN SUGAR
6 RENNET TABLETS
½ CUP LUKEWARM WATER
1½ TO 2 TABLESPOONS VANILLA (SEE NOTE)

2 CUPS HEAVY CREAM
1 CAN EVAPORATED MILK (12 OUNCES)
APPROXIMATELY 20 TO 25 POUNDS ICE
APPROXIMATELY 10 POUNDS COARSE SALT (CANNING, PICKLING, OR KOSHER)

Our family would not think a Christmas dinner was complete without homemade ice cream. Before Mom bought an electric ice cream freezer, we cranked out a gallon of ice cream by hand.

The whole family got into the swing of making ice cream. Dad brought two or three big buckets of pearly white snow into the basement, while Mom adjusted the dasher in the chilled custard inside the freezer can, and secured the cover and crank handle of the ice cream freezer. She packed snow down along the sides of the freezer can until it was full. Two cups of coarse salt were added, then more snow, more salt, and so on until the snow became "slush," and level with the top of the wooden freezer. We took turns, keeping the handle going in the same direction until the custard became ice cream. It was easy to tell when it was close to done; Mom or Dad had to finish the cranking because it was too difficult for us kids. Then Mom pulled out the dasher while Joel and I waited with spoons in hand, to catch any ice cream that fell off, and to "lick the dasher clean." Judy and Joany "suffered" the same delicious taste experience but didn't have to turn the crank, because Mom had an electric ice cream freezer by their time.

Once the lid was firmly sealed back on the ice cream freezer can, more snow and salt were added before Dad carried the whole affair outside and stuffed it into a snowbank by the back door to ripen (weather permitting . . . if the air was cold and the snow was deep). This custom is risky. Imagine Dad's disgust and Mom's fury when they discovered that our neighbor's dog had dug off the lid and eaten half the ice cream while we were eating dinner!

Unflappable Mom whipped up a big bowl of heavy cream as a substitute. Yet another year, our dog mistook the ice cream container for a fire hydrant and—well, you know the rest.

If the snowbank lay-away custom is too risky, either pack the snow according to the proportions given below or store (ripen) the ice cream in the freezer.

Start with a vanilla base, then add flavors once the ice cream is made. Vanilla was our "house specialty."

Rennet tablets are available in some health food stores and grocery stores, or at a local creamery or cheese maker's. A brand name "Junket" is put out by Salada Foods, Inc., a division of the Kellogg Company, Little Falls, New York. If you have a problem finding it in your area, write to them for the nearest retail store that carries it.

■■■■■■■■■■■■■■■■■■■■■■■■■■■■■■■■■

ONE DAY BEFORE SERVING In saucepan, warm milk over low heat, and bring to a simmer. Stir in sugars and continue to simmer, stirring until sugar is dissolved. Remove from heat and cool to body temperature.

Meanwhile, soak rennet tablets in lukewarm water; stir until dissolved. Once milk is neither hot nor cold, test like a baby's bottle with a drop on the wrist. (It should read 110° on a thermometer.) Add dissolved rennet tablets and vanilla to milk and mix thoroughly; refrigerate 4 to 6 hours or overnight. Cold mixture will look like loose yogurt or custard.

JUST BEFORE FREEZING Add heavy cream and evaporated milk; mix thoroughly.

NOTE
- For chocolate flavor, add 1 cup chocolate syrup with vanilla and proceed according to recipe.
- For coffee flavor, dissolve ¼ cup dry instant coffee in ¼ cup warm water, add with vanilla, and proceed according to recipe.

TO FREEZE Have on hand a 1-gallon electric ice cream freezer, 20 to 25 pounds ice or several gallons of snow, and 5 to 10 pounds coarse salt (canning, pickling, or kosher).

Place dasher inside ice cream container, securely seal lid, and attach electric motor. Pack snow or ice to come up to top of container, depending on your usage/storage plans, according to proportion chart below. Add salt and snow or ice alternatively until mixture becomes "slush."

Dry hands, plug in motor, and freeze according to manufacturer's directions. Stamp ice/salt and add ice/salt as necessary to keep level of "slush" at top. Once handle is difficult to turn or motor slows down (approximately 25 minutes), unplug machine. Remove motor and lid and check for proper consistency. If desired, add fruits, nuts, or flavoring according to variations now.

Replace lid and motor and continue to mix/freeze about 3 minutes. Stop machine. Remove dasher, give yourself a taste treat, and correct flavorings. Seal with plastic wrap underneath lid (remember the two dog stories) and securely fasten lid. Freeze in freezer; hold in container. Or, if you are brave, stick it in a snowbank (covered with a large heavy plastic bag) until serving time.

VARIATIONS
Shaved Chocolate Chunk With sharp paring knife or vegetable peeler, shave chocolate from block of semisweet chocolate and add 1½ to 2 cups before storing.
Maple-Walnut Add 3 tablespoons maple syrup plus 2 cups chopped walnuts before storing.
Peach Mix 2½ to 3 cups fresh peeled and diced peaches rolled in ⅓ cup orange juice and 2 table-

----

HINT I recommend these proportions of ice and salt to freeze, hold, and store (ripen) in the ice cream freezer:
TO FREEZE 8 parts ice to 1 part salt
TO HOLD UP TO 2 HOURS 4 parts ice to 1 part salt
TO STORE (RIPEN) OVER 2 HOURS 2 parts ice to 1 part salt

MAKES 1 GALLON

spoons lemon juice with ¾ to 1 cup sugar or to taste; mix thoroughly. Add before storing.
Peppermint Stick Place peppermint sticks in heavy-duty plastic bag and smash with hammer. (Mom smashed a 1-inch-thick-by-12-inch-long peppermint "stalk" placed in a clean work sock on the cement floor of the basement.) Measure 1½ cups; add before storing.
Fresh Raspberry Sweeten 3 cups fresh crushed raspberries with ½ to 1 cup sugar; add before storing.
Fresh Strawberry Sweeten 3 cups fresh crushed strawberries with ½ to 1 cup sugar; add before storing.

ICE CREAM "TRAPPINGS" (TOPPINGS)
"Mighty Good" Chocolate Sauce (approximately 1 cup) Heat 6 ounces semisweet chocolate chips with ¾ cup light corn syrup and ¼ cup heavy cream until chocolate is melted; mix thoroughly. Remove from heat; whisk in ½ teaspoon vanilla. Serve hot or cold.
Fresh Berry Topping (1½ cups) Crush 3 cups of fresh blueberries, raspberries, or strawberries with Foley food fork. Add approximately 1 cup sugar or to taste. Mix thoroughly.
Rhubarb Sauce (3 cups) Bring 4 heaping cups chopped rhubarb, 2 cups water, 1 cup sugar, and 1 teaspoon crystallized ginger to a boil. Cook 8 to 10 minutes, or until rhubarb is soft and sauce is thickened. Serve hot or cold.

1990s Old-Fashioned Vanilla Ice Cream

Well before folks thought about contaminated eggs, Grams, Mom, and most farm cooks "stirred a couple eggs plus a leftover yolk or two into the cream just before freezing!" To replicate that "French vanilla"–style flavor, the following recipe is not an imitation, but a super deluxe taste treat.

❖

2 CUPS HALF-AND-HALF
2 CUPS HEAVY CREAM
½ CUP WHITE SUGAR
¼ CUP BROWN SUGAR
3 TABLESPOONS CORNSTARCH
1 EXTRA LARGE EGG, BEATEN
1 TABLESPOON VANILLA

TWENTY-FOUR HOURS BEFORE SERVING Check manufacturer's directions for your ice cream freezer. If directed, put your freezer can/container in freezing compartment of your refrigerator.

EARLY IN THE DAY OR AT LEAST 2 TO 3 HOURS BEFORE FREEZING In heavy medium saucepan, warm half-and-half and cream over low heat, and bring to a simmer. Stir in sugars and continue to simmer, stirring until sugar is dissolved.

In small cup, blend cornstarch and 1 tablespoon cold water together, and whisk into hot cream. Over moderate heat, cook 4 to 5 minutes, stirring constantly.

In small bowl, beat egg. Gradually whisk half of hot mixture into beaten egg. Stirring constantly, return tempered egg to remaining hot cream in saucepan. Continue to whisk until well combined.

Return pan to heat, bring to a boil, and immediately remove from heat. Mixture will have soft-custard sauce consistency. Stir in vanilla, then refrigerate until completely cool to the touch. Freeze according to manufacturer's directions.

VARIATION
Grams's Fresh Peach Ice Cream Peel, core, and slice 3 to 4 fresh peaches. Add 1 teaspoon lemon juice and ½ cup sugar (or to taste) to peaches; let stand while freezing cream until soft "mush." Strain off accumulated juice and reserve for another use. Chop peaches (approximately 1 to 1½ cups), place fruit in clean linen napkin, squeeze out excess juice, and add to "mushy" ice cream. Continue freezing until firm.

M A K E S   1   Q U A R T

Hunter's Roast Venison

Darius Broadwater, Granddad's father, purchased "the farm" about 1850 from Kerwin who had cleared the land and homesteaded the property about 1800. No doubt they had a regular diet of venison, most probably spit-roasted over an open hearth. But Mom's modern version, with the marinade secret intact, renders venison a choice sporting entrée.

Plan ahead for this dish. Mom suggests that the venison (moose or bear meat, too) marinate at least two weeks for thin steaks, and three to four weeks for a roast. A side of venison needs six weeks to marinate. Marinated meat can be securely wrapped in plastic wrap, then in a freezer bag, and frozen up to six months.

Hunt up a large stone crock, glass, porcelain, or enamel vessel and reap the rewards.

■■■■■■■■■■■■■■■■■■■■■■■■■■■

TO MARINATE Place meat in vessel large enough to hold meat, preferably with lid.

Thoroughly mix buttermilk, onions, garlic, juniper berries, and peppercorns together. Pour marinade over raw meat, adding more buttermilk if necessary to cover completely. Cover container with lid or

1 VENISON ROAST, 4 TO 5 POUNDS
2 QUARTS BUTTERMILK
2 LARGE ONIONS, SLICED
4 WHOLE HEADS OF GARLIC, SMASHED WITH SKINS AND ALL
10 TO 12 JUNIPER BERRIES, BRUISED
2 TABLESPOONS BLACK PEPPERCORNS, CRACKED

1 TABLESPOON VEGETABLE OIL
½ TO ¾ CUP BEEF BROTH
¼ TO ½ CUP CURRANT JELLY

several layers of plastic wrap, plus plastic bag inverted over top. Refrigerate for at least 3 weeks. Turn and check every so often (once a week). The meat can be marinated up to 6 weeks.

TO ROAST Preheat oven to 350°. Remove venison from marinade; wipe dry with paper towel and discard marinade.

Heat oil in heavy casserole with lid (large enough to hold meat in one layer) until hot. Over high heat, sear venison on both sides until brown to seal in juices. Add broth and cover. Reduce oven temperature to 325° and bake 1¼ to 1¾ hours (approximately 22 to 25 minutes per pound) or until venison is tender to point of fork.

Remove from oven; place meat on warm platter. Strain pan juices into gravy strainer; allow fat to rise and discard. Pour defatted juices back into baking pan.

According to desired sweetness, swirl jelly into pan juices; taste and correct seasonings. Pour sauce into gravy boat.

Slice meat and garnish with parsley or watercress. Serve with raw cranberry relish . . . Mom's favorite.

SERVES 6 TO 8

Great-Grandmother Esther Mansfield Crowe's White Fruitcake

For generations this cake was traditionally baked by the mother of the bride to be served as the wedding cake for her daughter. Alongside this cake, a footed cake plate of pressed glass has held the wedding cake for every daughter in our family. At Mom's (and my) wedding, the cake in this recipe was the top layer of our wedding cake. The "public" layers were made from the traditional *Cerebral White Cake* recipe (page 330). After the wedding the top layer was stored or frozen. Then, according to unwritten tradition, on the first anniversary, it is defrosted and the couple eats this cake layer.

Adding her own personal statement to this tradition, Aunt Bets (with Grams's help) cut the fruitcake into small bite-sized pieces, wrapped them in white tissue paper, and tied them using a tiny blue bow. All the ladies attending her wedding were given these little gifts, along with the instructions to "make a wish and tuck it under your pillow before going to sleep tonight."

Not wanting to wait for another wedding, our family decided to serve this out-of-the-ordinary, magical fruitcake every Christmas as well. Having unclassified this information for posterity, I urge you to dig out your loaf pans, bake the cakes, and make a wish as you put a piece under your pillow tonight.

1 POUND BLANCHED WHOLE ALMONDS
1 POUND FLAKED COCONUT
1 CUP CHOPPED CANDIED CITRON
½ CUP WHOLE CANDIED RED CHERRIES
½ CUP WHOLE CANDIED GREEN CHERRIES
½ CUP DARK RUM

1 CUP BUTTER, SOFT
2 CUPS SUGAR
1 TEASPOON SALT
2 TEASPOONS VANILLA
2 TEASPOONS ALMOND EXTRACT
3½ CUPS SIFTED FLOUR, DIVIDED INTO ½- AND 3-CUP AMOUNTS
2 TEASPOONS BAKING POWDER
8 EGG WHITES
PINCH SALT

¼ CUP RUM (OPTIONAL)

ONE DAY AHEAD Mix nuts and fruits together thoroughly. Macerate mixture at least 2 to 3 hours or overnight in rum.

NEXT DAY Preheat oven to 300°. Prepare baking pans: Grease and line four 8-by-4-by-2-inch loaf pans with waxed paper, grease again, and heavily flour paper. On lowest rack position, place 9-by-13-inch cake pan half filled with warm water; refill as necessary during baking time.

Cream butter until fluffy. Gradually add sugar; continue to beat until light and fluffy. Add salt, vanilla, and almond extract; mix thoroughly.

Toss ½ cup flour into fruit and nut mixture.

Add baking powder to remaining 3 cups flour and sift together. Mix into butter mixture, blending thoroughly.

Beat egg whites until frothy. Add salt; continue to beat until stiff, but not dry. Fold egg whites into batter until evenly dispersed.

With wooden spoon, add fruit-nut mixture into batter; it will be very thick.

Spoon batter equally into 4 prepared loaf pans. (I weigh them.)

Place filled loaf pans on center oven rack, over pan of water. Bake for 60 to 80 minutes, or until toothpick inserted into center comes out clean. Do not expect them to be brown. This is a white fruit cake with a hint of brown around the edges. The top should be dull.

Remove from oven. Immediately tip cakes out from pans; if desired, drizzle 1 to 2 tablespoons rum over warm cake and finish cooling on rack. Wrap in cheesecloth that has been soaked in rum and wrung out. Then cover in plastic wrap.

TO STORE Seal in plastic bags and leave in cool dry place to "ripen" at least 1 month, refrigerate 2 to 3 months, or freeze indefinitely.

Five Wedding Waitresses Prairie Queen Classmates, circa 1950

TO GIVE AS A GIFT Unwrap and garnish with row of whole glacéed red cherries down middle of cake. Snip bits of green cherry to resemble leaves. Rewrap in several layers of plastic wrap. Wrap in foil and tie with gingham ribbon.

**MAKES 4 LOAF CAKES
(EACH SERVING 10 TO 12)**

Opal's Strawberry Preserves

Whenever Mom entertained, a cut-glass bowl of bright beautiful jam was on the table to accompany the customary bread and butter. Nearly everyone commented on the flavor, clarity, and consistency of her jam. Mom openly gave them the simple directions, but theirs never quite came out the same. So, here and now: The real secret of Opal's Strawberry Preserves.

■ ■

SPECIAL EQUIPMENT One 3-to-4-quart, nonreactive heavy bottom saucepan, 3 pint-sized mason jars.

Wash, hull, and drain berries. Measure and place in saucepan. Over high heat, stirring and smushing constantly, bring berries to a boil. Boil exactly 3 minutes. Add 3 cups

**1 QUART RIPE STRAWBERRIES
5 CUPS SUGAR, DIVIDED INTO
3- AND 2-CUP AMOUNTS**

of sugar, stirring constantly as fast as you can; boil exactly 3 minutes longer. Add remaining 2 cups sugar, stirring constantly as fast as you can; boil exactly 3 minutes longer.

Continue stirring, remove from heat, and pour into large mixing bowl. Place uncovered on counter for 3 days; stir every now and then during that time.

TO STORE Pour jam into sterilized jars following manufacturer's instructions, seal, and process for 5 minutes in hot water bath for safe shelf life. Refrigerate 2 to 3 months or freeze indefinitely.

Use the same recipe and procedure for Raspberry Preserves.

MAKES 1 TO 1½ QUARTS PRESERVES

From the Family Pharmacy

Old remedies, some sounding hysterically funny now, were applied, swallowed, and used because doctors were not readily available. A doctor was either "fetched" or called for only when "you were darn near death's door"!

Part of the mystical and miraculous healing qualities of these remedies lies within the blind faith that it will "cure whatever ails you!" Grams often said, "It will either kill or cure you!" One wants to believe they cure.

(I repeat these secret remedies here mostly for amusement and not as prescriptions.)

CURES

BURNS Immediately plunge the body part into cold water. Keep it in an hour if not improved before. Apply salve of aloe plant directly on body part after removing from the water.

CROUP Drop two or three drops of peppermint oil onto a soup spoon of sugar. Feed to the "patient."

HEAD COLD AND ALLERGIES Add a few drops of peppermint oil to a large kettle of boiling water. Stick your head over the kettle, with a heavy towel forming a tent, and steam breathe deeply for 15 minutes.

BAD COUGH/CHEST COLD Take 2 teaspoons dry mustard, 2 tablespoons flour, and 1 egg white.

Mix together to form a plaster, spread on the chest, and cover with a thin cloth. Wrap the "patient" in a heavy blanket. "This can take the skin and everything off your chest. You feel so bad from the burning that you no longer are sick!" Aunt Rubye says.

CORNS Add enough fine bread crumbs to ¼ cup cider vinegar to make a good poultice after standing ½ hour. Apply the poultice when retiring at night. In the morning the soreness will be gone and the corn can be picked out. For an obstinate corn, two or more applications may be required to effect a cure.

EARACHE Place a drop or two of warm almond oil in the sore ear.

HEADACHE Put a cold cloth to the head and a bottle of hot water to the feet.

HICCUPS Take three or four preserved damson plums in your mouth at a time and swallow them by degrees.

OLD SCARS To remove old scars, rub them every day with pure olive oil. To prevent scars forming, keep the parts wet with pure olive oil.

POISON IVY AND MOSQUITO BITES Wet a bar of brown soap, "Fels-Naptha," and rub on the affected part until itching stops. Or: Make a paste of baking soda and water, and rub on the part until itching stops.

TOOTHACHE Soak a piece of cotton with oil of cloves; apply directly on the tooth.

PREVENTIVE MEDICINE

TO PREVENT CHAPPED HANDS After cleansing, rub mutton tallow over your hands.

TO PREVENT A COLD Drink a pint of cold water lying down in bed.

IF A COLD IS COMING ON Wash your hair in hot water; rinse in a cold vinegar rinse.

FARM FRAGRANCES

"Lavender blue, dilly dilly; lavender green . . ." Grams's flowerbeds contained lavender, not only for color, but to dry for sachets and scented linen drawers. Both Mom and I grow lavender and lemon sage in our home gardens for the same reason. Bags and bags of dried rose petals, spiked with the petals from blue delphinium, bachelor buttons, and purple-tinted clover, plus a kaleidoscope of blossoms, fill the North closet (that she uses as an attic) to be blended for color and fragrance, then bagged and tied with satin ribbons as gifts.

Every fall Grams stalked the creek beds and along the streams for the large leaves of the "skunk plant" that she in turn used for floral arrangements. "Her basement always had a few 'weeds' hanging upside down on a string," remarked Rubye. "She was big in the weed department!"

Do not throw out those old rose petals. Lay them out in a single layer on screening or a flat basket to dry. Add different colors and fragrant petals to make a bowl of home-scented potpourri. Oils and scents can be purchased at an apothecary store—a specialty drugstore—or a health food store, or write to Caswell-Massey Company, 518 Lexington Avenue, New York, New York 10022, for specialty oils and essence of fragrances.

Cedar chests were given to baby girls with the idea of her embroidering linens and filling the chest by the time she got married: a hope chest. The durability and fragrance of cedar was not only pleasant and thrifty, but it repelled insects as well.

Bartering—a common practice on the farm—his finished baskets, berry carriers, and magazine racks for raw cedar planks, Dad has a cedar-crafted "cottage business" in his retirement stage. He also makes cedar "sticks" that hang in a closet, "blocks" that tuck into sweater drawers (to keep out the moths naturally), and "chips or shavings" that are added to a bowl of pine cones, resulting in a natural room fragrance. There is nothing secret about his work.

Grandmother Schrock's Miraculous Salve

❖

The Schrock kids walked barefoot during the summertime for economical reasons that we all can understand. On Sunday, they wore shoes, but during the week, barefoot children were the rule, not the exception, in their part of the country.

"Boys will be boys." At the age of twelve, Dad cut his foot on a piece of barbed wire. The injury went unchecked by his parents (he did not bother to tell them), and as time went on, his leg became swollen, red, and very painful. Dad, being stoic by nature, continued to pull his share of the workload.

As miracles often happen, he was working in a field near a woods where an old Native American woman lived. Some people thought she was a witch; others did not think of her at all. After observing Dad's limp, she knew how to help him get well. (He by this time had blood poisoning.) Sharing her sageness and her salve, she instructed him how to apply it and sent him home with enough extra to heal it.

The salve drew the infection out of his leg and he was soon back on

1 POUND MUTTON TALLOW (LANOLIN)
¼ POUND ROSIN
¼ POUND BEESWAX
10 DROPS CARBOLIC ACID
1 OUNCE OIL OF SPIKE

his feet again. Having a truly generous spirit, she also gave the recipe to Grandmother Schrock. And now I pass it on to you. . . .

In heavy saucepan, over low heat, melt tallow, rosin, and beeswax together. Remove from heat; allow to cool.

When mixture is partially cool, before it hardens, add carbolic acid and oil of spike; mix thoroughly. Pour mixture into clean, dry, recycled cold cream jars or other small containers.

TO USE Apply small amount on top of any infected sore or cut. Cover with Band-Aid or bandage. Leave on overnight. Change bandage and add a bit more salve with each change, once a day (after bathing). Continue treatment until redness and tenderness is gone. Once the infection is gone, discontinue use of the salve, and the skin will heal by itself, miraculously!

MAKES ABOUT 1½ CUPS

Grandmother Crowe's Uncanny Homemade Soap

✦

Nothing pleased Grams more than a clothesline full of spanking white linens drying in the breeze. She took great pride in her laundering ability on "Monday, wash day." Not only was the water boiling when she washed the clothes, but her homemade soap had the best cleaning power imaginable.

And for that purpose, annually on a sunny clear day in September or October, Grams made soap. The black cast-iron caldron—a large kettle, just like a witch's "brew" kettle—was uprighted out west of the house in a grove of trees. After the wood, kindling, and other debris were readied, she mixed up the ingredients with a long-handled paddle, which looked like an oar. She lit the fire and continued to stir the mixture until it was thoroughly mixed and came to a boil. Every so often, she "gave it a good stir." The soap brewed for six to seven hours, or until the mixture was thickened and the carefully measured fire burned out.

The best part of making soap was eating wieners. We roasted them

15 POUNDS MUTTON OR BEEF TALLOW (THE FAT SHOULD BE UNRENDERED)
3 CANS LEWIS LYE
15 GALLONS RAINWATER
1 ONE-POUND BOX 20 MULE TEAM BORAX
1 PINT SALT
1 CUP AMMONIA

over the soap-making fire as they were stuck on the end of whittled long green twigs that Grams fashioned for this purpose. We used only green wood, so it would not burn over the hot coals. Throwing Emily Post out the window, we slathered mustard on the roasted wieners and ate them while standing in front of the fire—sans napkins too! This magical midday snack ended with a marshmallow roast for dessert.

As the sun set, Dad lifted a heavy wooden board to cover the warm kettle. Uncannily, the next morning, beautiful snow-white soap was inside that kettle!

Using a long sharp knife, Mom cut the firm soap into large chunks and divided them among Grams, Rubye, Bets, and herself—supplying everyone with laundry soap for a year. To use the soap, they tied a small piece of it in the toe of a clean heavy-duty work sock, knotted the top, and tossed it into the hot water tub of the washing machine. (I am talking here about a wringer washing machine . . . the kind of machine that only *washed* the clothes.

Rinsing was done in separate tubs, by hand. The clothes were then put through the wringer, rinsed in the next tub of cold water, wrung out for a last time, and finally carried out of the basement and hung on the clothesline to dry!)

In case you make this super-powerful soap, toss the "soap sock" in with the white laundry to see the difference!

Mix tallow, lye, rainwater, borax, salt, and ammonia together. Bring to a boil, stirring constantly. Continue to boil, approximately 5 to 6 hours, stirring every so often, or until thick and the fire dies out. Cool. Cover and allow to "set up" at least 12 hours before cutting into blocks or portions.

For a "small batch," divide the amounts in half, and share some with a friend for an extraordinarily clean laundry.

MAKES 1 "LARGE BATCH"

Backyard Business Brewing   Mansfield and Frisby Women, Foley, Minn., 1890s

BIBLIOGRAPHY

Better Homes & Gardens New Cookbook, first edition. New York: Meredith Publishing Company, 1953.

Crist, Genevieve, and Elizabeth Weigle, eds. *Granddaughter's Inglenook Cookbook.* Elgin, Illinois: Brethren Publishing House, 1942.

The Holy Bible, King James Version, Red Letter Edition. Nashville: Thomas Nelson, Inc., 1901.

Mariani, John F. *The Dictionary of American Food and Drink.* New York: Ticknor & Fields, 1983.

Sisters of the Brethren Church, Subscribers & Friends of the Inglenook Magazine, *Inglenook Cook Book.* Elgin, Illinois: Brethren Publishing House, 1901 and 1911 editions.

Sullivan, Lenore. *What to Cook for Company.* Ames, Iowa: Iowa State College Press, 1952.

ADDITIONAL READING

Beard, James. *James Beard's American Cookery.* Boston: Little, Brown and Co., 1972.

Aunt Becky, ed. *Amish Cooking.* La Grange, Indiana: Pathway Publishing Corp., 1977.

Betty Crocker Picture Cook Book, first edition. New York: McGraw-Hill, 1950.

Hooker, Margaret Huntington. *Early American Cookery or Ye Gentlewoman's Housewifery.* Scotia, N.Y.: Americana Review, 1981.

Landin, Margaret, ed. *The Farmer Country Kitchen Cook Book.* New York: Gramercy Publishing Co., 1894.

Nichols, Nell B., ed. *America's Best Vegetable Recipes.* New York: Doubleday, 1970.

Nichols, Nell B., ed. *Cooking for Company.* New York: Doubleday, 1968.

Tyree, Marion Cabell. *Housekeeping in Old Virginia.* Louisville, Ky.: John P. Morton & Co., 1879.

Villas, James. *American Taste.* New York: Arbor House, 1982.

Index